MICRONESIA
HANDBOOK

DIANA LASICH HARPER

MICRONESIA
HANDBOOK

FOURTH EDITION

NEIL M. LEVY

MOON
PUBLICATIONS, INC.

MICRONESIA HANDBOOK
FOURTH EDITION

Published by
Moon Publications, Inc.
P.O. Box 3040
Chico, California 95927-3040, USA

Printed by
Colorcraft Ltd., Hong Kong

© Text and photographs copyright Neil M. Levy, 1996.
All rights reserved.
© Illustrations and maps copyright Moon Publications, Inc., 1996.
All rights reserved.

Some photographs and illustrations are used by permission and are the property of the original copyright owners.

ISBN: 1-56691-077-3
ISSN: 1088-095X

Editor: Emily Kendrick
Assistant Editors: Patricia Reilly, Lisa Stowell
Copy Editor: Deana Corbitt Shields
Production & Design: Carey Wilson
Cartographers: Chris Folks, Mike Morgenfeld
Index: Deana Corbitt Shields

Front cover photo: Rock Islands, Palau, by Donna Carroll
All photos by Neil M. Levy unless otherwise noted.

Distributed in the U.S.A. by Publishers Group West
Printed in Hong Kong

Please send all comments, corrections, additions, amendments, and critiques to:

**MICRONESIA HANDBOOK
MOON PUBLICATIONS, INC.
P.O. BOX 3040
CHICO, CA 95927-3040, USA
e-mail: travel@moon.com**

Printing History
1st edition — November, 1985
2nd edition — May 1989
3rd edition — September 1992
4th edition — February 1997

All rights reserved. No part of this book may be translated or reproduced in any form, except brief extracts by a reviewer for the purpose of a review, without written permission of the copyright owner.

Authorization to photocopy items for educational, internal, or personal use, or the internal or personal use of specific clients, is granted by Moon Publications provided that the appropriate fee is paid directly to Copyright Clearance Center, 222 Rosewood Drive, Danvers, MA 01923, U.S.A., tel. (508) 750-8400.

Although the author and publisher have made every effort to ensure that the information was correct at the time of going to press, the author and publisher do not assume and hereby disclaim any liability to any party for any loss or damage caused by errors, omissions, or any potential travel disruption due to labor or financial difficulty, whether such errors or omissions result from negligence, accident, or any other cause.

CONTENTS

MAPS

═══════ Road	○	Village / Town	Water
	•	Accommodation	
	▪	Sight	Reef
	▲	Mountain	
--------- Trail	𝍕	Waterfall	Mangrove
	✕	Airport	

NOTE: CONDITION OF ROADS MAY VARY.

CHARTS AND SPECIAL TOPICS

ABBREVIATIONS

A$—Australian dollars

AA—antiaircraft

a/c—air conditioned

AMI—Air Marshall Islands

B.C.E.—Before Common Era

C—Celsius

C.E.—Common Era

d—double

EEZ—Exclusive Economic Zone

FSM—Federated States of Micronesia

km—kilometer

mph—miles per hour

MV—motor vessel

no.—number

NZ—New Zealand

pop.—population

s—single

SPF—South Pacific Forum

t—triple

tel.—telephone

TTPI—Trust Territory of the Pacific Islands

U.S.—United States

US$—U.S. dollars

WW I—World War I

WW II—World War II

YHA—Youth Hostel Association

ACKNOWLEDGMENTS

First I wish to give thanks to and express admiration for the work of David Stanley, author of the prior three editions of *Micronesia Handbook,* the first guidebook to the region. I could not have written this edition without relying on his work, his files, and his advice.

I am grateful to the staff of Moon Publications for their assistance. I particularly wish to thank Emily Kendrick for her editorial encouragement and judgement. Thanks also to Dave Hurst and cartographer Chris Folks. And thanks to Bill Newlin, Moon's publisher and my friend, who took the chance that a law professor could write plain English.

Thanks to Kirin Malvede, editorial assistant, for her careful research and editorial support.

A number of scholars and writers shared their expertise with me. John M. van Dyke, Professor of Law, University of Hawaii, helped me understand the legal problems facing Micronesia. Pia Anderson, Univeristy of California at Berkeley, was a great resource on the archaeology and anthropology of Micronesia. And F. Brian Wruble taught me all I know about deep submergence vessels, and just how deep they go.

My appreciation also goes out to Giff Johnson of the *Marshall Islands Journal* and to Gene Ashby, author of *Pohnpei: An Island Argosy,* who both provided valuable input. Tim Rock and Stefanie Brendi of *Pacific Below* magazine shared their knowledge of diving and of Guam. I'm especially grateful for the expertise of Jack D. Haden of Australia, who shared extensive information on Nauru and Kiribati.

My most special thanks go to Jane Levy, my wife, who not only accompanied me to parts of Micronesia, but also used her knowledge as a librarian, museum curator, and basket weaver to contribute to the arts and crafts sections of this handbook, as well as the Booklist.

One of the main joys of travel is, of course, meeting other travelers. I met many, but mention only a few. Thank you Albert Schmitz and Albertien Korma, from the Netherlands, for sharing your time, knowledge of diving, and your photographs. Thank you Warren Cownie, seemingly on a one-man campaign to modernize Micronesia's phone system. Thank you Michael Keltos of the Pacific Business Center, University of Hawaii at Manoa, for your support of local businesses and for sharing your knowledge of Kosrae and Yap.

Many people within the travel industry supplied me with ideas and facts. Mike Musto of Trip-N-Tour Micronesia was a very useful source of information about travel, as was Hillary Kaye, tourism representative for the

Marshall Islands. My sincerest thanks to Remy Meraz of Continental Air Micronesia, who helped ensure that I could provide accurate airline information.

Many people living in Micronesia added to the enjoyment of my travels and helped me get to know the region. On Guam, thanks to Anthony Corn of the Guam Art Council and to artist Anita D. Bento. On Kosrae, thanks to Madison T. Nena, Division of Tourism, Thane Messinger, Scott Benbow, and my former student Charles Greenfield, all of whom introduced me to the charms of that island. In the Marshall Islands, thanks to Angela deBrum of the Tourism Office and to Alfred Capelle of the Alele Museum. On Saipan, I wish to thank Bill Stewart, Micronesia's preeminent cartographer, and Nancy Weil and Kurt D. Burkhart of the Public Information Office. I was aided on Palau by Danny Ongelungel, Dorji Roberts, and Barry Gorelick. And thanks to Dr. Dianne Pratt, who kept me in stitches.

Special Credit

Many of the antique engravings included in this book were taken from *Oceanie, ou Cinquième Partie du Monde* by M.G.L. Domeny de Rienzi. Domeny, a colorful French adventurer, self-proclaimed soldier of fortune, and professor of geography, published several books. *Oceanie* was first published by the prominent 19th-century French publishers, Firmin Didot Frères, as part of a multivolume work on the history of the peoples of the world.

HOW WAS YOUR TRIP TO MICRONESIA?

Micronesia is constantly changing. Have you made new and interesting discoveries you wish to share with readers of future editions? I'd love to here from you. Of course, everything will be field-checked, but you might help me discover fascinating aspects of Micronesia that I might otherwise miss. Moon Publications strives to make each edition better than the last and you can be part of the process.

Keep in mind that between the time this book went to press and the time it reached the shelves, hotels have opened and closed, restaurants have changed hands, and roads have been repaired or fallen into disrepair. Also, prices may have increased; therefore, all prices herein should be regarded as approximations and are not guaranteed by the publisher or author.

Note: Authors, editors, and publishers wishing to see their publications listed in our Booklist can send review copies to the address listed below. Hotel owners, tour operators, and divemasters: The best way to keep your listing in *Micronesia Handbook* up to date is to submit current information about your business. There is never any charge or obligation for a mention.

Address all correspondence to:

Micronesia Handbook
Moon Publications
P.O. Box 3040
Chico, CA 95927
U.S.A.
e-mail: travel@moon.com

PREFACE
THE TRAVEL WRITER

Preparation

To expand the universe of the possible,
> the travel writer records events that have not occurred
> and even events that could not occur.

Words define the travel writer's journey,
> but the journey composes his words.
> Intuition cannot replace investigation.

Heisenberg's Uncertainty Principle
> complicates the travel writer's task,
> as he tries to capture a languid, tropical vacation
> while meticulously gathering reliable information.

Commitment

The travel writer heads West,
> towards the sunset,
> towards island countries whose names he cannot pronounce
> towards islands he thought existed only in World War II movies
> —hoping to find Amelia Earhart,
> —hoping to find J.C. Penney.

The travel writer appears
> to move about with a sense of purpose,
> but is as purposeless as life's other travelers.
> Having no sense of direction, however,
> he never knows he's lost.

The travel writer sees all,
> questions all,
> assumes nothing,
> fears he would become confused
> in a universe he understood.

"Who am I to judge?"
> he asks.

Undertaking

The travel writer permits himself
        the silly questions
        he always has been too repressed to ask.

The travel writer leaves phrases,
        not footprints,
        on the pathways.
        He wonders whether to use the word "landmark"
        to describe what he sees underwater.

Frightened in a five seat Cessna,
        the travel writer knows that
        if he does not look out the window,
        he is not up in the air.

The travel writer is used, confused,
        but seldom knowingly abused.
        He has perfected the art
        of plagiarizing unwritten sources.

When hotel owners learn he is the travel writer,
        they tell him their dreams,
        believing that in doing so,
        their dreams become reality.

The travel writer believes those dreams,
        but omits writing them,
        to preserve the mystery of travel.

The travel writer says,
        "Conception is easy.
        Details are killing me."
        His pregnant wife agrees.

Like Gregor Samsa,
        the travel writer is a commercial traveler.
        The travel writer shares rooms with gigantic insects,
        but never awakened to find himself metamorphosed.

GORDY OHLIGER

INTRODUCTION

Halfway between the real and the make-believe lies the magical.

Micronesia's land area covers about 1,245 square miles, and the ocean area 4,500,000 square miles. There are plenty of things to enjoy in Micronesia, but if you don't like water, this is probably the wrong destination for you.

Micronesia is *the* diver's paradise, and much more. The land, though small in area, is tremendously varied. Soft ocean breezes rustle coconut fronds seemingly at will. There are high volcanic islands and flat sandy atolls. These far-flung islands host a great diversity of cultures as well: cultures alive today and cultures that left mysterious archaeological remains.

Today, Micronesia's people, definitely citizens of the global village, combine traditional values with Western culture. Micronesia is exotic, but not altogether foreign. As one hotel owner said, "where else can you find anyplace this exotic, where people speak English and use American currency?"

Although many people have never heard of Micronesia (you may be the first on your block to

visit it), this vast region includes thousands of lush tropical islands scattered between Hawaii and the Philippines. The name means "Little Islands." The total landmass of Micronesia is about that of Rhode Island or the Los Angeles basin.

While Tahiti and Fiji are household words, most Americans are unaware of this enormous area, which the United States administered after World War II. Today Guam remains a United States territory; the Northern Marianas are part of the American Commonwealth; and the Federated States of Micronesia, the Republic of the Marshall Islands, and the Republic of Palau, though independent—by "Compacts of Free Association"—have a special relationship to the United States in which the U.S. is in charge of their security and defense.

Six colonial powers, in turn, have controlled parts of Micronesia through the centuries. Spain, Germany, and Japan were forced out in wars, while Britain and Australia left voluntarily.

You have in your hands the new edition of the original travel guidebook to Micronesia. It may no longer be virgin territory for tourists, but parts are still as remote as you can get. The mysterious ruins of an ancient culture on Pohnpei and Kosrae rival those of Easter Island; tradition-oriented Yap and Kiribati seem lost in time; Palau and Chuuk rank among the world's premier diving locales; and Guam and Saipan offer comfort and luxury.

Countless unspoiled places exist. At some, you won't meet another visitor, yet access is relatively easy. Hotels and rental cars are available in all major towns. English is understood throughout and the only currencies used are American and Australian. The people are friendly and the available travel experiences varied.

To understand most fully the "micro" in Micronesia, you must leave the towns where Western influence is strongest and visit outer islands. This takes time and energy, but the payoff is unquestionably worth the effort. As the 21st century closes in on Micronesia, traditional ways are disappearing under a flood of United States payments under the Compacts, Japanese investment capital, and Filipino and Chinese workers. The modern world has penetrated even the most remote atolls—the time to go is now.

THE LAND

Micronesia contains four great archipelagos: the Marshalls, Gilberts, Carolines, and Marianas, largely north of the equator. Of Micronesia's thousands of islands, 125 are uninhabited. The largest volcanic islands are Guam (209 square miles), Babeldaob in the Republic of Palau (153 square miles), and Pohnpei (129 square miles). In lagoon area, Kwajalein is the world's largest atoll (839 square miles), while in land area Christmas Island (150 square miles) is the biggest of the coral islands.

There is great geologic variation in Micronesia's islands. Some are high, with volcanic peaks, others low islands of sand and coral. All of the Marshalls and Gilberts are coral atolls or islands. In the Northern Marianas, Micronesia's only active volcanoes erupt. Nauru and Banaba and half of Guam are uplifted atolls. The Caroline Islands include both volcanic and coral types. Kosrae, Pohnpei, and Weno (Chuuk) are high volcanic islands. Guam and Palau are exposed peaks of an undersea ridge stretching between Japan and New Guinea, volcanic in origin but partly capped with limestone. Yap is an uplifted section of the Asian continental shelf, which floated away. This surprising variety of landforms makes Micronesia a geologist's paradise.

Tectonic Plates

The westernmost islands of Micronesia flank some of the deepest waters on earth. The 4.2-mile-deep Marianas Trench is the western edge of the vast Pacific Plate, the only one of earth's six plates that doesn't bear a continent. As this

plate gets wedged under the Philippine Plate just east of the Marianas, volcanoes erupt along this section of the Pacific "Ring of Fire." The clashing plates have uplifted parts of Guam, Rota, Tinian, and Saipan.

Atoll Formation

In 1952 scientists at Enewetak in the Marshalls managed to drill through to volcanic rock, 4,244 feet deep, for the first time on any Pacific atoll, confirming Charles Darwin's Theory of Atoll Formation. The famous formulator of the theory of evolution surmised that atolls form as high volcanic islands that then subside into lagoons. The original island's fringing reef grows into a barrier reef as the volcanic portion sinks. When the last volcanic material finally disappears below sea level, the coral rim of the reef, now an atoll, remains to indicate how big the island once was.

Of course, all this takes place over millions of years, but deep down below any atoll is the old volcanic core, as the researchers at Enewetak found. Darwin's theory is well illustrated at Chuuk, where a group of high volcanic islands remains inside the rim of Chuuk's barrier reef; these islands are still sinking. Return to Chuuk in 25 million years and all you'll find will be a coral atoll like Majuro or Kwajalein.

Hot Spots

High or low, all the islands have a volcanic origin best explained by the Conveyor Belt Theory. A crack or "hot spot" opens in the sea floor and volcanic material escapes upward. A submarine volcano builds up slowly until the lava finally

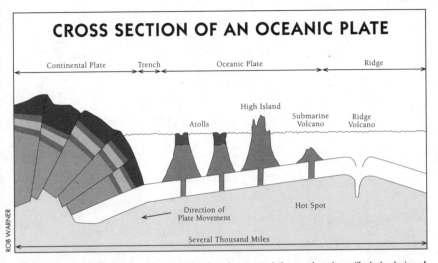

CROSS SECTION OF AN OCEANIC PLATE

Continental Plate Trench Oceanic Plate Ridge

High Island

Submarine   Ridge
Volcano   Volcano

Atolls

Direction of
Plate Movement

Hot Spot

Several Thousand Miles

ROB WARNER

breaks the surface, forming a volcanic island. The Pacific Plate moves northwest approximately four inches a year; thus, over geologic eons a volcano disconnects from the hot spot or crack from which it emerged. As the old volcanoes move on, new ones appear to the southeast, and the older islands are carried away from the cleft in the earth's crust from which they were born.

The island then begins to sink under its own weight, perhaps only half an inch a century, and erosion cuts into the volcano—by this time extinct. In the warm, clear waters a living coral reef begins to grow along the shore. As the island subsides, the reef continues to grow upward. In this way a lagoon forms between the reef and the shoreline of the slowly sinking island. This barrier reef marks the old margin of the original island.

The process is helped along by rising and falling ocean levels during ice ages. Rainwater causes a chemical reaction, which converts the porous limestone into compacted dolomite, giving the reef a more dense base. Eventually, as the volcanic portion of the island sinks completely into the lagoon, the atoll reef is the volcanic island's only remnant.

As the hot spot moves southeast, in an opposite direction to the sliding Pacific Plate (and shifting magnetic pole of the earth), the process

is repeated, time and again, until whole chains of islands ride the blue Pacific. In the Marshall, Gilbert, and Line Islands this northwest-southeast orientation is clearly visible. Although the Carolines are more scattered, the tendency, from Namonuito to Kapingamarangi or Kosrae, is still discernible. In every case, the islands at the southeast end of the chains are the youngest. This rule also applies in the South Pacific.

Life of an Atoll

A circular or horseshoe shaped coral reef bearing a necklace of sandy, slender islets of debris thrown up by storms, surf, and wind is known as an atoll. Atolls can be up to 63 miles across, but the width of dry land is usually only 600-13,000 feet from inner to outer beach. The central lagoon can measure anywhere from one to 31 miles in diameter; huge Kwajalein atoll has a width of 80 miles. Entirely landlocked lagoons are rare; passages through the barrier reef are usually found on the leeward side. Most atolls are no higher than 13 to 20 feet.

A raised or elevated atoll is one that has been pushed up by some trauma of nature to become a coral platform rising as much as 200 feet above sea level. Steep, cave-pocked oceanside cliffs frequently surround raised atolls. A good example of this type is eight-square-mile Nauru.

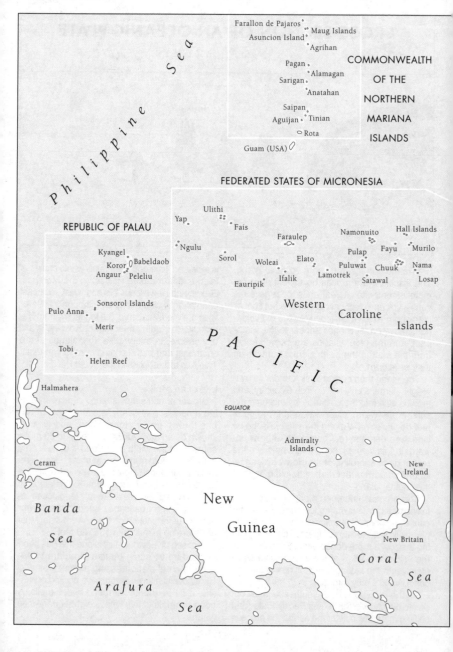

Philippine Sea

Farallon de Pajaros
Maug Islands
Asuncion Island
Agrihan

COMMONWEALTH
OF THE
NORTHERN
MARIANA
ISLANDS

Pagan
Alamagan
Sarigan
Anatahan

Saipan
Aguijan   Tinian
Rota

Guam (USA)

FEDERATED STATES OF MICRONESIA

REPUBLIC OF PALAU

Ulithi
Yap
Fais
Ngulu
Faraulep
Namonuito
Hall Islands
Fayu   Murilo
Pulap
Kyangel
Babeldaob
Koror
Angaur
Peleliu
Sorol
Woleai
Elato
Puluwat   Chuuk   Nama
Lamotrek
Satawal   Losap
Eauripik
Ifalik

Western   Caroline   Islands

Sonsorol Islands
Pulo Anna
Merir

Tobi
Helen Reef

P A C I F I C

Halmahera

EQUATOR

Admiralty
Islands

Ceram

New
Ireland

Banda

New

Sea

Guinea

New Britain

Coral

Arafura

Sea

Sea

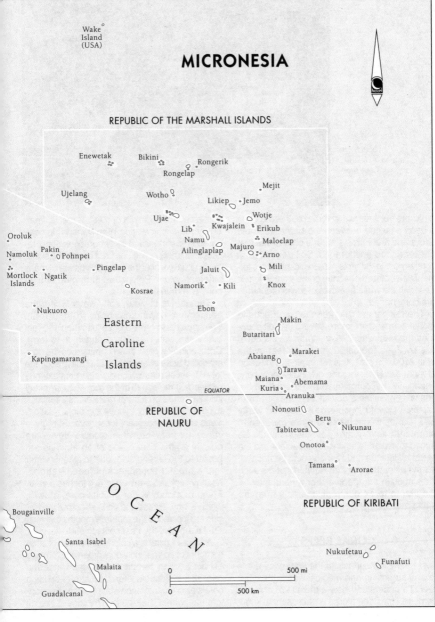

MICRONESIA

Wake Island (USA)

REPUBLIC OF THE MARSHALL ISLANDS

Enewetak Bikini Rongerik
Rongelap
Mejit
Ujelang Wotho
Likiep Jemo
Ujae Wotje
Lib Kwajalein Erikub
Namu Maloelap
Ailinglaplap Majuro
Arno

Oroluk
Namoluk Pakin Pohnpei
Mortlock Ngatik Pingelap
Islands
Jaluit Mili
Namorik Kili Knox
Kosrae

Nukuoro Ebon

Eastern
Makin
Caroline Butaritari
Islands
Abaiang Marakei
Kapingamarangi Tarawa
Maiana Abemama
Kuria
Aranuka
EQUATOR

REPUBLIC OF
NAURU
Nonouti
Beru
Tabiteuea Nikunau
Onotoa

Tamana Arorae

Bougainville

O C E A N

REPUBLIC OF KIRIBATI

Santa Isabel

Malaita
Nukufetau Funafuti

0   500 mi
Guadalcanal
0   500 km

© MOON PUBLICATIONS, INC.

beach on
Falealop Island,
Woleai atoll

PAUL BOHLER

Where volcanic island remains, there is often a deep passage between the barrier reef and shore; the reef forms a natural breakwater that shelters good anchorages. Soil derived from coral is poor in nutrients, while volcanic soil is fertile. Dark-colored beaches come from volcanic material; the white beaches of travel brochures are coral based.

The dangers of the greenhouse effect and global warming are more severe in atoll countries than anywhere else. Water levels could rise by three feet in 50 years, 10 feet by the year 2100. On atolls this will mean the intrusion of more salt water into the groundwater supply, especially if accompanied by droughts. If the sea level rises more quickly than the coral reef can grow upward, lagoons could lose their vitality and islands would become more exposed to storms. In time, entire populations could be forced to evacuate, and whole countries like the Marshall Islands and Kiribati could be flooded. It's the ultimate irony that isolated specks such as islands in the Marshalls or Kiribati may be the first to feel catastrophic effects from the smog of Beijing or Detroit.

CORAL REEFS

Just below the surface of the water lies a different, surprising and magical world: the coral reef. To understand how a basalt volcano becomes a limestone atoll, it is necessary to know a little about the growth of coral. A reef is created by the accumulation of millions of tiny calcareous skeletons left by generations of microscopic animals called polyps. Though the skeleton is usually white, the living polyps are of many different colors. Polyps live in the top of hard coral communities.

They thrive in clear, salty water where the temperature never drops below 70° F (21° C). They must also have a base less than 150 feet below the water's surface on which to form. Coral colonies grow slowly upward on the consolidated base of ancestors until they reach the low tide level, after which development extends outward on the edges of the reef. Virtually every living creature on a coral reef serves a function to others. The ability to have symbiotic relationships is a skill necessary for survival. Sunlight is critical for coral growth. Colonies grow more quickly on the ocean side of an atoll, as opposed to the lagoon side, due to clearer water and a greater abundance of food. A strong, healthy reef can grow up to two inches a year. Fresh or cloudy water inhibits coral growth, which is why villages and ports all across the Pacific are located at the reef-free mouths of rivers. These are also the best spots to surf.

A piece of coral is a colony composed of large numbers of polyps, individual organisms. Polyps extract calcium carbonate from the water and deposit it in their skeletons. Most reef-building corals also contain encrustations of microscopic algae within their cells. The algae, like all green plants, obtain their energy from the sun, and contribute this energy to the growth of the reef's skeleton. As a result, corals behave (and look) more like plants than animals, competing for sunlight just as terrestrial plants do. Many polyps are also carnivorous, supplementing their energy by capturing tiny planktonic animals and organic particles at night with minute stinging tentacles.

Coral Types

Corals belong to a broad group of stinging creatures that includes polyps, soft corals, stony corals, sea anemones, sea fans, and jellyfish. Stony corals such as brain, table, staghorn, and mushroom corals have external skeletons and are important reef builders. Soft corals, black corals, and sea fans have internal skeletons. Fire corals have a smooth, velvety surface and yellowish brown color. The stinging toxins of this group can penetrate human skin and cause swelling and painful burning. The many

The crown-of-thorns starfish (Acanthaster planci) *feeds on living coral.*

DIANA LASICH HARPER

varieties of soft, colorful anemones gently waving in the current might seem inviting to touch, but beware, many can inflict painful stings. All coral is fragile and can be destroyed by even casual, inadvertent touching. Keep your hands and feet off to contribute to the continuing health of the reef.

Corals, like most life-forms in the Pacific, colonized the ocean from the fertile seas of Southeast Asia. Thus the number of species declines as you move east: the Western Caroline islands have three times as many varieties of coral as Hawaii. Over 600 species of coral make their home in the Pacific, compared to only 48 in the Caribbean. The diversity of coral colors and forms is endlessly amazing.

Exploring a Reef

Exploring a healthy, thriving coral reef is one of life's great joys. While one cannot walk through pristine forests because there are no paths, it's quite possible to swim over untouched reefs—the most densely populated and ecologically complex living space on earth. This is our most unspoiled environment, a world of indescribable beauty. Enjoy it, treasure it, protect it. Use all precautions to avoid contact that will harm it.

Snorkeling over a reef is usually best at high tides. It is safest to snorkel inside the reef. However, snorkeling the outer "drop-off" is thrilling for its variety of fish and corals. Only strong swimmers with good ocean experience should do so, however. If you are swimming out, rather than being taken by a boat, come out only on a calm day to avoid being knocked back onto the reef by waves. Before going in, make yourself aware of any currents from channels that drain tidal flows. Observe the direction the water is flowing. If the flow is mild, swim into it so that your return, when you may be more tired, is easier. If the flow is strong, don't go in. If you misjudge, and get caught in a strong flow, swim across the current rather than against it. If you can't resist the pull at all, it is best to conserve your energy, let yourself be carried out, and when the current diminishes, swim along the outer reef face until you find somewhere to come back in.

Coral reefs are fragile and complex ecosystems, providing food and shelter for countless species of fish, crustacea (shrimps, crabs, and lobsters), mollusks (clams and mussels), and other living creatures. Hard coral grow less than two inches a year and it can take 10,000 years for a coral reef to form. Though corals look solid, they're easily broken, and by standing on them, breaking off pieces, or carelessly dropping anchor you can destroy in a few minutes what took so long to form. Once a piece of coral breaks off it dies and it may be years before the coral reestablishes itself.

We recommend you do not remove coral, seashells, plantlife, or marine animals from the

CORALS OF THE PACIFIC

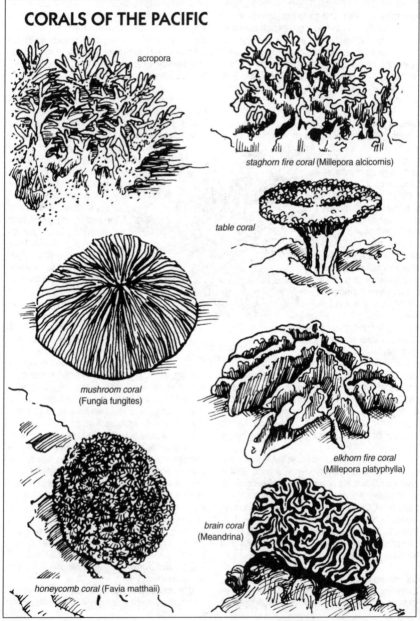

acropora

staghorn fire coral (Millepora alcicornis)

table coral

mushroom coral (Fungia fungites)

elkhorn fire coral (Millepora platyphylla)

brain coral (Meandrina)

honeycomb coral (Favia matthaii)

KAREN McKINLEY

RULES OF THE REEF

S am's Dive Shop on Palau recommends the following environmental protection rules for all divers and snorkelers:

- Avoid wearing gloves so that you will avoid the temptation to touch.
- Do not collect live or even dead coral or shells.
- Establish neutral buoyancy and keep fins off the bottom.
- Avoid damage to reef life through carelessly moving equipment.
- Never chase, ride, or harass aquatic life.
- Do not spear or collect fish while using scuba.
- Do not throw anything out of the boat, not cigarette butts nor pull tabs.

sea. In a small way, you are upsetting the delicate balance of nature. This is a particular problem along shorelines frequented by large numbers of tourists, who can strip a reef in very little time. If you'd like a souvenir, content yourself with what you find on the beach. Also think twice about purchasing jewelry or souvenirs made from coral or seashells. Limited-production traditional handicrafts that incorporate shells are one thing, but by purchasing unmounted seashells or mass-produced coral curios you are contributing to the destruction of the marine environment.

CLIMATE

Temperatures are uniformly high year-round, and rainfall is well distributed. The Gilbert and Line Islands in the Southern Hemisphere get less rainfall from July to November, while the Marshalls, Carolines, and Marianas are somewhat drier and less humid from December through April. The Northern Marianas enjoy Micronesia's most pleasant climate, with lower temperatures and moderate rainfall. Kosrae and Pohnpei are among the rainiest places on earth.

The Gilberts are much drier than the Marshalls and Carolines, and can even experience drought.

Travel during the rainy season is almost as easy as during the dry, since the rains are usually brief and heavy, instantly cooling the air and nurturing the thick vegetation. Also, much of the rain falls at night. For divers, though, the rainy season is slightly less favorable as rivers flush more sediment into the lagoons; however, the waters tend to be still at this time, allowing diving at places inaccessible during the windier dry season. The reduced number of visitors during the wet season also compensates for the higher precipitation.

The northeast tradewinds blow steadily west across much of Micronesia from December through March, changing to calms, easterlies, or southeast trades in summer. Throughout Micronesia, winds out of the west bring rain. The tradewinds are caused by hot air rising near the equator and then flowing toward the poles at high altitude. Cooler air drawn toward the vacuum is deflected to the west by the rotation of the earth. Micronesia's proximity to the equator explains the seasonal shift in the winds, as the intertropical convergence zone between the northeast and southeast trades (or doldrum zone— where the most heated air is rising) moves north of the islands in summer. The tradewinds cool the islands and offer clear sailing, making winter the most favorable season to visit.

A tropical cyclone or typhoon (hurricane) forms when thunderstorms release heat and the hot air rises. Cooler air rushes in toward the low pressure area created, spinning around the eye counterclockwise in the Northern Hemisphere, clockwise in the Southern Hemisphere. The main typhoon season in Micronesia is the rainy season, May through December, although typhoons can occur in any month. These storms are usually generated in the east and move west. Thus typhoons are far less common in the Marshalls than farther west.

Micronesia enjoys the cleanest air on earth— air that hasn't blown over a continent for weeks. To view the night stars in the warm, windless sky is like witnessing creation anew.

M.G.L. DOMENY DE RIENZI

FLORA AND FAUNA

The variety of animal species encountered in the Pacific islands declines as you move away from the Asian mainland. Island birdlife is more abundant than land-based fauna, but still reflects the decline in variety from west to east. The flora too reflect this phenomenon. Although some plant species spread by means of floating seeds or fruit, more commonly, wind and birds effect the movement. The microscopic spores of ferns, for example, can be carried vast distances by the wind.

Flying foxes and insect-eating bats were the only mammals to reach Micronesia without the aid of man. Ancient navigators introduced wild pigs, dogs, and chickens; they also brought along rats and mice. Jesuit missionaries introduced the water buffalo or carabao to Guam in the 17th century.

Birdwatching is a highly recommended pursuit for the serious Pacific traveler; you'll find it opens unexpected doors. Good field guides are few (ask at local bookstores, museums, and cultural centers), but a determined interest will bring you in contact with fascinating people and lead to great adventures. The best time to observe forest birds is in the very early morning—they move around a lot less in the heat of the day.

Toward the end of World War II, the Solomon Islands brown tree snake began to establish itself in Guam, probably having hitchhiked on a military supply plane. It proceeded to wipe out virtually all land based birds on Guam. Today, all Pacific tropical islands attempt to avoid the introduction of this voracious snake.

Micronesia's high islands support a great variety of plantlife, while the low islands are restricted to a few hardy species such as breadfruit, cassava (tapioca), pandanus, and coconuts. On atolls, taro must be cultivated in deep organic pits.

Mangrove forests are

*Seven days a week
fish dart among the coral.
Very clear water.*

common along high island coastal lagoons. The cable roots of the saltwater-tolerant mangroves anchor in the shallow upper layer of oxygenated mud, avoiding the layers of hydrogen sulfide below. The tree provides shade for tiny organisms dwelling in the tidal mudflats—a place for birds to nest and for fish or shellfish to feed and spawn. The mangroves filter and purify water flowing from land to sea and perform the same task as land-building coral colonies along the reefs: as sediment is trapped between roots, the trees extend farther into the lagoon, creating a unique natural environment. In this fashion, over the centuries, mangroves add to the size of their islands.

The past decade has seen widespread destruction of mangroves, which is tragic, considering that the ecological benefits of this fragile environment are not fully known. On many of the islands of Micronesia, canals have been maintained through mangrove forests. Canoe trips are a marvelous way to explore these wonderful ecosystems.

MARINELIFE

Micronesia's richest store of life is found in the underwater world of the lagoon and the surrounding ocean. While diving or snorkeling it is common to see angelfish, bonito, butterfly fish, eels, grouper, harp fish, jacks, mahi, mullet, parrot fish, stingrays, surgeonfish, swordfish, trumpet fish, tuna, and countless more. It's believed most Pacific marine organisms evolved in the triangular area bounded by New Guinea, the Philippines, and the Malay Peninsula. This "Cradle of Indo-Pacific Marinelife" includes a wide variety of habitats and has remained stable through several geological ages. From this cradle the rest of the Pacific was colonized. In a very real sense, unless the Pacific Ocean remains biologically viable, world civilization, and perhaps human life itself, will simply vanish. This ocean supplies the bulk of protein for the Pacific Rim, center of civilization for the 21st century. The oxygen provided to the atmosphere by the Pacific Ocean algae dwarfs that supplied by the Amazon rainforest.

Dolphins
While most people use the terms dolphin and porpoise interchangeably, true porpoises lack the dolphin's beak (although many dolphins are also beakless). There are 62 species of dolphins and only six species of porpoises, all highly intelligent mammals. Dolphins leap from the water and many legends tell of them saving humans, particularly children, from drowning (perhaps the most famous concerns Telemachus, son of Odysseus). Dolphins often follow schools of tuna. Net fishing of tuna, still practiced by some commercial fishing companies, drowns many dolphins.

Sharks
The danger from sharks has been greatly exaggerated. Of some 300 different species, only 28 attack humans. Most dangerous are the white, tiger, hammerhead, and blue sharks. Fortunately, all these usually inhabit deep water, far from coasts. Sometimes, however, attracted by wastes thrown overboard, they follow ships into port and create serious problems. Relatively few shark attacks a year occur worldwide. Considering the number of people who swim in the sea, your chances of being involved are pretty slim.

Sharks are least dangerous in waters such as those of Micronesia where food is abundant. If you see a shark, don't panic and thrash about—this could attract an attack. Get away as calmly and quickly as possible, unless you're with someone knowledgeable, such as a local divemaster, who says it's okay. Sharks normally stay outside the reef, but ask local advice. Avoid swimming in places where sewage or edible wastes enter the water or where fish have just been cleaned.

Barracudas
Swimmers need not fear an attack by barracuda. In these lush tropical waters where marinelife

The relatively harmless blacktip reef shark (Carcharhinus melanopterus) may be seen in shallow lagoon water.

DIANA LASICH HARPER

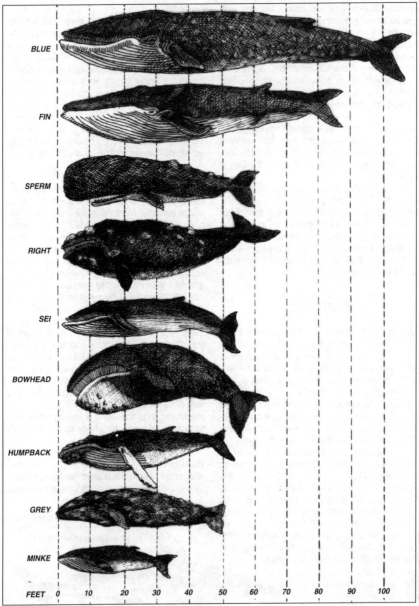

BLUE

FIN

SPERM

RIGHT

SEI

BOWHEAD

HUMPBACK

GREY

MINKE

FEET 0   10   20   30   40   50   60   70   80   90   100

DIANA LASICH HARPER

abounds, barracudas can find tastier food. Most cases of barracuda attack are provoked: a spearfisher shoots one in the tail, another is attracted by the spearfisher's catch.

Sea Urchins

Sea urchins (living pincushions) are common in tropical waters, most usually on rocky shores or reefs. The pins on some can even go through a fin. Quill punctures are painful and can become infected if not treated. The quills on many species have small barbs, like fish hooks, which make their removal difficult. The folk remedy for removal is to soak the area in vinegar or urine for 15 minutes. But if the quill is still in two weeks later, consult a doctor.

Other Marinelife

Among the troublesome sea creatures you may encounter, jellyfish are the most common. Their sting is painful, but rarely serious. Carry a bottle of meat tenderizer with you to the beach, and apply it to the affected area as quickly as possible.

Although stonefish, crown-of-thorns starfish, cone shells, and eels are hazardous, injuries resulting from any of these are rare. Stonefish

LOUISE FOOTE

The Pacific ridley turtle (Lepidochelys olivacea) is one of the rarest of the seven species of sea turtles. Pacific ridleys eat crustaceans, fish eggs, and some vegetation.

rest on the bottom and are hard to see due to camouflaging that makes them look like a sandy ocean bottom; their dorsal fins inject a painful, sometimes lethal poison, which burns like fire in the blood if you happen to step on one. Treat the wound by submerging it, along with an opposite foot or hand, in water as hot as you can stand for 30 minutes (the opposite extremity prevents scalding due to numbness). If a hospital or clinic is nearby, go there immediately. Fortunately stonefish are not common, and if you keep your feet off the bottom, you further reduce any risks.

Never pick up a live cone shell; some varieties have a deadly stinger dart coming out from the pointed end that can reach any part of the shell's outer surface. Eels hide in reef crevices by day; most are dangerous only if you poke your hand or foot in at them. Don't tempt fate by approaching them in a manner they might interpret as threatening.

REPTILES

Saltwater crocodiles live in the mangrove forests of the Western Carolines. They are so endangered it is almost impossible to find one, let alone be attacked by one. Six of the seven species of sea turtles are facing extinction due to overhunting and overharvesting of eggs. For this reason, importing any turtle product is prohibited in most Western countries.

Although the yard-long monitor lizard may look fearsome, it's no threat to humans and is beautiful to watch if you are lucky enough to

---

SAVE THE WHALES

The cetaceans (whales, dolphins, and porpoises) are divided into two suborders: the *Mysticeti* (baleen whales) and the *Odontoceti* (toothed whales, narwhals, and dolphins). The baleen whales (including all in the chart except the sperm whale) have a series of plates in the roof of the mouth which are used to strain plankton, krill, and fish from the water. Dolphins and porpoises use their teeth to catch squid or fish. In 1982, the International Whaling Commission voted to end commercial whaling around the world on 1 January 1986. Japan, Norway, and Iceland objected to the ban and continued to whale in the face of world opinion. Jacques Cousteau put it this way: "The only creatures on earth that have bigger—and maybe better—brains than humans are the cetacea, the whales and dolphins. Perhaps they could one day tell us something important, but it is unlikely that we will hear it. Because we are coldly, efficiently, and economically killing them off."

see one. The adaptable monitor can climb trees, dig holes, run quickly on land, and catch fish swimming in the lagoon. It'll eat almost anything it can catch, from insects to snails, smaller lizards, rats, crabs, birds, and bird eggs.

Geckos and skinks are small lizards often seen on the islands. The skink hunts insects by day; its tail breaks off if you catch it, but a new one quickly grows. The gecko is nocturnal and has no eyelids. Adhesive toe pads enable it to pass along vertical surfaces, and it changes color to avoid detection. Unlike the skink, which avoids humans, geckos often live in people's homes where they eat insects attracted by electric lights. Its ticking call may be a territorial warning to other geckos.

THE SNORKELER

Although he lived in an interactive universe turning toward pun, he resented being turned into a caterpillar as punishment for chasing a pair of butterfly fish.

HISTORY

History creates a community's past. To be comprehensible, it must employ a construct in order to simplify otherwise unmanageable amounts of data. By making sense, history differs from reality.

The Micronesians

The earliest arrivals to Micronesia left relatively few artifacts that withstood centuries of tropical weather. Thus, there is much guesswork in piecing together Micronesia's earliest human history. What follows is a summary of archaeologists', historians', and anthropologists' best theories, subject, of course, to continual revision.

Austronesian-speaking Micronesian peoples entered the Pacific from Southeast Asia over 3,000 years ago. The first islands they located were probably the Marianas, followed by the Western Carolines. From this base they settled the Eastern Caroline, Tungaru, and Marshall Islands. Trading beads uncovered at Yap prove that some contact was maintained with Southeast Asia. In the westernmost atolls of Micronesia, an Indonesian-style loom is still used to make hibiscus-fiber skirts.

The first Micronesians lived from fishing, gathering, and agriculture. Many islanders used pottery, and all made tools from stone, shells and bone. They cultivated breadfruit, taro, pandanus, coconuts, cassava, and (on the volcanic islands) yams. Pigs, chickens, and dogs were kept for food, but the surrounding sea yielded the most important source of protein. Most Micronesian societies were matrilineal; the husband and children became members of the wife's landholding matrilineage. Patrilineal Yap was an exception. From chiefly clans came the ruling male chiefs. The paramount chiefs of Palau, the Marshalls, Pohnpei, and Yap are still influential figures.

Micronesians were the greatest sea voyagers in the world and sailed huge outrigger canoes between the Carolines and the Marianas. To navigate they read signs from the sun, stars, currents, swells, winds, clouds, and birds. Yap was an important trading center, in regular con-

tact with Palau and the islands to the east. Annual expeditions brought tribute to the powerful islands of Ulithi and Yap.

Old stories in the Carolines tell of a great empire, of which we unfortunately know little. The magnificent ruins of Kosrae and Pohnpei, the stone money of Yap, the *latte* stones of Guam, Rota, and Tinian, and the basalt monoliths and terraces of Babeldaob add to the mystery, but testify to complex, wealthy cultures. It is hard to believe these extraordinary navigators did not keep some continual contact with the Philippines, Indonesia and perhaps even mainland Asia.

Magellan

Magellan was the first European to sail on the Pacific. He proved that one could sail around the world. In the late 15th century the Portuguese exercised control of the trade route around the tip of Africa to the spice islands of Indonesia and the riches of China, forcing the Spaniards to find another route for the trade they desired. The king of Spain outfitted Magellan with five ships for one of the greatest journeys in history.

In September 1519, Magellan's fleet of five ships sailed southwest across the Atlantic toward South America. On 21 October, Magellan sighted a cape, and then a bay-like opening. Two ships investigating the channel discovered that the flood tide was stronger than the ebb, indicating a passage. Magellan crossed what became known as the Strait of Magellan in a remarkable 38-day voyage, losing two ships in the process to the tempestuous weather.

On 28 November 1520, the three surviving ships entered the Pacific. The ships sailed northwest for months across this unimaginably vast sea. Worms reduced their biscuits to powder, and the crew had to hold their noses as they drank the water. The hides that kept the rigging from chafing on the yards were softened by being dragged overboard for days, and then eaten. Rats were a delicacy.

The ships finally sighted land on 24 January 1521, and 11 days later came upon people in swift outrigger canoes near Guam. The islanders

Colonial Intervention

Micronesia was not soon colonized. It was not an important objective of the Spanish, Portuguese, or even the later Pacific colonial power, the Dutch. No permanent base was set up on Guam until 1668. Even then, Spain's interest in Guam was to use it as a support base for their galleons trading the silver of Mexico for the tea, silk, and spices of the Philippines. Little attention was paid to the Carolines or Marshalls until 1864 when the first resident German trader set up shop

(Chamorros) took Magellan's skiff. In vengeance, he took 40 armed men ashore, burned 50 houses and boats, killed seven men, and recovered his skiff. By 9 March his fleet had arrived northeast of the Moluccas (Maluku, Indonesia) at Samar in the present-day Philippines. Magellan converted the rajah of Cebu and 3,000 of his subjects to Christianity. Magellan was killed while leading a similar expedition to convert and subdue the neighboring island of Mactan. One of the ships, however, sailed on alone across the Indian Ocean, around the Cape of Good Hope, and north through the Atlantic, reaching Seville, Spain, in September 1522. These survivors were the first men known to have circumnavigated the globe. One hundred seventy men died on the voyage.

The circumnavigation was perhaps not as important an event as is sometimes implied in history books. No one else bothered to do it until Sir Francis Drake in 1578. The Strait of Magellan remained a dangerous, difficult crossing. For centuries, the major direct route to Asia from Europe was around Africa. The predominant route for the Spanish was indirect: to Mexico and Central America by boat, across land to the Pacific, and then travel by its Pacific fleet.

in the Marshalls, followed in 1869 by a post on Yap. The Germans established a protectorate over the Marshalls in 1878 and attempted to extend this to all of the Caroline and Marshall Islands in 1885. The Spanish protested that they had already claimed the area. In 1874 the Pope mediated the Spanish-German dispute and ruled in favor of the Spanish, although the Germans were given trading rights and permitted to annex the Marshalls.

In the 1830s British whalers and traders from Australia became active in the Carolines and Marshalls. Americans arrived in the 1850s. These newcomers brought catastrophic epidemics and foreign control to the populations, further disrupting traditional life. Protestant missionaries established themselves on Pohnpei and Kosrae by 1852. The British established a protectorate over the Gilberts in 1892.

In 1898 the Spanish-American War shattered Spain's colonial empire, and the United States took advantage of the occasion to annex Guam and the Philippines. The Spanish had little choice other than to sell the Carolines and Northern Marianas to the Germans in 1899 for 25 million pesetas.

The Germans set about organizing the lucrative copra trade. To force the islanders to make

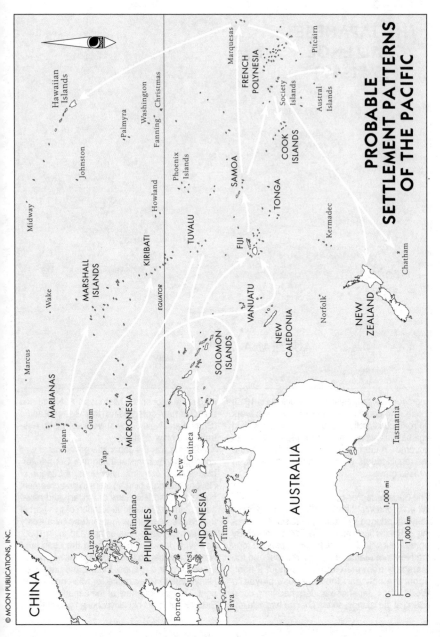

PROBABLE
SETTLEMENT PATTERNS
OF THE PACIFIC

© MOON PUBLICATIONS, INC.

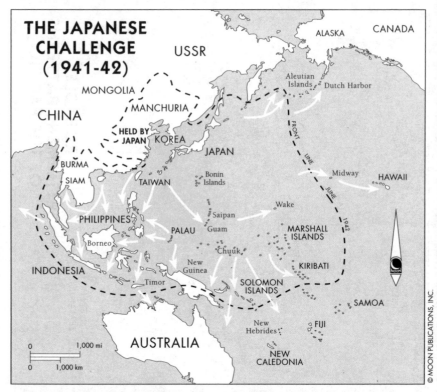

THE JAPANESE CHALLENGE (1941-42)

© MOON PUBLICATIONS, INC.

copra for sale, they established a poll tax in 1910; those who couldn't pay were required to work on road construction. The Pohnpeians revolted against this slave labor and killed the German governor. A German warship soon arrived, and the rebel leaders were executed and buried in a mass grave.

The Japanese Period

When World War I broke out, Germany essentially abandoned its Pacific possessions, bringing its Pacific fleet back to the European war. By agreement with the British, the Japanese took the Northern Marianas, the Carolines, and the Marshalls from the Germans without a fight, about the only part the Japanese played in World War I. Japanese traders had long been calling at the islands, so the change had little im-

mediate impact on the Micronesians. Nauru and the German colonies in the South Pacific (Samoa and New Guinea) were seized by Australia and New Zealand.

After the war the Japanese government was appointed to administer the former German territories north of the equator under a League of Nations mandate binding them to an agreement not to build "fortifications or military and naval bases." In 1922 the neutralization of this part of the Pacific was further guaranteed by a treaty between the United States and Japan. In 1935, however, Japan withdrew from the League of Nations and began building large military bases on some of the islands. Finally, they annexed Nanyo Gunto (their name for Micronesia) outright. The headquarters of the Japanese South Seas Government or Nanyochokan was at Koror.

Big Japanese business interests in 1921 founded the Nanyo Kohatsu Kaisha (South Seas Development Co., Ltd.). The Japanese built sugar mills in the Marianas and mined bauxite and phosphate in Palau. They also developed commercial fishing, trochus shell production, and agriculture. After 1931 Japanese citizens were allowed to purchase or lease Micronesian land and large tracts passed into their hands by dubious means.

Japan encouraged emigration to Micronesia. The number of Japanese colonists skyrocketed from 3,671 in 1920 to 84,476 in 1940, two-thirds of the total population. Japan had turned Micronesia into a part of Japan, with little regard for the indigenous people. Perhaps because it was closer to Micronesia than any other colonial power, Japan was the only one that had at-tempted to supplant the local population. The society they developed had three classes of people: Japanese at the top, Koreans and Oki-nawans in the middle, and Micronesians *(toming)* at the bottom.

Micronesians continued to live by subsistence agriculture or making copra, spectators on the sidelines of Japanese development. Interisland travel by canoe was banned and the authority of the traditional chiefs undermined. Before WW II, immigrants controlled almost all economic activities in the cash economy.

THE PACIFIC WAR

The First World War eliminated Germany from Micronesia, New Guinea, and Samoa, and gave

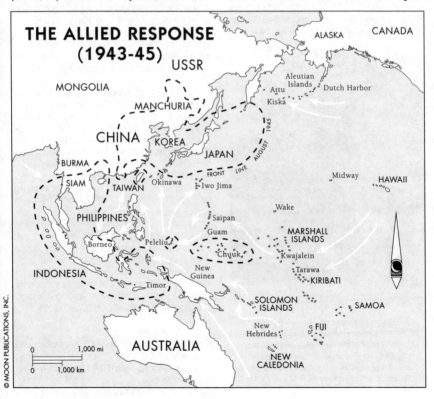

THE ALLIED RESPONSE (1943-45)

Japan the central Pacific. The Second World War expelled Japan and brought the United States.

In 1942 the Japanese used their military bases in Palau to attack the Philippines and Indonesia; Chuuk was a springboard for their assault on the Solomons and New Guinea. With the Japanese conquest of Guam, Nauru, and Tungaru the whole of Micronesia was under one rule for the first time in history. For the Micronesians the war years were ones of forced labor, famine, and fear. They watched as their islands were ravaged by foreign armies; 5,000 Micronesians died.

The Rising Sun

Japan had hoped to become the dominant power in Asia and the Pacific by establishing a "Greater East Asia Co-prosperity Sphere." The Japanese high command decided to achieve their ends through force. In July 1941, after

Admiral Isoroku Yamamotu planned the attacks on Pearl Harbor and Midway. He remained commander in chief of the Japanese combined fleet until a Betty bomber in which he was a passenger was shot down over Bougainville in the North Solomon Islands by American P-38s on 18 April 1943.

NAVAL HISTORICAL CENTER, WASHINGTON, D.C.

Japanese troops occupied French Indochina, the American, British, and Dutch governments declared an iron and oil embargo against Japan. When it became evident to the Japanese that they would have to fight to protect their oil supply from Dutch-held Indonesia, they prepared for war.

The Japanese planned to shatter the American fleet in one massive attack, creating a large defensive perimeter and thereby cutting off aid to opponents in China. The Pearl Harbor attack on 7 December 1941, for all its seeming brilliance, did not meet the Japanese tactical goal, since the main United States aircraft carriers were out of the harbor and survived the attack. The attack did not take the United States out of the war, as the Japanese high command had hoped. But it did delay the ability of the United States Navy to interfere with Japan's occupation of Southeast Asia. Hong Kong, Shanghai, Malaya, Singapore, the Dutch East Indies, Burma, and the Philippines all fell to the Japanese by April 1942. And China was temporarily cut off from much-needed assistance from the United States.

Then came the Doolittle bombing raid on Tokyo on 18 April 1942. The Japanese decided to widen the perimeter to protect the homeland. They occupied Tulagi in the Solomon Islands in May and started building an air base on Guadalcanal. Landings took place throughout New Guinea, and a Japanese fleet advanced toward Port Moresby. En route it was intercepted by Allied naval units, and although the ensuing Battle of the Coral Sea—the air battle between navies that never sighted each other—is now judged a draw, the Japanese invasion fleet turned back. Less than a month later on 4 June, another Japanese invasion fleet became locked in the Battle of Midway: American aircraft sank four Japanese carriers, with their planes and elite crews. Japan had lost its naval superiority in the Pacific. Its strategy of landing a knockout punch to the United States had failed.

The Setting Sun

From July to November 1942, Australian and Japanese armies fought back and forth across New Guinea's Kokoda Trail near Port Moresby. Simultaneously, Japanese soldiers struggled in the Solomons to recapture Guadalcanal

Task Force 38.3 enters the Ulithi lagoon in line ahead, returning from strikes in the Philippines, 11 December 1944.

from the Americans. By the end of 1942 the Japanese had lost both campaigns. A number of indecisive naval engagements accompanied the jungle war in the Solomons, but the end result was a further weakening of Japanese aerial strength. The spring and early summer of 1943 saw a stalemate between Australia and Japan, while the United States rebuilt its strength for the next phase: recovery of the Philippines.

In the wide Pacific, the advantage lies with the side on the offensive, as the Japanese learned when they tried to defend a vastly scattered front against overpowering mobile naval units. The Allied strategy was to approach the Philippines from two directions, with the United States and Australian armies fighting their way up through New Guinea, and the U.S. Navy thrusting across the central Pacific. By mid-1943 troops under Gen. Douglas A. MacArthur and Admiral Halsey began the long campaign in the Solomons (New Georgia, Bougainville) and New Guinea (Salamaua, Lae, Finschhafen, Madang). Large Japanese armies were bogged down in China and elsewhere, enabling the Allies to concentrate their forces at the weak points, neutralizing and bypassing entrenched strongholds (for example Chuuk) where the price of conquest would have been too great.

The central Pacific naval offensive under Adm. Chester W. Nimitz began in November 1943, with landings at Tarawa and Butaritari in Tungaru. Casualties were high at these battles, but they enabled the Allies to perfect amphibious landing techniques. In February 1944, the Americans captured Kwajalein and Enewetak. They destroyed the Japanese fleet in Chuuk lagoon. By this time, United States carrier forces were strong enough to overcome Japanese opposition, but at a heavy price if the plans entailed an amphibious landing, rather than mere aerial and naval bombardment.

The Philippines and Beyond

In June 1944 the United States landed on Saipan to secure advanced bases for bombing Japanese home islands. The Japanese Navy thus engaged the Allies in the Battle of the Philippine Sea, losing three carriers and 480 planes, and leaving the Philippines open to attack. Tinian and Guam were then taken by the Americans.

By July 1944, Japanese weakness was clearly evident, and United States submarines began to take a crippling toll on their merchant shipping. In September, the New Guinea and central Pacific offensives converged when Morotai (near Ternate) and Peleliu (Palau) were captured, providing dual springboards for the Philippines campaign.

The American landings at Leyte in the Philippines in October led to the largest naval battle of all time, the Battle of the Leyte Gulf. The Japanese lost 24 major warships, including all their

NAVAL HISTORICAL CENTER, WASHINGTON, D.C.

aviator's grave, Japanese Cemetery, Peleliu

remaining carriers, compared to a U.S. loss of only six smaller ships. For the first time, the Japanese made large scale use of kamikaze-piloted planes. In January 1945, the Americans landed at Lingayen on Luzon, and by early March the remaining Japanese had been driven into the mountains, where they would hold out until the end of the war, but not before Manila was destroyed in battle.

The next stage in the war was to be the invasion of Japan itself. The first of a damaging series of incendiary bombings of Japanese cities by Tinian-based B-29s occurred on 24 November 1944. In March 1945 over 80,000 civilians died in the incendiary bombing of Tokyo.

To gain advanced air bases able to provide fighter cover for the bombers, U.S. Marines landed at Iwo Jima on 19 February 1945. Although it took five bitter weeks, they finally cleared the island of defenders. In early 1945, the British reconquered Burma, reopening the road to China. In April, United States forces invaded Okinawa to secure an advanced naval base, but Japanese defensive positions and kamikaze attacks exacted serious casualties.

Finally, on 6 August 1945 the United States ushered in the atomic era, dropping an atom bomb on Hiroshima. Days later it dropped a second on Nagasaki. The planes had taken off from Tinian in the Northern Marianas. The Japanese, at the emperor's insistence, surrendered the day after the Nagasaki bomb. The United States has always justified this action with claims that had it invaded Japan instead, there would have been an even greater loss of life to American soldiers, as well as to Japanese military personnel and civilians.

Half a million Japanese soldiers and civilians died in this senseless war, far from their shores. Of the 50,000 Micronesians, 10% were killed as foreign armies fought back and forth across the islands in a brutal struggle the islanders could only lose. All Japanese military and civilians died in battle, committed suicide, or were repatriated at the end of the war. The prewar infrastructures and economies of Micronesia were obliterated. Bitter memories of the war are still vivid in the minds of the older people, who associate the destruction with the prewar Japanese occupation and militarization of the area.

THE POSTWAR PERIOD

Strategic Trust

In the Cairo Declaration of 1 December 1943, Churchill and Roosevelt announced that after the war, Japan would be stripped of all the island possessions it had obtained in 1914. Soon after the Japanese surrender, the United States Navy called for the annexation of Micronesia, but the Truman administration, sensitive to being branded neocolonialist, opted instead for a United Nations trusteeship, which it received in 1947. Included in the trusteeship were islands that now compose the Republic of the Marshall Islands, the Federated States of Micronesia, the Republic of Palau, and the Commonwealth of the Marianas.

The Trust Territory of the Pacific Islands (TTPI) was the last of the 11 trusteeships under the United Nations to attain self-government. It had been the only one designated a "strategic" trust, meaning that the United States could establish military bases and conduct nuclear tests. Originally administered by the U.S. Navy, in 1951 control over the trusteeship passed to the Department of the Interior, although the Northern Marianas remained under naval rule until 1962.

At first Micronesia was administered from Honolulu, but in 1954 the Office of the High Commissioner shifted to Guam, and in 1962 the Trust Territory headquarters moved to Saipan. There were six districts: Marshall Islands, Ponape (Pohnpei), Truk (Chuuk), Yap, Palau, and the Northern Marianas.

Military Use

Immediately after World War II, General MacArthur proposed an "offshore island perimeter" to defend American interests in the Far East. After the withdrawal from Vietnam in 1973, United States strategists resurrected plans for a chain of island-based military installations facing the Pacific Rim from Japan to the Indian Ocean. Micronesia offered a wide perimeter on islands that were immune from massive local opposition. The Pentagon obtained leases over much of the Northern Marianas in 1976. In a 1983 vote, the Marshallese approved a Compact that delivered the Kwajalein missile range to the United States for 30 years. For decades, only the Palauans resisted United States pressure for bases.

Currently, with the cold war over and conventional military deployments winding down worldwide, the United States has shifted to a strategy of a small number of high-tech bases, such as that at Kwajalein. Islanders often see themselves in a no-win situation. On the one hand, there are some continued antimilitary feelings. On the other hand, there is also fear of the economic hardship the islands would face if there were a precipitous, uncompensated withdrawal by the United States.

The American Role in Micronesia

It is clear that the United States objective in World War II was not to bring liberation to Micronesia. The goal was purely strategic—to rid the islands of Japanese bases. Nonetheless, the situation of Micronesians improved with the defeat of Japan. Japan, unlike previous colonial rulers, encouraged large scale emigration of its people to Micronesia. At the start of WW II, the population of Micronesia was two-thirds Japanese. Micronesians had been reduced to a politically impotent minority within their own homeland. With all the drawbacks of American rule, Micronesia today, with the exception of

Guam, is again overwhelmingly populated by its native population. Micronesians have the potential to fashion their own future.

This did not take place from American design, however. The United States, during its trusteeship, paid only lip service to the goal of preparing Micronesia for self-rule. From the start, United States policy was to preserve Micronesia for strategic use, while denying military access to foreign powers. The welfare of inhabitants was considered only in relation to this primary purpose, despite article six of the U.N. Trusteeship Agreement. That provision, at least in theory, bound the United States to "promote the economic advancement and self-sufficiency of the inhabitants."

Instead, two decades of neglect followed by two decades of often ill-conceived federal programs eroded the self-sufficiency of Micronesia's economies. In the early 1960s independence fever swept the third world, and it appeared the United States might lose control of its strategically located Trust Territory. In 1961 a visiting United Nations mission leveled heavy criticism at Washington for its neglect. In response, President Kennedy appointed a commission headed by economist Anthony M. Solomon to explore a future for Micronesia. The Solomon Report recommended agricultural development, capital improvements, and new health and welfare programs. The economic development proposals, which might have made the islands self-supporting, were never implemented.

In 1963 President Kennedy issued National Security Action Memorandum 145, setting forth as policy "the movement of Micronesia into a permanent relationship with the United States within our political framework." United States assistance to the TTPI jumped from $6.1 million in 1962 to $17 million in 1963, $67.3 million in 1971, and $138.7 million in 1979. Despite the flood of money, essential services (water, electricity, communications, sanitation) remained as bad as ever. Most of the money went into government salaries rather than into creating an economic infrastructure.

After 1966 large numbers of Peace Corps volunteers arrived in Micronesia; at the high point, 900 volunteers were at work on less than 100 inhabited islands. Today only about 60 Peace Corps volunteers remain in the Marshall

Islands and the Federated States of Micronesia. Many volunteers openly sided with the Micronesians, providing legal advice on how to defend their rights.

Political Development

The United States exported its political structures to Micronesia, undercutting the power of traditional chiefs. When the first Congress of Micronesia met on Saipan in 1965, American officials were taken aback by the political sophistication and solidarity displayed by the Micronesian legislators. In 1966 this Congress asked President Johnson to appoint a status commission to expedite the transfer of political control from American officials to elected Micronesian leaders. Negotiations toward a new status began in 1969. In 1971 the Micronesians rejected an offer of commonwealth status.

Frustrated United States officials fell back on a "divide and conquer" strategy, helping to fragment Micronesia into four separate entities. The CIA was brought in to spy on the Micronesian leaders (see front page, *Washington Post,* 2 December 1976). In 1975 the United States sliced off the Northern Marianas to form the Commonwealth of the Northern Marianas, with large tracts of land leased by the military.

Free Association

Despite the withdrawal of the Marianas delegates, a draft constitution for a "Federated States of Micronesia" was prepared. On 12 July 1978 a plebiscite was held throughout the Trust Territory. Voters in the Marshalls and Palau (the most strategically significant areas) rejected the constitution and elected to separate from the other districts, forming political entities of their own. This reflected, in part, an awareness of their stronger bargaining position and an unwillingness to share future benefits. A few months later the Congress of Micronesia was dissolved, and the four central districts (Kosrae, Pohnpei, Chuuk, and Yap) banded together, proclaiming the constitution of the Federated States of Micronesia on 10 May 1979. The Marshall Islands also attained self-government in 1979, and in 1980 Palau gained significant self-rule.

In 1983, voters in the Marshall Islands and the FSM approved Compacts of Free Association

with the United States. This phrase came from the fact that under the United Nations trusteeship, any continuing relationship with the United States had to be given with the "free" consent of the governed. The Compacts were formally adopted by the United States in 1986.

The 15-year Compacts granted two independent entities—the Republic of the Marshall Islands and the Federated States of Micronesia—full control over their internal and foreign affairs. In exchange for billions in financial support, the United States retained the right to use the islands for military purposes for 15 years. The U.S. has veto power over any Micronesian action in conflict with this right. Only the people of the Northern Marianas are U.S. citizens, although the others have the right of free entry to the States.

In 1986 the U.N. Trusteeship Council approved the termination of the U.S. trusteeship in the Marshall Islands, the Federated States of Micronesia, and the Northern Marianas, and—though the status of Palau remained unresolved—the U.S. declared the trusteeship terminated in the three in October 1986. Late in 1990 the Soviet Union withdrew its previous objections to these moves, and in December 1990 the U.N. Security Council voted 14 to 1 (with Cuba dissenting) to dissolve the Trust Territory in the Marshalls, FSM, and Northern Marianas. In 1991 the TTPI headquarters was moved from Saipan to Koror (Palau).

On 17 September 1991 the Federated States of Micronesia and the Marshall Islands were admitted to the United Nations. Palau finally ratified a Compact in 1994. Decades of opposition in Palau revolved around the United States' demand of the right to establish military bases and the islanders' opposition to allowing any nuclear weapons to enter its waters.

The Future

For the past several centuries, Micronesia's destiny was determined, in large part, by colonial powers that fought to control its strategic locations. Today, with the exception of Guam and the Commonwealth of the Northern Marianas, the islands of Micronesia are independent, though the nations of the former Trust Territory certainly can be said to remain within an American sphere of influence.

How will history judge the American administration of Micronesia? The Spanish came to use the islands of Micronesia as way stations for their far flung empire. They successfully spread their religion, often by murderous means. The Germans had little regard for preserving Micronesian culture and tried to force the Micronesians into plantation economies. The Japanese developed the islands by opening the floodgates to uncontrolled Asian immigration and militarization. Had they not started a disastrous war, Micronesia today would undoubtedly be as Japanese as Okinawa or Hokkaido, retaining an unassimilated Micronesian minority.

The American approach to Micronesia was subtle and effective. They instilled economic and political dependency, which served military ends. The United States, however, unlike the Japanese, protected Micronesian land rights. During the Japanese period much land was alienated to Japanese settlers. Under the TTPI most of this land went back to its original owners. And today, with the exception of Guam, Micronesians retain control of their homelands.

Today the United States seems almost in a hurry to be rid of Micronesia and to save the millions of dollars a year it spends on these islands. Its obligations to make Compact payments to the Marshall Islands and the Federated States of Micronesia expire in 2001. With the end of the cold war, it is not clear to what extent the United States still considers these nations crucial to its own defense. A precipitous, unplanned withdrawal of support, after years of economic dependence, would be disastrous.

Meanwhile, the Japanese are an increasing economic force in Micronesia. Even the Philippines, the People's Republic of China, and Taiwan are all anxious to exploit the region's resources.

International Relations

The Republic of the Marshall Islands, the Federated States of Micronesia, the Republic of Palau, the Republic of Nauru and the Republic of Kiribati all belong to the United Nations.

All are also members of the **South Pacific Forum** (G.P.O. Box 856, Suva, Fiji Islands), a regional grouping concerned with economic development, trade, communications, fisheries, and environmental protection. At their annual meetings, the heads of government of the SPF countries express their joint political views. Meetings held in Micronesia have included the 1976 and 1993 meetings on Nauru, the 1980 and 1989 meetings on Tarawa, and the 1991 meeting on Pohnpei. The 1996 meeting was planned for Majuro, Marshall Islands. At the 1985 Forum meeting the South Pacific Nuclear Free Zone treaty was signed. The 1989 meeting condemned driftnet fishing and set up a mechanism to monitor the greenhouse effect.

The **South Pacific Forum Fisheries Agency** (P.O. Box 629, Honiara, Solomon Islands), formed in 1979, coordinates the fisheries policies of the member states and negotiates licensing agreements with foreign countries. In 1988 the Federated States of Micronesia and Marshall Islands became parties to the **South Pacific Regional Trade and Economic Cooperation Agreement** (SPARTECA), which allows certain island products duty free entry to Australia and New Zealand; Kiribati and Nauru also belong.

All of the countries included in this book belong to the **South Pacific Commission** (P.O. Box D5, Nouméa Cedex, New Caledonia). The SPC was established in 1947 by the postwar colonial powers; Australia, France, the Netherlands, New Zealand, the United Kingdom, and the United States. The Netherlands withdrew in 1962. As the insular territories attained self-government they were admitted to membership. In October each year, delegates from the member governments meet at a **South Pacific Conference** to discuss the Commission's program and budget. The SPC promotes regional economic and social development through annual conferences, research, and technical assistance, and is strictly nonpolitical. Fields of activity include food, marine resources, environmental management, rural development, community health, education, and statistical studies.

The main nonprofit, nongovernmental organization active in the region is the **Micronesia Institute** (1275 K St. NW, Suite 360, Washington, D.C. 20005-4006, tel. 202-842-1140), particularly in the fields of health, education, entrepreneurship, private sector economic development, and cultural and historical preservation. The

School of the Pacific Islands (125 West Thousand Oaks Blvd., Thousand Oaks, CA 91360-4412, tel. 805-497-7691) is a nonprofit corporation that funds educational projects throughout Micronesia. The **Foundation for the Peoples of the South Pacific** (P.O. Box 85710, San Diego, CA 92186, tel. 619-279-9820) has a project in Kiribati.

ECONOMY

In 1994, the United Nations held a conference on Barbados to deal with the plight of the world's small island nations. Its final report, titled "Report of the Global Conference on the Sustainable Development of Small Island Developing States" dealt with problems the Micronesian nations share in common with similar ocean countries. The report focused on the importance of these countries, stating:

Small island developing States have sovereign rights over their own natural resources. Their biodiversity is among the most threatened in the world and their ecosystems provide ecological corridors linking major areas of biodiversity around the world. They bear responsibility for a significant portion of the world's oceans and seas and their resources. The efforts of small island developing States to conserve, protect and restore their ecosystems deserve international cooperation and partnership.

The report also focused on the competitive disadvantages these nations have:

Those disadvantages include a narrow range of resources, which forces undue specialization; excessive dependence on international trade and hence vulnerability to global developments; high population density, which increases the pressure on already limited resources; overuse of resources and premature depletion; relatively small watersheds and threatened supplies of fresh water; costly public administration and infrastructure, including transportation and communication and limited institutional capacities and domestic markets, which are too small to provide significant scale economies, while their limited export volumes, sometimes from remote locations, lead to high freight costs and reduced competitiveness. Small islands tend to have high

degrees of endemism and levels of biodiversity, but the relatively small numbers of the various species impose high risks of extinction and create a need for protection.

Because of the small landmass of small island countries, such as those of Micronesia, as well as their fragile ecologies, they face a problem with which the world has been unwilling to come to terms: economic growth must be sustainable. Civilization cannot exist for long by destroying resources through onetime use.

Regional differences within Micronesia are great, with the Marshall Islands and the FSM having a per capita gross domestic product of under $2000 a year, Palau about $4000 a year, and Guam and the Northern Marianas both over $15,000 a year. In Kiribati the GDP is less than $1000 per capita. About two-thirds of the population of the Marshall Islands and Palau lives in urban areas, while only about a third of the people of the FSM and Kiribati are in urban areas. By the same standards Guam and the Northern Marianas are almost totally urbanized.

Dependency

In 1961 imports to Micronesia led exports by two to one; by 1975 this had increased to 15 to one. In 1984 the U.S. provided $124 million in aid to the Trust Territory of the Pacific Islands, more than it spent in Guam and American Samoa combined. Most American aid went to

Cocoa and chocolate are made from the seed of the cacao tree.

LOUISE FOOTE

OCEANIA AT A GLANCE

Land areas and sea areas (the ocean area included within the 200-nautical mile Exclusive Economic Zone, or EEZ, of each country) are expressed in square miles. The Political Status category denotes the year in which the country became independent, or in which the territory or province fell under colonial rule by the power named. The sea areas (and various other figures) were taken from *South Pacific Economies: Statistical Summary*, published by the South Pacific Commission, Nouméa.

COUNTRY	POPULATION	LAND AREA	SEA AREA	CAPITAL	POLITICAL STATUS	CURRENCY	AIRPORT TAX
Tahiti-Polynesia	188,814	1,368	1,942,000	Papeete	France 1842	CFP	none
Pitcairn Islands	65	18	309,000	Adamstown	Britain 1838	NZ$	none
Easter Island	2,770	66	137,000	Hanga Roa	Chile 1888	peso	US$5
Cook Islands	18,543	93	707,000	Avarua	N.Z. 1901	NZ$	NZ$25
Niue	2,300	100	151,000	Alofi	N.Z. 1900	NZ$	NZ$20
Kingdom of Tonga	94,649	267	270,000	Nuku'alofa	ind. 1970	*pa'anga*	T$15
American Samoa	46,773	78	151,000	Utulei	U.S. 1900	US$	none
Western Samoa	161,298	1,097	46,000	Apia	ind. 1962	*tala*	WS$20
Tokelau	1,577	5	112,000	Fakaofo	N.Z. 1925	*tala*	none
Wallis and Futuna	14,000	106	116,000	Mata Utu	France 1887	CFP	none
Tuvalu	9,061	10	347,000	Funafuti	ind. 1978	A$	A$30
TOTAL POLYNESIA	**539,850**	**3,208**	**4,288,000**				
Fiji	758,275	7,055	498,000	Suva	ind. 1970	F$	F$20
New Caledonia	164,173	7,172	672,000	Noumea	France 1853	CFP	none
Vanuatu	149,739	4,706	263,000	Vila	ind. 1980	*vatu*	Vt2000
Solomon Islands	285,796	10,639	517,000	Honiara	ind. 1978	SI$	SI$30
Papua New Guinea	3,963,000	178,472	1,205,000	Moresby	ind. 1975	*kina*	K15
TOTAL MELANESIA	**5,320,983**	**208,044**	**3,155,000**				
Nauru	8,902	8	124,000	Yaren	ind. 1968	A$	none
Kiribati	72,298	313	1,371,000	Bairiki	ind. 1979	A$	A$10
Marshall Islands	43,380	70	823,000	Majuro	ind. 1986	US$	US$15
Federated States of Micronesia	98,071	271	1,150,000	Pohnpei	ind. 1986	US$	US$10
Palau	15,122	188	243,000	Koror	ind. 1994	US$	US$10
Guam	133,152	209	84,000	Agana	U.S. 1898	US$	none
Northern Marianas	43,345	185	300,000	Saipan	U.S. 1976	US$	none
TOTAL MICRONESIA	**414,270**	**1,244**	**4,095,000**				
TOTAL OCEANIA	**6,275,103**	**212,496**	**11,538,000**				

consumption rather than public investment. Large numbers of Micronesians continue to flock to urban areas to lead a lifestyle supported by United States payments. The average government worker earns much more than a villager.

Most of Micronesia is no longer self-sufficient. It has entered into consumer economies. Yet it is not clear that the islands can support today's dense populations, in a consumer lifestyle, on a sustainable basis. Micronesians today eat imported food—in many places the taro patches are abandoned, breadfruit is unharvested. Rice, the current staple, is imported.

Under the Compacts, the associated states are required to spend 40% of their U.S.-provided Compact payments on capital improvements such as roads, airports, harbors, sewers, and water supply systems. This of course does not insure that the money is effectively used to create a modern infrastructure. Japanese aid is tied to specific projects, with Japanese companies doing all of the work. Much Japanese aid to Micronesia is linked to fishing rights negotiations, and assistance is stopped to countries that cause problems for Japanese fishing companies.

Health and Welfare

Despite some impressive medical facilities, the quality of treatment is low. It's not unusual to be told at one of the showplace hospitals that all the doctors are at a "meeting" or have left for the day. Proper sewers and water systems are not in place. Large numbers of people fall victim to diseases that have been eradicated in Western countries. Health care is geared more toward curing disease than preventing it. Nutritional education is abysmal, though Pohnpei's drive to promote a return to breast feeding, rather than the continued use of formula, is a notable exception. Little emphasis is placed on family planning, thereby contributing to the population explosion. Imported foods of poor nutritional value have created new health problems. Cigarette smoking is almost universal.

Education

New schools have been built. Palau Community College at Koror offers vocational training. The College of Micronesia—FSM at Pohnpei handles teacher training. A school of nursing operates at Majuro. Practical technical and agricultural education has largely been left to Jesuit institutions, such as the Pohnpei Agricultural and Trade School (PATS). Micronesians also attend United States colleges. Many remain in the States, or return to the islands with few opportunities to use their education because of chronic underemployment.

DIANA LASICH HARPER

PANDANUS

Apart from the coconut tree, the pandanus shrub is one of the most widespread and useful plants in the Pacific. Among other things, the islanders use the thorny leaves of the pandanus, or screw pine, for weaving mats, baskets, and fans. The seeds are strung into necklaces. The fibrous fruit makes brushes for decorating tapa cloth and can be eaten. The aerial roots can be made into fish traps.

Law of the Sea

As plentiful as the oceans are, we human beings have proven ourselves sufficiently clever to rob them clean of fish. The great cod banks of the North Atlantic have been destroyed. With the technological advances of the last several decades, we can, with very little difficulty, wipe the Pacific clean of its tuna in a very short number of years.

The industrialized nations want tuna. Tokyo wants its sashimi. San Francisco wants its blackened ahi. Lower grade tuna still finds its way into cat food. As long as the industrialized nations put their short-term interests ahead of the long-term notion of sustainable yield, the destruction will continue. Even when treaties are passed to protect ocean environments, without a great deal of foreign assistance the small nations of Micronesia cannot adequately police their own waters.

States have traditionally exercised sovereignty over a three-mile belt of territorial sea along their shores. The high seas beyond these limits could be freely used by anyone. But on 28 September 1945, President Harry Truman declared United States sovereignty over the natural resources of the adjacent continental shelf. United States fishing boats soon became involved in an acrimonious dispute with several South American countries over their rich anchovy fishing grounds, and in 1952 Chile, Ecuador, and Peru declared a 200-nautical-mile Exclusive Economic Zone (EEZ) along their shores. In 1958 the United Nations convened a Conference on the Law of the Sea at Geneva, which accepted national control over continental shelves up to 650 feet deep. Agreement could not be reached on extended territorial sea limits.

National claims multiplied so much that in 1974 another U.N. conference was convened, leading to the signing of the Law of the Sea convention at Jamaica in 1982 by 159 states and other entities. This complex agreement of 200 pages, nine annexes, and 320 articles extended national control over 40% of the world's oceans. The territorial sea claims were increased to 12 nautical miles and the continental shelf ambiguously defined as extending 200 nautical miles offshore. States were given full control over all resources, living or nonliving, within this belt.

Largely due to other nations' objections to provisions for the strict regulation of undersea mining, the only industrialized country to sign so far is Iceland.

Many aspects of the Law of the Sea have become accepted in practice. The EEZs mainly affect fisheries and seabed mineral exploitation; freedom of navigation within the zones is guaranteed. The Law of the Sea increased immensely the territory of oceanic states, giving them real political weight for the first time. The

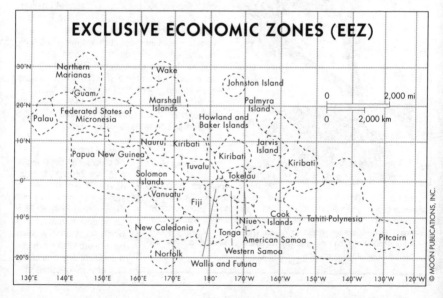

EXCLUSIVE ECONOMIC ZONES (EEZ)

© MOON PUBLICATIONS, INC.

land area of the seven political entities covered in this book comes to only 1,245 square miles, while their EEZs total 4,500,000 square miles!

Fisheries

Tuna is the second most important fishing industry in the world (after shrimp and prawns), and 66% of the world's catch is taken in the Pacific. The western Pacific, where most of the islands of Micronesia are located, is twice as productive as the eastern, with fish worth over a billion dollars extracted annually. Although tuna is one of the few renewable resources the Micronesian islanders have, for many years the U.S. government (at the behest of the tuna industry) attempted to deny them any benefit from it by claiming that since the fish were "migratory," they were not subject to protection by the EEZ nation. Thus American purse seiners claimed they were not subject to licensing fees for fishing within the 200-nautical-mile EEZs.

In 1985, when Kiribati signed a fishing agreement with the Soviet Union, the United States finally got the message. In 1987 the U.S. government agreed to a $60 million aid package, which included licensing fees for American tuna boats to work the EEZs of the 16 member states of the South Pacific Forum Fisheries Agency (including Palau, the Federated States of Micronesia, Kiribati, the Marshall Islands, and Nauru) for five years. The settlement, small potatoes for the U.S. but big money to the islanders, was seen as an inexpensive way of forestalling "Soviet advances" in the central Pacific. In 1990 the question of whether island governments would be allowed to control their valuable tuna resources seemed settled when the U.S. Congress voted overwhelmingly to impose management on tuna stocks in the U.S. EEZ. The "migratory" fish finally had owners.

The Forum Fisheries Agency, which negotiated the Tuna Treaty, now handles all fishing agreements between FFA member states and the United States, Korea, Japan, and Taiwan. Japan has resisted signing multilateral fisheries agreements, preferring to deal with the Pacific countries individually. As a means of buying influence, fisheries development in Micronesia has been sponsored mainly by Japan rather than the United States, with Japanese-built freezer plants established throughout the region. The Tuna Treaty now provides U.S. assistance to FFA countries in creating fishing industries of their own. The bitter irony of local fish being sent to Japan to be canned, then sold back to islanders at high prices, is all too real.

Until recently, purse seiner operations led to the drowning of tens of thousands of dolphins a year in tuna nets. Herds of dolphins often swim above schools of yellowfin tuna in the eastern Pacific; thus unscrupulous purse seine operators would deliberately set their nets around the marine mammals, crushing or suffocating them. In 1990, after a tuna boycott spearheaded by the Earth Island Institute (300 Broadway, Suite 28, San Francisco, CA 94133), H.J. Heinz (Star-Kist) and other American tuna packers announced that they would can only tuna caught using dolphin-safe fishing methods. Neither longline nor pole and line tuna fishing involves killing dolphins, nor do dolphins associate with tuna in the western Pacific. Because Micronesia has always been a dolphin-safe tuna fishing area, the number of U.S. boats operating here suddenly increased when the canneries stopped buying tuna caught off Central and South America.

Unfortunately, canneries in Italy, Japan, and some other countries continue to accept tuna from dolphin-killing Mexican and South American vessels without reservations. If you care about marine mammals, look for the distinctive "dolphin safe" label before buying any tuna at all. Earth Island Institute has also lobbied successfully to halt the use of "seal bomb" explosives to herd dolphins (and the tuna below them) into fishing nets.

Another devastating fishing practice, the use of driftnets up to 40 miles long and 50 feet deep, only began in the early 1980s. By the end of the decade 1,500 Japanese, Taiwanese, and Korean fishing boats were setting 18,600 miles of these nets across the Pacific each night. These plastic "walls of death" indiscriminately capture and kill everything that bumps into them, from whole schools of tuna or salmon, to dolphins, seals, whales, blue sharks, sea turtles, and many other endangered species. Thousands of seabirds are entangled as they dive for fish in the nets. Driftnets are extremely wasteful, as up to 40% of the catch is lost as the nets are hauled in, and an equally large proportion has to be discarded because the fish are too scarred by the net to be marketable. Lost or abandoned "ghost nets" continue their gruesome harvest until they sink from the weight of corpses caught in them. This practice, which makes fisheries management impossible, was strongly condemned by the South Pacific Forum at its 1989 meeting on Tarawa, and driftnet fishing boats were banned from the 11.4 million square miles of ocean included in the EEZs of the 16 member states. This act was mostly symbolic, as driftnetters often operate in international waters and don't pay licensing fees to anyone. In December 1989 the United Nations General Assembly passed a resolution calling for a moratorium on driftnetting in international waters after 30 June 1992, and in 1990 the U.S. Congress passed a bill prohibiting the import of any fish caught with driftnets beginning in July 1992. Under mounting international pressure, Japan agreed in 1991 to end its driftnet fishing by the U.N. deadline. Right from the start Japan had prohibited driftnet fishing by Japanese vessels within 1,000 miles of its own shores!

Tourism

Guam is the major tourist center of Micronesia, with over 800,000 (mostly Japanese) visitors a year. Saipan comes next with more than 500,000 (also mostly Japanese); the American-associated states altogether get about 80,000, with Palau alone accounting for about half of these. While less than 10% of tourists visiting Guam are Americans, the U.S. provides the majority of visitors to the Federated States of Micronesia.

Tourism to Guam and Saipan does not bring the benefits the numbers might imply, since the Japanese arrive on Japanese planes, stay at Japanese-owned hotels, eat Japanese food, ride Japanese tour buses, and buy Japanese-made products at duty free prices—mostly prepaid in Japan, preventing local operators from getting much of the action.

Tourism officials on Yap say they don't want high-pressure, high-rise tourist hotels owned by Japanese corporations, but that they might welcome smaller, low-key beach hotels constructed of local materials by investors willing to work with Yapese partners who supply the land and labor. Small locally owned hotels provide much of the lodging in the Marshall Islands and the FSM. Tourism to Kiribati is insignificant.

LOUISE FOOTE

THE PEOPLE

Micronesians are a mixed race, with strong Polynesian strains as well as Philippine influence. Many, though certainly not all Micronesians, are recognizable as such, sharing such common traits as copper skin, thin lips, comparatively short, slight builds, and straight black hair. Most of their societies were highly organized; the clans were led by hereditary chiefs who were most powerful in the Marshalls and Tungaru. Except in Yap and Tungaru, descent was largely matrilineal.

Contemporary Life

The landmass of Micronesia is small, making it one of the most densely populated areas on earth. The population growth rate is over three percent. More than half the inhabitants are under age 15. The demographic curve will make these islands even more crowded in the future, unless there is significant emigration.

Many Micronesians reside in Guam, Hawaii, and California, where employment opportunities are better. This is a pattern occurring over much of the Pacific. For example, considerably more Cook Islanders live in Auckland, New Zealand, today than live in the Cooks. Such migration may solve problems of individual families, but may also have disastrous cultural effects. Often it is young parents who move to earn a living and to remit earnings back to the islands where grandparents raise the young.

Language

Micronesians speak Austronesian languages different from those of Polynesia. Eleven major languages are spoken: Chamorro and Palauan are classified as Indonesian, while Yapese, Ulithian, Chuukese, Pohnpeian, Kosraean, Nauruan, Gilbertese, and Marshallese are Micronesian, and Kapingamarangi is Polynesian. Contemporary Chamorro is a mixture of the original tongue and Spanish. Frequently, one language is unintelligible to people from another island. Thus, at present, communication between people from different islands is most often in English.

Religion

Micronesia today is overwhelmingly Christian. Missionaries of many Christian denominations are active in Micronesia. Some, such as clean-cut young Mormons wearing white shirts and ties, are highly visible. Assemblies of God, Baptists, Catholics, Evangelicals, Jehovah's Witnesses, Lutherans, Methodists, Pentecostals, Presbyterians, Seventh-Day Adventists and Baha'is are also present. Only Palau maintains an indigenous religious movement, the United Sect (Ngara Modekngei).

M.G.L. DOMENY DE RIENZI

ARTS AND CRAFTS

Dance and song are the most important art forms of Micronesia, conveying the legends and history of the people. Dancing marks celebratory occasions. Single front line dances are common. Because of the generally differentiated roles of men and women in traditional Micronesian cultures, few dances involve men and women dancing together. Micronesian dance resembles Polynesian dance in many ways, including an emphasis on movements of arms, hands, and fingers, the prominence of group dances, and the use of sitting dances.

Simplicity of form is the cornerstone of Micronesian handicrafts. Although the region is culturally diverse, there is a common thread of design concepts emphasizing angular, geometric shapes. Patterns used in woven textiles on one island, for example, may show up in tattooing and woodcarving on another. Traditional art in the Micronesia region has similarities to Melanesian and Indonesian art, demonstrating Micronesian contacts with those areas. The primary media for traditional arts are woven fabrics (both loom and braided items) woodcarving, and architecture.

Except in the Marianas, handicrafts sold in Micronesia are authentic handmade products; they're easily distinguished from mass-produced Filipino knockoffs. Considering the time that goes into Micronesian handicrafts, prices are low (don't bargain). Many of the handicraft outlets are soft sell, low profit or cooperative ventures. When making purchases, avoid objects made from turtle shell. Such items frequently are manufactured from endangered species and are prohibited entry into the United States and many other countries.

In Micronesia today, particularly on Guam, a new school of painting is developing. Artists trained in Western art, often in the United States, are creating paintings using Western techniques but retaining an island influence.

Weaving

Textiles traditionally played an important public role. They marked rank and social status. Special textiles were worn for ritual occasions and life cycle events. Fabrics even served as currency. In parts of the Caroline Islands, banana and hibiscus-fiber fabrics were woven on a loom. Today, colorful cotton mill thread is frequently used. Both types of textiles may be purchased by visitors.

In the rest of Micronesia, as in most of the Pacific, braided or plait work predominates. Plaiting fashions a wide variety of utilitarian items, including sleeping mats, wall coverings, canoe sails, baskets, and clothing. Dried coconut fibers and pandanus leaves are the most common materials. Marshall Island plait work is elaborately and richly patterned. Traditionally, the fineness of the design indicated the origin of the mat makers and the family status. Some designs could only be used by royalty.

A Yap woman weaves with a simple backstrap loom, which in the Pacific is found only in the Caroline Islands. Only narrow material can be woven on this type of loom.

Woodcarving

Breadfruit is the wood most often carved (especially for model and actual canoes), although coconut, ironwood, and hibiscus are also used. In Palau, a great revival of hardwood carving took place this century. The finely carved war clubs of the South Pacific are not common in Micronesia, where men most often fought with sling and spear. But warriors in the Gilberts carried shark-tooth-edged swords and wore woven body armor. The only masks known in Micronesia were those of the Mortlocks.

Architecture

Architecture in Micronesia is an important art form. Not to be missed are the beautiful historic sites of Nan Madol on Pohnpei and Lelu on Kosrae. The *latte* stones of the Marianas are remnants of an architecture found nowhere else in Oceania. These physically impressive stones consist of columns larger at the base than the top, crowned by a capstone, usually of coral. Arranged in rows, the purpose of these monumental works is not known for certain, though many archaeologists believe they were used as foundations of aristocratic or communal dwellings.

Other prehistoric sites include the sculpted hills of Babeldaob in Palau, vast prehistoric terraces carved from natural formations. Also in Palau, the stone sculptures of Melekeok and Badrulchau, called "great stone faces," are worth a visit. Yap's ancient stone walkways should be thought of as horizontal archaeology, still serving their ancient purpose today.

Traditional buildings, particularly for community purposes, are still in use in Yap, Palau, and Kiribati. These beautiful structures are typically rectangular in shape, built on elevated platforms. Their steeply sloping roofs are made from coconut or pandanus leaves. The sides are built from local, natural materials and have shutters rather than glass. Thus, depending on weather conditions they can be open and breezy, or protected from the elements.

Shipbuilding

Micronesian large-scale voyaging canoes are probably the finest outriggers ever built and perhaps the world's fastest sailing crafts. They are superbly designed and crafted with superior sails, riggings, and steering apparatus. Common characteristics of Micronesian voyaging canoes include asymmetrical sides and double-ended hulls, with high ends and sharp bottoms. Forms and details of construction vary from island group to island group. Some canoes, particularly ceremonial ones, have beautiful prow ornaments. Many islands had a tradition of racing small model canoes, and these small models are now available for purchase in some localities.

Wishing to catch fish
a fisherman follows the birds.
Birds follow the boat.

M.G.L. DOMENY DE RIENZI

ON THE ROAD

Tourist activity for most of Micronesia dates back only to 1962. Beginning in the 1930s the Japanese cut non-Japanese visitors down to a trickle. The United States did the same from World War II until 1962. It was not until 1968 that Continental Airlines got together with local business interests to create a new joint venture, Continental Air Micronesia (known locally as Air Mike), which began service from Honolulu to Saipan in 1968.

Airstrips were gradually upgraded in all the district centers of the old Trust Territory of the Pacific Islands, and by 1970 Air Mike's Island Hopper, from Honolulu to Guam, was calling at Majuro, Kwajalein, Pohnpei, and Chuuk. Feeder services flew to Saipan, Yap, and Koror. Isolated Kosrae became part of Continental's world in 1986.

Guam is the second most important tourist destination in the Pacific islands (after Hawaii), with many more tourists than Fiji or Tahiti. Saipan, with excellent beaches, is the third. On Guam tourism now surpasses military spending as a source of island income.

ACCOMMODATIONS AND FOOD

Rooms
Moderately priced hotels can be found in most of the towns in Micronesia. Guam and Saipan also have large, high-rise tourist hotels. Prices range from $25 to $375. Many hotels in Micronesia, particularly the more expensive ones, will offer corporate and "local" discounts. Nobody is ever very clear about the exact requirements to qualify for each. Most likely, discount qualifications

are determined in part by how many vacant rooms the hotel has at the time. Be sure to inquire, particularly if you are calling from Micronesia to make the reservation.

During certain months, such as December, there can be an accommodation shortage, particularly in the Federated States of Micronesia. It is best to make arrangements in advance.

There aren't many hotels on the outer islands, but in the Marshalls and Federated States, island mayors or chiefs will help visitors find a place to stay. Most atolls in Kiribati have inexpensive Island Council rest houses. Radio ahead to let them know you're coming. Elementary school teachers in remote areas are often very hospitable and may offer to put you up. Always try to find some tangible way to show your appreciation, such as paying for groceries or giving a gift. Don't be afraid to offer cash if a stranger puts himself or herself out financially for you. Once you get home, don't forget to mail prints of any photos you've taken.

Camping

Camping is not common in Micronesia. A tent, however, can save the budget traveler a lot of money and prove convenient. It's rarely difficult to find people willing to let you camp on their land. Since most land is privately owned it's important to ask permission of someone like a village mayor or chief first; they're usually agreeable. Ensure this same hospitality for the next traveler by not leaving a mess.

On the main islands, if you find a place to camp, it is usually not safe to leave your tent unattended. Dismantle it daily and ask your host to store it for you, then erect it again at night. As yet the only regular campgrounds are on Guam, and the facilities at these are minimal. On the outer islands, however, there should be no problem: in fact, when you ask for a camping spot, you'll often be invited to stay in the family's house—an offer that can be difficult to refuse.

FOOD

All the towns have reasonable restaurants serving Island, American, Chinese, and Japanese food from $4 to $8. Sometimes they're surprisingly good. Grilled tuna and reef fish are delectable. The Japanese left Micronesians with an enduring taste for white rice, to which the Americans added white sugar, bread, and beer. Rice is still the staple, and on the outer islands you'll find a fare of rice, breadfruit, taro, lagoon fish, and sashimi (raw fish), plus the more prosaic canned mackerel and Spam. Guam and Saipan have a large number of excellent, though expensive, restaurants.

Breadfruit grows on trees. (Remember Captain Bligh? He was carrying breadfruit on his ill fated voyage.) Taro is an elephant eared plant cultivated in freshwater bogs. Its roots are a starchy staple. Although yams are considered a prestige food, they're not as nutritious as breadfruit and taro. Yams can grow up to 10 feet long and weigh hundreds of pounds. Papaya (pawpaw) is widely available. Atoll dwellers espe-

DIANA LASICH HARPER

BREADFRUIT

Breadfruit (*Artocarpus altilus*) grows on tall trees with large green leaves. From Indonesia ancient voyagers carried it to all of Polynesia. "Breadfruit Bligh" was returning from Tahiti with a thousand potted trees to provide food for slaves in Jamaica when the famous mutiny occurred. Propagated from root suckers, this seedless plant provides shade as well as food. A wellwatered tree can produce as many as 1,000 breadfruits a year. Joseph Banks, the botanist on Captain Cook's first voyage, wrote: "If a man should in the course of his lifetime plant 10 trees, which if well done might take the labour of an hour or thereabouts, he would completely fulfill his duty to his own as well as future generations."

cially rely on the coconut for food. The tree reaches maturity in eight years and then produces about 50 nuts a year for 60 years.

Tuna sashimi is cheap and available all over Micronesia. It is usually safe to eat, but, of course, it's safer to eat well-cooked food. Avoid unpeeled fruit and raw vegetables. And, except on Guam, do not drink tap water. Bottled water is available on all major islands. If you are going to an outer island, it is best to bring your own or carry purification material, as potable water may not be available. Also take as many edibles with you as possible. Imported foods are always more expensive there than in the main towns, and often staples such as bread are not available.

Keep in mind that virtually every food plant you see growing on the islands was planted by someone. Fishing floats or seashells washed up on a beach, or fish in the lagoon near someone's home, may also be private property under local laws and customs.

HEALTH

Micronesia's a healthy place, but it is in the tropics. Taking a few basic precautions minimizes risks.

Don't go from winter weather into the steaming tropics without a rest. Don't expect to be able to keep up the same pace here as you do at home. Airplane cabins have low humidity, so drink lots of water or juice and don't overeat on the flight coming over. It's also best to forgo coffee and alcohol, which will further dehydrate you. Divers must understand and follow the prescribed waiting period after diving before taking airplane flights.

Tap water is unsafe to drink in most of Micronesia other than Guam (check locally). If the tap water is contaminated, local ice will be too. Avoid brushing your teeth with water unfit to drink. Avoid raw vegetables. Peel fruit or wash it in bottled or treated water. Cooked food is less subject to contamination than raw. If you wish to avoid the cost of bottled drinks, take along water purification tablets or units, available at many sporting goods and travel stores. There are now tablets available that will take the bad taste out of water you have purified with iodine.

Medicine is often unavailable. If there are medicines you must take regularly, carry twice as much as you need. Split that supply in half and on travel days keep half on your person and half in your baggage to avoid the danger of losing your supply. Before the trip, speak to your doctor about carrying antibiotics and antidiarrhea medicine with you. Note: Even such basics as aspirin are often unavailable on outer islands, so be prepared.

You can always see a doctor at government hospitals in the towns, but although the cost of medical attention is low, on too many islands so is the quality. If you fall seriously ill get a flight home or to a country with higher medical standards as soon as possible. On the outer islands, clinics deal only in basics.

Sunburn

Though you may think you don't burn, everyone burns in tropical sun. Begin with short exposures, perhaps half an hour to an hour the first day, a bit more if it is overcast. Remember you can burn even on cloudy days. If you are a snorkeler, you can protect your back and shoulders with a T-shirt while in the ocean. Use a sunblock with a high sunscreen factor, remembering your nose, lips, forehead, neck, hands, and feet. If you go swimming, reapply periodically. Calamine ointment soothes burned skin, as does coconut oil.

Ailments

Cuts and scratches take a long time to heal in the tropics. An antibiotic cream speeds healing and helps prevent infection. To prevent infection from coral cuts wash the area with soap and fresh water, then rub vinegar or alcohol (whiskey will do) into the wounds—painful, but effective. Coral cuts can become inflamed if you enter salt water again, thus potentially spoiling your trip. All cuts can turn septic quickly in the tropics, so try to keep them clean and covered.

Many places in Micronesia, though not all, have mosquitos. If you (like most people) are susceptible to them, keep yourself covered when hiking. Be particularly careful around sunrise and sunset when they are at their hungriest. Bring mosquito repellent with you. (I owe unswerving devotion to Cutter's.) At night in your hotel room, keep all unscreened doors and windows closed. Most will be screened. And consider using the nearly universally available Chinese mosquito coils.

Prickly heat, an irritating rash, can be caused by wearing heavy clothing or synthetics that do not "breathe." If you are affected, take a cold shower, apply calamine lotion, dust with talcum powder, and take off those clothes!

Food spoils quickly in the tropics. You may experience diarrhea at some point during the trip. If so, be certain to keep up your intake of water. Particularly if you are sweating, be sure to replenish your salts. Most cases of diarrhea are self-limiting and require only simple replacement of fluids and salts. Before leaving, discuss with your doctor whether to take along prescription strength antidiarrhea medicine such as Lomotil. If the diarrhea is persistent or you experience fever, drowsiness, or blood in the stool, take these developments seriously. If you are at an island such as Palau where decent medical care is available, consult a doctor. If you are on an island without adequate modern medical care, consider flying elsewhere.

Toxic Fish

Over 400 species of tropical reef fish, including wrasses, snappers, groupers, barracudas, jacks, moray eels, surgeonfish, and shellfish, are known to cause seafood poisoning (ciguatera). There's no way to tell if a given type of fish will cause it: a species can be subject to being poisonous on one side of an island but not on the other. It doesn't matter whether the fish is cooked or raw. Local residents will have experience knowing which species to avoid. There's no treatment except to relieve the symptoms (tingling, prickling, itching, nausea, vomiting, erratic heartbeat, joint and muscle pains), which usually subside in a few days. If you suspect ciguatera, seek immediate medical care.

Several years ago scientists determined that a one celled dinoflagellate called *Gambierdiscus toxicus* was the cause. Normally these algae are found only in the ocean depths, but when a reef is disturbed by natural or human causes they can multiply dramatically in a lagoon. The dinoflagellate are consumed by tiny herbivorous fish and the toxin passes up through the food chain to larger fish where it becomes concentrated in the head and guts. The toxins have no effect on the fish that feed on them.

Vaccinations and Diseases

Malaria is nonexistent, and there have been no cholera outbreaks in over a decade. Many immunization centers refuse to administer the cholera vaccination because it's only 50% effective for six months and bad reactions are common.

Tetanus, diphtheria, typhoid fever, polio, and immune globulin shots are not required, but they're a good idea if you're going to remote islands. Tetanus and diphtheria vaccinations are given together and a booster is required every 10 years. Typhoid fever boosters are required every three years, polio every five years. Immune globulin (IG) isn't 100% effective against hepatitis A, but it does increase your general resistance to infections. IG prophylaxis must be repeated every five months. A yellow fever vaccination is required only if you've recently been in an infected area such as parts of South America or central Africa.

Infectious hepatitis A is a liver ailment transmitted person to person or through unboiled water, uncooked vegetables, or other foods contaminated during handling. Symptoms often include a yellowing of eyeballs or urine turning practically orange. Viral hepatitis B is spread through sexual or blood contact.

Dengue fever is a mosquito-transmitted disease. Signs are headaches, sore throat, pain in the joints, fever, rash, and nausea. It can last anywhere from five to 15 days, and although you can relieve the symptoms somewhat, the only real cure is to stay in bed and wait it out. It is painful, but dengue fever is rarely fatal to an adult. Of course, seek medical attention if you suspect this disease.

Leprosy and elephantiasis are hard to catch and are now found only on a few remote islands. Sexually transmitted diseases are rampant in much of Micronesia. AIDS has not reached epidemic proportions, though cases have been reported. But local public health authorities fear for the future unless there are radical changes in current sexual practices.

INFORMATION AND SERVICES

Regional tourist information offices and diplomatic posts are listed in an appendix at the end of this book. William H. Stewart, Economic Service Counsel, has designed an intriguing series of tourist maps, packed with interesting anecdotes on Palau, Guam, Kosrae, Pohnpei, Saipan, and Chuuk. These and a standard selection of tourist brochures are available from these offices. Also see "Periodicals" and "Booksellers and Publishers" in the Booklist.

Peace Corps volunteers are always good sources of information, and you'll find them in the most unlikely corners of the Marshall Islands and the Federated States.

Visas

Entry to Micronesia is easy. No visa is required to visit the Marshalls, Federated States, Palau, or Northern Marianas for a stay of up to 30 days. If you're leaving on the next connecting flight, you won't need a visa for Nauru either. Entry requirements to Kiribati are more complicated (turn to the Kiribati chapter for details). Citizens of most countries other than America and Canada should have a United States visa to enter Guam. Inquire from the American embassy or consulate in your home country.

Technically, United States citizens, with proper identification, can enter the Marshalls, Federated States, Palau, Guam, and Northern Marianas without a passport. But since individual customs officials have varying ideas as to what is proper, it's advised that everyone, Americans included, carry a passport when traveling in Micronesia. Passports are required for Americans to stay in Nauru or Kiribati.

All Micronesian countries require proof of onward passage upon arrival. If you arrive without it, you may be required to purchase a ticket on the spot or be refused entry. You may also be required to prove that you have sufficient funds. United States citizens don't require an onward ticket to enter Guam or the Northern Marianas.

Money, Measurements, and Mail

American currency (US$) is used throughout Micronesia, except in Kiribati and Nauru where Australian dollars (A$) circulate. In this book, prices are quoted in US$ in US$ areas and A$ in the A$ areas, unless otherwise noted. At last report US$1=A$1.26.

Credit cards are accepted at the large hotels and by car rental agencies in most US$ areas, but cash is easier at restaurants and shops. To avoid wasting time hassling at banks for cash advances, it's best to bring enough traveler's checks to cover your out-of-pocket expenses. On Yap, even some car rentals will not take credit cards. On the outer islands, only dollars are accepted and they should be in small denominations. Post offices in the US$ areas cash U.S. postal money orders, a good way to have money sent from the States.

A small stack of U.S. one- and five-dollar bills for minor expenses is always handy when traveling.

Make sure your traveler's checks are expressed in US$; other currencies may be difficult to exchange or subject to special service charges. To report stolen American Express traveler's checks call the Hong Kong office: tel. 2801-7300 or 2732-7327 (country code 852) collect (or on Guam, tel. 472-8884). If you'll be visiting Kiribati or Nauru, have your bank order a few Australian dollar traveler's checks.

Tipping has become widespread, though as yet it's a way of life only on Guam and Saipan. The serving staff in restaurants that cater mostly to foreign businesspeople or tourists expect to be tipped, but those in places patronized mostly by Micronesians do not. When in doubt, tip.

The electric current throughout the American portion of Micronesia is 110 volts, 60 cycles, with standard American outlets. In Kiribati it's 240 volts, 50 cycles, with Australian outlets.

Regular U.S. postal rates apply throughout Micronesia (except in Ki-

TOURIST

i

INFORMATION

MICRONESIAN TIME

	STANDARD TIME	
	HOURS FROM GMT	TIME 1200 GMT*
California	− 8	4 a.m.
Hawaii	−10	2 a.m.
International Date Line		**Sunday**
		Monday
Majuro, Kosrae	+12	midnight
Tarawa, Nauru	+12	midnight
Pohnpei	+11	11 p.m.
Chuuk, Yap	+10	10 p.m.
Guam, Saipan	+10	10 p.m.
Palau, Japan	+ 9	9 p.m.
Philippines	+ 8	8 p.m.
Hong Kong	+ 8	8 p.m.

*GMT is Greenwich mean time, the time at London, England. California adopts daylight saving time from May to October.

ribati and Nauru). Always specify airmail when posting a letter. Mail leaves Micronesia faster than it arrives. All the countries included in this book issue their own postage stamps (except Guam and the Northern Marianas, which use U.S. stamps). These stamps, available at local post offices, make excellent souvenirs. Many stamps will also be available on colorfully printed first day cover envelopes.

All mail is delivered to post office boxes. In this book you'll find the box numbers of most businesses we discuss. Postal codes appear in the "Micronesia Postal Codes" appendix and in each chapter. Micronesian post offices will hold general delivery mail. If you're mailing a letter to Micronesia from outside the United States, include "via U.S.A." in the address and be sure to use the correct five digit zip code.

Telephone

To call direct to a phone number in Micronesia from the United States, dial the international access code 011, then the country code, then the number. The country code for each island state is listed in the back of this book, as well as in each chapter.

WHAT TO TAKE

Packing
Decision number one is whether you wish to travel only with carry-on baggage. If you wish to do so, the trade-off will be worldly possessions for not having to stand in numerous lines. Assemble everything you simply must take and cannot live without—then cut the pile in half. Keep on cutting until it fits. Today, luggage is available that can be turned from a hand-carried piece into a backpack. If you decide to travel with more baggage, take along a day pack. Either way, when checking in for flights carry anything that can't be replaced with you.

If you are planning to dive almost anywhere in Micronesia other than Guam, you will want to take along all your gear other than weights and tanks. This will make it impossible to travel light.

Camping Equipment
A small nylon tent guarantees you a place to sleep every night. It must be mosquito- and waterproof. Get one with a tent fly. It's usually too hot to get into a sleeping bag in the tropics, so you could leave that item at home. A youth hostel sleeping sheet is ideal—all YHA handbooks give instructions on how to make your own. You don't really need to carry a bulky foam pad as the ground is seldom cold. A mosquito net could come in handy if you'll be visiting remote areas.

Clothing
For clothes take loose-fitting cotton washables, light in color and weight. Synthetic fabrics are hot and sticky, and most of the things you wear at home will be too heavy for the tropics. Coin-operated laundromats are found across Micronesia, so you don't need to take a lot of clothes. Be prepared for the humidity. Take along one lightweight long-sleeved shirt and long pants. They provide mosquito protection in the evenings and warmth in the occasionally over air conditioned restaurant.

Micronesians dress informally for both business and social occasions, but it's important to know that the dress code in the islands is strict. For women, in much of Micronesia wearing short skirts, halter tops, bathing costumes, and other brief attire in public places is considered offensive. Women should wear clothing that covers the knees. On outer islands especially, women should wear a knee-length dress or wrap a yard-long piece of cloth around their thighs. Shorts are usually are okay for men, as long as they are not too short. Men will want a clean shirt for evenings, but only Mormon missionaries wear ties. Topless or nude sunbathing can be done only with care in isolated, uninhabited areas.

Take comfortable, broken in shoes. Running shoes and rubber thongs (zoris) are very handy. Scuba divers' rubber booties are lightweight and perfect for both crossing rivers and reef walking, though an old pair of sneakers may be just as good.

Accessories
Micronesia provides wonderful scenery for photographers, both above water and below. It is best to bring along your own equipment and film. Consider taking an underwater camera with you. Several are now available for about $200. Not only will you be able to shoot underwater, these cameras are easier to care for above water since you do not need to take care against rain and humidity. Serious underwater photography for divers requires much more elaborate cameras and lights.

A mask, snorkel, and fins are essential equipment. Scuba divers should bring their own regulator, buoyancy compensator, and tank pressure gauge (tanks, backpacks, and weight belts can usually be rented locally). Throughout this book you'll find the frequencies of local AM and FM radio stations, should you choose to bring along a radio.

Much of travel entails cutting or tying. Bring along a Swiss army knife and a cord. A pocket flashlight, matches, and a water bottle are often handy. Sunglasses are a must. If you wear prescription glasses, bring along an extra pair since Micronesia does not have one-day eyeglass service.

Remember your driver's license and, if you dive, your scuba certification card.

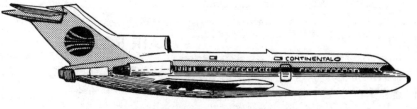

LOUISE FOOTE

GETTING THERE

Some principles for every Micronesia traveler:

- Unless you have unlimited time, flying is the only way to travel; boats take too much time.

- Distances are great. Even air travel takes time. Airfare is expensive.

- You cannot always get there from here. You cannot always pick a destination and choose a flight to get you there. It may not be possible to fly from one island to another without serious backtracking or waiting a week. The available flights and how they connect determines where you visit, unless you have unlimited time and money.

- Many travel agents are not knowledgeable about Micronesia flights. Try to find a specialist. Some are listed under "Organized Tours," below. As with travel anywhere, flights, routes, and prices change.

- Always think about the International Date Line when planning. A flight that leaves Guam one day may arrive in Honolulu the day before. In this book, the day of the week at the flight's place of origin is the one listed. The Date Line even moves around. The United States base at Kwajalein is now on the same date as the rest of the Republic of the Marshall Islands, one day later than the United States. All of Kiribati is now west of the Date Line.

- Understand the difference between inconvenience and tragedy.

- Travel inevitably entails time in transit: this time can be minimized, endured, slept through, or if all else fails—enjoyed.

Continental Air Micronesia
The main regional air carrier is Continental Air

Micronesia or "Air Mike" (Continental Air Micronesia, 300 N. Continental Blvd., Suite 600, Segundo, CA 90245) which has been offering convenient, reliable air service across the region since 1968. Their fare structure is complex and according to Rick Thom, Director of Sales for North America, if you are making your own arrangements, it is best to start inquiries through their toll free number, (800) 900-7657, or (310) 322-8100, fax (310) 322-8100. The Guam office is P.O. Box 8778, Tamuning, GU 96911, tel. (671) 646-0220. Air Mike's services are integrated into Continental Airlines' extensive worldwide reservation system, so booking can also be done through Continental's international toll free number at (800) 231-0856. In Canada call their ticket offices in Toronto (416) 690-7756, or in Vancouver (604) 222-2442.

In your planning, always remember the **International Date Line.** For example, an Air Mike Island Hopper that leaves Honolulu on Wednesday arrives in the Marshall Islands, the other side of the Date Line, on Thursday. Thus if you wish to stay in Majuro for a week, you take a flight out on a date eight days later than the date you left Honolulu. It somehow becomes more mystical in the opposite direction, when you may land the day before you take off.

Air Mike has a number of different fares. Under their regular fares, with no advance purchase necessary, the trip must be completed in 60 days from the purchase. They also have Visit Micronesia fares. Under these fares, the first flight must be confirmed at the time of ticketing and the trip must be completed in 30 days. This fare usually works out best for people who are only going to western Micronesia: Palau, Yap and Saipan, for example. Further, there are Circle Micronesia fares. Under these, tickets

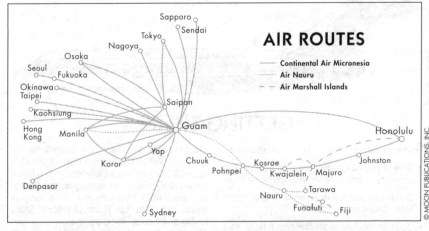

AIR ROUTES

——— Continental Air Micronesia
·········· Air Nauru
– – – Air Marshall Islands

Sapporo
Sendai
Tokyo
Nagoya
Osaka
Seoul
Fukuoka
Okinawa
Taipei
Kaohsiung
Hong Kong
Manila
Saipan
Guam
Honolulu
Yap
Koror
Chuuk
Pohnpei
Kosrae
Kwajalein
Majuro
Johnston
Denpasar
Nauru
Tarawa
Funafuti
Fiji
Sydney

© MOON PUBLICATIONS, INC.

must be purchased seven days prior to departure and the entire trip must be completed in six months. You can use the Island Hopper only in one direction, without any backtracking. This fare usually works best for any extensive tour of Micronesia. Finally, always inquire about family or senior discounts.

Although Continental Air Micronesia offers nonstop flights from Honolulu to Guam, the most popular routing among readers of this book is the Circle Micronesia fare, aboard the Boeing 727 Island Hopper service traveling Honolulu to Majuro to Kwajalein to Kosrae to Pohnpei to Chuuk to Guam, with flights leaving on Monday, Wednesday, and Friday in each direction. In Guam you can change to other Continental Air Micronesia flights continuing to Yap, Koror, or Saipan. If you know you're going to do this, buy a through ticket to your turnaround point—usually cheaper than buying a separate ticket in Guam.

A through ticket over the entire route Honolulu to Majuro to Kwajalein to Kosrae to Pohnpei to Chuuk to Guam to Yap to Koror will cost US$1250. If you only go Honolulu to Majuro to Kwajalein to Kosrae to Pohnpei to Chuuk to Guam, it's US$950. From Los Angeles or San Francisco the Island Hopper costs US$1230 to Guam and US$1650 if you continue on to Koror.

Continental Air Micronesia's nonstop fares are cheaper, so it will be less expensive to pay the higher Island Hopper fare in one direction only. Guam to Honolulu direct, depending on the flight and the season, can vary between US$585 one-way and US$889 roundtrip to Guam, and more to Koror. Guam to California direct varies between US$756 one-way and US$1067 roundtrip.

The sidetrip Guam to Saipan cannot be included in the Island Hopper but must be separately purchased. Sometimes Continental Air Micronesia's off-peak hour flights out of Guam to Chuuk, Pohnpei, Yap, and Koror are sold at a discount. To go to Rota or Tinian, contact Freedom Air or make arrangements for Pacific Island Air through Northwest Airlines.

Of course, Continental Airlines also has flights across the United States mainland and they'll be happy to quote you through fare. It's sometimes possible to save money by flying from the mainland to Hawaii on a special discount fare, then picking up Continental Air Micronesia there. This option is probably worth considering only if you want to include Hawaii in your trip anyway. Since you are often forced to spend a night in Honolulu or on Guam between connecting flights, you may have to spend whatever you "saved."

Flying times are six hours from Honolulu to Majuro or California, seven and a half hours from Honolulu to Guam nonstop, and around two hours on most flights within Micronesia itself. The Island Hopper takes almost 16 hours from Honolulu to Guam, so take it only if you want to stop somewhere.

Continental Air Micronesia is highly reliable with excellent on-time records and few baggage problems. The service on Continental Air Micronesia flights is friendly and personal. You begin to enjoy the charms of Micronesia from the time of takeoff on Air Mike.

Air Nauru

Air Nauru (80 Collins St., Melbourne, VIC 3000, Australia, tel. 03-9653-5703, fax 03-9654-4925), flag carrier of the tiny Republic of Nauru, provides service between Micronesia and the South Pacific, flying on Wednesday from Nauru to Pohnpei to Guam to Manila, returning the opposite route. This mostly aids travelers who are arriving from or traveling to Australia, New Zealand, or other South Pacific points via Nauru. Most Air Nauru fares are calculated point to point via Nauru. To work out a route, combine any two of these one-way economy fares out of Nauru itself: Brisbane ($328); Melbourne ($369); Sidney ($369); Guam ($257); Honiara, Solomon Islands ($138); Manila, Philippines ($414); Nadi and Suva, Fiji ($214); Pohnpei, FSM ($219); and Tarawa, Kiribati ($109). All prices are in U.S. dollars for a one-way economy ticket.

Here are a few Air Nauru offices: Shop 4, Level 5/17, Castlereagh St., Sydney, NSW 2000, Australia (tel. 02-9221-8622, fax 02-9231-2575); Sheraton Mall, 105 Symonds St., Auckland, New Zealand (tel. 09-379-8113, fax 09-379-3763); Ratu Sakuna House, Victoria Parade, Suva, Fiji Islands (tel. 313-731, fax 301-861); Ground Floor, Pacific Star Building, Makati Ave. at Gil Puyat Ave., Makati City, Philippines (tel. 02-818-7241, fax 02-817-7386); Pacific Star Hotel, P.O. Box 6097, Tamon Bay, GU 96911 (tel. 649-7106, fax 649-4856). For information in the United States, the best procedure is simply to call their Guam office. By the time you read this, Air Nauru may have closed some of the above offices. If that is the case, Air New Zealand or Qantas may be able to help you.

Air Marshall Islands

Air Marshall Islands (P.O. Box 1319, Majuro, MH 96960, tel. 625-3731, fax 625-3730, country code 692) can take you directly from Micronesia to the South Pacific. One-way fares out of Majuro on their weekly flight Majuro to Tarawa to Funafuti (Tuvalu) to Fiji run $197 to Tarawa, $472 to Funafuti, $589 to Fiji. Check if there are any cheaper. For more information on Air Marshall Islands, turn to "Practicalities" in the "Introduction" to the Republic of the Marshall Islands chapter.

From Europe

No direct flights connect Europe to Micronesia. The easiest access would be a cheap flight from Europe to California, Honolulu, or Manila, where you would join one of the Island Hopper routes described above and travel around the world. Prices quoted by European travel agents for a Continental through ticket from San Francisco or Los Angeles to Manila with all the stops vary considerably.

For the Continental portion of your ticket, go to a large professional travel agency specializing in business travel or call Continental Air Micronesia or Continental International. It may be cheaper and easier for Europeans to wait to buy their Continental ticket in California, but United States "ticket-to-leave" requirements are an obstacle. If you know a reliable travel agent in the States you might consider mail ordering your Continental ticket through them and paying by credit card.

Continental has ticket offices in some western European cities, including Athens (tel. 1-325-5061), Barcelona (tel. 3-412-2986), Britain (tel. 0293-776464), Brussels (tel. 2-640-3034), Copenhagen (tel. 3313-7277), Frankfurt (tel. 69-757-475), Lisbon (tel. 1-779-9614), Madrid (tel. 1-532-7410), Milan (tel. 2-749-2872), Oslo (tel. 02-837-800), Paris (tel. 1-225-3181), Rome (tel. 6-474-6634), Rotterdam (tel. 10-437-9911), Stockholm (tel. 08-240-080), Vienna (tel. 1-587-8057), and Zurich (tel. 01-811-0688).

European travel agencies specializing in round the world travel via Micronesia include **Reisbureau Amber,** Da Costastraat 77, 1053 ZG Amsterdam, Holland (tel. 20-685-1155); **Malibu Travel,** Damrak 30, 1012 LJ Amsterdam; **Trailfinders,** 42-50 Earls Court Rd., Kensington, London W8 6EJ, England (tel. 071-938-3366); and **Globetrotter Travel Service,** Rennweg 35, 8001 Zurich, Switzerland (tel. 01-211-7780).

The numerous flights between Guam/Saipan and Japan are described in the Territory of Guam chapter (see "Getting There," under "Practicalities"). The Manila to Guam route is served by both Continental Air Micronesia and Air Nauru. Continental also offers Manila to Koror.

Ticket Tips

Airline tickets are sometimes refundable only in the place of purchase, so ask about this before you invest in a ticket you may not use. Nearly every Pacific island requires that you have an onward ticket as a condition for entry, thus careful planning is necessary. A travel agent may be able to help you, provided the agent knows where Micronesia is!

Always reconfirm your onward reservations after arriving on an island, to minimize the possibility of being bumped from your continuing flight. When planning your trip allow a minimum two-hour stopover between connecting flights.

If your flight is delayed over four hours ask the airline for a meal voucher. If the flight is canceled due to mechanical problems with the aircraft, the airline should cover hotel and meals. If they reschedule the flight on short notice for reasons of their own, or you're bumped off an overbooked flight, they should also pay.

To compensate for no-shows, airlines often overbook. To avoid being bumped, check in early and go to the departure area well before flight time. In some airports, flights are not called over the public address system, so keep your eyes open. Overbooked airlines often offer meals, rooms, and even cash to volunteers willing to relinquish their seats.

Baggage

Continental Air Micronesia allows two pieces of checked baggage plus a carry-on on their big DC-10s and 727s, but the smaller commuter airlines may limit you to as little as 30 pounds. If you'll be changing aircraft at a busy gateway city, think twice before checking your baggage straight through to your final destination. Though a nuisance, it's safer to collect it at the transfer point and check it in again.

ORGANIZED TOURS

Scuba Tours

Many experienced divers consider Micronesia the world's ultimate diving destination. Chuuk,

Guam, Palau, Yap, and Pohnpei each offer totally different diving experiences. You can save money by

BOB RACE

booking scuba diving directly with the island dive shops listed in the individual chapters of this book. You can write or call ahead, or just wait to talk to them once you get there.

But unless you've got lots of time and are philosophical about disappointments, you may wish to go on an organized scuba tour. The list of companies offering such trips is long and growing, which says something about their popularity. In addition to the regular phone numbers given below, most have toll free numbers, which you can obtain by calling long distance information at (800) 555-1212.

Most of the prices quoted below are per person, double occupancy. To upgrade to a single room is about $50 extra per night. When booking your tour ask if meals are included. Ascertain what equipment you should bring with you. Of course, diver certification is mandatory. Unless otherwise stated, airfare is *not* included. Prices aren't cheap, but the convenience of having all your arrangements made for you by a company able to pull weight with island suppliers is sometimes worth it.

Mike Musto's **Trip-N-Tour** (2182 Foothill Dr., Vista, CA 92084, tel. 800-348-0842 or 619-724-0788, fax 619-724-9897) is the only scuba tour company that deals exclusively with Micronesia. Mike offers dive packages to the Marshalls, Chuuk, Pohnpei, Yap, Palau, Guam, Saipan, Tinian, and Rota. One-week dive packages, including airfare from the west coast, will be between $1500 and $2300, the biggest variable being the distance to the island to which you travel.

Poseidon Ventures (359 San Miguel Dr., Newport Beach, CA 92660, tel. 800-854-9334 or 714-644-5344; or 505 N. Belt, Suite 675, Houston, TX 77060, tel. 713-820-3483), offers monthly 11-night Blue Diving Tours to Chuuk and Palau. The price includes nine days of two-tank diving, hotels, taxes, and transfers (most meals extra). A three-night Pohnpei extension with two days of diving can be added on.

Tropical Adventures (111 2nd Ave. N, Seattle, WA 98109, tel. 800-247-3483 or 206-441-3483) occasionally has specials that slice $100 or more off regular scuba package prices, so call them up to compare. Tropical's president, Bob Goddess, claims he's always accessible by phone. Over 5,000 divers a year book through this company, which has been in business since 1973.

Innerspace Adventures (13393 Sorrento Dr., Largo, FL 34644, U.S.A, tel. 813-595-5296) has been operating scuba trips to Micronesia since 1971, longer than any other wholesaler. Innerspace's president, Tom Jacobus, specializes in offbeat dive sites, such as Jaluit atoll and Kosrae, so check with him if you have special requests.

Layne Ballard of **Central Pacific Dive Expedition** (29 Blazing Star, Irvine, CA 92714, tel. 714-440-3717 or 800-846-3483, fax 714-851-3111) can arrange independent travel or tours. He specializes in dive tours to the Marshalls. Working with Marshall Dive Adventures, he arranges diving in Majuro and on Bikini atoll.

If the thought of combining trekking or rafting in outback Indonesia or Thailand with scuba diving in Palau appeals to you, **In Depth Adventures** (P.O. Box 593, Eureka, CA 95501, U.S.A, tel. 800-452-3483 or 707-443-9842) is worth checking out. Co-owners Robert Cogen and David Walker—one a trial attorney and the other a licensed private investigator—have 80 years diving experience between them, and personally lead all trips. There are only a couple of departures a year and at $7250 (airfare included) it ain't cheap, but you should have a world-class experience.

Aqua-Trek (110 Sutter St., Suite 205, San Francisco, CA 94104, tel. 800-541-4334 or 415-398-8990, fax 415-398-0479) is another scuba tour operator to try.

See & Sea Travel Service (50 Francisco St., Suite 205, San Francisco, CA 94133, tel. 800-348-9778 or 415-434-3400, fax 415- 434-340) is *the* specialist for live-aboard diving. Their prices are slightly higher than the regular tours mentioned above, but you're offered three or more dives a day plus the selected cream of diving facilities, and all meals are included! See & Sea's current president is the noted underwater photographer and author Carl Roessler.

See & Sea (and most of the other companies above) will book passage on the two live-aboard dive boats based at Chuuk year-round. The newly remodeled Canadian-owned SS *Thorfinn*, a 160-foot former Norwegian whaling ship, is the world's largest live-aboard dive boat. The boat's outdoor hot tub, fireplace in the lounge, and shipboard photo lab add a touch of luxury. Divers are accommodated in 13 double cabins during five- and seven-day Chuuk lagoon cruises with 18 crew members serving the 26 guests. The *Truk Aggressor* (P.O. Box Drawer K, Morgan City, LA 70381, tel. 504-385-2416 or 800-348-2628, fax 504-384-0817) is also based at Chuuk. A week on either of these boats with meals, accommodations, and unlimited diving included will run about $1900, flight not included. Though more expensive than land-based scuba packages, these boats anchor right at the dive sights and tour prices include unlimited diving and meals. See & Sea can also arrange a stay on the **Ocean Hunter** out of Palau. This 60-foot motor sailer takes only six passengers and can anchor right at dive sites. The price is $2000 excluding airfare.

Ocean Voyages Inc. (1709 Bridgeway, Sausalito, CA 94965, tel. 800-299-4444 or 415-332-4681, fax 415-332-7460) arranges "share-boat" yacht tours throughout Micronesia, and scuba diving is often possible. This is worth checking out if you enjoy sailing as much as diving and want to get away from the usual scuba sites. Also try the yacht charter brokerage **Cruising Connection** (P.O. Box 31496, San Francisco, CA 94131, tel. 415-337-8330).

Tours for Naturalists
Oceanic Society Expeditions (Fort Mason Center, Bldg. E, San Francisco, CA 94123, tel. 800-326-7491 or 415-441-1106, fax 415-474-3395) is a 40,000-member, nonprofit environmental organization founded in 1972. Their 10-day snorkeling and natural history tour to Palau

is offered twice a year and is limited to 12 people. This expedition is led by expert naturalists and is ideal for individuals wishing to get close to nature, quickly and briefly, without sacrificing creature comforts. The $2490 price includes airfare from Honolulu, boat excursions, accommodations, and lunches. Participants sleep in standard tourist hotels.

Tours for Veterans

Valor Tours, Ltd. (P.O. Box 1617, Sausalito, CA 94966, tel. 415-332-7850) is one of the only American companies conducting escorted package tours to Tarawa (via Majuro). Their annual six night trip to Tarawa is designed for U.S. veterans who want to be present on Betio for the anniversary of the American landings there on 20 November 1943. This trip is always fully booked; when they run out of hotel beds on Tarawa participants are billeted in Marine Corps tents! Valor's president Robert Reynolds has also designed unique tours for veterans to the Solomon Islands, and extensions from Tarawa are possible.

Other Tours

Swingaway Holidays (22 York St., Sydney, NSW 2000, Australia, tel. 02-9237-0300) has beach holiday packages to Guam, Saipan, Pohnpei, Chuuk, Palau, and Yap from Australia. They use the best hotels available and prices include airfare but not meals. Participants travel individually on any flight departing Sydney or Brisbane for Guam. This may be cheaper than buying a regular ticket and paying for your accommodation directly. The **Pacific Island Travel Center** (91 York St., Sydney, NSW 2000, Australia, tel. 02-9262-6555), also offers these trips.

In Canada check with **Adventure Treks Ltd.,** in Calgary, Edmonton, Toronto, and Vancouver, for packages and plane tickets to Micronesia. Their Canada toll free number is (800) 661-7265.

GETTING AROUND

By Air

Local **commuter airlines** such as Air Marshall Islands, Air Mike Express, Air Tungaru, Caroline Pacific Air, Freedom Air, Pacific Missionary Aviation, Pacific Island Air, and Paradise Air operate domestic services within the individual island groups. These flights are described in the respective chapters.

By Ship

If you have a great deal of time, you can really get the feel of Micronesia by taking a field trip ship. These depart fairly frequently from Majuro, Pohnpei, Chuuk, Yap, and Tarawa; you should be able to get on if you're flexible. You'll also need a sense of humor because no one seems to know anything until just a few days prior to departure. It's useless to write ahead requesting reservations. If you happen to be there as the ship's about to leave, you're in luck.

The purpose of the field trips is to transport local passengers and freight. Field trips are for the adventurous: there are few comforts. Deck space is about seven cents a mile. The cabins are usually reserved by government officials, but if you manage to get one it's 10 cents a mile, plus another $10 a day for meals. The cheapest way to go is to stretch your own mat on deck and eat your own food. When buying your ticket, don't ask for a complete roundtrip as they'll compute it by adding up all the interisland fares. Pick one of the farthest islands and buy a ticket to there. Buy another one-way ticket at the turnaround point, or fly back. The ships visit many islands twice, on the outward and inward journeys, so you could stop off and pick it up on the return.

A ship might stop at each island for anywhere from a few hours to four days. You can sleep on board or go ashore and camp (ask the island mayor or chief for permission—usually no problem). As sailing time approaches, keep a close eye on the ship. Rely only on the captain or Field Trip Officer (FTO) for departure information. Even so, cases have been reported where a ship got an emergency call from another island, gave one blast of its horn, took up the ten-

der, and sailed away. Travelers off walking at the far end of the island have been left to catch a flight back. The ships are usually full at the beginning and end of the journey, but comparatively empty at the turnaround point.

The islanders and crew on board may give you food, so have something to give back. If you give the cook rice, he may be kind enough to cook it for you. A jar of instant coffee will come in handy as there's always plenty of hot water. The hot water is also good to heat up bags of Japanese ramen, but you'll need a bowl. You'll often be invited to feast ashore.

By Canoe

Never attempt to take a dugout canoe through even light surf: you'll be swamped. Don't try to pull or lift a canoe by its outrigger: it will break. Drag the canoe by holding the solid main body. A bailer is essential equipment. If you get off the beaten track on an island, it's likely that a local friend will offer to take you out in his canoe. Interisland travel by sailing canoe is sometimes possible in Kiribati.

By Ocean Kayak

Ocean kayaking is still new to Micronesia. But virtually every island has a sheltered lagoon ready-made for the excitement of kayak touring. On many islands, you can still be a 20th-century explorer. Continental Air Micronesia accepts folding kayaks as checked baggage at no charge.

Since 1977 **Baidarka Boats** (P.O. Box 6001, Sitka, AK 99835, tel. 907-747-8996) has been a leading supplier of mail order folding kayaks by Klepper and Nautiraid. **Aire** (P.O. Box 3412, Boise, ID 83703, tel. 208-344-7506) makes the Sea Tiger self-bailing touring kayak, which weighs only 7.2 pounds. Write these companies for their free catalogs.

For a good introduction to ocean kayaking, check your local public library for *Sea Kayaking, A Manual for Long-Distance Touring* by John Dowd (Seattle: University of Washington Press, 1981) or *Derek C. Hutchinson's Guide to Sea Kayaking* (Seattle: Basic Search Press, 1985).

By Road

In Micronesia, on all islands other than Guam and Saipan, roads are for walking and automobiles are merely tolerated. Wherever you are watch out for young children on the road. On many islands, the speed limit may be 15 miles per hour. This is for pedestrian safety as well as to avoid damage to your car, since the roads are often potholed and made of gravel.

Also be aware that your automobile insurance from home may not apply in Micronesia. Discuss this with your insurance agent before you leave. Not all car rental companies in Micronesia offer insurance.

Car rentals are available at all the airports served by Continental Air Micronesia. At Guam and Saipan several well-known rental companies compete for your trade, while operators on some of the other islands are of the rent-a-wreck variety. Generally, only the agencies on Guam and Saipan accept reservations. The price is usually calculated on a 24-hour basis (around $40), so you can use the car the next morning. Mileage is usually included in the price. Avoid any company that charges extra for mileage.

Shared taxis prowl the roads of Majuro, Ebeye, and Chuuk, offering lifts along their routes at low rates. You don't really need to rent a car on those islands. Taxi vans and minibuses on Pohnpei also charge per head. Yap, Guam, Saipan, and Tarawa have public bus services of varying quality, described further in those chapters. See the individual airport and hotel listings for information on airport transfers. Hitchhiking is fairly easy throughout Micronesia, except on Guam.

By Bicycle

Cycling in Micronesia? Sure, why not? You'll be able to go where and when you please, stop easily and often to meet people and take photos—really *see* the islands. It's great fun, but it's best to have bicycle touring experience. Most roads are flat along the coast but be careful on coral roads, especially inclines: if you slip and fall you could hurt yourself badly. Rainy islands like Pohnpei can start to seem inhospitable.

A sturdy mountain bike with wide wheels, safety chain, and good brakes might be best. Thick tires and a plastic liner between tube and tire will reduce punctures. Know how to fix your own bike. Take along a good repair kit (pump, puncture kit, freewheel tool, spare spokes, chain links, etc.) and a repair manual; bicycle shops are few to nonexistent in the islands. Don't try riding with a backpack; sturdy, waterproof bike bags are required. You'll also want a good lock. Refuse to lend your bike to anyone.

Continental Air Micronesia will carry a bicycle free as one of your two pieces of checked luggage within Micronesia. On domestic U.S. flights such as Los Angeles to Hawaii, however, Continental charges $30. You can avoid this charge by checking your bike straight through to your first stop in Micronesia. Interisland commuter airlines usually won't accept bikes on their small planes. Boats sometimes charge a token amount to carry a bike.

M.G.L. DOMENY DE RIENZI

REPUBLIC OF THE MARSHALL ISLANDS

INTRODUCTION

Ask almost any Marshallese what is the country's main tourist attraction and you will be told with pride, "the warmth of her people."

The Marshall Islands are as remote a chain of islands as exists on the planet. This remoteness allowed the Marshalls to avoid significant Western interest and control until the middle of the 19th century. But the isolation melted away in the face of modern transportation, when the 20th century landed on the Marshallese, who have retained an ambivalent attitude toward Western technology.

Twentieth-century waste litters the Marshalls. At the end of the runway of Majuro's International Airport sit the remains of a Western Pacific airplane, which has been lying on the ground for several decades. Through the years, the plane has been picked apart for spare parts, just for the sheer fun of it. A wing sits unattached to the fuselage.

The republic is composed of five islands and 29 atolls, narrow coral islands without much land, and few have extra space for garbage disposal. Throwing garbage onto infertile atoll land was functional when garbage was biodegradable, but this habit became quite dysfunctional with the emergence of nonbiodegradable garbage. Cans, building materials and plastic now lie everywhere on the narrow circle of sand that makes up Majuro atoll, the capital and commercial center of the Marshalls.

However, the Marshallese would like to turn their most spectacular garbage into treasure. As the United States pushed westward across the Pacific during World War II, it destroyed an enormous number of Japanese ships, planes, guns, and bunkers, which now litter sea and land. Many nations faced with such a situation would have considered it a problem to be solved, but the Marshallese look at it as an opportunity. Like their Micronesian cousins on the island of Chuuk in the Federated States of Micronesia, the Marshallese are attempting to build a tourist industry around wreck diving, confident that divers will come to view the refuse.

During the 1940s and 50s, the United States carried out a well-publicized series of nuclear tests on the Marshalls, dropping atomic and hydrogen bombs on Bikini and Enewetok atolls. Today, most Marshallese think the United States should be forced to attempt a cleanup. Others believe the radioactivity of these atolls must be accepted. They reason that since things could not be much worse, industrialized countries should be invited, for a price, to dump additional atomic and other toxic wastes here.

The Land

Majuro, the capital and commercial center of the Marshalls, will not please those seeking an

THE MARSHALLS AT A GLANCE

	POP. (1988)	LAND AREA (SQ. MI.)	LAGOON AREA (SQ. MI.)
RATAK CHAIN			
Ailuk	488	2.08	68.46
Arno	1,656	5.02	130.77
Aur	438	2.16	92.59
Bikar	0	0.19	14.44
Erikub	0	0.58	88.92
Jemo	0	0.08	none
Likiep	482	3.98	163.71
Majuro	19,664	3.56	113.94
Maloelap	796	3.78	375.56
Mili/Knox	854	6.14	294.71
Nejit	445	0.73	none
Taka	0	0.23	35.95
Tsongi	0	1.24	30.12
Utirik	409	0.93	22.12
Wotje	646	3.17	241.04
RALIK CHAIN			
Ailinginae	0	1.08	40.93
Ailinglaplap	1,715	5.68	289.69
Bikini	10	2.32	229.42
Ebon	741	2.20	40.08
Enewetak	715	2.28	387.99
Jabat	112	0.23	none
Jaluit	1,709	4.36	266.29
Kili	602	0.35	none
Kwajalein	9,311	6.33	839.30
Lae	319	0.58	6.83
Lib	115	0.35	none
Namorik	814	1.08	3.24
Namu	801	2.43	153.51
Rongelap	0	3.09	387.76
Rongerik	0	0.66	55.37
Ujae	448	0.73	71.78
Ujelang	0	0.66	25.48
Wotho	90	1.66	36.64
TOTAL	**43,380**	**69.94**	**4,506.64**

MAJURO'S CLIMATE

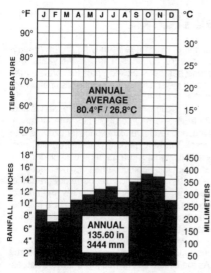

ANNUAL AVERAGE 80.4°F / 26.8°C

ANNUAL 135.60 in 3444 mm

unspoiled island paradise. It contains areas of tropical beauty, but most of the island is a vibrant, gutsy, overcrowded slum. Ebeye, an island on Kwajalein atoll, and the Marshall's second population center, has even greater overcrowding. Take the time to get away to outer atolls, however, and you'll soon discover islands of beautiful beaches, breadfruit, coconut palms, and pandanus. Services may be few, but the people are friendly and there is a sense of adventure in the air.

The 1,225 Marshall Islands are grouped together in 29 atolls (20 inhabited), five low islands (Jabat, Jemo, Kili, Lib, and Mejit), and 870 reefs. The atolls are narrow coral rings, usually with white sandy beaches enclosing turquoise lagoons. The southern atolls' vegetation is thicker due to heavier rainfall. Although the Marshall Islands comprise only 70 square miles, they are scattered over 775,000 square miles of central Pacific Ocean. Its position as the first island group west of Hawaii led to bitter battles during World War II. Its geographical isolation from industrialized countries and their media made them seem perfect to the United States as a place to test nuclear bombs too large or dirty for Nevada.

The Marshalls boast the largest atolls in the world, arrayed in two chains 150 miles apart and 800 miles long. The northeastern or Ratak ("Sunrise") Chain includes the large atolls of Mili, Majuro, Maloelap, Wotje, and Likiep; the southwestern or Ralik ("Sunset") Chain includes Jaluit, Ailinglaplap, Kwajalein (the world's largest atoll), Rongelap, Bikini, Enewetak, and others. The Marshall Islands' government also claims the United States-held island of Wake (Enenkio) to the north, but war over possession is not expected.

Climate

The Marshall Islands' climate is tropical oceanic, cooled year-round by the northeast trades. From January to March the climate is drier. The summer months are most likely to have the still air and water that divers prefer. The northern islands of the Marshalls are cooler than the southern atolls, and receive less rainfall. Typhoons are rare, although March, April, October, and November can be stormy.

HISTORY

Origin of the Marshall Islands

The first humans, Uelip and his wife, lived on the island of Ep. One day a tree began to grow from Uelip's head and split his skull. Through the crack were born his sons, Etau and Djemelut. Etau quarreled with his father and decided to build a home of his own. He took a basket of

FIELD MUSEUM OF NATURAL HISTORY, CHICAGO

MARSHALLESE STICK CHARTS

To travel to islands over the horizon, the people of the Marshalls learned to read the wave patterns of the sea. When uniform ocean currents and wind drifts are interrupted and reflected by numerous atolls and reefs, they form certain kinds of swells that show the direction of land. This phenomenon can be clearly seen today on aerial photographs and pictures taken from weather satellites. The patterns could be felt by an experienced navigator as waves slapped against the side of the canoe, and it's said that even a blind man could navigate by means of a Marshallese stick chart *(wapeepe)*. These charts were used to train young people in the art, and there were several types of these navigational aids.

soil and flew off through the air. The basket had a hole in it through which soil drained out, forming the Marshall Islands.

Discovery and Settlement

Micronesians arrived in the Marshalls thousands of years ago, though there is academic debate as to a more exact time of arrival. They were extraordinarily skilled navigators. Keen observers of the ocean, they discovered that the location of distant islands affected wave patterns. Thus, by studying those patterns, a Marshallese navigator could locate islands that were too low to be seen over the horizon. They created "stick charts" made of sticks and cowrie shells to help memorize the patterns. With this navigation system, far superior to anything Europeans possessed at the time, the Marshallese were able to sail their large outrigger canoes between distant atolls.

There is no record of any single chief ever controlling the entire group, although the Ralik Chain was occasionally united. Because land is so scarce in the Marshalls, it is highly valued. Traditionally, tribute in the form of the produce of the land was rendered to the chiefs.

European Contact

The first European on the scene was the Spaniard Alvaro de Saavedra, in 1528. Although Spain made a vague claim to the Marshalls in 1686, it never attempted to colonize the region. The islands were named for British captain John Marshall of the HMS *Scarborough,* who charted the group of islands in 1788. A Russian explorer, Otto von Kotzebue, made two trips to the Marshalls (in 1817 and 1825), and his careful observations provided Europeans with their first clear picture of the Marshallese and their atolls.

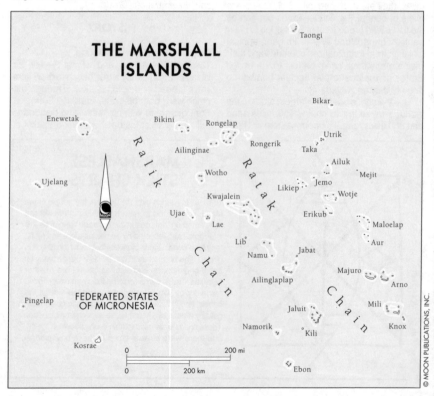

THE MARSHALL ISLANDS

M.G.L. DOMENY DE RIENZI

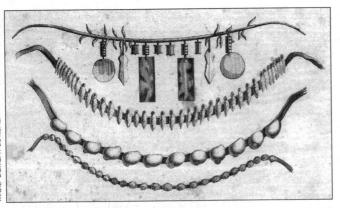

traditional jewelry

Ensuing whalers were repelled by the islanders.

The first German trader established himself on Ebon in 1861; in 1878 Chief Kabua of Elson and Jaluit, ancestor of the president of the Republic of the Marshall Islands, signed a treaty with the Germans giving them use of Jaluit and protection for their traders. In exchange, the Germans supported his supremacy among the islanders. The German government declared a protectorate over the Marshalls in 1885 and two years later arrived to set up headquarters on Jaluit. The Germans ruled indirectly through the Marshallese chiefs and did not attempt mass colonization. A small European business staff was in charge of copra production.

In 1888 the traders merged into the Jaluit Gesellschaft, which agreed to cover Germany's costs of administration in exchange for a monopoly. By 1899 the Jaluit company had 10 stations in the Marshalls and ships that purchased coconut meat throughout the Carolines. In 1905, a devastating hurricane swept across the Marshalls, destroying buildings and plantations. Unable to recover, the company returned control of the area to the German government in 1906, which joined it to other Micronesian islands it had purchased from Spain in 1899.

Japanese Contact

The Japanese, who had traded in the Marshalls since 1890, took the islands from the Germans in 1914, after the start of World War I. No fighting occurred because the Germans withdrew to strengthen their European war effort. The Japanese set up a naval administration. In 1920, Japan received a mandate from the League of Nations to administer Micronesia. The copra trade was turned over to a company called Nanyo Boeki Kaisha. Direct Japanese rule replaced the authority of the traditional chiefs and the number of Japanese officials steadily increased.

The Japanese began building military bases on some of the atolls in 1935. The Marshalls were a staging area for the 1941 Japanese invasion of what is now Kiribati, the Gilbert Islands. The United States captured Kwajalein and Enewetak from the Japanese in February 1944, after bloody battles. Japanese bases on Jaluit, Maloelap, Mili, and Wotje were neutralized by aerial bombardment, and the survivors, both Japanese and Marshallese, were left to sit out the war. From Kwajalein and Majuro, the United States Navy struck west into the Japanese-held Carolines and Marianas.

In 1947 the Marshall Islands became part of the Trust Territory of the Pacific Islands, administered by the United States. Although under United Nations auspices, the Trust Territory was made a "strategic" trust, meaning that the United States was allowed to create military bases. From 1946 to 1958 the United States carried out a massive nuclear testing program on the northern atolls of Bikini and Enewetak. In 1961, Kwajalein became the army's Pacific Missile Range, a target for Intercontinental Ballistic Missiles (ICBMs) test fired from California.

Recent History

In a vote of the people on 12 July 1978, Marshallese voters chose to separate from the other districts of the Trust Territory of the Pacific Islands. They approved a constitution of their own the following year, and on 1 May 1979 formed a Marshall Islands government. In September 1983, the Marshallese electorate voted for a Compact of Free Association with the United States that will bring in about $1 billion in United States aid over 15 years.

In December 1990, the United Nations Security Council formally terminated the trusteeship arrangement in these islands and the following September accepted the Republic of the Marshall Islands as a member.

GOVERNMENT

The legislature is modeled on the British parliamentary system. But the government, like all politics in the Marshalls, remains strongly influenced by the ancient, traditional hierarchy. The constitution provides for a 33-senator Nitijela (Parliament) elected every four years. Majuro has five seats, Kwajalein three, Ailinglaplap, Arno, and Jaluit two each, and 19 other districts one each. The voting age is 18.

The Nitijela elects the president from its ranks, and the president chooses his cabinet from elected members of the Nitijela. If the house passes two votes of no confidence, the president must dissolve the Nitijela and call new elections. Legislative powers are centralized in the Nitijela, there being no states or provinces.

The two political groupings are the ruling RMI party and the Ralik-Ratak Democratic Party opposition. Many of the elected members of the Nitijela are also customary chiefs (iroij). The traditional high chief Amata Kabua, first president of the Marshall Islands, has exercised firm personal leadership since self-government began in 1979. Members of his family hold key governmental positions.

The Council of Iroij (consisting of 12 hereditary traditional leaders) deliberates on matters relating to land, custom, and tradition. A Traditional Rights Court rules on land rights.

The capital of the Marshall Islands is D-U-D (Darrit-Uliga-Delap) on Majuro; Ebeye (on the Kwajalein atoll), Jaluit, and Wotje are adminis-

trative subcenters. Each of the 24 inhabited islands and atolls has a mayor and island council organized according to municipal constitutions, which govern the consumption of alcoholic beverages, among other things.

ECONOMY

The Republic of the Marshall Islands, like most small Pacific island nations, will have a great deal of difficulty regaining economic self-sufficiency. The republic is currently dependent on financial aid from the United States, which accounts for over half of the government's budget. The local economy, though not its social structure, is aided by Marshallese who work abroad, usually in the United States, and remit money back to family members still living in the Marshalls. The economy is hampered by one of the highest birthrates in the world. This has swelled population and created a great number of children who need to be supported. Much economic development money has not been effectively utilized, leading to a heavy burden of government debt. As stated by Rube R. Zackhras, Minister of Finance:

The problem facing RMI is colossal. There is not doubt that dependence of the economy on massive foreign aid, imported food, raw material and capital goods and on expatriate human resources has to be reduced if we are to reduce the negative impact of the eventual termination of Compact funding. We have to create alternative sources of employment, income and government revenue that would take the place of Compact funding. In addition, we have to meet the needs of a fast growing population more than half of which consists of young dependents who do not contribute to incomes of family.

Most of the monies received from the United States annually as grants, funding, and aid is spent on Majuro itself. In 1986, Ebeye began to get a larger piece of the pie. About one percent of the money in the Marshall Islands General Fund goes to the outer islands.

Government workers outnumber those in the private sector. Local government represents half of all economic activity. There is, however, still a degree of subsistence agriculture (coconuts, breadfruit, pandanus, bananas, taro, sweet potatoes, yams, pigs, chickens, reef fish), particularly on the outer islands.

In 1993 the Marshalls imported $62 million, and exported $9 million. Copra and coconut oil are the most significant agricultural exports. Almost all trade is with the United States and Japan.

The Kwajalein Missile Range brings in over $25 million a year in salaries paid to Marshallese workers at the base, $11 million annual rent paid by the military, and taxes on the salaries of American expatriates.

The Marshalls, like other nations of Micronesia, allow foreign fishing fleets, using foreign labor, to harvest enormous amounts of tuna from its waters. Thus the Marshalls receive relatively little income from the taking of perhaps their greatest natural resource. But income enterprises are underway to farm giant clams (Tridacna gigas) and to export live tropical fish to aquarium stores.

THE PEOPLE

Of the 34 atolls and islands, 24 are inhabited. Almost half the population of the Marshalls lives on Majuro and another quarter on Ebeye, making these islands among the most densely populated in the Pacific. From 1980-88, the birthrate was over 4.24%, close to the theoretical limits of population growth. Since then, aggressive family planning promotions have decreased the rate, which nonetheless remains high. Over half the population is under age 15, the highest such ratio in the Pacific.

Westernization and the breakdown of the traditional family have led to many of the problems often associated with urban poverty: alcoholism and high rates of teenage suicide and out-of-wedlock teenage pregnancy. What is perhaps more remarkable is the degree to which some traditional values have survived the effects of colonialism, the destruction of World War II, and the cold war era nuclear testing program.

For most people on Majuro, rice has replaced more nutritious traditional starches, such as taro and other root plants. Some families eat few fresh vegetables or even fresh fish, living instead on a diet of canned and processed foods. Such eating habits have led to obesity and even cases of blindness in children from lack of vitamin A.

Outer islanders, particularly the young, continue to migrate to Majuro and Ebeye, though they are often unable to find suitable employment once they arrive. Another important social development on the Marshalls is that many young adults will spend at least part of their life working in Hawaii, Guam, or the United States mainland. The cultural effect when they return cannot be minimized.

Most Marshallese are Protestant, but missionaries of many creeds are active on Majuro. Many social activities focus on the church. Eight grades of education are compulsory. High schools teach in English. For postsecondary education, students can go on to the College of the Marshall Islands (CMI), a teacher training facility on Majuro, which in 1991 became affiliated with the University of the South Pacific in Fiji. CMI offers a nursing program that serves all of Micronesia.

Marshallese society is matrilineal: chiefly titles descend through the mother. Under these traditional rules, each Marshallese belongs to the bwij (clan) of his or her mother and has the right to use the land and other property of the bwij. Alongside this is "blood" lineage (bodokodok), which is inherited from the father. The dri jerbal till the land. The head of the bwij is the alab, a spokesman between commoners (kajur) and the chiefly families (iroij). The paramount chiefs (iroijlaplap) are the Marshallese equivalent of royalty. As the money culture expands, Marshallese women are losing control of the land as family property is often sold to local men. Only Marshallese can own land in the Marshall Islands, although outsiders may lease it.

Language

Marshallese, the official language, belongs to the Austronesian family of languages (formerly known as Malayo-Polynesian) and is related to Gilbertese and some languages of the Carolines. People of the Ratak and Ralik Chains speak mutually comprehensible dialects. Yokwe (pronounced "YAG-way") is the Marshallese greeting; "thank you" is kommol. Kids often shout *belle* or *dribelle* (foreign people) at visitors; answer them with *yokwe*. If they are small you might try answering back *driMazjal* (Marshallese people)—it usually gets a laugh.

ARTS AND ENTERTAINMENT

Arts and Crafts

The Marshalls still produce a good supply of traditional handicrafts that are readily available for purchase by tourists. Plentiful supplies of pandanus and coconut fiber, plus the relaxed pace of atoll life, led to a variety of handicrafts. The best baskets in Micronesia are made in the Marshalls, especially those made by the Bikini refugees on Kili. You can also find woven coasters, wall hangings, pandanus hats, grass skirts, belts, purses, headbands, necklaces, fans, and mats, all made by Marshallese women.

The men do woodcarvings of sharks, eels, and canoes. Marshallese stick charts *(wapeepe),* which record the way ocean swells reflect and bend as they near land, make unique souvenirs. (See "Shopping" under "Majuro," below).

INSTITUT ROYAL DU PATRIMOINE ARTISTIQUE, BRUSSELS

a Jaluit fan made of coconut, pandanus, and hibiscus fibers

Holidays and Events

Public holidays include New Year's Day (1 January), Memorial Day and Nuclear Victim's Remembrance Day (1 March), Good Friday, Constitution Day (1 May), Fisherman's Day (first Friday in July), Labor Day (first Monday in September), Manit Day (last Friday in September), Independence Day (21 October), President's Day (17 November), Thanksgiving (fourth Thursday in November), and Christmas Day (25 December).

Constitution Day, commemorating the Marshallese constitution, which took effect 1 May 1979, is a good time to see Marshallese singing and dancing, canoe races, and other traditional activities. Aging Week (last week in May) features exhibitions of handicrafts, traditional Marshallese medicines, and cooking. Fisherman's Day marks the beginning of a famous game fishing tournament organized by the Marshalls Billfish Club in Majuro. Alele Week (last week in August) also hosts dancing, singing, handicrafts, and other cultural activities. At Christmas, singing and dancing unfold in the churches all day.

PRACTICALITIES

Accommodations and Food

The only regular hotels and restaurants are on Majuro and Ebeye. On either island, occasionally all rooms can be full. Taxes on rented rooms are three percent of the bill plus $2 a day. Outside D-U-D camping is generally acceptable, provided you first obtain permission of the landowner (usually no problem).

In Ebeye, the Marshalls' second-largest city, you can stay at a hotel with a state-of-the-art Meridian phone system that can record incoming and outgoing calls, turn itself on or off, and probably give a wake-up kiss. However, for reasons that no one could quite explain, if you want to call anyplace in the world other than the 1/10th square mile which is Ebeye, you must walk down to the local phone company to do it.

Accommodations for visitors are available on Mili and a few other outer atolls, but reliable information is hard to obtain. One way to arrange a stay on an outer island is to go to the Nitijela and ask for the senator from the atoll of your interest. The senator will be able to outline the

Marshall Islands
Country Code 692

accommodations situation and perhaps suggest local contacts. Although you can simply show up on the outer islands, to be assured of a good reception it's much better to make prior arrangements with the Island Council. The Ministry of Internal Affairs (P.O. Box 18, Majuro, MH 96960, tel. 625-3240) has a radio link with most of the atolls and is experienced in arranging stays. Give them as much lead time as possible to contact the island's mayor and make the arrangements.

If you arrange to stay with someone as a guest, ask whoever made the arrangements what to take along as a gift (a large jar of instant coffee, T-shirts, music cassettes, or flashlight and batteries, for example—but not alcohol). Although Marshallese hospitality is genuine, adequate reciprocation (monetary or otherwise) is customary. Airline baggage limits permitting, take your own food and bottled water or water purification system with you to the outer islands, as local cooperative stores carry only basics like sugar and flour.

Visas

Although United States citizens may not need a passport to enter the Marshalls, to avoid hassles it's best to carry one. No visa is required of United States citizens for stays up to 30 days, but anyone intending to stay over 30 days should obtain a Marshalls entry permit in advance through their local sponsor. Visa extensions beyond the initial 30 days are hard to come by without an adequate reason. Everyone other than United States and Canadian citizens must already have a United States visa if they are going east to Hawaii or west to Guam. All visitors must have an onward or return air ticket and are forbidden from engaging in political activity.

After clearing customs at Majuro, visiting yachts must obtain a permit from the Ministry of Interior and Outer Islands Affairs to cruise to the other atolls.

Money, Mail, and Measurements

American currency is used. Food and essentials can cost almost twice as much on the outer islands as they do in Majuro, if they can be found at all. Bargaining is not customary in the Marshalls and tipping is done only in tourist-oriented establishments.

The Marshall Islands issues its own colorful postage stamps. Domestic United States postal rates apply. Packages mailed to the United States are frequently opened for postal inspection. Address mail to Majuro, MH 96960; or Ebeye, MH 96970. The electric voltage is 110 volts/60 cycles, and American appliance plugs are used.

The Marshall Islands is the first country west of the International Date Line. If you are coming from Hawaii, you lose a day. Whatever the day,

guest cottages on
Mili-Mili

you'll be on Marshallese time, which means slow down! Government offices are most reliably open weekday mornings.

Health

A vaccination certificate against cholera or yellow fever is required if arriving from an infected area. Typhoid and polio immunizations are not required, but recommended. There's a large new hospital on Majuro and a field hospital at Ebeye. Only dispensaries are available on the outer islands. Be aware: The sexually transmitted disease and tuberculosis rates on Majuro and Ebeye are high!

The Marshall Islands experiences cases of *ciguatera* (seafood poisoning) much more than other parts of Micronesia. There is little if any danger, however, in restaurants. And on outer islands, where it is most prevalent, older residents can offer guidance on which fish to avoid.

Don't drink the tap water in D-U-D or on the outer islands. At best the water is brackish, and it may well be contaminated. Buy bottled water if you can. From January through April water is rationed on Majuro. Be thoughtful and minimize your use.

Information

Upon request, the Tourism Office (P.O. Box 1727, Majuro, MH 96960, tel. 625-3206) will send you their brochures. The Hawaii office is at 1888 Lusitania St., Honolulu, HI 96813, tel. (808) 545-7767.

Hillary Kaye, tourism representative for the Marshall Islands, is a wealth of information. Contact her at 4000 Westerly Place, Suite 210, Newport Beach, CA 92660, tel. (714) 851-5150, fax (714) 851-3111.

The Alele Museum (P.O. Box 629, Majuro, MH 96960, tel./fax 625-3226) sells hard to find books such as *Collision Course at Kwajalein* (1984, $8), by Giff Johnson, and *Man This Reef* (1982, $11), by Gerald Knight. They will also have the *Marshall Islands Guidebook,* which includes a Marshallese dictionary, maps of all the atolls, and much background information on the country. These books can be shipped by airmail. You can write for a complete list.

The weekly, privately owned *Marshall Islands Journal* (P.O. Box 14, Majuro, MH 96960) comes out on Friday (50 cents) in English and Marshallese. Annual subscription rates to the *Journal* are $81 to the United States, $205 elsewhere (airmail). The *Journal* includes a wealth of interesting local news from an independent perspective, so be sure to pick up a copy first chance you get. It advertises itself as "The World's Worst Newspaper" (which it's not).

The Guam-based *Pacific Daily News* is usually available in D-U-D. Two AM and two FM radio stations broadcast in English and Marshallese. Cable TV is available, including CNN.

The many Peace Corps volunteers in the Marshalls are an excellent information source on the outer islands.

What to Take

You're allowed to bring in one bottle of liquor and two cartons of cigarettes—a good idea if you need them, as they're heavily taxed. Cosmetics are also expensive locally. Color print film can be purchased in D-U-D. Women visitors should be aware that local women dress conservatively, the custom is against wearing shorts above the knees.

Getting There

Majuro Airport (MAJ) is eight miles west of town and has no bank or tourist information. Handicrafts are sold at two shops that sometimes open at international flight times. A shared taxi to D-U-D costs $2 pp, although most of the hotels offer free shuttles. The airport departure tax is $15 on international flights. The HNR Restaurant at the airport does not overinflate prices. Since service is often slow, do not assume you can fit in a quick bite right before a flight. Flights are announced in a gentle, unamplified voice so pay attention to the time, particularly if you are in the restaurant.

Continental Air Micronesia (tel. 247-3209) offers flights to Majuro three times a week from Honolulu and from Guam. It costs about the same to fly Honolulu to Majuro as Honolulu to Guam, with stops in Majuro, Kwajalein, Kosrae, Pohnpei, and Chuuk. You can get instant confirmations on flight bookings out of Majuro. Reconfirm your onward flight well in advance at the Air Mike office.

There are three **Air Marshall Islands** (tel. 625-3733) flights a week from Majuro to Tarawa ($197 one-way), Funafuti ($472 one-way), and

Fiji ($589 one-way), which allows a sidetrip to the Republic of Kiribati or a connection to the South Pacific. Check for any reduced roundtrip excursion fares. This airline also flies between Honolulu and Majuro/Kwajalein a number of times each week ($563 one-way). Special roundtrip fares from Honolulu are available. For toll free information on Air Marshall Islands, if calling from the United States, dial (800) 543-3898.

Layne Ballard of **Central Pacific Dive Expedition** (29 Blazing Star, Irvine, CA 92714, tel. 714-440-3717 or 800-846-3483, fax 714-851-3111) can arrange independent travel or tours. He specializes in dive tours to the Marshalls. In conjunction with Marshall Dive Adventures, he can arrange diving in Majuro or in exotic locales such as Bikini atoll.

Getting Around

By Air: Government-owned **Air Marshall Islands** (P.O. Box 1319, Majuro, MH 96960, tel. 625-3733) uses safe, reliable 19-seat German-made Dornier propeller aircraft to provide punctual service to all 26 airstrips in the Marshalls weekly or twice a month. AMI flies from Majuro weekly to Airok ($89) and Jeh ($82) on Ailinglaplap, also weekly to Likiep ($120), Maloelap ($69), Wotje ($93), and Tinak on Arno ($41), twice weekly to Mili ($56), Jaluit ($85), and Kili ($93), and six times a week to Kwajalein ($125). All fares are one-way. Their current schedule appears in the *Marshall Islands Journal* each

week. Checked baggage limits are 30 pounds on domestic flights, 44 pounds international. Often the flights are full.

Special services sometimes allow weekend trips to Arno and Jaluit. Occasionally AMI offers Sunday day trips to outer islands like Maloelap or Mili for about $75 including a lunch of local foods—a great opportunity if your travel plans coincide. A flight arrival on an outer island is the main social event of the week.

By Boat: Time permitting, a leisurely way to experience the Marshall Islands is on a field trip aboard the *Micro Chief* or *Micro Palm.* These 600-ton ships make five different field trips from Majuro: west (1,510 miles), north (695 miles), south (680 miles), central (530 miles), and east (175 miles). Theoretically the ships visit all the atolls every month or two. Fares run about 25 cents a mile with cabin, 15 cents a mile on deck. The cabins are usually full. Meals are $10 a day extra, but the food served is poor, so it's best to take along your own.

To find out what's available, inquire at the **Government Transportation Office** (tel. 625-3469) beside the dock as soon as you arrive on Majuro. If something's leaving that same day, jump on it—otherwise, you might have to wait a couple of weeks. Another possibility is to fly to an island that the field-trip ship will be visiting shortly and ride back to Majuro. Note that alcoholic beverages are prohibited on many outer islands.

a supply ship at Majuro

DAVID STANLEY

THE RATAK CHAIN

MAJURO

Majuro, 2,273 miles southwest of Honolulu, is a long finger of islands joined together by causeways that enclose the south side of the Majuro lagoon. Originally, 64 islands surrounded the oval lagoon; causeways now enable you to drive the 35 miles from Rita to Laura. Some say Rita and Laura—World War II code names for Darrit and Majuro Islands respectively—are named after Hollywood stars Rita Hayworth and Lauren Bacall.

Before the war Majuro was just another outer atoll, but on 1 February 1944 the Americans landed unopposed on Majuro and built a fighter strip near where Gibson's Department Store is now, while naval units anchored in the lagoon. Take the time to explore and you'll find Majuro an interesting place to spend a few days.

D-U-D

The present capital of the Marshall Islands bears the title D-U-D Municipality—the initials stand for Darrit-Uliga-Delap, originally three islands but now joined into one road-linked strip. D-U-D is three miles long and at most places 650 feet wide. It's a conglomeration of administrative buildings, businesses, department stores, supermarkets, small groceries, beer outlets, and densely packed houses of plywood and corrugated iron or tin roofs. Don't expect a pristine paradise: it is heavily littered and cars outnumber coconuts palms. Well over 20,000 Marshallese from every atoll in the country and a couple of hundred Americans now live here.

Rita, the residential community at the northeast end of D-U-D, is quite lush with many mature breadfruit, papaya, and plumeria trees. You can easily walk the several miles to Rita from Uliga, the commercial center of the island, or you can take a cab out for about 50 cents and walk back. It is probably the best place to get a feel for daily life in Majuro. The lushness of the area causes a mosquito problem, however, so bring along the bug juice.

Uliga features the Reimers store and hotel, the post office, the library and courthouse, as well as many restaurants and bars.

The small **Alele Museum** (open Monday 10 a.m.-noon, Tuesday and Wednesday 9 a.m.-noon and 1-4 p.m., Thursday closed, Friday 9 a.m.-noon, Saturday 10 a.m.-1 p.m., Sunday closed) has a collection of models of traditional sailing ships and stick charts, as well as a display of traditional weaving and ropes.

A few books on the Marshalls, first day postal covers, and T-shirts depicting local legends are sold in the museum. The T-shirts make excellent

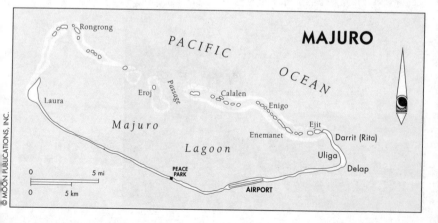

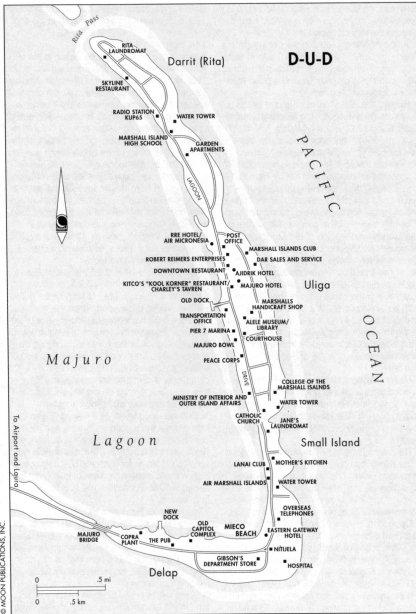

D-U-D

Rita Pass

Darrit (Rita)

RITA
LAUNDROMAT

SKYLINE
RESTAURANT

RADIO STATION
KUP65

WATER TOWER

MARSHALL ISLAND
HIGH SCHOOL

GARDEN
APARTMENTS

LAGOON

PACIFIC

RRE HOTEL/
AIR MICRONESIA

POST
OFFICE

MARSHALL ISLANDS CLUB

ROBERT REIMERS ENTERPRISES

DAR SALES AND SERVICE

DOWNTOWN RESTAURANT

AJIDRIK HOTEL

KITCO'S "KOOL KORNER" RESTAURANT

MAJURO HOTEL

Uliga

CHARLEY'S TAVREN

OLD DOCK

MARSHALLS
HANDICRAFT SHOP

TRANSPORTATION
OFFICE

ALELE MUSEUM/
LIBRARY

PIER 7 MARINA

COURTHOUSE

MAJURO BOWL

Majuro

PEACE CORPS

DRIVE

OCEAN

COLLEGE OF THE
MARSHALL ISALNDS

MINISTRY OF INTERIOR AND
OUTER ISLAND AFFAIRS

WATER TOWER

CATHOLIC
CHURCH

JANE'S
LAUNDROMAT

Lagoon

Small Island

LANAI CLUB

MOTHER'S KITCHEN

AIR MARSHALL ISLANDS

WATER TOWER

To Airport and Laura

OVERSEAS
TELEPHONES

NEW
DOCK

OLD
CAPITOL
COMPLEX

MIECO
BEACH

EASTERN GATEWAY
HOTEL

MAJURO
BRIDGE

COPRA
PLANT

THE PUB

NITIJELA

GIBSON'S
DEPARTMENT STORE

HOSPITAL

Delap

0   .5 mi

0   .5 km

© MOON PUBLICATIONS, INC.

souvenirs; children's sizes sell for $5 and adult sizes $12. They come with a printed card explaining the legend depicted.

Adjoining the museum is the **library** (Mon.-Thurs. 10 a.m.-6 p.m., Friday 10 a.m.-5 p.m., Saturday 9 a.m.-1 p.m.), which has recent American news magazines and a good reference section on Micronesia.

Behind the Alele Museum is one of the island's great institutions—the **Marshalls Handicraft Shop** (P.O. Box 44, Majuro, MH 96960, tel. 625-3566). This enormous crafts store is now over 25 years old and was largely responsible for the revival in Marshallese handicrafts. It is cooperatively owned and run by women. Of the purchase price for crafts, 80 cents of each dollar goes directly to the artist. Mary Lanwi, one of the guiding spirits of the Handicraft Shop, is keenly aware of the degree this institution has empowered women of the Marshalls who otherwise had few economic options. The enormous inventory allows you to learn of the diversity of handicrafts being produced throughout the Republic. Baskets sell for $15-20, stick charts are in the same price range, and items such as woven coasters are as little as $1.35. Craftswomen are frequently at work at the store, and with an advance request, the store can often arrange particular demonstrations. They can mail purchases home and will also accept mail orders.

Next to **Robert Reimers Enterprises** is a covered table area that pretty much serves as the town square. Old men play checkers (coral vs. pop-tops). It's the easiest place in town to sit down and get to know locals—everyone is quite friendly.

The most interesting architecture on the island is the newly completed **Nitijela** (Parliament) complex in Delap. This thoroughly modern building is monumental in feeling; its steel-green windows set into the sand-colored structure echo the dominant colors of the atoll and its lagoon.

Opposite the new Nitijela is **Gibson's Department Store,** which, like Reimers, is a general store, selling clothing as well as food. **Mieco Beach,** between Gibson's Department Store and the old Nitijela complex, is the best beach D-U-D has to offer. At times it has been strewn with empty beer cans and refuse. This presumably will change in late 1996 when Outrigger

Hotels and Resorts opens a newly constructed 150-room government-owned hotel at the spot.

To Laura

A mile and a half past Mieco Beach is the **Majuro Bridge,** built with Japanese aid money in 1983. It's the highest point on the atoll, roughly 12 feet above sea level at high tide. A channel was cut through the lee side to allow better access to the sea for small boats, which could then avoid the long detour around Calalen Island. On the ocean side, on both sides of the channel are often some pretty clean waves. When the waves reach four feet, a nice left forms off the red buoy to the left of the channel (looking out from the bridge). Some caution though; aside from the channel, the bottom is a very hard reef that should not be surfed, and there are frequently dangerous currents in the channel as the tide goes out. This is not a place for anyone but experts. As always, if possible, check conditions with a local.

As you continue around the island toward Laura, you won't find many public beaches. Do not go to a beach in front of someone's home without asking permission, since the beach is considered the homeowner's property. If you find an owner, however, permission to use the beach will usually given. A thank you will go a long way, and perhaps a drink or candy for any kids, but no money should be offered. If you are hoping to camp, you should also ask landowners for permission. Your tent will be pretty safe, but don't leave valuables out when you are gone.

Opposite the airport, on a clear day, you can look across the lagoon and see small islands dotted along the circumference of the lagoon. Right past the runway is a place to park, a nice spot to picnic or to snorkel. The **Japanese Peace Park,** created a couple of miles past the airport in 1984, is another nice spot for a picnic or a snorkel.

You are now in the area the people of crowded D-U-D call the "countryside," an area of coconut and pandanus plantations, a tremendous change from the bustle and dense population of nearby D-U-D. The island here widens to a quarter of a mile across, then broadens still further at the end, Laura town.

Laura had been the big town on the atoll until the United States arrived during the war and chose to concentrate development on the D-U-D side. Now it is a very laid-back community. You'll often see people hanging out enjoying midday barbecues. It is very lush with many banana, taro, and pumpkin patches. There are a number of stands for snacks and drinks. Once the road gets to Laura, it is unpaved for the last mile or so, but it is still easily passable by any car or bike. The road splits to a lagoonside road and one on the oceanside. The lagoonside road comes back to meet the oceanside road, so either road leads to the beach at the end of the island.

Just beyond the end of the paved road is the 10-foot-high Japanese **typhoon monument**, which memorializes Emperor Hirohito's assistance to Majuro after a typhoon in 1918. At the end of the island, you'll come to a beautiful beach and **snorkeling** locale. Ask for Atlan Tobey, a local teacher who lives just beyond the typhoon monument; he can help you find a place to camp.

Laura retains an outer island flavor despite its accessibility to raucous D-U-D. Admission to the beach is $1 for adults, 25 cents per child. It's clean, has both a shower and an outhouse, and is one of the few white-sand beaches on the island. It is a fairly easy place to snorkel but watch out for tidal movements, particularly as you get closer to the channel. At high tide, the reef begins about 300 feet from shore and can be easily spotted from shore by its darker color amid the turquoise.

Accommodations

Although Majuro is nothing but island, it has no beach resorts in the usual sense of those words, in part because there are so few white-sand beaches. Even hotels on the lagoon are usually built behind a seawall, which protects the hotel but makes access to the water more difficult. Oceanside hotels also have relatively poor access to the water.

Budget hotels in Majuro are not particularly cheap. This does not mean that owners are making a fortune; it is costly to build and maintain even a rudimentary hotel out here. Unless indicated otherwise, rooms have private baths, are air conditioned, will probably have a small refrigerator, and may even have a television.

All things considered, the **Ajidrik Hotel** (P.O. Box E, Majuro, MH 96960, tel. 625-3171, fax

625-3712), centrally located in Uliga, is probably the best bet for a budget traveler. Its 15 rooms go for $50 s, $56 d.

Sitting in the shade of its uncompleted (and probably never to be completed) three-story monolith are some older units of the **Eastern Gateway Hotel** (P.O. Box 106, Majuro, MH 96960, tel. 625-3337 or 625-3512). These units have the forlorn look of being in a permanent construction zone. They are located on a nice lagoonfront beach in Delap, a couple of miles south of the business center, but opposite the new government building. The rooms are $55 s, $60 d.

The **Majuro Hotel** (P.O. Box 185, Majuro, MH 96960, tel. 625-3324), in the center of Uliga, charges $47 s, $49 d, for its 15 rooms. It is in disrepair and should only be used as an emergency place to sleep.

Finally, past the airport and near the Japanese Stone House is the **Beach Lodge Motel** (P.O. Box 477, Majuro, MH 96960, tel. 625-3664, fax 625-3663). It has 10 units for $50 or so. You'll definitely wish to have a car if staying out here.

The best hotel in the Marshall Islands, by a long shot, is **Hotel Robert Reimers** (P.O. Box 1, Majuro, MH 96960, tel. 625-5131, fax 625-3783) known to everyone on Majuro as the RRE Hotel. The main portion is on the second floor, above the Ace hardware store, in the center of Uliga. It has 12 units with lanais overlooking the lagoon (our favorite units) at $90 s, $95 d, as well as six windowless rooms at $75 s, $80 d. In addition there are prefabricated beach units that cost $75 s, $100 d. The location is convenient for any business in Majuro. Its restaurant, the Tide Table, is the best on the island and serves breakfast, lunch, and dinner. Go up to the bar at happy hour, 5 p.m. Here it is easy to meet local government officials or expats on business. Any visiting tuna boat captain or outer island teacher volunteer will probably pass through; it's a great place to meet the quirky adventurers who have chosen such lives. RRE is also probably the best place in town from which to arrange fishing or diving trips.

Less lively, but also a good choice, is **Royal Garden Hotel** (P.O. Box 735, Majuro, MH 96960, tel. 247-3701, fax 247-3705), on the ocean a couple of miles west of the Majuro

Bridge. The 24 rooms rent for $78 s, $95 d (including tax). It's located on a stretch of ocean that offers good reef walking at low tide, but not really any swimming. It's in clean, pleasant surroundings and has a restaurant with a beautiful ocean view. You'll need to rent a car to get around.

For a longer stay on Majuro, call Brian and Nancy Vander Velde of the **Garden Apartments** (P.O. Box 1603, Majuro, MH 96960, tel./fax 625-3811). They rent apartments in Rita, prices starting at $350/month or $150/week.

In order to accommodate visitors to the South Pacific Forum in 1996, the government built an upscale 150-room hotel at Mieco Beach. Run by the Outrigger chain and called the **Outrigger Marshall Island Hotel,** tel. (800) 688-7444, it opened in July 1996. Rooms begin at $125 and suites at $235.

Food

Majuro has a good choice of restaurants, at varying price ranges. **Kitco's "Kool Korner" Restaurant,** near the Majuro Hotel, serves dishes like hotcakes and eggs ($2) and fried chicken with chips ($3). The **Downtown Restaurant** near the Ajidrik Hotel offers a similar menu. **The Deli,** between Robert Reimers Enterprises and the post office, sells takeaway breakfast foods, sandwiches, and Chinese dishes that can be eaten at their sidewalk picnic table area. Thursday and Friday at noon the Deli sets up a barbecue that serves up some of the best food in town: a chicken or beef teriyaki plate with a soda is under $5.

The **Tide Table Restaurant** at the RRE Hotel, though fairly expensive, is undoubtedly the best restaurant on the island. Dinner with a couple of beers will cost you about $18. Try the seared blackened ahi, very rare inside, in spicy mustard sauce. Tide Table serves a great local draft beer, Premium Wheat Beer by Republic, amber in color with a sweet yet smoky taste. The restaurant has been upgraded since it was taken over in April 1995 by Tertius Yarbrough from Hawaii.

The **Skyline Restaurant** in Rita and the **FAB** in Delap, both owned by Prianga Fernando, an immigrant electrical engineer from Sri Lanka, offer the same menu, featuring local, Chinese,

and American dishes as well as curries from his homeland. Huge portions are reasonably priced, most $4-5. Beer is served.

The chopped tuna or tuna steak ($3.50) at **Mother's Kitchen,** next to Momotaro's store in Delap, is good, but the restaurant is less than spotless.

The **Royal Garden Hotel** serves meat and seafood. The food is not exceptional and the dinner bill will run $8 to $10. Lunch is cheaper with burgers at about $3.

Japanese Flavor Garden Restaurant, open for lunch and dinner, is located near the Royal Garden Hotel one mile west of the Majuro Bridge. It serves reasonably priced meals (primarily Japanese, but also hamburgers), which you may carry back into their lagoonside garden and eat at the covered picnic tables. It's a good place to stop if you're driving. The restaurant is called the "Stone House" by locals because of the coral on the outside of the building.

A favorite spot with locals is the **Quik Stop Coffee Shop** located near Gibson's. It bills itself as "Home of Local, Filipino and International dishes." The ambience is shopping mall eclectic. It serves breakfast lunch and dinner. Particularly good are the noodle dishes for around $5. Full dinners are not much more.

Blue Lagoon, near the airport, offers local takeaway foods, ready-made for picnics. It is located about one mile from the airport, heading toward D-U-D.

Located in the building next to the Air Marshall Islands office, **Lanai Bar and Oriental Restaurant** (Lanai Club) offers mediocre but filling Chinese rice plate lunches for $5. It has beautiful views out to the lagoon. Food is cooked outside and can be eaten there or inside the air conditioned restaurant.

Food is served at the new **Majuro Bowl.** Also new is **Da Ohana** in Uliga. Al Wong, former manager of the Tide Table, is offering up some excellent food here.

Tipping is expected at American-style restaurants, such as the Tide Table, the Royal Garden, and the Quik Stop Coffee Shop, but not in the Marshallese restaurants.

Entertainment

Majuro has two great bars, the Tide Table at the RRE Hotel, which is *the* place to meet other travelers, and the Marshall Islands Club. The **Tide Table** has a great view out over the lagoon and serves on tap two wonderful beers from local Republic Beer brewery. There is frequently a live band on Saturday night.

Nearby, but on the ocean side of the island, is the **Marshall Islands Club.** Cool breezes blow in from the ocean when, as usual, the storm shutters are up. It is a big barn of a place, with pool tables, shuffleboard, a classic bar, and music blaring from large speakers. It is the perfect vision of a tropical bar. It is a proven fact that if you sit at a table alone, with a pen and paper, you will instantly become a writer. It is that type of place.

The white sand beach curved into the distance, a cruel reminder that I am no more a coconut than a leaf of spinach is a can of sardines.

The Marshall Islands Club often serves free *pu pu* (snacks) during happy hour. Order a pizza or try their $2 snacks anytime: sashimi, fried fish pieces, chicken wings, nachos, and giant-clam meat. A live band plays after 10 p.m. certain nights ($3 cover), as advertised on signs at the door.

Other drinking spots include **Charley's Tavern,** next to Kitco's Restaurant, a cocktail lounge that is retro without effort; the **Lanai Club,** on Delap's Small Island; **The Pub,** near the new dock in Delap; and the lounge above the **Majuro Bowl.** All are bars that have music late on weekend nights. The Pub is a favorite late night dancing spot for the younger crowd.

Most bars on Majuro have a happy hour, with reduced prices weekdays from 5 to 6:30 p.m. On weekend nights, the streets are active and the discos start hopping around 11 p.m. Most bars are closed on Sunday.

Sports and Recreation

Majuro is a good place to go diving, as the underwater attractions beat the above-water sights fins down. The lagoon offers coral pinnacles, abundant sea life including sea turtles and reef sharks, and there are fine walls, channels, and wrecks to visit. There is even good shore diving. Laura is an exceptionally good place for shore diving or snorkeling. Take special care with

ocean currents if you do any snorkeling or diving on the ocean side of the atoll or near a pass!

The United States dumped a large number of jeeps and trucks off Rita as it was leaving the island. Known as the "parking lot," divers can swim to it from land. Because of difficult currents at times in the channel, it is best to visit it only with a local dive professional. There are also oceanside walls to dive at the 25-mile marker and at the 28-mile marker.

Operating out of the RRE Hotel, **Marshall Dive Adventures** (P.O. Box 1, Majuro, tel. 625-3250, fax 625-3505), managed by Fabio Amaral, is the premier dive operation on Majuro. MDA charges $75 for a two-tank dive, $100 to dive neighboring Arno atoll. They will take snorkelers for considerably less. They will soon offer trips to Bikini atoll.

There are also small, independent operators on Majuro. Before using one it's a good idea to verify its reliability with local sources. You might ask at the Tourism Office.

Majuro is becoming known for its sportfishing, and game fish such as blue marlin, mahimahi, sailfish, tuna, and wahoo abound off the east tip of Arno. Line fishing in the lagoon and night fishing for flying fish are also possibilities. One of the biggest events on Majuro is the annual **Billfish Tournament** during the first weekend in July. If you plan to compete, be sure to arrange a boat before making the trip.

Charter boats for deep-sea fishing can be arranged through the RRE Hotel ($150 half day, $300 full day) or the fisheries office. You might also try to reach Wally Milne through the Lanai Club.

Shopping

The largest department stores and supermarkets are **Robert Reimers Enterprises** in Uliga, the **Long Island Grocery Store,** and **Gibson's Department Store** in Delap. A three percent government sales tax is added to all sticker prices at the cash register.

The best spot for purchasing traditional handicrafts is the **Marshalls Handicraft Shop** (open weekdays; P.O. Box 44, Majuro, MH 96960, tel. 625-3566), just behind the Alele Museum. They have a great selection of baskets, fans, coasters, mats, Kili bags, wall hangings, stick charts, and model canoes at reasonable prices.

Crafts are also sold at the **Busy Hands Club,** next to the Catholic church, and at the RRE Hotel.

Services

The **Bank of Guam** (tel. 625-3322) and the **Bank of Marshall Islands** (tel. 625-3636) have branches opposite one another near Robert Reimers Enterprises in Uliga. The **Bank of Hawaii** (tel. 625-3741), at the Gibson's complex in Delap, is the only place you can get a cash advance with a credit card. The banks are open weekdays 10 am.-3 p.m., Friday till 5 p.m.

The downtown post office next to the RRE complex in Uliga has Marshallese stamps and first day covers (open weekdays 8 a.m.-noon and 1-4 p.m., Saturday 8-10 a.m.). There's a branch post office at Gibson's in Delap.

Collectors abroad can order Marshall Islands stamps from the **Stamp and Philatelic Center of the Republic of the Marshall Islands,** One Unicorn Center, Cheyenne, WY 82008-0009, tel. (800) 443-4225.

Calls to the U.S. are $2.50 a minute, station to station, to Guam $3 a minute, to Europe $5 a minute. There's a three-minute minimum to Europe.

To place radio telephone calls to the outer islands, go to radio station KUP65 near Marshall Islands High School in Rita. They're open 24 hours a day and the charge is 50 cents a minute.

The **Consulate of Israel** is on the ocean side behind Robert Reimers Enterprises, the **United States Embassy** (tel. 625-4011) is on Long Island between the airport and D-U-D, and the Chinese Embassy (tel. 625-3275) is near the airport.

There are a number of laundromats (50 cents) around D-U-D, one of the best of which is **Jane's Laundromat** in Delap; it's air conditioned. Others are opposite the Bahai Center near the tip of Rita, next to the Pub out toward the new dock, and next to the MBC TV station in Uliga.

There's a small coin laundry directly between the Majuro and Ajidrik Hotels. Take along some reading material, as the lines can be long. You often see local women occupying four or five machines at a time, though the laundromats are less crowded in the morning.

Health

The **Majuro Hospital** (tel. 625-3399) in Delap provides X-ray, laboratory, emergency, outpatient, and inpatient services. The staff includes American Health Service Corps, Filipino, and Marshallese doctors. Outpatients are treated 1-9 p.m. There's also a pharmacy at the hospital.

D-U-D tap water is unsafe to drink unless boiled for 20 minutes or treated. You may buy bottled water at any market.

Information

You can pick up brochures at the **Tourism Office** (tel. 625-3206), located south of Mieco Beach in the old Nitijela complex.

TV station METV, beside the Marshalls Handicraft Shop behind the library, rents videocassettes of Marshallese dancing and singing at $2 a day. They'll also copy the tapes for $30 apiece.

AM radio stations broadcast at 1100 and 1560 on the dial.

Getting Around

Swarms of shared taxis prowl up and down Lagoon Drive in D-U-D, 25 cents to $1 pp a ride within the town, depending on the distance. Flag one down anywhere, though the taxis are often full. Cruising buses charge 25 cents a ride within D-U-D. A taxi to Laura is $10 pp each way.

Blue and white minibuses run four times a day between D-U-D and Laura ($1.50 pp one-way), but there is no service on Sunday. Look for them in the parking lot in front of the RRE Hotel in Uliga; the stop is marked with a sign reading Bus Parking Only.

OFFICIAL FIRST DAY COVER

Undersea Glory

Small cars rent for $40-45 a day (extra for insurance) at **DAR Sales and Service** (P.O. Box 153, Majuro, MH 96960, tel. 625-3174) behind Robert Reimers Enterprises and at the airport. It's convenient because you can drop the car off at the airport. **RRE Hotel** in Uliga also rents cars, as well as **Deluxe Rent-a-Car** (tel. 625-3665) opposite the Pub in Delap.

Foreign driver's licenses are accepted for one month. At most agencies you must be at least 25 years old to rent a car. The excellent taxi service and limited roads make renting a car optional. One possibility is to rent a car just for one day, to drive to Laura. In fact, Majuro (along with Chuuk) has the best public transportation in Micronesia.

ARNO

You can see Arno, one of the five most populous atolls in the Marshalls, as a thin line along the horizon east of D-U-D; small outboard motorboats often journey between the old dock on Majuro and Arno ($10). If you have to arrange to go with a sportfishing, diving or snorkeling boat, the trip will be much more expensive. Both Ine and Tinak Islands have airstrips, with flights from nearby Majuro about once a week—the easiest way to escape city life. Surprisingly there's no guesthouse on Arno, so if you wish to stay, you have to camp or stay with friends.

Over a hundred islets sit on Arno's peculiarly shaped barrier reef, which twists around three la-

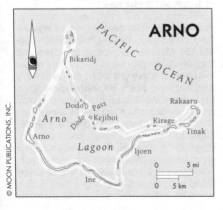

goons! The beautiful beaches and quiet communities make a visit worthwhile. Arno lobsters are famous. With persistence, you can visit the oyster and clam farm on Enerik Island. Black pearls are harvested here. A Japanese fishing project functions on Arno, with local fishermen using small boats to supply a cold storage facility.

MILI

On Mili-Mili, the major island on Mili atoll, you will soon discover that the tourist is the main attraction. You will probably be the only one on the island and you will be fussed over, particularly by the school-age children who will want to practice their (limited) English with you. Mili-Mili is the picture perfect atoll, from coconut palms to white-sand beaches.

After Kwajalein, Mili, 93 miles south of Majuro, is the largest atoll in land area in the Marshalls. During the war, the Japanese brutally suppressed a local revolt. Mili has many Japanese war relics, including submerged wrecks for diving enthusiasts, cannons, bunkers, and intact Zero aircrafts. A giant clam hatchery is on Wau Island. The Knox Islands, just southeast of Mili, are uninhabited.

There are Air Marshall Islands (AMI) flights from Majuro ($56 one way) twice a week. A speedboat also arrives every two weeks ($5). Camping is no problem, but food supplies on Mili are very limited so it's best to bring your own. Take care with the drinking water.

The plane to Mili, a 19-seater Donner 228, lands in a narrow slot through a thicket of breadfruit, coconut palms, and pandanus. Prevailing winds are off the lagoon. Since the plane lands into the wind, it usually lands facing the lagoon and close to it. It will seem that half the island greets your plane. There are only a few vehicles on the whole island, but they will be out to meet the plane to see if you need help with your luggage. Toward your right are four thatched huts on the beach, run by Neija Daniel, who also has a small store next door. The huts rent for $28 a night. This is a great opportunity to see, from the inside, the ingenious design of traditional Marshallese house construction. Cooling breezes come in when you lift the thatched window coverings. Running water is outside and

© MOON PUBLICATIONS, INC.

toilet facilities are in an outhouse. Marshalls Dive Adventures may be able to help you line up a stay in advance.

When the lagoon is still, often the case during summer, there is wonderful snorkeling in the lagoon, off to the right of the cottages as you face the beach. When the wind has been blowing, you can actually get a small, sloppy, but makeable wave in the lagoon.

Remnants of the Japanese military occupation—wrecked Zeros, bunkers, and large guns—are scattered in the bush and difficult to find. It is best to use a guide. You might try Emos Kimej, who lives in a two-story structure just on the other side of the airplane slot from the cottages. He is old enough to tell you about life under Japanese rule and the American invasion.

Take a walk down Main Street parallel to the lagoon. Most life on Mili-Mili is on the lagoon, not the ocean. Main Street is a wide dirt lane with virtually no traffic. Past the schoolhouse, you'll

see an old Japanese bunker. The remains of Japanese roads and runways are visible everywhere. Today grass grows up through them: the island itself is defeating the material remains of Japanese Imperial rule.

RRE Hotel (tel. 625-5131) runs an interesting, small eco-resort on privately owned **Wau Island,** on the opposite side of the lagoon from Mili-Mili. Most of their visitors are divers and they can take up to six at a time. You will fly into Mili-Mili, where you will be met by the dive boat and taken on a wreck dive. Depending on the weather, the boat will then take you to Wau across the lagoon or outside, on the ocean. There are three cabins for guests; all are simple, basic, and clean, with indoor toilets and running water most of the time. If you come in a group for diving, meals will be prepared for you.

At Wau you will be taken on drift dives to see turtles, stingrays and other large fish. RRE also runs a giant clam farm on Wau. You can reach the giant clams by snorkeling from shore. They are incredibly beautiful creatures, with enormous variations in the color and patterns of their mantels. Many have a brilliant luminescence.

MALOELAP

Maloelap atoll, 106 miles north of Majuro, has the largest lagoon in the Ratak Chain, with 71 islands on the reef. AMI flies from Majuro to Taroa ($197 one-way, $328 roundtrip) twice a week, to Kaven every other week ($62). Chartering a speedboat for the ride across the lagoon between the two islands costs about $60 (four hours).

The village on Taroa Island is only a few minutes walk from the airstrip. The mayor has a simple thatched guesthouse in the center of the village, where visitors can stay for about $10 pp a night. Toilet and washing facilities are outside. Advance arrangements must be made through the Ministry of Interior and Outer Islands Affairs on Majuro, which has radio contact with Taroa. In the past, during the summer, visitors could also sleep in empty classrooms.

In 1941, Maloelap became the easternmost Japanese bastion in the Pacific, but on 29 January 1944 a United States air strike from the carrier *Enterprise* against the X-shaped runways on Taroa terminated Maloelap's role as a fortified base. The United States forces never bothered to land on neutralized Maloelap. About two-thirds of the 3,000 Japanese stationed on Maloelap died in the original and subsequent air strikes or from starvation, as they were marooned on an island that could not support them.

Today numerous Japanese guns, bunkers, bombs, and large concrete buildings are hidden in the thick undergrowth of Taroa. Two Zero aircraft lie beside the airstrip. A large concrete Japanese power plant, its rusted generators still inside, sits between the airstrip and the village. Right in the middle of the village is a reinforced three-story Japanese radio station, presently used as a church and living quarters by locals. In the bush, not far from the village, is an aircraft graveyard, with over a dozen wrecked Japanese fighters and bombers. Along the ocean side, at the far end of the airstrip, are coastal defense bunkers and at least six large 150mm guns, three on each side of the airstrip. Many more Japanese ruins are half swallowed in the bush.

You can snorkel around the twin masts of a Japanese freighter, the *Toroshima Maru,* which poke out of the lagoon just off the beach, only about 300 feet from the large Japanese wharf in the middle of the village on Taroa.

WOTJE

Wotje is a large atoll between Maloelap and Likiep, 150 miles east of Kwajalein. During World War II Wotje was a Japanese military base. It is said that soil was brought in from Japan in an effort to make the atoll self-supporting, and Wotje is still known as the garden island of the Marshalls. Numerous war relics remain in the lagoon and on some of the 72 islands of Wotje. The Wotje people often travel to uninhabited Erikub atoll by speedboat to fish and make copra. Plan on camping or staying with locals if you visit.

LIKIEP

Likiep is another sizable atoll, with 65 islands arranged around its shallow lagoon. About a century ago, a German named Adolph Capelle and a Portuguese named Anton deBrum bought Likiep from the chief; their descendants still jointly own the atoll. The deBrum mansion, former

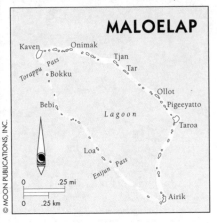

MALOELAP

Kaven Onimak
Torappu Pass Bokku Tjan
  Tar
Bebi Ollot
  Pigeeyatto
Lagoon Taroa
Loa
Enijun Pass
  Airik

0   .25 mi
0   .25 km

© MOON PUBLICATIONS, INC.

headquarters of Likiep's coconut plantation, has been restored with support from the Endowment for Historic Preservation of the Micronesia Institute, Washington, D.C. Thousands of glass plate photos taken by Joachim deBrum are kept at the Alele Museum on Majuro.

THE RALIK CHAIN

KWAJALEIN ATOLL

Kwajalein atoll, 274 miles from Majuro, is the world's largest atoll. Its 176-mile-long coral reef encloses a boomerang-shaped lagoon of 840 square miles. This atoll is a tale of two islands. Kwajalein Island, known as Kwaj, is home to the United States Army's Missile Range. Ebeye, a mere three miles away, is home to over 12,000 Marshallese, more than 1,000 of whom work on the base. Until 1958 the U.S. Navy used Kwajalein as the main support facility for its nuclear testing program on Enewetok and Bikini.

When the 1963 Limited Test Ban Treaty drove nuclear testing underground, the base on Kwajalein Island was converted to testing the accuracy of missile systems. In 1964 control of the atoll passed from the navy to the army, which set up the Kwajalein Missile Range now officially called USAKA (United States Army Kwajalein Atoll). For many years, the central two-thirds of the lagoon was closed to small crafts since it was used as a target for intercontinental ballistic missiles fired from California. Missiles aimed at Kwajalein were often themselves used as targets for antiballistic missiles. Since such tests are now quite infrequent, the entire lagoon is usually open for diving or fishing boats. Kwajalein is still an essential element in the Pacific Barrier radar system, which detects and tracks orbiting satellites. The army values Kwaj as a $4 billion facility.

The compensation of landowners for the base has been a bone of contention. A 1969 "sail-in" reoccupation of the test zone by 200 islanders won enhanced recognition of their rights. During a second sail-in in 1979, landowners occupied missile range facilities on Kwajalein and Roi-Namur, a smaller base on the north end of the atoll. As a result, the United States dramatically increased

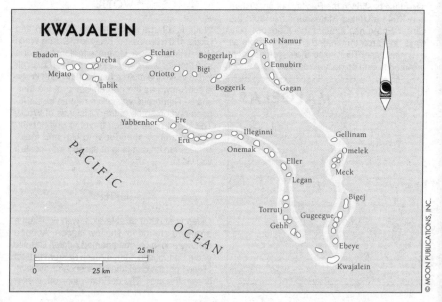

KWAJALEIN

Ebadon
Oreba
Mejato
Tabik
Etchari
Oriotto
Bigi
Boggerik
Boggerlap
Roi Namur
Ennubirr
Gagan
Yabbenhor
Ere
Eru
Illeginni
Onemak
Eller
Legan
Gellinam
Omelek
Meck
Bigej
Torrutj
Gehh
Gugeegue
Ebeye
Kwajalein

PACIFIC OCEAN

0   25 mi
0   25 km

© MOON PUBLICATIONS, INC.

lease payments. Nonetheless, in 1982 over 1,000 Marshallese launched Operation Homecoming, reoccupying 11 islands inside the security zone, where they camped for four months.

Under the 1986 Compact of Free Association, $11 million a year "rent" was to be paid for the military use of Kwajalein atoll for 30 years. However, it was unclear to whom the payments should be made. Monies had at first been distributed on a per capita basis. Today $7 million is distributed to senior landowners in proportion to their rank under the traditional system. These senior landowners theoretically held land for the benefit of all Marshallese, but since no mechanisms are in place to require fair distribution, often hundreds of thousands of dollars a year are used for nothing other than personal gain. The other $4 million a year goes to the Kwajalein Atoll Development Authority (KADA).

About 3,000 Americans live on **Kwajalein Island,** primarily employees of private American corporations doing research for the Defense Department. It is difficult to get advance permission to stay on the base unless you have business there or are visiting someone. If you ask the stateside army for permission, it will be denied with bureaucratic excuses. If you are staying on nearby Ebeye, it is relatively easy to take a boat to Kwajalein and walk around the nonrestricted areas of the base. If you know anyone living on Kwajalein, they will have little difficulty arranging overnight stays.

Kwaj has the reputation of being a wealthy American suburb lost in the middle of the Pacific Ocean. It is true there are swimming pools, baseball diamonds, and other amenities. The military did an excellent job landscaping; most apartments are set within stands of mature coconut and pandanus trees. Best yet, there are virtually no private cars on Kwaj. Everyone gets around on funky, rusty one-speed bikes. But Kwaj is not particularly opulent. Its upscale suburban reputation comes mainly from its proximity to the grinding poverty of nearby Ebeye.

Information

There is an AM and an FM radio station and two TV stations, one run by the Armed Forces Television Network.

Practicalities

There are a number of cafeterias on Kwaj where a meal will cost $3 or $4. At the **Pacific Dining Room** a cafeteria-style lunch buffet costs $5; the salads are safe to eat.

Kwaj Lodge is the only hotel on the island. Rooms for government travelers are $35 or less and for others $49 or less. There are 12 private rooms, 24 semi-private. Reservations *must* be made by your "personal point of contact" on the island. For information, though not reservations, call (805) 461-7422 or fax extension 3211 at that number. The Lodge can also arrange rooms in bachelor quarters for as little as $5 per night.

Getting There

All **Continental Air Micronesia** flights between Majuro and Kosrae touch down on Kwajalein. Ebeye does not have its own airport, and people going to Ebeye must also deplane here. On arrival, luggage is lined up by American authorities and sniffed by drug detecting dogs. The search holds up passengers for almost an hour, quite an inconvenience. Afterward, passengers proceeding to Ebeye are referred to Marshall Islands Immigration. After clearance, they're bused to a lagoonside wharf and sent on by free ferry.

In the past, to visit Ebeye one had to obtain an "Entry into Ebeye" permit from the Immigration office in the Nitijela building in Delap on Majuro. The permit was issued automatically if you had hotel reservations or some other place to stay on Ebeye. The Marshall government now appears to dispense with this requirement for American or Marshallese passengers on Air Mike, but it would be safest to confirm with the Immigration office.

If you have neither an American nor a Marshallese passport, and are going to Ebeye, you will be escorted from airport to ferry dock. With those passports, however, you will be allowed to walk around the base, including the restaurants.

Kwajalein serves as the northwestern hub of the Marshalls, with weekly **Air Marshall Islands** flights to Airok and Jeh on Ailinglaplap ($74), weekly to Ujai ($183) and Wotho ($190), and several a week to Majuro ($125). There are also flights twice a month to Enewetok ($154), and others; all fares are one-way.

EBEYE

About 10 minutes by boat from the Kwajalein base is the Marshallese community on Ebeye (pronounced "EE-bye"). Though on a tropical atoll island, it has the harsh, parched look of a Sonoran desert barrio that was picked up and dropped here so that Kwaj could have a supply of cheap labor. The best reason to visit Ebeye is if one is a truly avid diver.

As you walk the streets of Ebeye, the Marshalls' second-largest town, at dusk, you will be overwhelmed by the number of young children, almost as if a universe had been created containing only seven-year-olds. They sit, they run, they pick nits out of each other's hair. They play ball, often substituting sticks for bats or beach balls for the basketballs they cannot afford. They are poor, charming, and beautiful; they smile easily. I dread the thought of returning in six years to a universe populated solely by adolescents, made sullen by despair.

children of Ebeye

In 1951 construction of the naval station on Kwajalein Island forced the evacuation of the 450 Marshallese inhabitants to Ebeye, one-tenth the size of Kwajalein. By 1967, 4,500 people were jammed onto Ebeye's 80 acres amid appalling sanitary conditions. About one-quarter of the population of the Marshall Islands lives there now. After a disastrous storm in 1988, and with United States aid, the "reconstruction" of Ebeye began. Most dwellings now have water and electricity. The main streets are paved. There is a combination power/desalination plant. A small number of new residences were built, but most remain plywood shacks piled on each other. When a visitor remarks on the conditions of poverty, he or she is immediately told how much better things are since the reconstruction.

Over 1,000 Ebeye workers commute by boat to work on Kwaj. Due to the lack of other sources of employment in the Marshalls, and despite living conditions on Ebeye, its population continues to grow as Marshallese from other atolls arrive looking for jobs on the base or support from relatives already established here.

Ferries run by the United States Army leave Ebeye to Kwaj about every half hour 5:30-8:30 a.m. and return on a similar schedule in the afternoon.

Sights

Visitors can walk around Ebeye in an hour or two. There is little to see other than the people. The nicest time for a walk is dusk. As the sun sinks and the temperature cools, the children come out to play. On the south end of the island is a **beach park** with good snorkeling if you can bear the noise from the island's nearby electrical generator. The **post office** is about 50 feet south of the Anrohasa Hotel and the **new hospital** is about a quarter mile north of it. In the late afternoon and evening, people fish from the pier serving the boats from Kwaj.

As our boat approached the shore, I saw him seated on the dock playing checkers: the Senator, the Iroij, the King of Ebeye himself and I put on my shirt as was the custom.

A poorly maintained causeway links Ebeye to a series of smaller islands. The first island, with a bandstand and cabanas, is the private reserve of major landholders; the second island with hydroponically grown vegetables under glass is also privately owned.

Along the second causeway, the lagoon has a spectacular 200-foot wall to dive. It is pretty easy to spot from the causeway. All kinds of great snorkeling spots present themselves. To get here, it is probably best to arrange for a taxi to drop you off and to pick you up. Although taxi rides on Ebeye itself are only 25 cents, you will have to negotiate a price for a ride to the wall. There are no services on the causeway or these islands, so bring your own food and water.

KADA is planning a small diving resort on Ebwoj, the third island. The next island has some nice FEMA-built housing. On the lagoon side of the island, near the housing, is a well-preserved Japanese war relic, an armored personnel carrier. The causeway ends five miles from Ebeye.

Ebeye presents other opportunities for diving and snorkeling. There are some beautiful coral pinnacles, which can be seen while snorkeling. Divers can visit the 600-foot wreck of the *Prinz Eugen,* a pocket battleship that had been a companion ship to the infamous *Bismarck.* Its bow lies at 200 feet and its stern protrudes above the water. Arrangements are most easily made through KADA.

Accommodations

Be certain to make advance hotel reservations on Ebeye, as there are only two hotels. There is usually a vacancy, but there are *no* alternatives, not even a bus station or an airport in which to spend the night. The island is too crowded to find a place to pitch a tent. The newly expanded **Anrohasa Hotel** (P.O. Box 5039, Ebeye, Kwajalein, MH 96970, tel. 329-3161, fax 329-3248) should probably be your first choice. Located by the lagoon, just south of the ferry landing, it was recently expanded and now has 24 rooms, 18 in the new wing. All are air conditioned and offer a private bath. Rooms in the old wing are $65, and in the new, $85. The hotel has two rooms with cooking facilities for $95 and two suites for $150 each. There's a bar, restaurant, and laundromat on the premises.

The hotel discounts commercial travelers 10% but charges four to six percent for use of a credit card to pay the bill. Have traveler's checks ready.

At the south end of Ebeye is the **DSC Hotel** (P.O. Box 5097, Ebeye, Kwajalein, MH 96970, tel. 329-3194, fax 329-3310), run by Immigration officer Rudy Paul. The seven air conditioned rooms with private facilities are $57, $47 per night for stays of four nights or more. The rooms are on the third floor (no elevator) above the DSC grocery store.

Food

There are really only two acceptable restaurants on Ebeye. **Bob's Island Restaurant,** overlooking the ferry pier, is a local favorite. It serves breakfast ($3-4), lunch, and dinner (main course $7-10). Barbecue is their specialty and it's very good. The pleasant dining room overlooks the lagoon as does an outside patio. Bob's has a full bar; the clientele includes both locals and visitors from Kwaj.

Anrohasa Restaurant is also worth a visit but beware of the TV—always on and blaring. Try the sweet bread from their bakery for breakfast. The menu is mainly Chinese and mediocre, but a number of local dishes such as "U"—a coconut porridge—are served. No booze is served in the restaurant, though the hotel has a separate bar.

Entertainment

Mon La Mike is a nightclub that opens on the weekend at about 11 p.m. Admission for women is free; men pay $10. It can get rowdy as the patrons get increasingly drunk, so it is probably best to leave by 1 a.m.

Services

To make overseas calls on Ebeye, go to the NTA office on the south end of the island. It is open 24 hours a day and can accept a modem. Both the Bank of Guam and the Bank of Marshall Islands operate branches on Ebeye.

JALUIT ATOLL

The Germans set up a trading post on Jaluit in 1878, and when the Marshalls became a colony in 1885, the Germans headquartered here. In 1914 Jaluit became the Japanese administra-

© MOON PUBLICATIONS, INC.

tive center. Later, the Japanese built an airstrip on nearby Emidj Island and shipped tons of soil from Kosrae and Pohnpei to create vegetable gardens on the island. By 1941 the population of Jabwor village was 3,000. The United States bombed and bypassed the Japanese base on Jaluit during World War II; some war wreckage remains.

Today bananas and breadfruit are grown; copra, seashells, and handicrafts are exported. There's a public high school in Jabwor at the north end of Jaluit, one of 91 reef islands composing the atoll. Swept channels lead from three passes to lagoon anchorages off Emidj and Jaluit Islands. The new dock and petroleum storage facility at Jaluit sports a big Mobil Pegasus sign. Jaluit is accessible twice weekly by air from Majuro ($85 one-way), 56 miles northeast.

AILINGLAPLAP ATOLL

Ailinglaplap, 150 miles west of Majuro, is a large, copra-growing atoll. Several passages provide entry into the lagoon. Phosphate deposits have

been located on some of the 56 islands. Traditionally, the high chiefs of the Ralik Chain resided on Ailinglaplap, which is located halfway between Majuro and Kwajalein.

BIKINI ATOLL

From 1946 to 1958, 23 atmospheric nuclear blasts shook Bikini atoll. They left behind a legacy of contamination, cancer, leukemia, thyroid problems, miscarriages, and irreversible genetic damage. The full effects are not yet known.

For the initial series of tests, a captured Japanese war fleet and several U.S. naval vessels, including the aircraft carrier USS *Saratoga,* were positioned in Bikini lagoon to test the use of atomic weapons against naval forces. On 1 July 1948 "Able" was dropped on 90 ships by a B-29 from Kwajalein. On 25 July an underwater explosion code named "Baker" contaminated the atoll. "Charlie," the third test, was canceled when it became apparent that radiation would endanger U.S. personnel.

In February 1946 American officials informed the inhabitants of Bikini that their islands were needed temporarily "for the good of mankind and to end all world wars." The 166 Bikinians were taken to uninhabited Rongerik atoll, but in just two years it became apparent that Rongerik lacked the resources to support them, and they had to be evacuated again.

After a few months on Kwajalein, Bikinians were resettled on Kili Island, an isolated dot in the ocean just southwest of Jaluit. Most Bikinians remain there today, even though Kili is quite a step down. Bikini's 36 islands are six times larger than Kili in land area. Kili does not even have a protective lagoon, and fishing is often impossible due to weather conditions. Other Bikinians live on Ejit Island at Majuro.

In the 1960s the United States undertook a cleanup of Bikini so the people could return home. It's now clear that the cleanup was done in a haphazard manner, and the Atomic Energy Commission failed to take sufficient tests before they declared, in 1969, that Bikini was once again safe for habitation.

After lawsuits and pleas to American benevolence, a $6 million trust fund was set up by the U.S. government in 1978, and a further

$20.6 million placed in a resettlement fund. In 1984 the United States promised to spend $42 million on another cleanup, and in 1988, $90 million was allocated by Congress for a final cleanup. Decontamination alternatives include flushing sea water through the soil to leach out the contaminants, scraping off the top half yard and replacing it with uncontaminated soil, and applying potassium-rich fertilizer to block the uptake of cesium-137 by plants.

In April 1992, the scuba wholesaler Tom Jacobus of Innerspace Adventures (13393 Sorrento Dr., Largo, FL 34644) scored a first by leading a group to Bikini to dive on the Japanese battleship *Nagato,* the U.S. aircraft carrier *Saratoga* (the world's only divable aircraft carrier), the destroyer *Anderson,* and the submarine *Apogon.* These groups also got to stay on Ebeye and dive on Japanese wrecks in the Kwajalein lagoon—not your everyday diving tour!

Marshall Dive Adventures currently dives Bikini atoll. They can be contacted directly, or arrangements can be made through Central Pacific Dive Expeditions. For more information, see the "Getting There" section in this chapter's "Introduction."

ENEWETAK ATOLL

Enewetak (Eniwetok) is an almost perfectly circular atoll 20 miles in diameter. In December 1947, officials in Washington announced that it was to be used for nuclear tests, and the 145 inhabitants were immediately moved to Ujelang atoll, with one-quarter the land area and a fifteenth the lagoon area of Enewetak. From 1948 to 1958, 43 nuclear tests rocked Enewetak. On 1 November 1952 the world's first hydrogen bomb was tested here, unleashing more explosive force than all the wars of history combined, and completely vaporizing one of the islands of Enewetak; in 1958 another H-bomb destroyed a second.

In 1976, the United States Congress appropriated funds for a $110 million cleanup operation on Enewetak by the Defense Nuclear Agency. The contaminated waste was scraped off the surface of the atoll and buried in a bomb crater on Runit Island under a gigantic cement

dome 18 inches thick. The material will remain a hazard to human life for thousands of years, and there have already been reports that the dome is cracking.

The Department of Energy reports that the southern islands of the atoll are now safe for habitation, but the northern islands will be unsafe for the next 300 years. In 1980, 542 people returned from Ujelang to Japtan Island on Enewetak. Like the people of Bikini, the Enewetakese remain a disrupted community whose future is clouded by uncertainty. Added to the sociocultural disruptions is the volatile new ingredient of compensation money and how it should be divided.

RONGELAP ATOLL

On 1 March 1954, 15 megaton "Bravo," the largest and dirtiest of the hydrogen bombs, was tested on Bikini. This was the most colossal manmade explosion in history, with an explosive force equal to 1,200 Hiroshima-type bombs, more than twice what its designers expected. The blast sent up a 22-mile-high cloud, which dropped 1.5 inches of fine white dust on Rongelap atoll four to six hours later, turning the water yellow, contaminating the food, and burning the unprepared people standing in the open. Children played in the radioactive material as if it were snow. The United States Navy destroyer *Gypsy*, which had been stationed a mere 19 miles from Rongelap lagoon on the day of the test, quickly sailed off. The population of Rongelap was not evacuated for 48 hours. The evacuees experienced all the symptoms of radiation exposure. At the time United States officials blamed the contamination on an unexpected wind shift, but 27 years later four retired U.S. airmen who had operated the weather station on nearby Rongerik shed new light on the matter. They reported that the test was allowed with full knowledge that for weeks previous the prevailing wind had been blowing directly at these islands. United States government documents declassified in the mid-1980s confirmed that U.S. officials knew that the wind was blowing toward Rongelap before the Bravo test.

I have gone to the ends of the earth,
where innocence is nourished by nuclear waste,
where names are clear, but not their purpose.
How can I explain the smiles of the children,
smiles that go dim when eyes go blind,
smiles that go sullen from blameless poverty.
I have gone to the ends of the earth,
but I can return untouched
if only I can harden my heart.

FEDERATED STATES OF MICRONESIA

INTRODUCTION

The Federated States of Micronesia (FSM) is the largest and most populous (about 100,000 people) political entity to emerge from the Trust Territory of the Pacific Islands. It includes all of the Caroline Islands except for what is now the Republic of Palau. International flights fly to the state capitals: Pohnpei, Kosrae, Chuuk, and Yap. Pohnpei (formerly Ponape) is a lush, volcanic island with much to entice the hiker and historian, while Kosrae has better beaches and friendly, easygoing people. Chuuk (formerly Truk) is best known for its spectacular underwater wreck sites. Yap remains a stronghold of traditional Micronesian culture.

Each of these four islands offers some of the conveniences, and some of the drawbacks, of modern Western life. Everywhere in the Federated States you'll encounter a natural, relaxed affability. The outer islands of the country offer the adventuresome a glimpse of a more traditional way of life—it's idyllic and always slow.

Most outer islands lack hotels, cars, and electricity. But don't expect to find "happy natives" without knowledge of the world around them—today it's difficult to find any place where the young, at least, are totally unfamiliar with Western music or movies.

The Land

The Eastern Caroline Islands include Kosrae, Pohnpei, and Chuuk States, while Yap and Palau form the Western Caroline Islands. More than 1,550 miles lie between Kosrae and Yap, yet the FSM totals only 270 square miles in land area, with Pohnpei alone accounting for almost half that land.

This huge island group, named for King Charles II of Spain, includes almost every type of oceanic topography: a myriad of outer island atolls and high volcanic islands such as Pohnpei and Kosrae; Yap, a large island of sedimentary rock; Fais, a raised atoll; and Chuuk, an atoll to be, with remnants of its volcanic core still poking out of the lagoon. Nearly a thousand smaller coral islands and reefs complete the scene.

The vegetation is also varied. Coconut palms, pandanus, and breadfruit flourish on the low islands. On the high islands, mangrove forests along the coasts are home to salt-resistant plants; inland you'll find coconut groves on the flats, rainforest up the slopes, and ferns or grasslands near the summits. Other than fruit bats, often endangered, most of the terrestrial fauna was introduced by man. Numerous shore- and seabirds make up for the lack of land birds. Marinelife in the lagoons, on the reefs, and in the open ocean is truly what Micronesia is about.

Climate

Heavy rainfall drenches the Carolines, although the quantity decreases as you move west from Pohnpei to Yap. Pohnpei gets measurable rainfall 300 days a year—it's wet Jan.-Feb. and even wetter March-December. At Chuuk the rain falls mostly at night, hardest just before sunrise. The rain often comes in short, heavy downpours, presenting only a temporary inconvenience to travelers, while providing the inhabitants with water for crops, washing, and cooking. Humidity is high year-round.

The northeast trades blow across the Eastern Carolines Dec.-April; southeast winds prevail July-September. Yap gets northeast winds Nov.-May, changing to southwest July-October.

The Western Caroline Islands spawn more tropical typhoons than any other area on earth, an average of 19 a year! Sept.-Nov. is peak typhoon season, and most of the storms move northwest toward Asia. Typhoons rarely occur in the Eastern Caroline Islands, although Typhoon Nina raged across Chuuk in November 1987. On Pohnpei, near the equator, the sun rises near 6 a.m. and sets just after 6 p.m. every day of the year.

Toward Self-Government

Until 1978 the FSM, along with most of Micronesia, was administered as part of the Trust Territory of the Pacific Islands, a United Nations trusteeship area administered by the United States. Thus the history of the region up to that point must be treated as a whole (see "History" in the Introduction chapter). In July 1978 a draft FSM constitution was approved by voters in Kosrae, Pohnpei, Chuuk, and Yap. The constitution was defeated in votes in Palau and the Marshalls, which then became separate political entities.

On 1 October 1982, American and FSM negotiators at Honolulu signed the Compact of Free Association, which was approved by the United States Congress in 1985. Under the terms of this 15-year treaty, the FSM will receive a total of about $1.3 billion through the year 2000 when, presumably, a new agreement will be reached. In exchange, the Compact gave the United States military access to the FSM, while

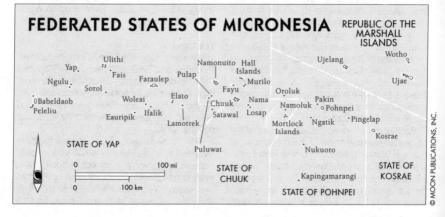

THE FSM AT A GLANCE

	POP. (1989)	LAND AREA (SQ. MI.)
State of Kosrae	7,177	42.31
State of Pohnpei	32,884	133.34
Ant	nil	0.73
Kapingamarangi	577	0.50
Mwoakilloa	305	0.46
Ngatik	644	0.66
Nukuoro	450	0.66
Oroluk	nil	0.19
Pakin	nil	0.42
Pingelap	840	0.69
Pohnpei	30,068	129.03
State of Chuuk	47,871	49.18
Chuuk Lagoon	38,341	38.57
East Fayu	nil	0.15
Etal	420	0.73
Houk	346	1.08
Kuop	nil	0.19
Losap	795	0.39
Lukunor	1,279	1.08
Murilo	694	0.50
Nama	897	0.27
Namoluk	310	0.31
Namonuito	994	1.70
Nomwin	624	0.73
Pulap	541	0.39
Pulawat	477	1.31
Satawan	2,230	1.78
State of Yap	10,139	45.72
Eauripik	99	0.08
Elato	70	0.19
Fais	253	1.08
Faraulep	182	0.15
Gaferut	nil	0.04
Ifalik	475	0.39
Lamotrek	278	0.39
Ngulu	26	0.15
Olimarao	nil	0.08
Pikelot	nil	0.04
Satawal	465	0.50
Sorol	nil	0.35
Ulithi	847	1.81
West Fayu	nil	0.04
Woleai	794	1.74
Yap	6,650	38.69
TOTAL	98,071	270.55

denying such access to other powers. In 1991 the FSM was admitted to the United Nations.

Government

The FSM constitution went into effect on 10 May 1979—now celebrated as Constitution Day. Under it, each of the four states has a locally elected governor and legislature, while the central government meets at Palikir on Pohnpei. The 14-member National Congress of FSM includes one member at large elected from each state for a four-year term. The president and vice president are chosen by the Congress from among these senior members, thus president and vice president cannot be from the same state. The other 10 members serve two-year terms, apportioned according to population: Chuuk, five members; Pohnpei, three; Kosrae, one; and Yap, one. There are no political parties. The national government has primacy over state governments. In Chuuk, Pohnpei, and Yap states, the role of traditional chiefs is recognized by the state constitutions.

Economy

Payments from the Compact of Free Association have bolstered FSM's standard of living. It is only because of them that FSM maintains a balance of trade, since imports dwarf exports. These payments are made to the government, which consequently is bloated, employing two-thirds of the workforce. Employment is often based more on politics than on governmental need. Compact payments far surpass local taxes, though revenue also comes in through fishing licenses and tourism. FSM's main exports are tuna and copra, but most tuna fishing for the export market is carried on by foreign boats using foreign crews. In 1989, for example, a couple hundred foreign fishing boats paid $10 million in fees to take $200 million in tuna from the FSM's 200-nautical-mile Exclusive Economic Zone. Clearly FSM has not maximized its potential income from this source.

There are few private businesses other than retail outlets, which sell consumer goods, and a few service industries, such as tourism. Under the Compact, textiles manufactured in the FSM may be imported into the United States free of quotas. One Taiwanese company set up a factory on Yap in 1989 to take advantage of this.

The company's entire workforce, however, came from mainland China and Sri Lanka.

Food and almost all the elements of modern life are imported. Outside the towns, reef fishing and subsistence agriculture continue to be the main occupations. Tourism is being encouraged—wisely, slowly. There's no rush to jump on the Guam/Saipan bandwagon. Instead smaller, locally controlled developments are going ahead. Land can only be leased (not purchased) by outsiders, and new businesses must have 51% local ownership. In 1990 Pohnpei received 9,534 visitors, Chuuk 7,654, and Yap 3,984, nearly half of them from the United States and another quarter from Japan.

With the cold war over and payments running out in 2000, the United States may not feel the same need to provide itself with a forward line of defense. It's doubtful the U.S. will be willing to outlay the same amount of funds in the future as it did in the past. However, a precipitous drop in payments would have a devastating effect on the economy of FSM since it is unlikely that the islands could become self-sufficient before the close of this century.

The People

Ethnically, the Federated States' population is overwhelmingly Micronesian, with several thousand Polynesians on two outlying atolls in Pohnpei State and in Kolonia. There are small but significant American and Asian expat communities on the major islands. Less than a third of the population lives in urban or semi-urban areas. Eight different languages are spoken in the FSM: Chuukese, Kosraean, Kapingamarangi, Nukuoran, Pohnpeian, Ulithian, Woleaian, and Yapese. Many are totally dissimilar, making English the common language for interisland communications. Traditionally most of the societies have been matrilineal, although the influence of missionaries has created a patrilineal system on Kosrae. The Polynesian islands of Kapingamarangi and Nukuoro have always been patrilineal.

Most Yapese are Catholic, most Kosraeans Protestant. Pohnpei and Chuuk are split between Catholics and Protestants, with Chuuk leaning toward Catholicism. Nearly half the population is under 15, three-quarters under 25, and the total population is growing at the as-

KARL PARTRIDGE

Gayan, a chief of Maap, Yap

tounding rate of 3.5% annually. The life expectancy is 58-59 for men, 62-64 for women. The suicide rate among young Micronesian males ages 15-24 is high. FSM citizens have unrestricted entry to the U.S. and its territories, including Guam. U.S. citizens don't have such rights in the FSM.

Holidays and Events

The list of national public holidays changes from year to year according to the will of the legislature, but days to watch out for include New Year's Day (1 January), President's Day (third Monday in February), Traditional Culture Day (31 March), FSM Constitution Day (10 May), Micronesian Day (12 July), United Nations Day (24 October), FSM Independence Day (first Friday in November), and Christmas Day (25 December).

There are also state holidays such as Kosrae Constitution Day (11 January), Sokehs Rebellion Day (24 February, Pohnpei), Yap Day (1 March), Kolonia Independence Day (17 May),

Kosrae Liberation Day (8 September), Pohnpei Liberation Day (11 September), Chuuk Charter Day (26 September), Kosrae Self-Government Day (3 November), Pohnpei Constitution Day (8 November), and Yap Constitution Day (24 December). Try to be in Colonia on Yap on 1 March or in Kolonia on Pohnpei on 11 September to see canoe races, customary dancing, and other traditional events. There are the various municipal Constitution Days on Pohnpei. On Kapingamarangi, Taro Patch Day is celebrated on 15 March.

Conduct
Micronesians expect Western women to dress modestly. Male visitors calling on government offices should avoid dressing too casually. Observe how the officials are dressed. Micronesians are friendly, so a big smile and a hello are never out of place.

PRACTICALITIES

Accommodations and Food
The only regular hotels are in the state capitals, although resorts are now springing up in outlying areas. You'll find inexpensive restaurants in all the towns. In rural areas you'll have a choice of camping or staying with local families; both require permission from the local landowner, householder, chief, or government representative. Try to find some way to repay any kindnesses received. Nonmonetary gifts are always very welcome.

Visas
Since the FSM is not part of the U.S., its entry requirements are not the same as those of Guam and Hawaii. Tourists don't need a visa for a stay of up to 30 days, although officials may want to see your passport and onward ticket. If you don't have an onward ticket they may insist that you purchase one on the spot (this applies to everyone, Americans included).

United States citizens are not required to have a passport, only proof of citizenship such as a birth certificate or naturalization papers. But Americans should carry valid passports to ease entrance and save time. All nationalities other than Americans and Canadians going on

to Hawaii must have a valid United States visa in their passport.

Each state has its own immigration controls, so you get a new entry permit every time you cross a state boundary; $10 exit fees are the norm. Thus each time through immigration control earns you another 30 days without leaving the Federated States. Visa extensions are a nuisance, so when you arrive, always ask for 30 days (the maximum) upon arrival.

Anyone considering arriving by yacht should apply for an FSM vessel permit in advance from: Chief Immigration Officer, FSM National Government, Palikir, Pohnpei, FM 96941 (tel. 320-5844, fax 320-2234). Ports of entry are Lelu and Okat on Kosrae, Kolonia on Pohnpei, Weno on Chuuk, Ulithi, and Colonia in Yap. Upon sailing from one state to another, yachts must clear customs.

Money, Measurements, and Phone
U.S. currency is used. Credit cards are now fairly well accepted at hotels and car rentals, except in Yap. It is most convenient to carry U.S. cash or traveler's checks in small denominations.

Standard American 110-volt, 60-cycle appliances are used. The FSM issues its own postage stamps, but U.S. domestic postal rates apply. To call direct from the U.S. to a telephone number in the FSM dial 011-691 and the regular seven-digit number. To call from one FSM state to another, put a one before the seven digit number. Calls within the FSM are $1 a minute, cheaper at night. But calls out of the country are quite expensive. There's a time difference of one hour between Kosrae/Pohnpei and Chuuk/Yap.

Most public telephones in the FSM accept FSMTC telephone cards, which can be purchased at phone company offices. The same card can be used in Kosrae, Pohnpei, Chuuk, and Yap, so consider investing in a $10 card (good for 40 local calls) if you'll be using the phone much.

Getting There
One must change planes at Honolulu if coming from the United States mainland., Most visitors come to Micronesia on **Continental Air Micronesia** Island Hopper (Air Mike) service between Hawaii and Guam. The flights originate on

Wednesday and Friday in each direction. From the west it runs Honolulu to Majuro to Kwajalein to Kosrae to Pohnpei to Chuuk to Guam. Remember each flight begins on Monday, Wednesday, or Friday, at the place the flight originates, but crosses the International Date Line between Hawaii and the Marshall Islands.

There are additional flights Wednesday, Friday, and Sunday between Guam, Chuuk, and Pohnpei. Yap is on the Guam to Palau route and a change of planes at Guam is necessary.

Flights are Wednesday, Friday, and Sunday to Yap, returning Monday, Wednesday, Friday, and Sunday.

Air Nauru has cut back its service to FSM and now flies only to Pohnpei. The Wednesday flight runs Nauru to Pohnpei to Guam to Manila. This pertains mostly to those traveling to or from traveling to Australia, New Zealand, and other South Pacific points via Nauru. For more information "Air Nauru" under "Getting There" in the On the Road chapter.

STATE OF KOSRAE

Because of its profile, Kosrae is called the "Island of the Sleeping Lady." Legend tells that Kosrae was shaped by the gods from the transformed figure of a sleeping woman. Her good looks might make you want to linger, to know her better. And she won't disappoint.

Particularly if you are coming from the crowded, flat islands of the Marshalls, you can't help becoming excited by this island's central mountains enshrouded in dense, green jungle. In some places, the mountains run directly to the ocean; more frequently they run to low-lying plains created over eons by mangrove trees reaching into the ocean, trapping runoff soil, and creating their own landfill.

Views are reminiscent of Rarotonga in the Cook Islands, or Oahu's windward side 30 years ago. Breadfruit, papaya, mango, taro, coconut palms, bananas, Kosrae's famed green tangerines, jacaranda, and colorful flowers grow everywhere.

Formerly Kusaie, Kosrae (pronounced "korshy") is a single 42-square-mile island, the easternmost of the Carolines and, after Pohnpei, the second-largest island in the Federated States. It fulfills the tropical island fantasy: lush green interior circled by alternating coral beaches and mysterious mangrove forests. The rugged interior, inaccessible except with a guide, is crowned by Mt. Finkol (2,069 feet). A broad valley between Mt. Finkol and Mt. Mutunte divides the island in two, with a deep harbor at each side.

Orientation

Five traditional villages lie along the coast. Heading clockwise around the island from the air-

port, they are: Tafunsak, Lelu, Malem, Utwe, and Walung (which is part of Tafunsak municipality). A road circles most of the island but does not reach Walung. The road to Walung has become a political hot potato, some villagers preferring privacy to the "progress" a road would bring.

Lelu, the largest village, sits on Lelu Island, connected to Kosrae by a causeway. The view from Lelu of jungle-covered volcanic peaks in profile on the western horizon is majestic. The

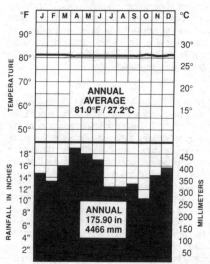

KOSRAE'S CLIMATE

ANNUAL AVERAGE 81.0°F / 27.2°C

ANNUAL 175.90 in 4466 mm

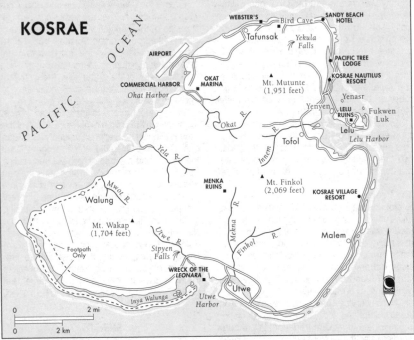

KOSRAE

© MOON PUBLICATIONS, INC.

skyline from here resembles the sleeping lady of the legend.

Most government offices, the hospital, tourist office, post office, communications center, police station, banks, Continental Air Micronesia, high school, and library are located at Tofol, Kosrae's administrative center, about 2.5 miles from Lelu by road. Tofol is not so much a town as it is a stretch of road where buildings are strung somewhat close together.

History

Hundreds of years ago a feudal aristocracy ruled Kosrae from Lelu Island. The rulers built themselves a great stone city called Insaru, the ruins and canals of which you see today. These ruins give a feel for the aristocracy's material wealth—such prosperity allowed the legendary Isokelekel and his 333 warriors to conquer Nan Madol, Pohnpei's capital.

Whalers brought diseases that reduced the number of Kosraeans from 10,000 or more to a

mere 300 in just a few decades. The whalers were followed in 1852 by Congregational missionaries from Hawaii who came to convert the survivors. Perhaps those few survivors had lost faith in their old gods and were receptive to a new religion. Today, Kosraeans are much more likely to think of this conversion as the beginning of their redemption, rather than the death of their old culture. The survival of the Kosraean people and their language, in the face of the devastation brought by the West, is a tribute to the vitality of traditional Kosraean culture.

Unscrupulous traders came as well, including the notorious Bully Hayes, whose ship *Leonora* sank at Utwe Harbor in 1874. Hayes is thought to have buried his treasure in the vicinity, but nothing has been found—yet.

Thousands of Japanese immigrants came to Kosrae in the period between the two world wars, outnumbering Kosraeans and forcing them to abandon their villages and move to the interior. During WW II this Japanese community was reinforced by Japanese military troops. Although the U.S. bypassed strategically isolated Kosrae, it did bomb the island, killing three Kosraeans in the attack on the Japanese forces, including the mother of a future governor of Kosrae, Thurston Siba. Before the bombing, and particularly afterward, the Japanese subjected Kosraeans to forced labor and made it a criminal act for a native Kosraean to pick fruit from trees.

Kosraeans are linguistically separate from the people of Pohnpei. Nonetheless, Kosrae was part of the district of Pohnpei until January 1977. At that time, Kosrae demanded and was granted status as a separate state of the FSM.

The People

Kosraeans are a warm and friendly people, usually quite eager to meet tourists. Most Kosraeans speak English. Much of the island is underemployed. Many women do some subsistence farming while many men still fish. Life is slow and entertainment is often a meal with family or friends. There are no movie houses, nightclubs, or bowling alleys.

Church services are an integral part of Kosraean culture and social circles. The population is overwhelmingly Congregationalist, though there are also three Mormon churches, a Baptist church, and a Seventh-Day Adventist school. As the *Kosrae Visitor's Guide* points out, there are rules of expected behavior, even for tourists, on Sundays:

- *Do* wear long pants and a shirt (men).

- *Do* wear a dress (women).

- *Do* feel free to attend church (the Kosraeans are noted for their choral singing), visit friends, read, and relax.

- *Do not* collect seashells, snorkel, water-ski, or scuba dive.

- *Do not* drink alcoholic beverages.

It is illegal to drink or fish on Sunday and stores and offices are shut. Commercial dive shops and fishing boats do not operate. So sit back and relax—this might be the day you discover the joy of a peaceful Sabbath. If you are not up to the rigors of such leisure, Sunday is a good day to visit the Lelu ruins, but no guide will be available.

Each of the villages has a blue and white Congregational church. They are surprisingly large for the size of the population and they are invariably packed on Sunday. Services begin at 10 a.m. (this appears to be the one Kosrae event that begins punctually). Men and women sit on opposite sides of the center aisle. Most churches have an additional 4 p.m. Sunday service and also welcome visitors to choir practice.

One cannot pretend to know Kosrae without taking part in the church experience. Much of the hour is filled by sensational, uniquely Kosraean choral singing. One solo woman singer will set the tone, using a series of high-pitched wailing notes. The rest of the choir then joins in. Men and women sing separate parts, sometimes in a call-and-response mode, other times in very complex harmony. The rhythms and phrasing sound more like Pacific Island music than the New England hymns from which the songs were derived. The Kosraeans took what they were taught and adapted it to their own culture. Regardless of your own religious beliefs (or lack of them) you will be moved by the spiritual feel around you. It is an experience not to be missed.

SIGHTS

Around the Island

As you drive round the island from the airport in a clockwise direction, you will come upon a road to the left in about a mile. This road leads to the village of **Tafunsak.** It has a great feel—not much going on, but that's the whole point. It's a funky, old, quiet town with a beautiful large church.

If you turn left when you get to the coast, the road is quite scenic, going through mangroves and densely verdant small hills. The road eventually runs out—turn back along the coast. If you continue straight, less than a mile past Tafunsak this road rejoins the round-the-island road.

Several hundred yards past the junction, to the right, you can see a large **cave** at the base of the hill where swarms of swiftlets live. Local legend tells that a giant also lives at the back of the cave. Nearby is **Yekula Falls,** not very impressive except after a rain when it is possible to bathe in the pool at the base. Ask permission of anyone you see to enter this private land.

Prismatic basalt "logs" stacked atop giant volcanic blocks demonstrate the architectural evolution of Kosrae's Lelu ruins.

Lelu

Lelu town occupies a peninsula across the harbor from Tofol. One drives to Lelu from the main island across a causeway. On the left of the causeway you'll find a ladder that leads down to a swimming hole used by local kids. On the right is the Aquaculture Center, with its giant clams growing. A local market is in the middle of the causeway six days a week.

Lelu is a relaxed town. The tall concrete building on the main street near Thurston's Enterprises dates from 1915. It served as the storehouse of an American trader who dumped stones from the nearby ruins into Lelu Harbor to extend his dock. This historic building is now the **Kosrae Museum** (tel. 370-3078, fax 370-3767), a good place to begin your visit as the museum focuses on the ruins and their excavation. It's open Mon.-Thurs. 9 a.m.-3 p.m. Call ahead to verify that it actually will be open when you visit. At other times, the museum may be opened in response to your call. You can arrange to hire a guide to the ruins here or through your hotel.

Lelu Ruins

When they built their fortress at Lelu, Kosrae's rulers thought they were building a stronghold, a sanctuary. They never dreamt they were constructing an archaeological site.

Kosrae's leading land attraction is the Lelu ruins, located in Lelu town. Lelu flourished as the feudal capital of Kosrae from 1400 to 1800; the king and high chiefs had their residences here. The city once covered the entire flat portion of Lelu Island and included 100 large, walled compounds. Its power was such that warriors from Lelu were able to invade Pohnpei, overthrow the Saudeleurs, and conquer Nan Madol in the 17th century.

One of the most impressive archaeological sites in the Pacific, the ruins are similar in style to, and predate, Pohnpei's Nan Madol, yet they are much more accessible since they sit right in the center of town. The heart of the site is just a few minutes' walk down a footpath that begins beside Thurston's Enterprises on the main street and runs along the security fence on the side farthest from the museum. Parts of the ruin are quite muddy after rain, so wear good walking shoes. Because parts are so overgrown, to get the most out of your visit hire a guide. As soon as you get deep enough into the site to be unable to hear the refrigerator at the Thurston store, the centuries roll back. You see the enormity of the material culture, the wealth and organization that allowed such massive construction.

Ancient coral and rock walkways run through the ruins. The crisscrossed basalt logs permit a striking glimpse of the ancient city. Archaeologists believe they were floated on rafts all the way from Utwe. Many Kosraeans, assuming their ancestors were too intelligent to do this much work to construct a monument, maintain that the city was built in one night by two magicians.

The prismatic, stacked basalt architecture often rests on walls of massive basalt boulders. These walls reach as high as 20 feet and, like Incan architecture, the stones were carefully fitted so that mortar was unnecessary. The height of the base of each residence corresponded to social rank. You can still see the network of canals that brought ocean-bound canoe traffic through the city.

Note the flat grooved *sakau*-pounding stones at Pensa-1 and at the entrance to Insaru. **Insaru** holds the truncated pyramid tombs of the kings whose bodies were placed in crypts. When a corpse completely decayed, the bones were taken to a reef off Lelu and dropped into a deep hole. These ocean-going people believed that life came from the sea. The ancient Kosraean burial process reflected this belief by returning the remains to their origin.

Lelu Hill

A trail behind a small cemetery not far from the old wharf leads to the summit of Lelu Hill (355 feet), which the Japanese fortified during WW II. You pass a couple of their air raid shelters near the trailhead, then proceed straight ahead on the main trail until reaching a switchback as you approach the summit. A short distance along this trail, a **tunnel** hewn from solid rock winds 100 feet back into the hill. Continue along the same overgrown track toward the south side where another tunnel, a little more difficult to find, cuts through the hill. Japanese trenches, foxholes, and caves still girdle Lelu Hill in rings, but all known wartime guns have been removed. Be prepared to do some bushwhacking if you want to explore Lelu Hill, and take along a flashlight. Better yet, ask the museum or your hotel to help find a guide for you.

Tofol

For an easy glimpse of the interior, take a ride or

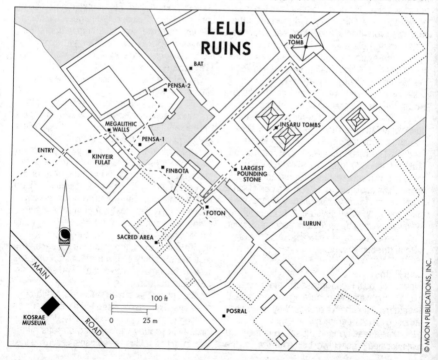

early 19th-century houses at Kosrae

M.G.L. DOMENY DE RIENZI

a stroll up the dirt road that leaves the main Tofol-Lelu highway; it's before Tofol, just beyond a small bridge near the **** Star Construction Company (formerly a Mobil station). The way leads past lush tropical gardens onto the plateau between Mt. Finkol and Mt. Mutunte. It is probably best not to leave the road unless you are with a guide. Almost all seemingly unused land is privately owned. Moreover, it is very easy to get lost in the interior, particularly under the jungle canopy when it's raining or misty. Paths are not regularly maintained so bring a machete or go with a guide who carries one.

About two miles past the turnoff to Lelu is Tofol, the site of all governmental and most private business on the island. There is a new public library within the high school complex. It's open Mon.-Thurs. 8:15 a.m.-4:30 p.m. and Friday 10 a.m.-2 p.m. In addition to its regular collection, it has an excellent Micronesia reference section including many government documents.

As you continue around the island, the road will get progressively worse. About two miles past Tofol, the road turns to fairly well-maintained gravel with progressively more rough spots. Still, even in an ordinary car, one can drive to Utwe. Drive *slowly*. Never think you should drive faster than a local in a pickup truck. The drive is beautiful and your patience will be well rewarded. Toward the water you'll see beautiful vistas of mangroves growing on reefs, literally forming the island. Inland you'll find great views up deep jungle canyons towards the mountains. Most beaches are privately owned,

and you should ask permission at a nearby house before using one. Permission will most usually be granted.

Allow three hours for the roundtrip from the Kosrae Village Resort to Utwe and back, even with only minimal sightseeing.

Malem

Malem itself is not a particularly picturesque town, but opposite the Municipal Building you can see one of the best waves on the island. Winds are frequently offshore and peel off to both the left and right. The reef is hard and you should only be out there at high tide. Bodysurfers and spongers, please take particular care.

Right past Malem lie reefs extending out a great distance. At low tide they make for interesting tidepool viewing. Wear good sturdy footwear.

Utwe

Utwe is a pleasant village at the mouth of the Finkol, Kosrae's largest river. It serves as a good base for exploring the south side of the island, but there is no hotel. The Tourism Office in Tofol can arrange canoe rentals, a guide for Mt. Finkol, camping, and paid accommodations with a local Utwe family.

The backwater canoe journey arranged through the tourist office in Tofol travels on the **Inya Walunga** (Walung Channel) from Utwe to Walung. You begin by traversing a wide lagoon with a magnificent view of the jungle-clad mountains, then enter a shallow channel through a mangrove swamp of fantastically twisted roots. If the tide is low you'll have to travel along the coast outside the lagoon, which is much less interesting.

It's also possible to scale **Mt. Finkol** (2,069 feet), the highest peak on Kosrae, and return to Utwe in a day. You need to be an expert hiker and you'll need a guide. You wade up the Finkol River quite a distance, then scramble through the slippery rainforest to the top. Wear rubber booties or some old tennis shoes. The sweeping view of the entire island from the grassy summit compensates for the exhausting climb.

A less ambitious, though wonderful hike, out of Utwe is up Mt. Finkol to the **Menka ruins.** This hike is a good hour through the jungle and should be undertaken only with a guide. In Kosraean lore Menka, even older than Lelu, is the home of Sinlaku, goddess of breadfruit.

Walung

Walung is not connected to the rest of the island by road. This makes it difficult to reach but keeps it an "unspoiled" spot: a long palm-fringed beach, no electricity, no stores, no roads, no cappuccino, and the *New York Times* is delivered only twice a decade. It is possible to walk into Walung either from Utwe or from Okat Harbor, near the airport. From either direction, the hike is beautiful but arduous and should not be attempted without a guide.

Easier is a boat from the **Okat Marina** (tel. 370-2629), just past the bridge from the airport. A roundtrip costs about $35, depending on how long you want the boat to wait for you in Walung. The trip takes about an hour each way. If you coordinate the trip with a tide table, you will be able to go through the mangroves at high tide and outside the reef at low tide. You can also negotiate for the boat to stop en route for handline fishing or snorkeling. This trip can also be arranged through your hotel.

Okat Marina also offers a once-in-a-lifetime experience: for $50 you can fish all night. It is for the hardy only: no cabin, probably no sleep, and certainly no sympathy if you become seasick. But when else might you have the chance to fish by handline for large bottom fish with people who do this for a living, not for an experience?

ACCOMMODATIONS

Hotel accommodations on Kosrae have been upgraded over the past several years. Some low-end hotels became longer-term residences, often for immigrant workers. Other hotels improved while three interesting hotels opened. Each appeals to a slightly different market and thus there is a fair amount of choice considering that the island only has six hotels, less than 60 rooms total. It is only during summer and holidays that one need fear being unable to find a room.

The first hotel you reach if heading from the airport clockwise toward Tofol is the **Sandy Beach Hotel** (Donald Jonah, P.O. Box 6, Kosrae, FM 96944, tel. 370-3239, fax 370-2109). It's about halfway between the airport and Tofol. All of its 16 beachfront rooms are air conditioned and have refrigerators. The downstairs rooms are $40 s, $55 d; upstairs rooms, all overlooking the ocean, are $45 s, $60 d. The hotel still maintains an old one-room thatch cottage that rents for $35. Rooms are clean and spacious, but plain with little decoration. The charms of the hotel outweigh this drawback. At the beach you can view tidepools during low tide or go snorkeling during high tide to enjoy the interesting ecology of sea grasses directly in front of the hotel. The tide usually pulls to the left as you face the water. Head out into the current so that you have an easy return, going with the flow. If you are skilled in ocean swimming, you may be able to traverse the reef if the breakers are *small* by walking at low tide and swimming at high. The reward lies in deep-water snorkeling over coral. Best of all, Mr. Jonah, his son Ronald, and daughter-in-law Ruth are fantastic hosts. The **Dive Caroline** shop is on the premises.

About one-half mile before the turnoff to Lelu is the **Pacific Tree Lodge** (P.O. Box 51, Lelu, Kosrae, FM 96944, tel. 370-2102, fax 370-3060). This hotel, built in 1992, is uniquely designed. Six cottages, each with two units, surround a

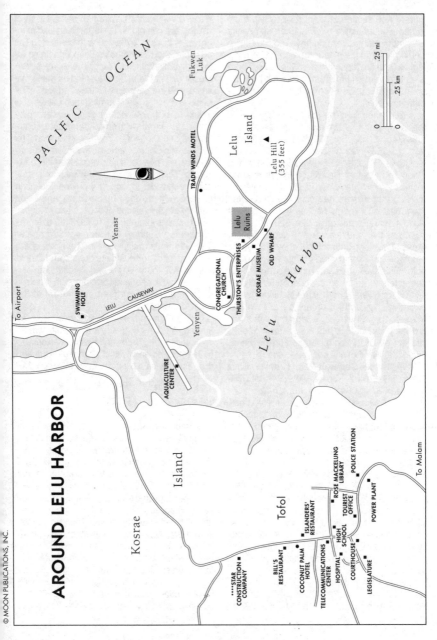

AROUND LELU HARBOR

© MOON PUBLICATIONS, INC.

PACIFIC OCEAN

Fukwen Luk

Lelu Island

Lelu Hill
(355 feet)

TRADE WINDS MOTEL

Lelu Ruins

Lelu Harbor

Yenasr

CONGREGATIONAL CHURCH

THURSTON'S ENTERPRISES

KOSRAE MUSEUM

OLD WHARF

SWIMMING HOLE

To Airport

LELU CAUSEWAY

Yenyen

AQUACULTURE CENTER

Kosrae Island

Tofol

STAR CONSTRUCTION COMPANY

BILL'S RESTAURANT

COCONUT PALM HOTEL

ISLANDERS' RESTAURANT

TELECOMMUNICATIONS CENTER

HIGH SCHOOL

HOSPITAL

COURTHOUSE

LEGISLATURE

ROSE MACKELUNG LIBRARY

TOURIST OFFICE

POLICE STATION

POWER PLANT

To Malam

25 mi
.25 km
0

squared-off section of mangrove forest, a joy to see with its active birdlife. Each unit backs onto more mangroves that have grown right up to the glass doors. The rooms are quite comfortable and are a bargain at $55 s, $75 d. There is a restaurant on the premises; reach it via the boardwalk that has been built deeper into the mangroves.

A half mile down the road, 350 feet before the Lelu turnoff, is the modern **Kosrae Nautilus Resort** (P.O. Box 135, Kosrae, FM 96944, tel. 370-3567, fax 370-3568), recently constructed by Aussies Doug and Sally Beitz and Geoff and Heather Raaschou. All 16 modern rooms are comfortable and clean. Undaunted by the fact that Kosrae has no TV station, each room has a TV that is hooked up to a central video player. Rooms are $75 s, $90 d.

Across the road is a very interesting beach. Close in is a long flat reef, but about 150 yards out, there is a sharp drop-off into a very deep hole. This wall presents an opportunity for snorkelers to enjoy an experience usually reserved for divers. The Kosrae Nautilus has its own dive shop and will organize night dives to the hole as well as canoe trips through mangroves. The Nautilus has a swimming pool. It also has one of the top restaurants on the island, one of the two that sell beer and wine.

The 11-room **Coconut Palm Hotel** (William Tosie, P.O. Box 87, Kosrae, FM 96944, tel. 370-3181, fax 370-3084) in Tofol is a reasonable choice at $40 s, $55 d, if you are here on business. It is not scenic, but it's clean and reasonably comfortable. If there doesn't seem to be anyone around, ask next door at Bill's Restaurant as it's under the same ownership.

Close to the Lelu ruins but off the island's main road is **Trade Winds Motel** (Thurston K. Siba, P.O. Box TE, Kosrae, FM 96944, tel. 370-3254, fax 370-3047). Although most of the units now rent on a long-term basis, units with kitchens are often available for the economical price of $30 s, $40 d. This motel is managed by Island Office Supply in Tofol, so if you show up unexpectedly, you may find no one around to help you.

Kosrae Village Resort (P.O. Box KV, Kosrae, FM 96944, tel. 370-3483, fax 370-5839) is Kosrae's newest hotel and its first full eco-resort.

It's small with only 12 planned units, seven of which were completed by 1995. Built amid mangroves with as little disruption to the ecology as possible, the resort succeeds in remaining almost invisible from the beach. The cottages, built mostly with native materials, stand on mangrove timber and are covered with thatched roofs. The rustic and extremely charming resort stays cool thanks to all the overhead mangrove. Owned by American expats Katrina Adams and Bruce Brandt, and Director of Tourism Madison Nena and his wife Christiana Nena, the resort relies on screens and overhead fans rather than air conditioning. Toilets are indoors, but each shower is partially outside, though fully private. Mosquito protection is provided by mosquito lamps and netting, which is placed over each bed at night.

The daily room rate is $105 s, $165 d; rooms are free on Sunday. For an extra $30 pp per day, all meals are included. The hotel offers reduced rates for business guests and for extended dive tours. Bruce and Katrina, both certified by PADI, offer a full dive program. There is even a nice drop-off right out in front of the hotel for shore diving.

This hotel is committed to the physically challenged. All parts of the resort are fully wheelchair accessible. Bruce and Katrina are licensed to instruct and dive with challenged divers and they can devise a program to meet all needs.

FOOD

Until recently, Kosrae's restaurants were its greatest drawback. Few restaurant menus feature local dishes, and even fresh local produce is rare. This is particularly disappointing because a fair amount of food is grown or caught on the island and its surrounding lagoon. At local get-togethers there are mounds of ahi sashimi, boiled lobsters, and mangrove crabs, and plates of smoked reef fish. The local sukiyaki contains papaya as well as meat. Also popular are nutritious starch dishes including rice mixed with coconut meat; breadfruit cooked in taro leaves; sliced taro; and a gelatin tapioca made by chopping tapioca and mixing it with poi and copra, then covering it with sweetened coconut milk. On special occasions, *fafa* might

a river on Kosrae as
seen by French visitors
in 1824

be served. This fantastic dish of chopped taro balls served in a sweet coconut sauce by tradition may only be prepared by certain families.

Two restaurants, one at Kosrae Village Resort and the other at the Nautilus Resort, are improving the level of restaurant fare on the island.

In 1995, the Kosrae Village Resort opened the **Inum Restaurant.** The architecture and atmosphere are splendid and the food is very good. Local ahi is served both as sashimi and tempura style for $5; tasty mangrove crab is $11. The restaurant rotates local dishes such as *um mas,* breadfruit cooked in an outdoor oven between hot basalt rocks and pandanus leaves. Kosrae Village Resort also opened the first full-service bar on the island. For the lowest prices, join the happy hour, Mon.-Sat. 4-6 p.m.

At last, a $2 glass of wine (Almaden jug), probably the cheapest in Micronesia, can be found at the **Kosrae Nautilus Resort** restaurant. First, cross the lobby of the hotel and buy your very own mandatory drinking permit for $3, good for one month. For dinner, try a huge sashimi appetizer followed by an ahi steak. If you have a sweet tooth, leave room for the crepes a la mode.

The Nautilus has a happy hour on Monday, Wednesday, and Friday. Friday is a particularly good day to meet expats and other travelers there.

Bill's Restaurant (tel. 370-3181), opposite the Coconut Palm Hotel in Tofol, serves breakfast, lunch, and dinner. It's clean and has a lun-cheonette look to it. Most full breakfasts run $5. A ramen lunch will set you back three bucks. For dinner, there is a good assortment of fish and chicken dishes. A treat at Bill's any time of day is frigid coconut milk served in the shell for $1.

Islanders' Restaurant, just up the street from the Coconut Palm, is closed weekends. But during the week, particularly at breakfast or lunch, it's a good place to get a feel for the local working community, native and expat. The cook does very well with local fish. Lunch probably will not cost you more than $5.

You get to the **Treelodge Restaurant** by walking over a boardwalk that begins at the back of the Pacific Tree Lodge. The restaurant is beautifully set in the mangroves, and the view is a pleasure during the day. The aesthetics, however, are not helped by the plywood floors or the plastic chairs. Don't go there if you are in a rush as service can be painfully slow. Portions are big and you can fill up on fried chicken for $5. The restaurant is open-air and not air conditioned.

Primarily used by its guests, but open to the public, is the restaurant at the **Sandy Beach Hotel.** It's in a small, simple room with a wonderful view out to the beach. Breakfasts are good and reasonably priced. Try the pancakes. Mangrove crab is an occasional treat; ask in advance and they probably can arrange some for you.

If you have access to cooking facilities or are staying with a local family, buy fish, crabs, and lobster at the **Okat Marina** across the bridge from the airport or at the occasional market on the Lelu causeway near the old airstrip.

OTHER PRACTICALITIES

Sports and Recreation

Whatever Kosrae may lack in nightlife, it makes up for in outdoor, daytime recreational activities. In addition to hiking, there are incredibly varied water activities including fishing, canoeing through mangrove forests, snorkeling, surfing, and reef walking.

What attracts most of Kosrae's tourists is undoubtedly its superb drift diving. There are also a number of walls to dive as well as several wrecks. Visibility is often 100 feet, and much more during summer. There are four dive shops on Kosrae. Prices are comparable, usually about $75 for a two-tank dive; price may vary depending on how many other divers go out that day. All dive shops will also take snorkelers at a much lower rate, usually about $20 per person, but again price depends on how many other people are going out.

Dive Caroline (P.O. Box 6, Kosrae, FM 96944, tel. 370-3239, fax 370-2109) is a full-service dive shop based at Sandy Beach Hotel. The shop also fills tanks and rents equipment. **Kosrae Nautilus Resort** (P.O. Box 135, Kosrae, FM 96944, tel. 370-3567, fax 370-3568) is a good spot for anyone. **Kosrae Village Resort** (P.O. Box KV, tel. 370-3483, fax 370-5839) is a good diving establishment for anyone, but *the* place for divers with disabilities. **Phoenix Sports Club** (P.O. Box PHM, Kosrae, FM 96944, tel. 390-3100, fax 370-3509) is Japanese owned, a branch of the company on Pohnpei. There are a good number of Japanese-speaking guides and instructors, as well as those with some knowledge of English. Ask Max to show you how he can attract fish using air bubbles.

Shopping

Although church singing is perhaps the most important folk art of Kosrae, there is also a live handicraft tradition. Work includes woven bags, hats, fans, headbands, trays, food utensils, taro pounders, purses, model canoes, carved sharks,

coconut- or pandanus-fiber carrying cases, and decorative wall hangings.

The **Kosrae Community Action Program** can put you in touch with local artisans. Call 370-4496 or drop into the Division of Planning in Tofol. Most hotels also sell reasonably priced handicrafts. If you are interested in seeing a carver at work, go see Peter Lick in his workshop. It's inland from the road, on the airport side of the Sandy Beach Hotel.

Services

A Bank of Hawaii branch (tel. 370-3230) is next to the Islanders' Restaurant at Tofol. Below the nearby Coconut Palm Hotel are the Bank of the FSM (tel. 370-3225), the post office, and Continental Air Micronesia (tel. 370-3024).

Overseas calls can be placed at the Telecommunications Center (open 24 hours) in Tofol. Address mail to Kosrae, FM 96944.

There's a coin laundry at Thurston's Enterprises in Lelu.

Most Kosrae state government employees are on a four day work week, so *don't* count on getting much business done on Friday. Some national government offices, including the post office, however, are open.

Information

You can pick up brochures on Kosrae at the tourist office (tel. 370-2228), in a traditional-style thatched building at Tofol. The tourist office also sells the book *Kosrae, The Sleeping Lady Awakens* by Harvey Gordon Segal ($14), and William H. Stewart's *Tourist Map of Kosrae* ($2.50). You're most likely to find someone there Mon.-Thurs. early in the morning. Madison Nena and Justus Alokoa in this office are good sources of information and can help with practical arrangements.

Radio station V6AJ-AM broadcasts from Kosrae over 1500 AM.

TRANSPORTATION

Getting There

Flights land at the **airport** (KSA) at Okat, five miles west of Tofol. Visitors with hotel reservations are usually picked up at the airport; those without reservations will have no trouble hitching a lift. There's a $10 departure tax.

Able to grow in salt water, mangroves trap runoff from the interior and thus, over centuries, expand the size of the island.

Continental Air Micronesia Island Hopper heads west from Hawaii Monday, Wednesday, and Friday, and leaves Guam heading east the same days. You can reconfirm your onward flight at their Tofol office (tel. 370-3024). Remember that because of the International Date Line, you lose a day between Honolulu (or the Marshall Islands) and Kosrae.

The **Kosrae Terminal and Stevedoring Company** (tel. 370-3085) at Okat Harbor near the airport runs a monthly cargo/passenger ship, the *Mutunlik,* to Pingelap ($9.36), Mwoakilloa ($13.50), Pohnpei ($18.30), Ebeye ($20.70), Majuro ($30), and Nauru ($25.20). The quoted fares are deck class, and three meals are an extra $10 a day (optional). No cabins are available. For information on departures call the office or the Public Works Department (tel. 370-3011) in Tofol.

Private yachts can dock at either Lelu or Okat Harbor.

Getting Around

Kosrae's public transportation is virtually nonexistent, unless you include hitching in your definition of public transportation. There is a bus, but its main function appears to be to take government workers to and from work. There is one taxi cab company (AA Taxis, tel. 370-2639), with several sedans and one van. From Tafunsak village to Tofol the charge is $1 per person, with a minimum charge of $2 per cab. If you flag down a cab with room, it will pick you up for $1. The price of longer trips, past Tofol, should be negotiated with the owner, Alik Albert.

Hitchhiking is an option on Kosrae—it is that sort of place. If you are walking, people will often offer a ride, even if you haven't asked. Additionally, hotel owners will often take you for short rides if they are not too busy. Most hotel owners, for a fee, will also arrange longer trips and tours.

Nonetheless, if you plan on extensive sightseeing, you will probably want to rent a car. The going price seems to be about $45 per day. Many rental cars have manual shifts, while some imports have right-hand drive; specify what you want. Your hotel management can arrange a rental for you at a fair price. If you wish to arrange a car yourself, try calling **Thurston's Enterprises** (tel. 370-3245, fax 370-3047), **Webster's** (tel. 370-3116, fax 370-2116), or **Bill and Sue's Auto Rental** (tel. 370-3181, fax 370-3084).

STATE OF POHNPEI

INTRODUCTION

Pohnpei is mysterious—mountain jungles, mist-shrouded waterfalls, coastal mangrove forests—particularly after 5 p.m., when it is most usually seen through one's drug of choice: paralyzingly potent *sakau* made from the roots of a pepper plant, alcohol, betel nut, or locally grown (illegal) marijuana.

The island of Pohnpei (spelled Ponape until 1984), eight outlying atolls, and Minto Reef make up the State of Pohnpei, about halfway between Honolulu and Manila. Pohnpei Island, 12 by 14 miles, is the largest in the FSM. Local author Gene Ashby calls Pohnpei "the outer edge of Paradise."

The rugged, rainforested slopes of the interior rise to 2,540 feet at Nahnalaud ("Big Mountain") and Ngihneni ("Giant's Tooth"), shroud-

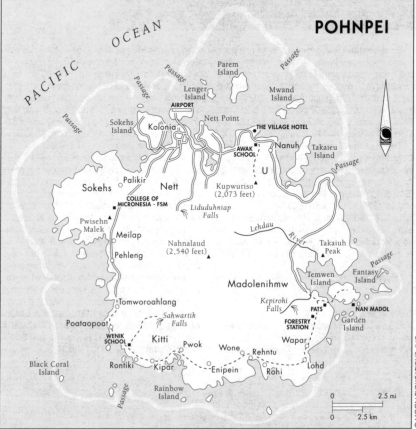

POHNPEI

PACIFIC OCEAN

Parem Island

Mwand Island

Lenger Island

AIRPORT

Sokehs Island

Kolonia

Nett Point

THE VILLAGE HOTEL

Nanuh

Takaieu Island

AWAK SCHOOL

Palikir

Nett

Kupwuriso (2,073 feet)

Sokehs

COLLEGE OF MICRONESIA - FSM

Liduduhniap Falls

Lehdau River

Pwisehn Malek

Meilap

Nahnalaud (2,540 feet)

Takaiuh Peak

Pehleng

Madolenihmw

Temwen Island

Fantasy Island

Kepirohi Falls

NAN MADOL

Tomworoahlang

Sahwartik Falls

PATS

Poataopoat

FORESTRY STATION

Garden Island

WENIK SCHOOL

Kitti

Pwok

Wone

Wapar

Rehntu

Black Coral Island

Rontiki

Kipar

Enipein

Rohi

Lohd

Rainbow Island

0   2.5 mi

0   2.5 km

© MOON PUBLICATIONS, INC.

INDONESIA REGIONAL TOURISM COUNCIL

Pohnpei's Kepirohi waterfall is a great place to swim.

of the mangrove forests, there are no beaches on Pohnpei itself. However, there are some great beaches from which to snorkel and dive on nearby reef islets. There are three types of islands in Pohnpei's lagoons: coral, volcanic, and artificial. Creating artificial islands through landfill is not just a modern activity. The ancient residents of Pohnpei did so also.

Aside from the main town, Kolonia, the most heavily populated areas on Pohnpei are Sokehs Island and Madolenihmw (pronounced "mad-o-LEN-ee-um"). Under the Germans, Pohnpei was the capital of Micronesia.

Pohnpei is one of the few islands in the Pacific with monumental ruins from every period of its history: Micronesian, Spanish, German, Japanese, and American.

Kaselehlia, like *aloha,* translates into hello or goodbye, but to visitors it means "Welcome to Pohnpei."

Climate

An island does not contain a lush, tropical forest without a lot of rain. Kolonia gets roughly 16 *feet* of annual rainfall, but twice that amount falls on the mountains of the interior. Much, though by no means all, of the rain falls at night.

ed in lush tropical vegetation nurtured by endless precipitation. Pohnpei's peaks generate the island's heavy rains by catching passing clouds and wringing the moisture from them. The torrential rains swell the 42 streams and rivers, which thunder down from the uplands in high cascades. Pools at the feet of the falls, and the rivers themselves, allow excellent freshwater swimming. When Pohnpei's bright orange hibiscus flower falls prey to the tropical sunlight, it turns saffron yellow, tinged by burgundy, more elegant in death than in life.

Nearly all the shore is skirted by intact mangrove forests. At Kitti, for example, the forest is almost a mile wide. Canoes must wind through twisting channels to reach the lagoon. Because

POHNPEI'S CLIMATE

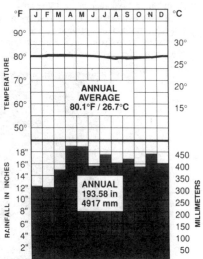

The Founding of Pohnpei

According to one Pohnpei legend, long, long ago people sailed from a distant island in search of new land. On their way they met an octopus who told them of a shallow place in the sea stretching from north to south. They reached the place, but found only a tiny coral islet that fit between canoe and outrigger. So they used magic to call coral and rocks to help build the island. Since waves broke the stones, they planted mangroves to protect their work and put a reef around the island to keep the sea away. As they brought more soil, the island grew. They built an altar and piled rocks on top of it. Thus Pohnpei got its name from *pohn* (on) *pei* (the altar).

All the people returned to their home island, except for one couple who remained and had many children. A second group arrived and helped enlarge Pohnpei, but all still lived in caves. Finally, a third group landed on the island bringing vegetables. They taught the others how to build houses of grass and small trees. Later groups came, each contributing to the Pohnpei of today.

History

Pohnpei was divided into three kingdoms by a line of native kings, the Saudeleurs, who ruled from Nan Madol, beginning in the 13th century. The Saudeleur dynasty was overthrown by the legendary warrior Isokelekel, who arrived with 333 comrades. Isokelekel established the first line of Nahnmwarkis, who are the current tradi-tional chiefs. In the legends of Pohnpei (though not Kosrae) Isokelekel was actually a descen-dant of Pohnpei's earlier rulers who had been banished to Kosrae by usurpers.

Pohnpei was sighted by Alvaro de Saavedra in 1529. Pedro Fernando de Quirós, leader of a Spanish expedition, passed Pohnpei on 24 De-cember 1595 but didn't land. The islanders were left in peace until the second quarter of the 19th century, when whalers arrived. In 1854 the Ameri-can whaler *Delta* brought a smallpox epidemic to Pohnpei, wiping out half the population and lead-ing the Pohnpeians to abandon Nan Madol. A few years later the American ship *Pearl* brought measles, which killed many more. Whaling de-clined after 1865 when the Confederate raider *Shenandoah* sank 40 Yankee whaling ships in the North Pacific, four of them at Pohnpei.

One chance arrival, James F. O'Connell, ship-wrecked here off the *John Bull* in 1827, entered local lore as the "Tattooed Irishman." O'Con-nell danced an Irish jig to ingratiate himself with the local chiefs. His book, *A Residence of Eleven Years in New Holland and the Caroline Islands,* is a colorful mix of sailor's tales and in-teresting facts about old Pohnpei.

The Spanish laid vague claim to these is-lands in the 16th century but only arrived to oc-cupy Pohnpei after the Germans claimed the Carolines in 1885. The Spanish built a town wall and fort at Kolonia, the remains of which you can visit today. The Germans bought the is-lands from Spain in 1899, took over the outpost at Kolonia, and developed the copra trade.

a Japanese AA gun in a bamboo thicket on Sokehs Mountain (Pohndolap)

DAVID STANLEY

German rule was often harsh. In 1910 members of the Kawath clan of Sokehs killed four German officials in a rebellion brought on by forced labor for road building. The Germans brought soldiers from New Guinea to capture those responsible for the rebellion. Seventeen Pohnpeians were executed and 426 exiled to Angaur Island, Palau, to work in phosphate mines. Land owned by the rebel clans at Sokehs and Palikir was confiscated and given to outer islanders.

The Germans were forced off Pohnpei at the start of World War I in 1914 and the Japanese occupied the island. In a short period, they completed a road fit for vehicles around part of the island.

Thousands of Japanese colonists arrived and by 1941 they outnumbered the Pohnpeians three to one. Pohnpei was not a strategic base for the Japanese during World War II. The United States chose to bypass it, after bombing its airfields. During much of the Trust Territory period Pohnpei was a quiet backwater.

Pohnpei is now the capital of the FSM. Considering its relative isolation it is surprisingly cosmopolitan. Micronesians from other states come to attend to the business of government. There is a fairly large expat community, primarily Americans and Filipinos. On any given day, a great number of Chinese from fishing boats may also be in town.

Economy

Since Pohnpei is the capital of the Federated States of Micronesia, government plays the dominant role in the local economy. Education is important because Pohnpei is home to the main campus of the College of Micronesia—FSM. It recently moved from Kolonia to a new complex out at Palikir. The Pohnpei Agricultural and Trade School (PATS) is the only one of its kind in the region.

In 1995, at the inauguration for his second term, Pres. Bailey Olter called for an economy based upon the notion of "sustainable living." This concept is critical for all nations on this consumer-oriented planet. But the problems created by consuming more than nature can produce hit the limited ecologies of small island nations particularly painfully. President Olter maintains that for Pohnpei, sustainable living must revolve around agriculture, tourism, and the fisheries.

Over the past decades, agriculture has not fared well. There was a clear decline in subsistence farms. However, Pohnpei is famous for its yams *(kehp)*, which grow up to 10 feet long—a cluster can weigh a thousand pounds. Other traditional crops are taro, breadfruit, cassava, and sweet potatoes. Pohnpei's black pepper is thought by many to be the tastiest in the world.

A few local processing industries around Kolonia may be of interest to visitors. Pohnpei black pepper is bagged and exported by Island Traders (P.O. Box 704, Pohnpei, FM 96941), beside the Public Market in Kolonia. A branch of Island Traders behind the Chinese Embassy makes buttons from trochus shells. You're welcome to wander in and inspect both these small factories set up by Bob and Patti Arthur, of the Village Hotel.

Kaselel shampoo and Oil of Pohnpei soap are made from coconut oil by Pohnpei Coconut Products Inc. (P.O. Box 1120, Pohnpei, FM 96941), near PATS in Madolenihmw. This company also produces Marekeiso oil for use on body and hair and Oil of Pohnpei suntan oil. All these excellent products are sold at handicraft outlets around Kolonia.

Genuine Pohnpei pepper can be ordered through the mail from Albert Roosevelt, Pohnpei Agricultural Development, Inc., P.O. Box 1479, Pohnpei, FM 96941. Both white and black pepper, ground or whole, is available.

The People

The state's population is approximately 33,000, about a fifth of which lives in Kolonia. Pohnpeians outside Kolonia don't live in compact villages, but in groups of individual houses with land around each. The people are easygoing and friendly.

Influential lines of chiefs and nobility control the five municipalities other than Kolonia: Sokehs, Nett, U, Madolenihmw, and Kitti. Each has a Nahnmwarki, or High Chief, and a Nahnken, or Talking Chief. Below the hereditary nobility are other social classes of landowners and commoners, a complex social hierarchy. Descent is matrilineal, with children becoming members of the mother's clan and inheriting their prestige and property from it. It's hard to discern differences in caste from appearances; whenever in doubt, visitors should

M.G.L. DOMENY DE RIENZI

Pohnpei is also noted for its unique stools, a seat with a built-in coconut grater.

SIGHTS

Kolonia

Kolonia is more a town than a colony or city. You can look for downtown Kolonia, only to realize you are in it. One is never more than a couple of dozen feet from the nearest chicken or pig.

At the same time, Kolonia has a cosmopolitan feel. About 500 Western expatriates and as many Filipinos live on Pohnpei on a more or less permanent basis. Because Pohnpei is the capital of the Federated States, everyone in town seems to speak English; in this way someone from Kosrae can communicate with someone from Yap or Chuuk.

Before World War II, Kolonia had a population of 10,000 Japanese nationals (in all there were 13,000 Japanese on Pohnpei and only 5,900 Micronesians). Kolonia is again approaching that size in population, and it's mostly Micronesians this time.

The **Pohnpei Lidorkini Museum** (open Mon.-Fri. 10 a.m.-5 p.m.) is a good place to start a visit to Kolonia. The small museum has excellent model canoes, some six to eight feet long. Inside the museum is also a small Pohnpeian assembly house *(Nahs)* with tools of *sakau*-making and an explanation of *sakau's* ritual importance to the culture. Because of its artifacts from Nan Madol, it's great to visit the museum before going to that site.

Perhaps the museum's strongest feature is its focus on uses of native materials, particularly uses of the coconut palm. The meat, of course, can be eaten, or it can be made into oil for cooking. Coconut cream becomes a sauce and coconut milk a cool drink. Leaves of the coconut palm are shown used in hats and mats. The coconut husk in the hands of skilled craftspeople becomes twine *(sahl twehl)*. Coconut shells were made into containers for water, fish, and bait. The palm tree itself was a valuable source

address or greet older people first. Pigs are a symbol of wealth, so you see them everywhere on Pohnpei.

Immigrants from outer islands such as Pingelap, Mwoakilloa (formerly Mokil), and the Mortlocks make up about a quarter of the population of Pohnpei Island. Some formed separate communities, each with its own language, on Sokehs Island, where they were resettled in 1912 on lands seized by the Germans during the 1910 rebellion. At Porakiet, on the west side of downtown Kolonia, some 1,000 Polynesians from Kapingamarangi atoll now live.

Crafts

Pohnpei has an outstanding tradition of loom woven sashes of intricate patterns. Certain patterns and colors belonged to specific families and copying was not permitted. In fact, some sashes belonged to the nobility, and a commoner could be put to death for wearing such a belt. Sashes were sometimes heavily decorated with glass beads and tiny shells.

Still available for purchase is the dance paddle. Dance paddles in Pohnpei come in various sizes, typically with a white line design of an intricate geometric pattern on the flat of the blade. The edges of the blade are decorated with pandanus fiber. Other local crafts include carefully scaled model canoes, wooden sea animals and fish, and woven items such as wall hangings, trays, handbags, baskets, fans, and mats.

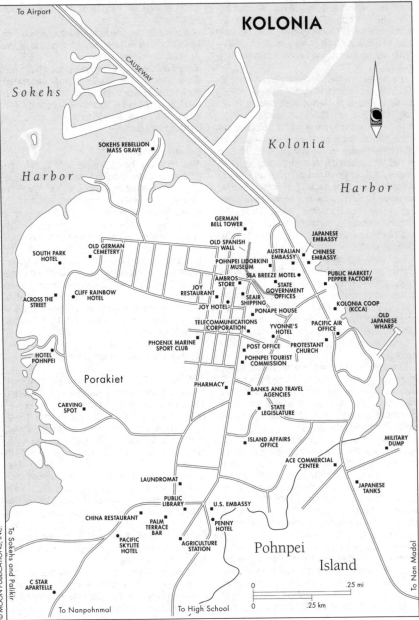

KOLONIA

To Airport

CAUSEWAY

Sokehs

Kolonia

SOKEHS REBELLION
MASS GRAVE

Harbor

Harbor

GERMAN
BELL TOWER

OLD SPANISH
WALL

JAPANESE
EMBASSY

OLD GERMAN
CEMETERY

POHNPEI LIDORKINI
MUSEUM

AUSTRALIAN
EMBASSY

CHINESE
EMBASSY

SOUTH PARK
HOTEL

SEA BREEZE MOTEL

PUBLIC MARKET/
PEPPER FACTORY

AMBROS
STORE

STATE
GOVERNMENT
OFFICES

CLIFF RAINBOW
HOTEL

JOY
RESTAURANT

SEAIR
SHIPPING

KOLONIA COOP
(KCCA)

ACROSS THE
STREET

JOY HOTEL

PONAPE HOUSE

OLD
JAPANESE
WHARF

PACIFIC AIR
OFFICE

TELECOMMUNICATIONS
CORPORATION

YVONNE'S
HOTEL

HOTEL
POHNPEI

PHOENIX MARINE
SPORT CLUB

POST OFFICE

PROTESTANT
CHURCH

Porakiet

POHNPEI TOURIST
COMMISSION

PHARMACY

CARVING
SPOT

BANKS AND TRAVEL
AGENCIES

STATE
LEGISLATURE

ISLAND AFFAIRS
OFFICE

MILITARY
DUMP

ACE COMMERCIAL
CENTER

LAUNDROMAT

JAPANESE
TANKS

PUBLIC
LIBRARY

U.S. EMBASSY

CHINA RESTAURANT

PALM
TERRACE
BAR

PENNY
HOTEL

Pohnpei

PACIFIC
SKYLITE
HOTEL

AGRICULTURE
STATION

Island

C STAR
APARTELLE

To Nanpohnmal

To High School

To Sokehs and Palikir

To Nan Madol

0   .25 mi

0   .25 km

© MOON PUBLICATIONS, INC.

of lumber, while the roots yielded medicine and the outer husk could become charcoal. In the words of an old Pohnpei saying: *"Sohte wasa ehu ni turke nih me sohte ah doadoahk"*—"There is no part of the coconut tree to throw away."

For further information on the museum, contact Museum Director Henter P. Lawrence (P.O. Box 250, Education Department, Kolonia, Pohnpei, FM 96941, tel. 320-5299, fax 320-5155).

In the park on the north side of Kolonia is the **old Spanish wall,** which now doubles as the center field fence for the little league field. Built in 1887, it marked the western boundary of Fort Alfonso XIII, which extended north and east to the lagoon. Just across the park is the **Catholic mission.** Only the apse and belfry remain from the original church erected 1909-14 by the Capuchin fathers. During World War II the Japanese used material from the structure to build defense works.

Due west, in a clearing directly behind a new Protestant church, is the **old German cemetery,** with the graves of sailors off the cruiser *Emden,* who died putting down the Sokehs revolt of 1910. The mass grave site of 17 Pohnpeians, executed by a German firing squad in 1911, is marked by a simple enclosure on the left, near the end of a dirt road at the north end of Kolonia.

One can catch a good view of Sokehs Island from the terrace behind the **South Park Hotel.** Better still, enjoy the same view from the bar next door, called **Across the Street** because it is across the street from the Cliff Rainbow Hotel, which owns and operates it.

You can then take a stroll through the Polynesian village of Kapingamarangans at **Porakiet** on your way back to town. Ninety Polynesians settled here in 1918 after a severe drought on their native island, Kapingamarangi. Open thatched houses sit on stone platforms and the residents have an outdoor lifestyle. There are several meetinghouses, a tribute to the cohesiveness of this small community.

In the village, about 300 feet past the Hotel Pohnpei is the **Carving Spot** of artist Heyger Paul, who welcomes visitors to see him work. He makes the famed Pohnpei stools used for grating coconut ($100-150). He also carves fish and porpoises from local woods. They cost about

$1.25 an inch. Mr. Paul takes phone orders (tel. 320-3648).

A massive **Japanese meteorological building** stands abandoned on the grounds of the Agriculture Station in Kolonia.

Just a little up and across the road from Ace Commercial Center are three small **Japanese tanks** beside the road. Other small tanks are lined up in a pit in the bush directly behind these three. The driveway opposite Ace leads to a large military dump.

Sokehs Island

After crossing the causeway onto Sokehs Island, one has the choice of several interesting hikes, the easiest of which is to the right. The road is paved for about a mile and a half, and dirt tracks continue farther. The road presents a great slice of island life. You will be joined by happy children and see well-kept, simple homes. You obviously are not in the wilderness, but the island has a wonderful overgrown feel. Looking inland, one sees fantastic volcanic outcroppings. Toward the right are ever-changing views of the water seen through mangroves. At the end of the road, a footpath continues along a stone trail through the mangroves from Danipei to Peilong. The west side of Sokehs Island is less heavily populated than the east. It will take approximately two hours to hike around the island.

A more difficult hike, great for scenery, war relics, and birdwatching, is to the top of **Sokehs Mountain** (823 feet), locally known as Pohndolap. Just after the causeway, instead of taking the road to the right, take the road straight ahead that winds up the hill. When the paved road turns left, go straight on the overgrown Japanese military road. Follow this for about 25 minutes until it switchbacks steeply to the mountaintop.

You'll know you're getting there when you start seeing good views of Kolonia. Take care to note which way you came so you can find your way back down. On top are two large double-barreled Japanese AA guns to the right and a six-inch naval gun in a concrete bunker at the back of the hill to the left.

At the north end of the mountain, some distance beyond the AA guns, is a metal Japanese searchlight platform that offers stunning views of Sokehs Rock and Kolonia.

Massive volcanic plugs poke skyward just below the summit of Sokehs Rock (Paipalap).

The climb to the top of **Sokehs Rock** (658 feet), or Paipalap (Peipapap), is easier than one would imagine from the look of its sheer basalt sides when seen from Kolonia. Nonetheless you should be experienced and in excellent shape to make this climb. The trail has signposts, but it's best to make this hike with someone who has done it before. You might consider hiring (for a few dollars) a young local to guide you. The trail begins by a house just before Danipei church, near the end of the peninsula. The rock itself belongs to Pohnpei State but the access trail crosses private land and a $1 pp toll is sometimes collected at the trailhead.

Go across the right side of a taro and banana plantation, past and around two large caves, then up to a big tree. Here comes the tricky part—to scale the cliff, you must climb the tree, which provides handholds. By this time you'll have encountered a black power cable. Follow this up the back of the rock to the top. The view from the summit is the best on the island, all the way out to Pakin atoll to the northwest. Go slowly, as the rock can be slippery.

Southeast of Kolonia
A dirt road runs four miles south from Kolonia past the rock crusher along the dirt road to **Liduduhniap Falls** at Nanpil (admission at several dollars may be charged). The dirt road follows the Kahmar River (good swimming) then climbs, affording a good view of the island's lush interior. The area around the falls has been cleared; the road runs right up to it. After rains, the way can be muddy and cars can bog down. You pass a hydroelectric project on the way to the falls.

Two more Japanese naval guns are atop **Kupwuriso** (2,073 feet), a tough four-hour roundtrip climb through the jungle opposite Awak School at U. Ask around for someone to guide you (offer $10).

Around the Island
The potholed roads of southern Pohnpei are among the worst in Micronesia. The 50-mile, 80-bridge, round-the-island road, begun by the Spaniards in the 1890s and continued by the Japanese in the 1930s, was finally completed in 1985. Eastbound the pavement ends at Awak School; the paved road west reaches five miles past the capital complex. Do not plan to drive around the island unless you are an experienced off-road driver and can rent a pickup or a four-wheel-drive. The road is often steep and slippery on the southeast side of the island.

West on the round-the-island road, about a half-mile past the junction with the road from Sokehs Island, is Panasang Heights and a local takeout snack bar with a nice view from the property.

Farther on is a well-marked turnoff to the impressive nine-building **FSM capital complex** opened at Palikir in 1989, which houses the national government offices, the Congress of the FSM, and the FSM Supreme Court. The buildings are completely modern, but the roof lines,

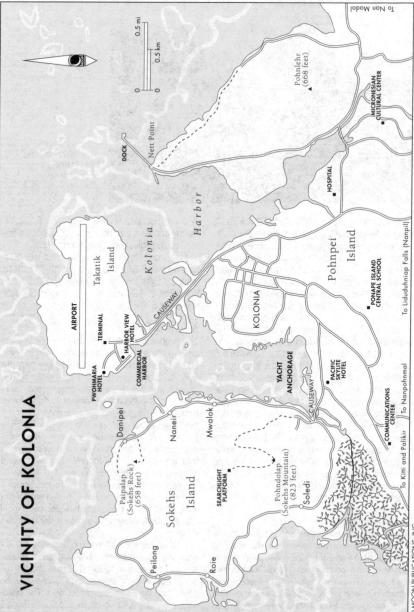

VICINITY OF KOLONIA

© MOON PUBLICATIONS, INC.

the color of material, and the basalt-shaped supports are reminiscent of traditional meeting-houses. The area is open and quite attractive, well worth the detour.

One and a half miles beyond Palikir is the new campus of the College of Micronesia—FSM. It replaced the old campus in town that will remain a part of the college extension service. The school is next to a volcanic plug known as **Pwisehn Malek** ("Chickenshit Mountain") that towers above the road and can be climbed. The prismatic basalt formations are striking when seen from above and indicate the availability of materials to build Nan Madol. When a lava flow is very deep, the material cools slowly into these columnar basalt crystals. Pwisehn Malek got its name from a legendary rooster who relieved himself here (and thereby created the mountain) while racing around the island on an errand from the gods.

Two uncommercialized waterfalls flow off the southwest side of Pohnpei, an hour's hike up a muddy track from Wenik School. Water that feeds the first falls, **Sahwarlap**, passes under the first suspension bridge you encounter. Trouble is, you're above the falls so it's hard to get a clear view. Just beyond the bridge, work your way over to the edge of the cliff for a view of **Sahwartik**, the higher of the two falls. There's a very tricky path to the bottom of the falls where you'll find a spectacular deep swimming pool, but a guide is necessary. Swimming on top is possible, but not outstanding. This hike gives you a glimpse of the interior few tourists ever see. Go even farther up the trail if you have time.

Every Saturday there's a day tour from Kolonia to **Enipein Marine Park** (tel. 320-2693) on the south side of the island ($40 pp including lunch and transportation). Participants tour the mangroves in a small boat, snorkel on a nearby reef, and get to try the intoxicating native pepper plant drink, *sakau*. Advance reservations must be made through the Tourist Commission in Kolonia or your hotel. Also at Enipein, a couple of miles east of the Marine Park headquarters, is a large river with a good swimming hole just above the highway bridge.

LOUISE FOOTE

Madolenihmw
The **Pohnpei Agricultural and Trade School** (PATS) at Madolenihmw is a Jesuit secondary school, offering 160 Micronesians four-year courses in construction, mechanics, horticulture, and animal husbandry. Tours of PATS are offered 1-4 p.m. A small **coconut products plant** near the Temwen Causeway produces excellent coconut oil soap, shampoo, and skin cream. Sold in tiny pandanus baskets, they make wonderful souvenirs.

Four huge **Japanese naval guns** intended to protect the entrance to Madolenihmw Harbor rest in jungle around the top of Temwen Island. After crossing the causeway, go straight about three miles and ask for Bernard Perez, who owns the land where the guns are. Bernard is a kind man and will probably offer to show you around.

Kepirohi Falls (admission $3), just before the turnoff to PATS, pours over basalt cliffs into an idyllic swimming pool. Take the path near the bridge where the boats dock. Pyramid-like **Takaiuh Peak** rises across Madolenihmw Harbor: The secure yacht anchorage just west of the point of land opposite Temwen's north end makes this a good port of call for yachties.

Nan Madol
If you ever visit Pohnpei, if you are ever even close to Pohnpei, you *must* see Nan Madol. Period.

This celebrated archaeological site is located on artificial islands in the lagoon off Temwen Island off the east side of Pohnpei. These islands

the mysterious ruins of Nan Madol

NAN MADOL RUINS

Temwen Island

KONDEREK

NAN
DOWAS

NAN
MWOLUHSEI

PEHI
EN
KITEL

PEHIKAPW
SAPWAWAS

KARIAHN

PEINERING

Passage

PAHN
KADIRA

IDEHD

DARONG

KELEPWEL

Lagoon

PAHNWI

0   .1 mi

0   .1 km

© MOON PUBLICATIONS, INC.

are home to impressive stone compounds and varied basalt buildings. Legend tells how Nan Madol was formed by the magicians Olsihpa and Olsohpa, who caused stones to fly into place.

The most usual means of visiting Nan Madol today, as it was in traditional times, is from the sea. One enters a break in the seawall and comes to the monumental plaza on Nan Dowas surrounded by basalt logs, forming walls that are 25 feet high. As you approach the island, you will be overwhelmed by the grandeur of the construction. You can only imagine the feeling it inspired in visitors from other islands when they arrived for commerce or to pay tribute to Nan Madol's rulers. Thus, like Piazza San Marcos

in Venice, the grandeur of the city made a foreign policy statement.

A mighty seawall flanks the site on three sides, with open channels between the 80 artificial islands. Those who reject the magician theory will feel awe toward the society that was able to construct Nan Madol; all of the huge basalt logs that went into the project had to be brought in on bamboo rafts! Carbon dating at the earliest levels indicates they were built between 1285 and 1485. When Europeans began to colonize Pohnpei, Nan Madol had only recently been abandoned.

The main islets to visit are Pahnwi, with a seawall of monoliths; Kariahn, the burial place of priests; Pahn Kadira, the administrative center; Kelepwel, housing servants for Pahn Kadira; Idehd, the religious center; Pehi en Kitel, the burial place of chiefs; Darong, center for ceremonial clamming; Peinering, coconut oil-producing center; Pehikapw Sapwawas, the communication or drumming center; Nan Mwoluhsei, a huge boulder from which warriors jumped to prove their bravery; Konderek (place of funeral rites), and the greatest ruin of all, Nan Dowas, the war temple or fortress.

Nan Dowas is the most spectacular island, the only one surrounded by monumental walls. Some of its walls have partially collapsed, most likely from the long, steady pressure of breadfruit tree roots. Many of the other islands of Nan Madol have not been excavated, or even properly surveyed. One would need a lifetime to explore the entire compound, particularly since some of the islands are completely overgrown today. If you can, time your trip to high tide; many islands are accessible by boat only at that time. Walking across the canals at low tide is a more difficult alternative. You must choose between walking in mud or using tricky underwater coral stepping stones.

The best method to get to Nan Madol is by boat. These trips can be arranged by many of the hotels in Kolonia, most charging about $50. The Village Hotel is the closest to the site. Most tours also take you snorkeling in the lagoon and conclude with a swim in the Kepirohi waterfall. If you prefer to spend additional time at the site, discuss this with your guide and boatmates before taking off.

Alternatively, you can wade or snorkel to the ruins from Joy Island or Temwen Island. This is much more difficult and should be done at low tide. If you wish to explore the site thoroughly, this is one method of seeing some of the islands closest to land.

The high chief of Madolenihmw, Ilten Selten, 23rd Nahnmwarki since the fall of the Saudeleur dynasty, lives on Temwen and charges a $3 pp fee to visit the ruins. A representative of the chief may approach you on the site to collect the entrance fee.

FSM Country Code 691

ACCOMMODATIONS

Pohnpei has a six percent room tax. Most hotels offer free transfer service from the airport, so ask. There's no suitable place to camp in Kolonia itself—you have to go a bit outside. Whenever camping on Pohnpei, get permission from the landowner, especially if houses are near your campsite. Occasionally every hotel room on Pohnpei is full.

Hotels
If you are hardy and wish an away-from-it-all experience while in the middle of it all, you can't do any better than the **Hotel Pohnpei** (Mercedes Santos, P.O. Box 430, Kolonia, Pohnpei, FM 96941, tel. 320-2330, fax 320-5983). On a hillside near the Polynesian village of Kapingamarangans, yet an easy walk from town, you'll be housed in one of 15 thatched cottages cascading down the hillside. The rooms are not air conditioned, but they all have ceiling fans and garden baths at $35 s, $45 d. The hillside location provides spectacular views across the water to the Sokehs. Not all the rooms have the same views, so ask to see the room before checking in. Borrow one of the hotel's outrigger canoes and paddle around the lagoon. This hotel is an experience in all senses. Certainly fun, but not the place to stay if you are in town on business.

Close to the U.S. Embassy is the new and immaculately clean **Penny Hotel** (P.O. Box 934, Kolonia, Pohnpei, FM 96941, tel. 320-5770, fax 320-2040). The hotel is well situated, overlooking an upscale residential neighborhood that might be fun to walk through. It's also across the street from the old agriculture school, where you'll find many plants not grown elsewhere on the island as well as famous Pohnpei pepper plants. This 15-room hotel charges $65 s, $75 d. Although there is not a restaurant on the premises, there are a good number nearby.

The friendly, modern **Joy Hotel** (P.O. Box 484, Kolonia, Pohnpei, FM 96941, tel. 320-2447, fax 320-2478) could be said to be in the heart of town if Kolonia were the type of town that could be said to have a center. The 10 a/c rooms with fridge and TV are $69 s, $90 d (tax included). With this differential, it is a comparatively better buy if you are traveling alone. Excellent Japanese meals are served in the dining room.

The **South Park Hotel** (P.O. Box 829, Kolonia, Pohnpei, FM 96941, tel. 320-2255, fax 320-2600) has six rooms in the old wing at $40 s, $45 d; 12 rooms in the new wing at $65 s, $75 d. All rooms are a/c, but the new rooms have better beds, cable TV, and refrigerators. Most rooms have unsurpassed views of the Sokehs. The South Park is undergoing extensive development and may be bigger by the time you get there. At the prices quoted above, it is a bargain.

Across the street on the same hill, though lacking the view, is the larger **Cliff Rainbow Hotel** (P.O. Box 96, Kolonia, Pohnpei, FM 96941, tel. 320-2415, fax 320-2417). Rooms are comfortable, though not exciting. It works fairly well for either English or Japanese speakers. Rooms start at $40 s, $45 d in the old wing and go as high as $85 s, $95 d in the newest wing. The least expensive rooms are the best value. It is a 10-minute walk or a $1 cab fare to almost anyplace in town. There is a small restaurant on the premises open for breakfast, lunch, and dinner. A full-service hotel, it can make arrangements for your touring or diving needs.

Sea Breeze Hotel (P.O. Box 371, Kolonia, Pohnpei, FM 96941, tel. 320-2065, fax 320-2067), next to the Australian Embassy (reportedly the scene of the best parties in town), is a clean but rather spartan place. Rooms that overlook the water are $55 s, $65 d, five bucks less for rear rooms.

Serious drawbacks plague both the **Harbor View Hotel** (P.O. Box 1328, Kolonia, Pohnpei, FM 96941, tel. 320-5244, fax 320-5246), with rooms for $45 s, $60 d, and **Pwohmaria Beach Resort** (P.O. Box 1416, Kolonia, Pohnpei, FM 96941, tel. 320-5942, fax 320-5941) with rooms for $69 s, $80 d. Both isolated hotels are near the airport but removed from town life. The Pwohmaria bungalows are nice, but despite the name it is near the commercial harbor and is not a beach resort. The Harbor View is on the docks, noisy, and suited only for those who are truly harbor freaks. The Harbor View can smell quite ripe when the wind blows from the tuna wharf.

The newly opened **Pacific Skylite Hotel** (P.O. Box 1687, Kolonia, Pohnpei, FM 96941, tel. 320-3672, fax 320-3708) is overpriced, beginning at $95 for single rooms and doubles for $110. It is expensively furnished in poor taste. Although most rooms face the Sokehs Rock (and those rooms are more expensive), the hotel was not designed to maximize the ability to enjoy the view from the rooms. It feels isolated, and this feeling is exacerbated by the high prices of its restaurant.

The Village Hotel (P.O. Box 339, Pohnpei, FM 96941, tel. 320-2797; fax 320-3797), six miles east of Kolonia at U, is undoubtedly the best vacation hotel on Pohnpei—nothing is a close second. It's probably the most romantic hotel in all of Micronesia: great lodging, great food, everything seems to get done for each guest. Its 20 Pohnpei-style thatched bungalows with bamboo walls, oversized waterbeds, ceiling fans, and private bath run $80-95 s, $90-105 d (depending on the view from the room). Air conditioning is unnecessary here as the tradewinds blow through the screening surrounding the rooms. Patti and Bob Arthur wisely opted for ceiling fans instead. They also wisely opted to leave telephones out of the rooms.

It is hard to believe this hotel is almost 20 years old. The Village, awarded for its accomplishment as an ecotourism hotel, was ahead of its time when founded and has been able to maintain the edge.

Also out of town, but near to Kolonia, is the **Nantehlik Hotel** (P.O. Box 225, Kolonia, Pohnpei FM 96941, tel. 320-4981, fax 320-4983). Rooms at this riverfront hotel go for $55 s, $75 d.

Apartments

Pohnpei has a number of apartment hotels that take day guests. Their prices are quite economical, particularly if you are traveling with a family. If you cook at home, your savings will increase.

In the heart of town is the new **Yvonne's Hotel** (P.O. Box 688, Kolonia, Pohnpei, 96941, tel. 320-4953), with many units having kitchens. Rentals start at $45.

Across the street from the library, and near the U.S. Embassy, is the **Nihco Apartments** (tel. 320-2135, fax 320-3800), with two-bedroom units going for as low as $50.

Farther from town on the road to the communications center is the 12-unit **C Star Apartelle** (P.O. Box 279, Kolonia, Pohnpei, FM 94961, tel. 320-3460, fax 320-3399). Prices start at $60 s, $75 d, with a three-bedroom unit going for $125. Discounts are offered for commercial travelers there for a longer stay.

Resort Islands
There are a number of islands in the Pohnpei lagoon with guest facilities. These "resorts" provide simple cottages, usually without indoor plumbing or electricity. They are inexpensive and provide a chance to slow down, if you don't mind roughing it a bit.

Heg's Garden Island (formerly Joy Island, P.O. Box 175, Kolonia, Pohnpei, FM 96941, tel. 320-3686) is set on a sandy reef islet near Nan Madol on the southeast side of Pohnpei. The swimming is great—bring snorkeling gear. Accommodations are $10 pp in one of 12 unfurnished thatched cottages. There's ample fresh water for washing, and an electric generator is used at night. Bedding (if required) is $2 pp extra. There's no restaurant or snack bar so bring your own food, unless you've made advance arrangements.

Black Coral Island (P.O. Box 1519, Kolonia, Pohnpei, FM 96941, tel. 320-4869) off the southwest side of Pohnpei, is similar to Heg's Garden Island and roughly the same price. But at $35 roundtrip, the boat over is more expensive if there are only one or two of you. For information call 320-2440 or ask at the Tourist Commission in Kolonia. Black Coral also welcomes day guests at $5 pp.

At Enipein ask for Joseph Paulus, who sometimes provides basic accommodations in thatched huts on Laiap or **Rainbow Island**—he'll take you across in his boat. For advance information about staying on Rainbow Island ask at the Cliff Rainbow Hotel (tel. 320-2415) in Kolonia.

FOOD

Pohnpei has a number of interesting and reasonably priced Japanese restaurants.

The **Joy Restaurant** (lunch Mon.-Sat., dinner Sunday only) is the most interesting spot in town

SAKAU

Listen for the rhythmic pounding leading to a *sakau* house. *Sakau*, made from a pepper shrub root, is pounded on a flat stone and squeezed through hibiscus fibers to produce a mildly narcotic, powerfully anesthetizing drink similar to Fijian *kava*, but stronger. The *sakau* is generously served in a half coconut shell. The taste is a combination of woodiness and chalk. Getting *puputa* (high) on *sakau* is a strange experience: your head may stay coherent, but when you try to get up, your knees have disappeared.

You can try it in the villages on Pohnpei or at a *sakau* house in Kolonia (25 cents a cup). A *nahs* is an assembly house for drinking *sakau*. For genuine hand-pounded *sakau*, visit the **Nan Uht Sakau Bar** a few blocks up the street running directly north from the Palm Terrace: their slogan is "we pound it on the rock." Others are the **Happy Landing**, opposite the Hotel Pohnpei, and the **JW Bar** down the hill from the old Community College. Most nights some form of live music materializes at Happy Landing. *Sakau* bars are continually changing locations, so ask around if these places seem closed. Arrive early because the houses often run out of *sakau* by 8:30 p.m. In Micronesia, *sakau* is found only on Pohnpei.

One health concern is that *sakau* may be made with untreated water. Unless you have a cast-iron stomach, you may wish to make inquiries before drinking.

for lunch. Terrific Japanese-style bento box lunches are $5-7. It is a popular restaurant with expats, local business people, and government workers. On crowded days someone may be seated with you at your table, which is a great way to meet people.

The nearby **Joy Hotel Restaurant** serves a similar though less extensive menu at prices similar to the Joy Restaurant. The food is as good (or better) than at the Joy Restaurant, though the atmosphere is missing the energy.

The **South Park Hotel Restaurant** serves mediocre Japanese food, which with a beer will set you back about $20 for dinner. From the lanai is a great view of the Sokehs. But a better way to enjoy the view is to skip the meal here and get a happy hour beer ($2) next door at the Cliff Hotel's Across the Street bar.

The most elegant restaurant on Pohnpei is the **Tattoed Irishman** at the Village Hotel. The restaurant is covered but open-air with a view out over the mangrove forest to the ocean below. In the distance, even Sokeh Rocks can be seen. The food is good and plentiful. Dinner with a beer or two will cost you about $25. The restaurant also serves breakfast and lunch.

Sei's Restaurant is about 50 feet before the turnoff to the U.S. Embassy. It's housed in a wonderful room, quite spacious, with a high beamed ceiling and planked floor. The tables are large and well spaced. Most of the menu features Japanese food, which is quite good, though not inexpensive. The best buys are Wednesday lunch ($6.50) and Saturday dinner ($12), advertised as:

Viking Dinner
(Smorgasbord)
Hawaiian style
All you can eat

The **China Restaurant** (closed Sunday) offers fairly good, though expensive, Chinese food. Their special group menus for four or more are the best buys.

The **PCR Restaurant,** just down the road from the China Restaurant, features a little bit of everything: Japanese food, steaks and seafood, pizza, spaghetti and chicken. Try the seafood pizza.

The **Cafe Ole** is a small luncheonette next to the Ambros Store. It serves lunch from a steam table. It also serves breakfast, but the best working definition of eternity is the time it takes to get a cup of coffee here.

OTHER PRACTICALITIES

Entertainment
Pohnpei is blessed (or from another perspective—cursed) with some of the great bars of the Pacific.

Across the Street, across the street from the Cliff Rainbow Hotel, which operates it, overlooks the water and beautiful Sokehs Rock. This comfortable, open-air room serves beer for $2 during happy hour.

Pres. Bailey Olter (left) and local author Gene Ashby at the Palm Terrace, Kolonia

The **Tattoed Irishman** at the Village Hotel also has an open air bar with an unsurpassed ocean view. Its elegant island ambience makes it a fantastic place to watch the sunset.

Down by the small boat marina, **Rumors** sits at the edge of the mangroves. Happy hour is 4-6 p.m.; Saturday and Sunday it opens at noon. Snacks are available, but there is no meal service.

The **Palm Terrace Bar** (which survived the demise of the Palm Terrace Hotel and restaurant) is a hot, crowded, wonderful local watering hole. On weekday afternoons a delightful mix of island characters saunters in after work (ask for author Gene Ashby). By 5 p.m. it'll be full of American expats but by 9 p.m. their places will have been taken over by Micronesians. This is the place to be if you want to meet people.

The **Micronesian Cultural Center** at Nett offers programs for visitors including local dancing, *sakau* pounding, and craft demonstrations for $12.50 pp (five person minimum). Another similar cultural center is found in U. You cannot just drive out and expect anything to be happening. Ask the Tourist Commission, your hotel, or a travel agent to make arrangements at least 24 hours in advance.

STATE OF POHNPEI 111

Sports and Recreation

The biggest dive shop on Pohnpei is the **Phoenix Marine Sport Club** (PMSC) (P.O. Box 387, Pohnpei, FM 96941, tel. 320-5678). Diving on the dropoffs just outside the reef passes costs $95 for two tanks including lunch and drinks (four-person minimum). This includes tanks but you will have to pay extra for any other equipment you rent. Diving at Ant and Pakin atolls is $105 for two tanks. A full day of picnicking and snorkeling, usually at Black Coral Island or Ant, is $55 pp, lunch $5 extra (five-person minimum). PMSC also offers deep-sea trolling at $500 half day, $700 full day (lunch and drinks included) for up to seven persons. Pickups are made at all hotels upon request. Trolling or reef fishing can also be arranged through **Micro Tours** (P.O. Box 459, Pohnpei, FM 96941, tel. 320-3683, fax 320-5528) or **Pohnpei Sport Fishing** (tel. 320-5417).

Joy Ocean Service, based at the Joy Hotel (P.O. Box 484, Pohnpei, FM 96941, tel. 320-2336), also offers diving. Scuba diving from the Village Hotel is $70 pp for three persons, $75 pp for two persons, or $100 for one person.

Divers should bring their own regulator, buoyancy compensator, and gauges with them. A certification card is required for all equipment rentals and scuba trips. Too much sediment from heavy rainfall runoff precludes beach diving off the main island, but the channels through the barrier reef offer excellent possibilities to ~ caves and sharks in good weather. From

December through February waters are more likely to be rough.

There are a fair number of small tour and diving operators that open and close with some regularity. The Pohnpei Tourist Commission keeps a fairly up-to-date list (P.O. Box 66, Kolonia, Pohnpei, FM 96941, tel. 320-2421, fax 320-6019).

Enipein Marine Park, located on Pohnpei's southern coast, offers a unique opportunity to explore coastal mangrove ecology. This ecosystem is vital not only to the sea life of the coast, but to that of the nearby reefs. For about $50 you will be picked up in Kolonia and driven to Enipein where you will ride a canoe through the canals of the mangrove forest to a reef for swiming and snorkeling. Afterward, you're served an island style meal before being brought back to Kolonia. There are not trips everyday, so when you arrive in Kolonia, make arrangements. If the park has enough requests, it will organize additional trips. You can contact the park directly at P.O. Box 264, Kolonia, Pohnpei, FM 96941, tel. 320-2693. The Tourist Commission or your hotel can also make arrangements for you.

A local nonprofit organization, **Micronesia Bound, Inc.** (Aramas Kapw Program, P.O. Box 326, Kolonia, Pohnpei, FM 96941, tel. 320-2365), can provide guides for a mountain trek across the center of the island. Prices begin at $100 (two days) and $150 (three days) for two persons. They also have five- and fourteen-day expeditions that may include jungle survival training,

Boathouses and kitchens line the lagoon side at Mwoakilloa; the people sleep in houses on the breezier ocean side.

DAVID STANLEY

RAUTENSTRAUCH-JOEST MUSEUM, COLOGNE, GERMANY

An imposing figure from Nukuoro, 400 km south-west of Pohnpei. Abstract female images of this kind were draped with flowers and mats during island ceremonies.

wilderness treks, "ocean expeditions" (canoe trips—paddling around the island), camping, community service, and more. A less demanding one-day tour around the island by car including stops at two villages, Sokehs Rock, a waterfall, and a mangrove swamp costs $25 pp. The organization is located next to the Immigration office, not far from the old Spanish wall.

Shopping

Handicrafts such as baskets, grass skirts, wall hangings, trays, model canoes, and woodcarvings are sold at shops in the **Public Market** on the lower east side of town. Behind this is **Pohnpei Products Mart,** selling local fruits and vegetables plus a few handicrafts and local coconut oil shampoo and soap. Next to this store is the pepper processing factory where Pohnpei pepper is graded, sorted, and bagged. It's okay to go inside and look around. Several general stores are also found in this area. Stock up on supplies and color print film at the **Kolonia Coop,** a Wild West general store.

Excellent Polynesian handicrafts such as woodcarvings of dolphins and sharks, shellwork, woven wall hangings, coconut graters, model outrigger canoes, canoe bailers, mobiles, food and oil bowls, tackle boxes, and fish or eel traps are available at the **gift shop** at Porakiet. You may see some carvers at work near here. (See "Kolonia" under "Sights," above). Joy Restaurant also sells crafts.

The **Pohnpei Public Library** (P.O. Box 284, Kolonia, Pohnpei, FSM 96941) near the Palm Terrace sells calendars, postcards, and posters of Micronesian birds and fish. **Phoenix Marine Sports Club** has colorful T-shirts.

For more mundane needs, the newly expanded **Palm Terrace Store** and the Ambros store are probably the best places to shop. Downstairs at **Ambros** is a grocery store, and upstairs is clothing and sundries.

Services

The Bank of Hawaii (tel. 320-2543) and Bank of Guam (tel. 320-2550), both open Mon.-Thurs. 9:30 a.m.-2:30 p.m. (till 4 p.m. on Friday), have adjacent branches in the commercial block just below the Pohnpei legislature. A couple of good travel agencies are in offices above them. The Bank of FSM (tel. 320-2724) is in lower Kolonia.

You may place long distance telephone calls from the Telecommunications Corporation on the main street near the post office, weekdays 8 a.m.-2 p.m. The cost for calls to the U. S. is dropping, but still can be quite expensive. Address mail to Pohnpei, FM 96941.

The FSM Immigration office (tel. 320-2606), across from the baseball field and next to the old Spanish wall, will give visa extensions 30 days at a time, up to 90 days maximum.

Several countries have diplomatic missions in Kolonia. The Chinese Embassy (tel. 320-5575) near the Public Market is hard to miss, and above the Bank of FSM across the street is the Australian Embassy (P.O. Box S, Kolonia, Pohnpei, FSM 96941, tel. 320-5448). The new Japanese Embassy is across the street from the Australian Embassy. The United States Embassy (P.O. Box 1286, Kolonia, Pohnpei, FSM 96941, tel. 320-2187) is near the old Japanese meteorological station on the south side of town.

Information

The Pohnpei Tourist Commission (open weekdays, P.O. Box 66, Kolonia, Pohnpei, FM 96941, tel. 320-2421, fax 320-6019), beside the small Japanese tank on the main street, can provide current information on local resorts on reef islands and cultural events. It also sells William H. Stewart's excellent *Map of Pohnpei and the Ancient Ruins of Nan Madol* ($2.50).

The Pohnpei Public Library is near the Palm Terrace store.

One of the best travel books you can ever read is *Pohnpei, An Island Argosy* by Gene Ashby (Rainy Day Press, P.O. Box 574, Kolonia, Pohnpei, FM 96941). Gene explores every aspect of Pohnpei, and copies are usually available at souvenir shops and restaurants in Kolonia. Other good local books are *Micronesian Customs and Beliefs* and *Never and Always,* which include fascinating tales told by students at the Community College of Micronesia, and edited by Gene.

Radio station WSZD-AM broadcasts at 1450.

GETTING THERE

Pohnpei Airport (PNI) is on Takatik Island, two miles northwest of Kolonia. Most of the hotels offer shuttles to meet the flights. Car rental booths and a snack bar open for arrivals and departures. Airport departure tax is $10. Signs warn against the spitting of betel nut juice.

Continental Air Micronesia Island Hopper heads west from Hawaii Monday, Wednesday, and Friday, and leaves Guam heading east on Monday, Wednesday, and Friday. Remember that because of the International Date Line, you lose a day between Honolulu and Pohnpei. Reconfirm your onward reservations at the Air Mike

office (tel. 320-2424) at the airport upon arrival.

Air Nauru has a flight a week from Nauru to Pohnpei, Guam, and Manila. From Nauru you can make connections to or from Kiribati and to the South Pacific.

Pacific Missionary Aviation (P.O. Box 517, Pohnpei, FM 96941, tel. 320-2796) has an office in a hanger behind the main airport terminal. Their shuttle operates between Pohnpei and Pingelap ($70 one-way) Monday and Friday, and between Pohnpei and Mwoakilloa on the same days ($60 one-way). Book ahead if possible as the flights are often full. This company has done commendable work in Micronesia, providing air-and-sea rescue, medical evacuations, and flying health clinics.

GETTING AROUND

Field Trips

The **Island Affairs Office** (tel. 320-2710), near the governor's office behind the Pohnpei legislature, offers two monthly field trips on the MV *Micro Glory.* The four-day eastern trip visits Mwoakilloa and Pingelap ($31 cabin roundtrip), while the nine-day southern trip calls at Ngatik, Nukuoro, and Kapingamarangi ($89 cabin roundtrip). Cabin passengers must pay $2 pp daily extra for berthing. The ship has seven double cabins, usually booked well in advance; deck fares are about one-third these amounts.

Check with **SeAir Transportation Agency** (tel. 320-2866) downtown for boat tickets to Mwoakilloa ($6.24), Pingelap ($9.78), and Kosrae ($18.30). All fares are deck class (no cabins available) and meals are extra.

Boats to the outer islands routinely leave anywhere from 48 hours to a week late. If you're not prepared for this, *take a plane.* Complaining will not be productive.

By Road

Taxis and minibuses around Kolonia or out to the airport charge a flat fare of $1 pp. Just flag down any taxi you see cruising the streets around Kolonia. To Palikir the taxi fare is $2 pp; or to the Village Hotel, $5.

Minibuses to Madolenihmw and Kitti can usually be found in the lower town around the market or near Ace Commercial Center. On their regular runs these charge about $2 pp to anywhere on the island, and the easiest time to catch them is early morning or late afternoon weekdays. They only leave every couple of hours, so be prepared to wait. The minibuses don't run all the way around Pohnpei: eastbound they run as far as PATS, westbound as far as Enipein. Other minibuses run to Sokehs for 50 cents pp.

Hitching on the roads to and from Kolonia isn't too difficult; there's not much traffic, but drivers will take you if they have room. Assume, however, that any pickup truck that stops to give you a ride outside Kolonia will expect you to pay a couple of bucks.

Pohnpei Bicycle Rental (tel. 320-2875), on the main street next to Ponape House, rents bicycles for $10 a day.

Car Rentals

About a dozen agencies, large and small, rent cars for $40 and up a day with unlimited mileage. Check the rental time and fuel level marked on your contract before you drive off—and make sure there's a spare tire. Insurance is not always available. Be particularly careful driving off paved roads since it is easy to ding the car. Most car rentals will deliver and pick up at your hotel. It is easiest to have your hotel make the arrangements for you. If you wish to do so yourself you might try: **Penny Rent A Car** (tel. 320-2940), with offices at the airport and in the lower town; **Hervis Rent-A-Car** (tel. 320-2784) located nearby; **Jerry's Car Rental** (tel. 330-2769), below the Chinese Embassy near the market; or **H & E Car Rental** (tel. 330-2413) behind the Australian Embassy.

Speedboats

Speedboats for the islands east of Kolonia (Lenger, Parem, Mwand) leave from the dock near the market. The **Pohnpei Island Transportation Co.** or PITC (P.O. Box 750, Kolonia, Pohnpei, FM 96941, tel. 320-2409) by the Public Market rents a speedboat at $150 per day (gas included) for up to three people (additional persons extra). Take this boat right around Pohnpei, visiting the old Japanese seaplane ramp at Lenger Island, Nan Madol, and Rainbow Island on the way.

If the PITC boat is unavailable, try **Joe Henry** (P.O. Box 788, Kolonia, Pohnpei, FM 96941, tel. 320-2339). Joe charges about $50 pp (lunch included) for the Nan Madol trip (half an hour at Nan Dowas and a boat ride around the rest).

THE OUTER ISLANDS

Pakin and Ant, two small atolls off the west coast of Pohnpei, have wonderful beaches and excellent diving. Numerous seabirds nest on **Ant,** and the diving in the S-shaped pass is superb during slack water (beware of strong currents when the tide is running). Ask about trips to Ant at any dive shop. Yachties should obtain permission from the Nanpei family in Kolonia before visiting.

Ngatik (Sapwuahfik), southwest of Pohnpei, was resettled by Pohnpeians after the crew of a British whaler massacred all the male inhabitants in 1837. Only a few people share **Oroluk** atoll with hawksbill and Pacific green sea turtles.

Mwoakilloa (Mokil)

This clean, jewel-like atoll 97 miles east of Pohnpei consists of three islands: Coconut, Taro, and Home (where the 300 atoll residents live). Lined with coral stones, Main Street runs right down the middle of Home, from the elementary school to the airstrip at the far end. Canoe houses and kitchens line the lagoon side of the road, while sleeping houses are on the ocean side. There's only one store in the village, often completely sold out. No dogs are allowed on this island.

The eastern field-trip ship from Pohnpei often calls at Mwoakilloa, both on the outward and inbound journeys, allowing a stop in between of a couple of days. Camp at the airstrip or ask about accommodations at the Municipal Building. Mwoakilloa is mostly for avid snorkelers, as you can soon exhaust the above-water attractions. Red coral washes onto the ocean beaches.

Pingelap

Pingelap, between Pohnpei and Kosrae, is a three-island atoll (pop. 520) with a big sunken taro patch *(inipwel)* behind the village. The snorkeling is good off the east end of the airstrip. The wide main island would take several hours to walk around at low tide. At night, Jan.-April, is-

DAVID STANLEY

Sunday school at Pingelap

landers using hand-held nets catch flying fish they attract with burning torches.

The chief magistrate can arrange accommodations at the Municipal Building, or ask for storekeeper Larry Lundstrum, who sometimes takes in guests. There are several small stores on Pingelap.

Polynesian Islands

The people of Nukuoro and Kapingamarangi atolls are Polynesians. There are 42 tiny islands on the **Nukuoro** reef but most of the 820 people live on the largest.

Although 33 islets compose **Kapingamarangi** atoll, 366 miles southwest of Pohnpei, the population lives on the adjacent islets of Touhou and Ueru, which are linked by a concrete bridge. Tiny Touhou, which you can walk around in 10 minutes, houses the majority. The homes are arranged in clusters, each of which belongs to a different family. Yachts require a pilot to enter the lagoon, where an American plane and a Japanese ship lie submerged. Overwater toilets are a quaint part of Kapinga. Kapingamarangi has suffered Hanson's disease (leprosy) epidemics.

Often doctoral students and other researchers into Pohnpeian culture are stymied by incomplete answers from Pohnpeian informants. Traditionally, to tell all that one knows about a subject or a story is thought to cause the informant to lose part of himself. Legends, like knowledge of traditional medical cures told by elders, might only be passed on in their complete forms to selected family members, oftentimes the youngest male member. Since it is unlikely that the youngest will inherit land, the secret knowledge could be his legacy from the family.

—GENE ASHBY, *AN ISLAND ARGOSY*

STATE OF CHUUK

INTRODUCTION

Driving around Weno's lush north shore, the road though paved is deeply potholed. I slowed down as I saw two children and their young mother sitting in the roadway, cutting coconuts with machetes. Behind them stood a corrugated metal shed on which had been spray-painted 90210.

Near the lagoonside market sat a brown-skinned woman, gold encircling her two front teeth. She was wearing a flower garland, a lava lava, and a Snapple T-shirt.

The State of Chuuk (known to generations of sailors and other foreigners as Truk) consists of 11 high, mangrove-fringed volcanic islands in the sapphire blue Chuuk lagoon and a series of 14 outlying atolls and low islands. The Chuuk lagoon, 40 miles across at its widest point, is circled by one of the world's longest barrier reefs. Submerged in the lagoon is a Japanese fleet, destroyed by United States air power in 1944.

The reef-locked islands in the lagoon, the heart of the state and home to 80% of its people, compare with Pohnpei's or Kosrae's lush peaks. The state's outer island groups, the Halls, Westerns, and Mortlocks, resemble the palm and sand atolls of the Marshalls. Visitors can explore three aspects of Chuuk: Weno (formerly Moen), the state's administrative center; the other islands in Chuuk lagoon, all rural; and the outlying atolls—in all, 290 islands from which to choose.

Most visitors to Chuuk (other than those who come to do business on Weno) come for its unique wreck dive sites. This leaves all that is above sea level an unexplored land of adventure for tourists. There are many opportunities to escape to the outliers. Boats constantly leave for lagoon islands and there are several departures a week to the even more remote outer islands.

Wartime Chuuk

In Chuuk, World War II is simply called *the* World War, or even *the* War. What the rest of the world calls World War II hit Chuuk with particular brutality. Chuuk was the main Japanese naval base in the central Pacific, the "Gibraltar of the Pacific," protected by the encircling reef and giant guns in caves and tunnels guarding the passes. Most of the entrenched firepower was taken off obsolete cruisers and battleships and positioned on the hillsides. The Japanese had four airstrips in Chuuk lagoon, two on Weno and one each on Etten and Parem.

On 17 February 1944, the United States unleashed Operation Hailstone, one of the most devastating aerial attacks in history. For two days and one night, aircraft from nine carriers hammered the islands in 30 waves. Submarines posted outside the passes caught fleeing vessels. Japan lost 250 planes, nearly 60 vessels, and thousands of men, compared to a United States loss of only 26 aircraft. The 180,000 tons of shipping sunk set a two-day World War II record.

This defeat would have been even more devastating except for an American reconnaissance flight over the lagoon on 4 February that tipped the Japanese off to the impending attack. On 10 February all the Japanese warships present (including a battleship, two aircraft carriers, five heavy and four light cruisers, and 20 destroyers) withdrew to Palau. Most of the ships wrecked in the lagoon were merchant ships converted to war use. It is difficult to understand, however, how the same Japanese Navy that three years earlier had realized the vulnerability of American ships in Pearl Harbor could think that Chuuk Lagoon could be protected from a massive air assault.

The 45,000 Japanese survivors on Chuuk were bypassed as the United States forces moved on to capture Saipan. Both Japanese and Chuukese suffered famine due to an American blockade. In 1946 the United States Navy established the present administrative center on Weno, replacing the earlier center on Tonoas Island (Dublon).

Under Chuuk lagoon lies the Japanese navy. Sailors presumed dead.

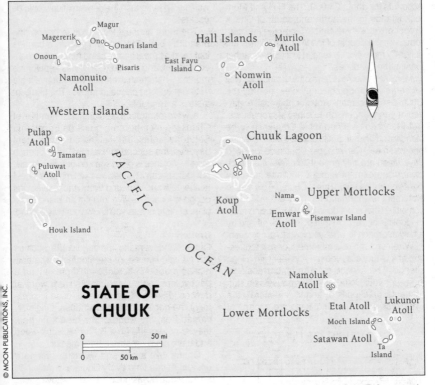

Magur
Magererik   Ono   Onari Island   Hall Islands   Murilo
Onoun   Pisaris   East Fayu   Atoll
                           Island   Nomwin
Namonuito   Atoll
Atoll

Western Islands

Pulap   Chuuk Lagoon
Atoll
   Tamatan   Weno
Puluwat
Atoll

PACIFIC

                    Koup   Nama   Upper Mortlocks
                    Atoll   Emwar   Pisemwar Island
   Houk Island   Atoll

OCEAN

STATE OF   Namoluk
CHUUK   Atoll

          0   50 mi   Lower Mortlocks   Etal Atoll   Lukunor
          0   50 km   Moch Island   Atoll

                                          Satawan Atoll   Ta
                                                         Island

© MOON PUBLICATIONS, INC.

Economy

On Weno, businesses are scattered but are primarily located on or near the road between the airport and the boat dock. Small, scarcely stocked stores can be found in the other villages of Weno, with even fewer stores on onter islands in the lagoon. Weno is home to a tuna fleet, but sees little benefit from it. With approximately 200 hotel rooms, tourism is not a major economic force. The state government is often on the verge of not paying its bills, despite the money it receives from the United States under the Compact (see "Toward Self-Government" in the "Introduction" to the Federated States of Micronesia chapter).

There are no credible statistics concerning the economy of the other islands within the lagoon. Some people commute to Weno either for government jobs or to sell farm products.

On some of the islands, such as Fefan, people have substantial gardens. But the line between someone considered "unemployed" and someone who is a "subsistence" fisherman is a fine one. Western economic concepts are difficult to apply to this third world economy.

Many Chuukese lack the sufficient education and management skills needed by the cash economy. Consequently, a number of Americans remain in positions of management and increasingly, as in other states of the FSM, Filipinos are taking jobs of middle management. This threatens to become a vicious cycle, with the Chuukese feeling further alienated from the cash economic sector.

The People

Approximately half of the 100,000 inhabitants of the FSM live in the State of Chuuk. Weno

accounts for about 25,000. The Hall and Mortlock Islands to the north and south of Chuuk
proper are closely related in language and customs, but the people of the Western Islands are
culturally more closely related to islanders farther
west in the Carolines.

Many Micronesians from other islands, as well
as some anthropological studies, portray the
Chuukese as cantankerous or aggressive, particularly in comparison to other Micronesians.
But the visitor will find most Chuukese to be
friendly and helpful. Smile and say hello to everyone you meet. *Ran annim* is Chuukese for "good
day." If you are silly enough to provoke a direct,
clear disagreement with a Chuukese, at some
point you will be told, "This is Chuuk." This simple
statement is shorthand for "You are asking for
something that is not done here. Stop being rude,
the topic is closed." At that point back off and try
a new approach to what you wish to accomplish.

When you make a statement or ask a question of a Chuukese, you may be met with a long
silence. The silence may be embarrassingly
long—for you. Do not take this pause as a sign
of mental weakness or anger. It is merely the
Chuukese way. The Chuukese are experts at

waiting. To try to rush the conversation would be
useless.

The most unusual local food is *oppot,* ripe
breadfruit buried for up to a year in a banana
leaf-lined pit *(nas)* before being removed, knead-
ed, cooked, and served. *Oppot* was kept for the
months when fresh breadfuit was not available
or to eat on long canoe journeys. The pungent
taste is memorable.

A word of caution: A significant number of
Chuukese men become drunk on Friday and
Saturday nights, particularly on government
paydays, the second and fourth Friday of each
month. Violence is often sparked between locals,
but tourists can also become victims so it's best
neither to wander around Weno those evenings
nor go to local bars. Weno is not an island to explore at night unless you know your way around.

Crafts

Outer islanders make fine handicrafts, such as
the *tapwanu* masks of the Mortlocks, the only
masks made in Micronesia. Representing a
benevolent spirit, these masks were worn at
dances to ward off typhoons, or used to orna-
ment the gable of the men's house. Originally
carved from the wood of the breadfruit tree,
they're now made from lighter hibiscus wood
and have been renamed "devil masks."

Chuuk love sticks and war clubs also are
unique. At one time every Chuukese male had
an individually designed love stick. Love sticks
were up to 13 feet long, so the young man could
thrust the object through the wall of a hut and
reach the girl of his affections, who might be
sleeping on the other side of the room. He would
then entangle her hair in the long stick and tug to
wake her. She would know by the feel of the
stick whose it was; if she pulled it inside the hut
he could enter; if she shook it she was coming
outside; and if she pushed it out, he was rejected. Dr. Freud would have had a field day ana-
lyzing this custom.

The frightening wooden war bludgeons and
shark-tooth-studded knuckle-dusters of Chuuk
were designed for less romantic encounters.
Handbags, baskets, trays, stools, wall hangings,
lava lava, and grass skirts complete the crafts
scene. Note that many nontraditional objects,
such as carved faces and story boards, are also
sold. Some are quite decorative and interesting.

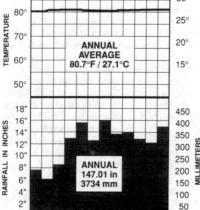

CHUUK'S CLIMATE

ANNUAL
AVERAGE
80.7°F / 27.1°C

ANNUAL
147.01 in
3734 mm

Many women in Chuuk wear truly beautiful tortoiseshell combs in their hair. They are occasionally seen for sale and in all honesty look more beautiful than imitation plastic ones. However, the real material often comes from severely endangered species and should not be bought for that reason. Further, it is illegal to import this material into the United States and most European countries.

Health

Take extra care with the water on Weno. Don't drink tap water without first boiling or chemically purifying it. Be careful with raw fruit or vegetables you suspect were washed in local, untreated water.

SIGHTS OF WENO

Weno is a dirty island nestled in one of the most beautiful settings on earth. Trash and wrecked cars lie scattered along potholed roads. Seawalls wreck the visual unity of the lagoon shore. But the view from Weno across newly forming mangrove forests as the sun sets behind the Tol group can be sublimely beautiful. The commercial center, an industrial zone amid housing, stretches along the west shore of Weno from the airport to beyond the port. Nantaku, the governmental center of Chuuk State, is on the saddle road heading east. Dense forests and grasslands fill the interior of this, the second-largest island in the lagoon.

Western Weno

If this island has a downtown, it is the small-boat harbor and the market in front of it. Outer island women come by boat to sell avocados, pineapples, and beautiful leis made of plumeria and soft green leaves. Rice, clothing, and other goods are sold out of panel trucks. The area is jumpy, dirty, quirky, and filled with tropical energy. Men sit in the boats they used to transport people in

The tapwanu mask of the Mortlock Islands is the only type of mask known in Micronesia, and may once have ornamented the gable of a men's house. Carved from the wood of the breadfruit tree, it was thought to protect the fruit of that tree during storms.

from the outer islands, waiting to return them at the end of the day. The Seaside Restaurant overlooks it all.

Nearby is the **Chuuk Ethnographic Exhibition Center,** upstairs and accessible from the Chuuk Visitors Bureau (open weekdays 8 a.m.-5 p.m., admission $1.50). Here you'll see *tapwanu* devil masks of hibiscus wood, *fenai* love sticks of mangrove wood, *tor lava lava* skirts of hibiscus fiber, model canoes, war clubs, fish traps, war relics, and other crafts. World War II artifacts take up half of the museum.

For groceries, head to the metal-corrugated **Truk Trading Company** (TTC) or nearby **Shigeto's.** TTC is the best place in town to get hardware, clothing, or photography supplies. Shigeto's store is on the inland side of the road, about 150 feet past the commercial pier when coming from the airport.

A big **Japanese gun** is in a tunnel dubbed "Nefo Cave," a short walk up from the governor's residence at Nantaku. Follow the road due south from the courthouse as far as a large, green water tank. The tunnel is 150 feet to the right. There's an excellent view of Weno center and the lagoon from here.

The Japanese had an airstrip at **South Field,** the level area just east of the Truk Continental Hotel. As you approach this part of the island, the land gets more lush and you will see occasional taro patches as well as bananas and breadfruit trees. A **coconut processing plant** now sits on the vast concrete platform that once sloped into the lagoon to permit seaplane traffic. Inside you can see soap, body oil, and shampoo being made from copra. Drop into the Continental Hotel and its beachside bar to enjoy the superb lagoon view.

Roads run along the north and west sides of Weno. It's a three-hour walk on a level footpath along the southeast coast between the ends of these roads. Eastbound you get a good view of grassy Mt. Witipon. There's a beach at **Nukanap** where you can stop for a swim.

Northern Weno

To climb to the grassy summit of **Mt. Tonachau** (750 feet), take the road beside the rock crusher past the airport up as far as the U.S. Air Force Civic Action Team (CAT) headquarters. The overgrown trail follows the power lines that run up the ridge just before the "Cat House." It's a stiff climb that can be slippery near the top, and high sharp grass on the slopes forces you to stay on the trail. Bring your camera. One story explains that Tonachau is a great octopus whose arms once stretched across the lagoon; another claims the hero Soukatau brought the great basalt knob atop Tonachau with him from Kosrae. Soukatau's son, Souwoniras, built his *wuut* (meetinghouse) on the mountain.

Tunnuk holds the major Catholic enclave in Micronesia. At **Fairo** village on the lagoon near Tunnuk is a traditional *wuut* built by Puluwat islanders in 1990, with support from the Micronesian Institute, as a community center. A canoe house stands alongside.

To reach the small, attractive **Wichon Falls** and swimming hole on the northeast side of Weno, walk about a third of a mile up a dirt road from Peniesene and ask directions—it's unmarked. You'll see a cross-section of village life along the way.

As you head farther north round the island, the scenery becomes very lush with many old, wild mango trees. Unfortunately, as on much of the island, junk and garbage is ever present by the side of the road and the ocean. In another 50 years, tourists may come to see the remains of old Chevy's and Ford's left to rot by the side of the road, much as they now come to see naval wrecks.

Eastern Weno

There are some interesting sights in eastern Weno, but the pavement ends before the high school. After that, the dirt road is extremely rough and we recommend against driving it in a con-

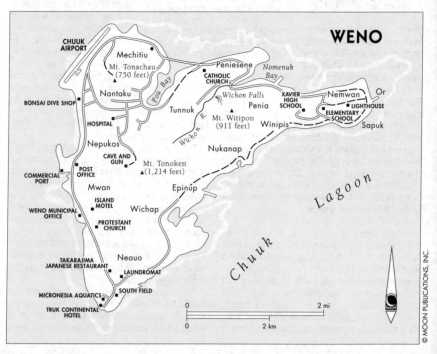

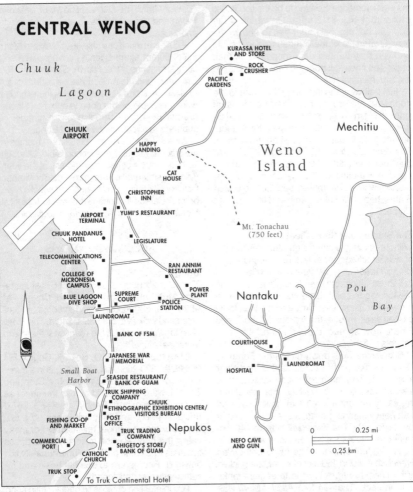

CENTRAL WENO

Chuuk

Lagoon

CHUUK AIRPORT

KURASSA HOTEL AND STORE

ROCK CRUSHER

PACIFIC GARDENS

Weno Island

Mechitiu

HAPPY LANDING

CAT HOUSE

CHRISTOPHER INN

AIRPORT TERMINAL

YUMI'S RESTAURANT

CHUUK PANDANUS HOTEL

LEGISLATURE

TELECOMMUNICATIONS CENTER

▲ Mt. Tonachau (750 feet)

COLLEGE OF MICRONESIA CAMPUS

RAN ANNIM RESTAURANT

Pou

Bay

BLUE LAGOON DIVE SHOP

SUPREME COURT

POWER PLANT

Nantaku

POLICE STATION

LAUNDROMAT

BANK OF FSM

COURTHOUSE

JAPANESE WAR MEMORIAL

LAUNDROMAT

Small Boat Harbor

SEASIDE RESTAURANT/ BANK OF GUAM

HOSPITAL

TRUK SHIPPING COMPANY

CHUUK ETHNOGRAPHIC EXHIBITION CENTER/ VISITORS BUREAU

FISHING CO-OP AND MARKET

POST OFFICE

Nepukos

TRUK TRADING COMPANY

COMMERCIAL PORT

SHIGETO'S STORE/ BANK OF GUAM

NEFO CAVE AND GUN

CATHOLIC CHURCH

TRUK STOP

To Truk Continental Hotel

| 0 | | 0.25 mi |
| 0 | | 0.25 km |

© MOON PUBLICATIONS, INC.

ventional car. Because there are no pickups or 4WD cars regularly available for rent on Chuuk, your options are limited: you can drive as far as you are able and then walk, or you can go on a tour. Most hotels will be able to arrange a tour, and the going rate seems to be about $15 pp.

Near the east end of Weno is **Xavier High School,** once a fortified Japanese radio communications center, to which the thickness of the cement walls and the steel hatches on the windows attest. After the war the Jesuits purchased the building for $1000 and made it into the best four-year high school in Micronesia, with students coming from throughout the region. The view of the lagoon from the roof is excellent.

An abandoned **Japanese lighthouse** *(totai)* in reasonably good condition stands on the highest point of the Sapuk Peninsula. Get there by following a footpath from the elementary school near Xavier High School, or from Or village to the east. Someone claiming to be the lighthouse owner may ask $1-2 pp at Or, which is fair enough, but pay only after you're shown the way. Ownership of the lighthouse is in dispute and you may be asked for money more than once. The fine view from the lighthouse makes it worth the nuisance.

Just below, at the bottom of the slope to the northeast, are several huge **eight-inch naval guns** in big metal housings. The guns are off an Italian armored cruiser purchased by Argentina and sold to Japan. One bears the imprint Stabilimento Armstrong Pozzuoli 1902. These guns point straight out toward Northeast Pass. Looking at these fearsome weapons you'll appreciate what a wise military decision the United States made in 1944 to bomb and then bypass Chuuk.

The Sunken Japanese Fleet

Without doubt, the world's greatest assortment of war wreckage for divers to visit lies under Chuuk lagoon. A ghost fleet of 180,000 tons of Japanese ships and over 270 planes litter the shallow lagoon bed. Little was salvaged from the wartime air strikes; almost all the wrecks lie as they sank, most of them around Tonoas and Fefan, now shrouded in coral and home to schools of fish.

Sixty ships went down during the February 1944 air strike, and 40 others sank during other attacks. Among the most important wrecks is the *Shinkoku Maru,* a 503-foot oil tanker standing eerily upright just 40 feet down, covered with heavy marine growth, a site where a night dive is possible. The *Yamagiri Maru* is a 440-foot munitions ship loaded with 18-inch shells, now in 50 to 120 feet of water. The holds of the *San Francisco Maru,* in 150 feet of water, are packed with mines and trucks, while three light tanks rest on deck. The 494-foot *Aikoku Maru* was blown in half by an American dive-bomber, itself destroyed in the explosion. The largest wreck in the lagoon, the *Heian Maru,* a 526-foot submarine tender, lies 50 feet down.

Near Etten, and accessible to snorkelers, is the *Fujikawa Maru,* a 437-foot armed aircraft ferry still containing Zero planes. Its stern is perhaps 20 feet below the surface at low tide. The front gun is clearly visible from the surface, as is the hoist for loading the ship, now dubbed the

"Devil's Altar." The *Dai Na Hino Maru,* between Fefan and Uman Islands, is also accessible to snorkelers.

A 372-foot munitions ship, the *Sankisan Maru,* full of 50mm ammunition, is covered with soft coral formations 50 feet down. Submarine I-169 *Shinohara* was lost because someone forgot to close the storm ventilation valve in the bridge when the 330-foot sub dove to avoid an air raid in April 1944. You can also visit a number of submerged Japanese planes off Etten.

June to September are the calmest months in the lagoon, with all wrecks accessible, although visibility may be better other months of the year. (Micronesia Aquatics recommends September, October, February, and March). All wrecks have been declared parts of an Underwater Historical Monument and it is illegal to take souvenirs.

ACCOMMODATIONS

Budget

The most economical stay in Weno is at the **Island Motel** (P.O. Box 728 Weno, Chuuk, FM 96942, tel. 330-4220). The 10 rooms, all carpeted and with TVs, are $35 s, $40 d. The motel is on the inland side of the road, past the Weno Municipal office.

Christopher Inn (P.O. Box 37, Chuuk, FM 96942, tel. 330-2652, fax 330-2207) is in a three-story concrete building above the Stop and Shop, toward the left and across the street as you leave the airport. Rooms are $47 s, $57 d (including tax), and they will knock off a few bucks for rooms without televisions. For many years, this hotel was the mainstay for business travelers to Chuuk, but it has unfortunately slid downhill. Rooms are extremely basic and insufficiently air conditioned.

Two interesting choices lie about a mile north of the airport. The **Pacific Gardens** (P.O. Box 494, Weno, Chuuk, FM 96942, tel. 330-4639, fax 330-2334) opened in 1993 in a well-kept, modern building. A room that rents for $50 s, $60 d, is actually a double room; there is a small kitchen but no oven or stove. Manager Levy I. Banadera is a gracious host who tries his best to please guests. Unlike most hotel rooms in Chuuk, there is even some color used to decorate the rooms. A word of caution: The

Pacific Gardens is right next to a rock crusher. On days that it is running (reportedly a day or two a month), it creates much noise and raises a great deal of dust.

The Quiet Corner restaurant is in the building, as is a bar that serves as a disco on the weekend—it's been said that things can get a bit rambunctious on those nights. There's an on-site laundromat where you can do your own wash or pay extra to have the hotel do it for you.

Across the street is **Kurassa Hotel** (P.O. Box 64, Weno, Chuuk, FM 96942, tel. 330-4415, fax 330-4355), where all the rooms have kitchenettes at $48. To rent a room, walk into the Kurassa Store, where someone will pass you off to someone else in the back office. Old men hang out in front of the store and one gets the feel and pace of a time gone by. This hotel defines funky and is definitely not for everyone. But it has an interesting oldtime feel to it. Try to get one of the older units above the store, rather than a newer unit to the side. The hotel has a fair number of permanent, local residents. Kurassa is not a rural village, but an interesting slice of urban-island, working-class life. The lagoon facing Kurassa looks fun to snorkel.

The **Chuuk Pandanus Hotel** (formerly the Chuuk Star Hotel; P.O. Box 1230, Weno, Chuuk, FM 96942, tel. 330-2040, fax 330-2045) is the newest hotel in Weno. It provides clean, safe rooms at $55 s, $65 d. The hotel has a sterile, unlived-in feel that hopefully will improve as it ages.

Expensive

Truk Continental Hotel (P.O. Box 340, Weno, Chuuk, FM 96942, tel. 330-2727, fax 330-2439) is the last hotel owned and operated by Continental Airlines. Regular room rates are $106 s, $118 d, but for commercial or government travelers who make their own reservations the rate drops to $88 s, $100 d; it's expensive, but a good value for Chuuk. The hotel is beautifully set in a coconut grove on the beach at the southwest corner of the island. There is great snorkeling right in front of the hotel's beach. It is the best hotel on the island and will fill up, so make reservations if possible.

Specify whether you want a sunrise or sunset unit. The sunrise units' views are less expansive, but to many are more interesting because they face neighboring islands. Also specify whether you want a room with a television. On a map, it may look like the hotel is isolated, but, at least during the day, it is only a 10-minute taxi ride all the way to the airport for a 50-cent fare. The Truk Continental has the best restaurant on the island and a separate bar with a deck onto the beach.

The **Truk Stop** (P.O. Box 546, Weno, Chuuk, FM 96942, tel. 330-4232, fax 330-2286), formerly Truk Travel Unlimited, located about one mile south of the airport, has added 19 upgraded rooms in a new wing onto its former four units. The hotel is well run and clean, with a good restaurant on the premises. Its clientele tends more toward business and government travelers than tourists. The hotel's only drawback is its prices—rooms start at $90 and go to $115 for lagoonfront rooms. These prices are comparable to those at the Continental, which is a far superior hotel.

Falos Beach Resort is now run through the Pacific Gardens (P.O. Box 494, Weno, Chuuk, FM 96942, tel. 330-4639, fax 330-2334). It's located on a lagoon island surrounded by a white-sand beach, a bone-crunching 30-minute ride from Weno if the wind is up. A night's stay is $50 s, $100 d. It is only for the hardy and the not easily bored. Cottages are concrete and square; rooms do have screens and occasional electricity. There are two outhouses and a "shower" consists of a bucket and some fresh water.

The island can be a lovely spot for a day trip. The price is $35 per person, with a two-person minimum. This includes lunch and transportation to and from the island. The snorkeling is great and the property fun to explore.

FOOD

Rainbow Restaurant is on the first floor under the Christopher Inn. Lunch and dinner average $7, but a good bowl of ramen is $3.50. The menu includes fish, Filipino, Japanese, and Chinese dishes. The restaurant is quite clean, but not suf-

---

FSM Country Code 691

ficiently air conditioned. **Yumi's Restaurant,** opposite the airport, also has Filipino dishes.

About the cheapest and friendliest place on Weno is the **Ran Annim Restaurant.** It's beside the bakery between Christopher Inn and the police station—there's no sign, so ask. Don't be put off by the ramshackle appearance.

The **Seaside Restaurant** overlooking the small boat harbor is a nice place to stop for coffee and to get a feel for Weno. It is not particularly clean so take care ordering food.

The best deal in town is the luncheonette in the corrugated metal Truk Trading Company (TTC) building, opposite the large-boat pier, two buildings north of Shigeto's Store. There is no big sign on the street as the building's main entrance is on the side. Its little snack bar serves a filling and delicious bowl of chicken jook (Chinese rice porridge) for 60 cents.

Breakfast or lunch at the **Quiet Corner Restaurant** in the Pacific Gardens hotel runs about $6. It has a good selection of Filipino, American, and Chinese dishes. For dinner, $13 will get you anything on the lunch menu along with soup, salad, and dessert.

The **T & S Cafeteria,** located on the road between the FSM Supreme Court and the power plant, offers breakfasts and lunches at reasonable prices.

The expensive **Takarajima Japanese Restaurant** is on the west side road, near the Truk Continental Hotel. Dinner with a couple of beers will cost $20 or more. It has a nice Japanese decor, including some great saltwater aquariums, but the food is not special.

The restaurant at the **Truk Stop** is quite good and overlooks the lagoon. Lunches cost about $6. Try the "local plate," a sampling of chicken, fish, tapioca, and cooked bananas. In the evening, the restaurant often serves mangrove crabs.

The best and most festive restaurant on the island is at the **Truk Continental Hotel.** The restaurant takes particular pride in its Pohnpei pepper steak and also does a good job with fish. It is the only restaurant on Chuuk where the cleanliness of salad can be trusted.

THE CHUUK LAGOON AT A GLANCE

	POP. (1989)	AREA (ACRES)	HIGHEST POINT (FEET)
Eot	279	119	201
Fanapanges	447	388	392
Fefan	3,902	3,265	1,030
Fono	369	81	201
Parem/Totiw	350	484	237
Patta	1,299	832	648
Polle	1,327	2,240	681
Romanum	679	185	168
Tol/Wonei	5,720	5,375	1,487
Tonoas/Etten	3,870	2,300	1,171
Tsis	438	151	250
Udot	1,513	1,218	799
Uman	2,895	1,161	951
Weno	15,253	4,668	1,237
other lagoon islands	nil	200	13
reef islands	nil	1,015	13
TOTAL	**38,341**	**23,682**	**1,487**

OTHER PRACTICALITIES

Entertainment

Prohibition of a sort has existed on Weno since 1977. Regardless of the official legal status, today alcohol is served in restaurants and bars and it's no longer necessary for tourists to purchase drinking licenses.

Local bars open and close with some regularity. It is probably safest for tourists to avoid these spots, particularly on payday Fridays—the second and fourth Friday of each month. Hotel restaurants and bars are more likely to be safe. If you must disco, try Yumi's or the bar beneath the Pacific Gardens, and keep alert as the evening progresses. Fights have been known to occur.

Sports and Recreation

Chuuk offers the best **wreck diving** in the world. There is no place else to see this many wrecks in such a small area—and all in a warm ocean. Wreck diving poses technical challenges to divers beyond those usually encountered in other types of diving. Know your limits. Do not explore inner passages that make you uncomfortable. There is less supervision of divers in Chuuk than at many other dive locations. Thus, even more than usual, you must set your own limits.

As is the case in most of Micronesia, other than Guam, it is best for divers to bring all their own equipment, other than tanks and weights. **Micronesia Aquatics** (Clark Graham, P.O. Box 57, Chuuk, FM 96942, tel. 330-2204) has offered reliable scuba services since 1974. Diving is $45 pp (one tank) or $65 pp (two tanks), snorkeling from the boat $30 pp. This company also offers waterskiing ($45 an hour pp) and windsurfing lessons ($25). Rental of windsurfing equipment is $10 an hour. The office is just inside the gate of the Truk Continental Hotel.

Blue Lagoon Dive Shop (Gradvin K. Aisek, P.O. Box 429, Chuuk, FM 96942, tel. 330-2796) offers diving at a similar price. Gradvin's father, Kimiuo Aisek, was an Operation Hailstorm eyewitness. He is a local legend for locating most of the lagoon wrecks. He founded this company in 1973.

Sundance Tours and Dive Shop (P.O. Box 85, Chuuk, FM 96942, tel. 330-2204, fax 330-4096), located next to the Truk Stop, opened in 1990 and also offers an array of diving packages.

If you wish to snorkel, it will be cheaper to go to the small-boat harbor and bargain for someone to take you to one of the many nearby wrecks. Make sure they know of a wreck in shallow water; this way four people can go for about $30.

Two live-aboard dive boats, the SS *Thorfinn* and the *Truk Aggressor,* serve visiting scuba divers. The SS *Thorfinn* charges $1700 for a one-week package (accommodation, meals, and diving included). The *Truk Aggressor* also offers a week package for $1895. At those prices, the live-aboard boats are more expensive than staying at a hotel and diving with the companies mentioned above, but you get almost unlimited diving and save time not having to shuttle back and forth from the dive sites each day. Of course, you also miss the opportunity to explore Chuuk. Passage on these boats must be booked ahead, either through one of the dive wholesalers listed under "Organized Tours" in the "Getting There" section of the On the Road chapter,

or by contacting **Seaward Holidays Micronesia Inc.** (P.O. Box DX, Weno, Chuuk, FM 96942, tel. 330-4302, fax 330-4253) for the SS *Thorfinn,* **Aggressor Fleet** (Drawer K, Morgan City, LA 70381, tel. 504-385-2416) for the *Truk Aggressor* only, or **Live/Dive Pacific** (74-5588 Pawai Place, Building F, Kailua-Kona, HI 96740, tel. 800-344-5662, fax 808-329-2628) also for the *Truk Aggressor* only.

Many hikes around Weno involve crossing private property, and property owners may be upset if you undertake such a walk without permission. Ask directions of any adults you meet, then ask if it's okay to continue.

Shopping

Sundance Tours beside the Truk Stop sells baskets, fans, wall hangings, coasters, shell necklaces, T-shirts, love sticks, and woodcarvings. Beware of the black coral and turtle shell products sold here, which are prohibited entry to the United States and many other Western nations for environmental reasons. Handicrafts can also be purchased at Yumi's opposite the airport and the **Small Industries Center** near the Truk Trading Company. **Big Mama's Nupoko Barker Co.** sounds more like a biker's bar than a handicrafts store, but a good assortment of handicrafts is displayed in the window. Unfortunately, store hours are sporadic at best.

The post office sells attractive FSM first day covers. Both Blue Lagoon Dive Shop and Micronesia Aquatics sell Chuuk T-shirts. Camera film is usually available at the Truk Continental Hotel.

The **Chuuk Coconut Authority** (P.O. Box JQ, Chuuk, FM 96942, fax 330-2777) on Weno produces Misimisi body oil, Tirow suntan oil, Saram shampoo, and Afata bath soap from local copra. These quality products are exported worldwide. You can visit the factory adjacent to the Truk Continental Hotel.

Three percent sales tax is added to all sticker prices in Chuuk.

Address mail to Chuuk, FM 96942.

Services

The Bank of Guam (tel. 330-2331, open Mon.-Fri. 10 a.m.-3 p.m.) and the Bank of FSM (tel. 330-2353, open Mon.-Thurs. 8:30 a.m.-2:30 p.m., Friday 8:30-4 p.m.) have branches on

Weno. Only the Bank of Guam will change foreign currencies.

You can place long distance phone calls at the Telecommunications Center (open 24 hours) near the airport. Long distance calls can be placed from many hotel rooms, but you must go through an operator and must charge the call to your hotel, rather than a calling card.

Avoid the Chuuk Hospital if at all possible.

Information

The Chuuk Visitors Bureau (P.O. Box FQ, Chuuk, FM 96942, tel. 330-4133, open weekdays 8 a.m.-5 p.m.) is a good place to ask questions. It sells maps and leaflets including William H. Stewart's *Dive Map of the Ghost Fleet of the Truk Lagoon* ($3.50). The staff can help arrange for you to stay as a paying guest with families on outer islands.

Radio station WSZC-AM broadcasts at 1600.

GETTING THERE

Chuuk International Airport (TKK) is within a mile of the business center on Weno. A small counter serves cold drinks and coffee at flight times. The only phone at the airport is a card phone (no coins). To get a taxi from the airport, turn left as you leave the terminal and walk out to the main street where cabs pass frequently during daylight hours. The high security fence around the airport terminal is locked at night, so forget trying to crash here if you arrive late from some outer island. Reconfirm your onward flight at the Air Mike office (tel. 330-2424) at the airport, open daily 8:00 a.m.-5:00 p.m. There's a $10 departure tax.

Continental Air Micronesia Island Hopper heads west from Hawaii Monday, Wednesday, and Friday, and leaves Guam heading east on Monday, Wednesday, and Friday. Remember that because of the International Date Line, you lose a day between Honolulu and Chuuk. Additional flights, including several on Sunday, connect Chuuk to Pohnpei and Guam, sometimes at reduced rates. Reconfirm your onward reservations at the Air Mike office at the airport upon arrival.

Caroline Pacific Air (P.O. Box 960, Kolonia, Pohnpei, FM 96941, tel. 320-4735, fax 320-

5736; or P.O. Box 960, Weno, Chuuk, FM 96942, tel. 330-4457) flies roundtrip Monday, Wednesday, and Friday to the Mortlocks. The plane goes to Onoun ($64 one-way) and Ta ($74 one-way).

GETTING AROUND

Field Trips

The field trip ships *Micro Trader* and *Micro Dawn* depart Weno approximately every two weeks on a weeklong journey along one of four different routes: Upper Mortlocks, Lower Mortlocks, Hall Islands, and Western Islands. The trip to the Westerns is the best, but it only goes once a month at most. There are basically three types of trips: medical evacuations, trips to pick up or drop off high school students, and regular field trips, when the boat becomes a sailing supermarket, bringing supplies to the residents of the islands it visits.

Schedules don't matter much on these trips as the ship can be diverted at any time for emergency evacuations. The ships usually leave in late afternoon, but they're often delayed until the next day at the last minute, even after the ship is fully loaded and all passengers aboard. In this case everyone has to get off and find somewhere else to spend the night. As a general rule the ship will leave a day or two late and get back a couple of days later than expected.

Passage costs nine cents a mile deck, 30 cents a mile cabin (plus $2 a night for berthing). The *Micro Trader* has eight two-berth cabins, but government officials have priority on these. Even though you may have been promised a cabin you can't really be sure you actually have one until just before the ship leaves. And once you're underway you may be asked to give up your cabin in case of medical need. You can always travel deck.

Three meals are provided at $13 a day. Passengers who take meals with the ship's officers pick up morsels of useful information along with what they get on their plates. There's no obligation to take every meal (you only pay for those you consume). Take along a good supply of food and bottled water, and get a cabin if at all possible as the local color of deck passage will wear off after a couple of nights.

Other Boats

Smaller municipal boats make more frequent trips from Weno to the outer islands, for example the *Ik No. 3* to Kuttu in the Lower Mortlocks, the *Ik No. 1* to Puluwat, the *Toku* to Tamatam, and the *Fuun Matau* to Pulap. The large motor vessel *Miss Nama* sails to Nama twice a week, leaving Weno Tuesday and Friday afternoons (four hours, $5 one-way), and there are similar services to Losap and Pis.

Some of the above are actually fishing boats owned by outer islanders and offer no comforts or safety standards.

By Road

By day, Weno has one of the best public transportation systems in the Pacific. Pickups with taxi signs in the front windows continually cruise the roads, so getting around is cheap and easy. These shared taxis charge 50 cents pp within the town area. At night, however, everything stops running. Do not be caught far from your hotel at night unless you have arranged for your return.

Rental cars from **VJ Car Rental** (tel. 330-2652) at Christopher Inn are $35 a day. **Truk Stop Car Rentals** (tel. 330-2701 or 330-4232) has older cars at $35 a day, newer cars at $40-45 a day, plus 13% tax. **Kurassa Hotel** (tel. 330-4415) rents a few cars for $45 including tax. Considering the excellent taxi service, it's not really necessary to rent a car on Weno.

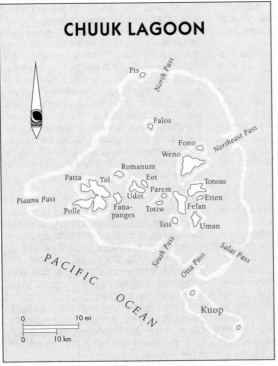

CHUUK LAGOON

The ship usually stops at each island on its route for a couple of hours, and you're free to go in on the ship's boat for a look around. In rough weather, landing on some islands gets dicey through the crashing surf. Take along small gifts to give to people who show you around their island.

For field trip information check with the **Transportation Office** (tel. 330-2592) in the warehouse beside the commercial port, as only they can give definite information on cabin availability. The **Truk Shipping Company** (P.O. Box 669, Chuuk, FM 96942, tel. 330-2455), upstairs in the back of the two-story building opposite the gasoline station beside the small-boat harbor, sells deck tickets and is a good place to make initial inquiries about departures. The field trips are a great experience, not to be missed if you have the opportunity and time.

ISLANDS IN THE CHUUK LAGOON

Chuuk lagoon's islands form the largest island group in the Carolines. Ninety-eight islands and islets are in the group, 41 of them on the barrier reef encircling the lagoon. Five major passes allow ships to enter. All the other large volcanic islands within the lagoon offer a simpler, more traditional lifestyle than Weno; each is beautiful in itself and for its views of the others. Although mangroves predominate along the shores, there are also beaches.

During the Japanese period, the lagoon islands were divided into two groups: the Shiki Islands (including Weno, Tonoas, Etten, Fefan, Parem, and Uman) and the Shichiyo Islands (Udot, Fanapanges, Tol, and the others). The present administration divides these islands into Northern Namoneas (Weno and Fono), Southern Namoneas (Fefan, Parem, Tonoas, Totiw, Tsis, and Uman), and Faichuk (Eot, Fanapanges, Polle, Patta, Romanum, Tol, Udot, and Wonei).

Transportation

Go to the small-boat harbor to catch a ride to other lagoon islands. Serving commuters who work, shop, or sell their produce on Weno, the boats leave the Chuuk lagoon islands in the early morning and depart for the return trip in the afternoon. All of the small *yamma* boats based in remote villages operate this way. One can usually find a boat to Fefan, Uman, Parem, Udot, or Tol for about $3 one-way. But you must spend at least one night on each island. Tol is the farthest away, so boats going there leave earlier. Different boats serve the east and west sides of Fefan, and there are several routes to Tol. Be sure to clarify exactly where the boat is going. Since the lagoon islands have no hotels, some boat owners may hesitate to take you if they think you'll expect them to provide free accommodations on the island. You could get around this by explaining that you'll be camping, or ask if they know of anyone willing to accommodate a paying guest. About $10 pp a night would be fair.

However, there is a more convenient, but slightly more expensive, way to visit these islands. Go down to the small-boat harbor around 9 a.m. During the day, the boatmen who brought people into Weno usually just sit in their boats waiting to return. Some will be quite happy to take you to another island, wait for you to explore, and then return (before their afternoon customers finish work). You can also negotiate snorkeling sidetrips or trips to the barrier reef and its islets.

A word of caution: Some of the boatmen view tourists as easy pickings. Be certain that you

and the boatman agree on an itinerary and a price before you leave. Specify clearly whether the price is per person or for the whole boat and write it down. Don't let the boatman try to change it at the end of the day because of a "misunderstanding." If during the trip you wish to change the itinerary, agree to a new price in advance of the change. A four- or five-hour trip to one of the closer islands should not cost more than $25 per boat, $35 to Tol or the outer reef. You should be willing to pay some in advance for the boatman to buy gasoline, but have him quote one all-inclusive price. Some will want to charge you an additional amount for fuel, but you really have no idea how much gas is needed.

Tonoas

From the look of it today, it's hard to believe that Tonoas, the Japanese Natsu Shima or Summer Island, once housed the largest Japanese naval installation outside the home islands. As you walk around the island, however, evidence surfaces: wrecked buildings, melted oil tanks, an abandoned Japanese hospital, piers, and torn-up railway tracks.

In 1814 a Spaniard, Manuel Dublon, arrived to collect bêche-de-mer, and from that time until the official change back to the original Tonoas in 1990, the island was called Dublon, a name still in common use.

In 1899 the Germans made Tonoas a base for the copra trade. The Japanese also built their Chuukese capital, Tokyo, here, centering on the area between the present Municipal Building and Catholic mission. Until late 1946 thousands of Japanese prisoners were held on Tonoas awaiting repatriation. The overcrowding forced the U.S. Navy to build their base on Weno, which has been Chuuk's administration center ever since.

Don't miss the old **Japanese seaplane base,** now the junior high school, with its vast fields of concrete sloping into the lagoon, bomb shelters, and view of the old airstrip.

A $2.2-million wharf called **Ichimantong** juts into the lagoon on the south side of Tonoas, within sight of the crumbling remains of a Japanese dock built 40 years earlier.

Two **Japanese AA guns** sit at the top of the peninsula beyond the hospital ruins, but you'll need a guide to find them.

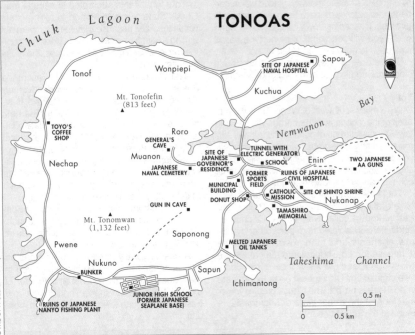

TONOAS

Chuuk Lagoon

Lagoon

Tonof

Wonpiepi

Sapou

SITE OF JAPANESE
NAVAL HOSPITAL

Kuchua

Mt. Tonofefin
(813 feet)

Bay

TOYO'S
COFFEE
SHOP

Roro

Nemwanon

GENERAL'S
CAVE

Muanon

Nechap

JAPANESE
NAVAL CEMETERY

SITE OF
JAPANESE
GOVERNOR'S
RESIDENCE

TUNNEL WITH
ELECTRIC GENERATOR

SCHOOL

Enin

TWO JAPANESE
AA GUNS

FORMER
SPORTS
FIELD

RUINS OF JAPANESE
CIVIL HOSPITAL

MUNICIPAL
BUILDING

DONUT SHOP

CATHOLIC
MISSION

SITE OF SHINTO SHRINE

Nukanap

GUN IN CAVE

TAMASHIRO
MEMORIAL

Mt. Tonomwan
(1,132 feet)

Saponong

Pwene

MELTED JAPANESE
OIL TANKS

Takeshima   Channel

Nukuno

BUNKER

Sapun

Ichimantong

0   0.5 mi

RUINS OF JAPANESE
NANYO FISHING PLANT

JUNIOR HIGH SCHOOL
(FORMER JAPANESE
SEAPLANE BASE)

0   0.5 km

© MOON PUBLICATIONS, INC.

The most unusual sight on Tonoas is a little
out of the way and generally overlooked. It's the
General's Cave—actually a network of tunnels beginning beside the road at Roro. Still
used as a typhoon shelter, the cave can easily
accommodate the entire population of Tonoas.
Bring a flashlight and go under the hill and out
the other side. Then climb to the top and find
your way down to the nearby Protestant
Church.

Across the road from the church are two
meeting halls. The one nearest the water is the
Hall of the Magic Chickens. A legend tells that
an ancient sorcerer called all the chickens of
Tonoas together and had them level the top of
the hill behind the church in a single night. Even
today it is said that anyone who eats chicken
in this hall will assume fowl (foul?) characteristics
and suffer other terrifying consequences. Because of this legend, people on Tonoas would
rather starve than eat a local chicken. Imported
chickens are apparently okay.

Fefan

Fefan is a center for market gardening and
handicrafts. Most of the boats from Weno stop at
Mesa on the east side.

For strong hikers, from Sako Store at Fason,
just south of Mesa wharf, hike up to the center of
the island along an old Japanese road that leads
to Unufouchy, where five large **Japanese naval
guns** congregate and afford fine views. After
visiting the guns continue down the other side to
Saporanong on the west coast. Many other
Japanese guns still sit in caves on the sides of
Fefan's mountains, such as those above **Inaka.**
You can see these if you're very keen. There are
also three small field guns near the road just
north of Mesa wharf.

An easier hike is along the flat, round-the-island road. You could walk around the entire island in about five hours. To take a shorter hike,
have your boatman drop you at one pier and
pick you up at another. This walk is a delightful
series of smiles, greetings, and sights. Simple,

nice homes sit along the way, placed within gardens, taro patches, papaya trees, and pineapple terraces. Cascading down hillsides, or in stone walls, you will see some of same type basalt rock used to build Lelu and Nan Madol.

The stores on Fefan are few and poorly stocked. Bring in your own food and drink.

Tol

Only 18 miles southwest of Weno, Tol is the outback of the lagoon, with numerous villages and few visitors. A throng of curious children will surround you as you disembark and follow wherever you go. Be prepared to experience a little culture shock if you visit Tol. No matter what happens, don't get angry or show any irritation.

Tol (13 square miles, pop. approx. 6,000) is actually three islands—Tol, Polle, and Patta—known collectively as the Faichuk Islands, partially isolated from each other by narrow channels and mangrove forests. The Japanese forced Chuukese to dig canals between the islands to allow their patrol boats free circulation. The highest peak in the state (1,457 feet) is on Tol. The Chuuk greater whiteeye, one of the rarest birds of Micronesia, is found in the jungles of Tol.

Tol's inhabitants attempted to secede from Chuuk State a few years ago to form a state within the FSM because they felt they were not getting a fair share of the state budget. Although the move passed the FSM Congress, the president vetoed it.

The Tol administrative center is Fason; the Susumu boat drops you there. More adventurous would be to take a boat over to Polle, leaving Weno almost daily at 1:30 p.m. The best beaches on Tol are at Sapou and Malaio villages, at the west end of Polle. Ask the local assistant magistrate for permission to camp. Giant **Japanese cannons** meant to defend Piaanu Pass still lie in huge caverns chiseled from solid rock, two above Sapou, two more above Malaio. All four can be seen in a morning.

The boat from Malaio to Weno stops at Epin on Patta along the way. If you decide to stop, visit the **cave** dug by the legendary turtles, Nukaf and Sapota, a short walk from Epin.

A relatively easy three-hour walk along an old Japanese road from Malaio brings you to the Netutu Catholic mission, set on both sides of a canal. Netutu is less than an hour's walk from Fason. Hiking north toward Patta is much more difficult.

Dive-bombers fly over Fefan, 29 April 1944.

NATIONAL ARCHIVES, WASHINGTON, D.C.

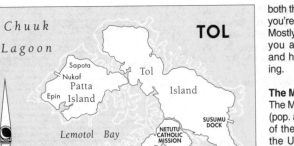

OUTSIDE THE CHUUK LAGOON

The Outer Islands

Sizable populations inhabit the 11 atolls and three single islands of the Mortlocks, Halls, and Westerns. No cars clog these very traditional islands, so no highways are needed. People are extremely hospitable and you'll be invited to stay with embarrassing frequency. Keep in mind, however, that some islands have a limited food supply and are unable to accommodate visitors.

To stay on an outer island, make advance arrangements by radioing ahead to an island mayor. If it's known you're coming there will be time to spread the burden among several households. It is diplomatic to work through the Chuuk Visitors Bureau on Weno.

Each outer island has both an elected mayor and a hereditary chief. Either can give permission for visitors to stay on the island. If you arrive unannounced on an island it may be better to ask to see the chief, but if arrangements are made prior to your arrival you'll probably work through the mayor, who will be in closer contact with Chuuk. The mayor will often speak better English than the chief. Pay a courtesy call on both the chief and the mayor if you're planning to stay awhile. Mostly they want to know who you are, why you've come, and how long you'll be staying.

The Mortlocks

The Mortlock or Nomoi Islands (pop. approx. 6,000) southeast of the Chuuk lagoon include the Upper Mortlocks (Nama and Losap), the Mid-Mortlocks (Namoluk, Etal, and the northernmost islands of Satawan atoll), and the Lower Mortlocks (Lukunor and southeastern Satawan). **Nama** (pop. approx. 900) is a single island without a lagoon. Many in the Mortlocks feel alienated from and dominated by the rest of the State of Chuuk and periodically argue for their own state within FSM.

Satawan atoll's land area totals only a couple of square miles, but its lagoon is the second largest in Chuuk State. The old Japanese airstrip was on Satawan Island (pop. approx. 900) but it's now completely planted with coconut and breadfruit trees and the new airstrip is on Ta (pop. approx. 300). At low tide, you can walk on the Satawan reef from Ta Island to Satawan Island in two hours. **Japanese guns** still lurk beneath Satawan's lush vegetation.

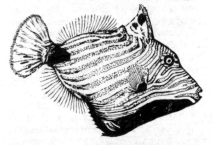

The undulate triggerfish (Balistapus undulatus) gets its name from a triggerlike mechanism controlling the dorsal fin, which the fish uses to wedge itself into coral crevices when threatened.

You can continue northwest on the barrier reef along the east side of the atoll from Satawan to Moch (pop. approx. 600) in five hours at low tide, passing many small islands along the way. Satawan is one of the only atolls of Chuuk where this is possible.

The Japanese government has built a modern plant to freeze fish on Oneop Island (pop. approx. 550) on Lukunor atoll.

The Hall Islands

Sixty miles north of Chuuk lagoon, the Hall Islands (Pafeng) consist of the twin atolls of Nomwin and Murilo, each with under a thousand residents, and the uninhabited single island, East Fayu. The Hall Islanders are closely related to the people of the Chuuk lagoon and speak the same dialect. The houses in the group have tin or concrete roofs, and boats are made of fiberglass with outboard motors.

THE WESTERN ISLANDS

Some of the last vestiges of old Pacific culture persist on the western Chuuk and eastern Yap Islands. The inhabitants of the central Carolines have much more in common with each other than they do with the high islanders on Yap proper or those of the Chuuk lagoon. Here amid the sapphire blue waters and smell of plumeria, nearly every house is built of native materials (few tin roofs), most of the men wear loincloths, and many women walk about barebreasted.

You can still see outriggers carved from breadfruit logs, though the use of fiberglass boats with outboard motors has increased. Large thatched canoe houses serve as men's social clubs, workshops, and schools. You'll still find old navigators here, men who can travel hundreds of miles to islands they've never seen, without a compass or charts, just from watching the sun, stars, wind, waves, birds, and fish. They travel in sailing canoes between the states of Chuuk and Yap and can predict a typhoon when all seems calm. Yet the young, like young everywhere, appear eager to adopt at least the outward trappings of "world village" culture.

© MOON PUBLICATIONS, INC.

The Westerns include Namonuito, Pulap, and Puluwat atolls, plus Houk (Pulusuk) Island. Chuuk's most skilled navigators reside on Tamatam, Houk, and Puluwat.

Puluwat

Puluwat atoll (pop. approx. 500) is a cluster of five islands, the largest of which are Puluwat and Alet. The one passage into Puluwat's small lagoon leads to an excellent protected anchorage between these two, where cruising yachts sometimes can drop anchor.

All people live on Puluwat Island. The Puluwat islanders were once feared warriors, but missionaries changed that. These days the large thatched canoe houses lining the lagoon are more likely to shelter one of the island's dozen fiberglass outboards than traditional canoes. The atoll's vegetation is dense and there's an ample supply of fish and vegetables.

A tall concrete **Japanese lighthouse,** pocked with bullet holes from wartime strafing, still stands at the west tip of uninhabited Alet, just above the beach. You can climb the spiral stairway almost to the top, but the upper platform is now closed as the lighthouse recently returned to service. It's a 90-minute walk along the reef from the village to the lighthouse; many harmless small blacktip reef sharks patrol the shore on the ocean side. A new junior high school has been built beside the lighthouse.

Houk

Houk (Pulusuk) is a relatively large, heavily vegetated island with only a fringing reef (no lagoon). Ships sailing between Chuuk and Houk usually call at Pulap or Puluwat first, as the direct route from Weno to Houk is obstructed by dangerous reefs.

Houk is one of the most traditional and isolated islands of Micronesia. Magnificent outrigger canoes are kept in large thatched boathouses along the beach. The breadfruit trees of Houk are incredibly tall and the food supply is adequate. A brackish lake, home to small fish, is used for bathing and washing clothes.

Pulap Atoll

Pulap and Tamatam are small islands on the Pulap reef, each with a single, sparsely populated village. They lie on opposite sides of the atoll, with about five miles of lagoon between them. Both are so small you can look right across them. When typhoons strip the coconuts and breadfruit from the trees and the residents are forced to depend on taro, they can suffer serious famines.

Tamatam is a very traditional island, clean and breezy with houses along the ocean side and a friendly, welcoming people. The two verdant ends of Tamatam are separated by a narrow sandy strip. The island's many huge outrigger canoes can carry as many as 10 men or more to the outer islands of Yap.

Namonuito Atoll

Namonuito's huge triangular lagoon is the largest in the Caroline Islands. The atoll's five inhabited islands are Onoun (Ulul), Magur, Ono, Onari, and Pisaris. Namonuito is somewhat less traditional than the other Western Islands to the south.

Onoun Island (pop. approx. 500) is a long, broad coral strip at the west end of the lagoon. Coconut-covered Onoun is the largest of the Namonuito islands and the best able to receive visitors. Taro is planted in swampy pits in the center of the island and the food supply is adequate. It's a "developed" island with roads (no cars), stores (closed), an airstrip (no scheduled service), and a large, modern junior high school (many students). The concrete-surfaced airstrip, a 15-minute walk north of the main village, was completed by a United States Air Force Civic Action Team in 1991. There's good snorkeling on the lagoon side, cool breezes and fiery sunsets on the ocean side.

The other four Namonuito islands have small populations and limited food supplies. Magur is the northernmost island of Chuuk State. Landing on Ono is dangerous during rough weather. At tiny Pisaris, in the southeast corner of the Namonuito lagoon, visiting ships must anchor far from the island due to treacherous coral shoals in this corner of the lagoon. The shallow waters on the lagoon side protect Pisaris from heavy seas, so landing itself is easy at high tide. Magur and Onari are also reasonably approachable.

STATE OF YAP

INTRODUCTION

The State of Yap consists of three islands interconnected by bridges (Yap, Gagil-Tomil, Maap), nearby Rumung (closed to tourists), and 15 outer islands. Together the outer islands stretch 625 miles east but total only seven square miles. All the outer islands are atolls except Fais, a raised atoll. The northeast tradewinds make sandy beaches more common on the western and southern shores, but none are near Colonia, the main town.

A barrier reef surrounds the main island cluster, limiting shore snorkeling opportunities. Yap is not volcanic and the land and hills are more gentle than, for example, Palau. The landscape varies from coastal villages flanked by majestic palm trees to the open pandanus and scrub meadows of the upland interior. There are a few sandy beaches, but most of the coast is fringed by mangrove forests.

YAP'S CLIMATE

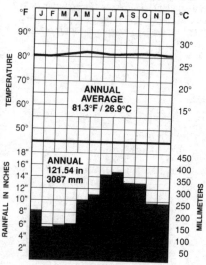

One of the most exciting aspects of Yap is that villages and taro patches are often linked by ancient stone paths, many of which are raised. The builders took dirt from adjoining land to raise the road bed. The depressed, nearby land therefore became easier to irrigate for taro. The paths are so well engineered, with stones holding up the edges and a system of culverts allowing drainage, that they have withstood centuries with only minimal upkeep. As you walk these paths, usually well shaded, you feel the presence of an early, great civilization that was able to produce the abundance needed to sustain massive public works. Life on Yap continutes to revolve around its villages—most still have meetinghouses—even when the lifestyle in some respects does not remain traditional. The main roads bypass the villages, but you can reach them by driving or hiking on lanes that connect with the roads or by using the ancient stone walkway system.

Yap is the most traditional corner of Micronesia, and things operate at a much slower pace than on Guam or even Koror. The state constitution gives the island chiefs veto power over state legislation relating to culture or matters of tradition. Yapese tourism officials say they want "controlled tourism," rather than the uncontrolled growth that occurred on Guam and Saipan. If this is inconvenient at times, remember that it's *they* who are in charge, not tourists. A public outcry stopped a major Japanese resort development. If you think everything isn't arranged just to please you, you're right.

History

The Yapese were, and the outer islanders still are, the greatest voyagers of the Western Pacific, able to travel incredible distances in outrigger sailing canoes, using only stars and waves as their guides. The Yapese name for Yap Proper is Wa'ab, while the outer islands are Remetau. Traditionally, all of the outer islands that now belong to Yap State, plus the Westerns and Halls in Chuuk State, and the Marianas, were under the rule of the high chief of Yap.

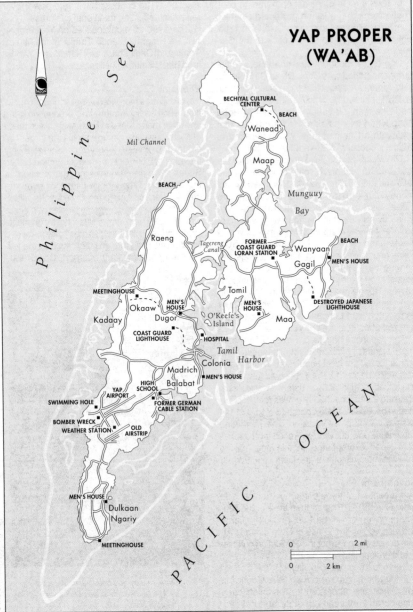

YAP PROPER
(WA'AB)

Philippine Sea

Mil Channel

BECHIYAL CULTURAL
CENTER
BEACH
Wanead

Maap

Munguuy Bay

BEACH

Raeng
Tagereng Canal
FORMER
COAST GUARD
LORAN STATION
Wanyaan
Gagil
BEACH
MEN'S HOUSE

MEETINGHOUSE
Okaaw
MEN'S HOUSE
Dugor
Tomil
MEN'S HOUSE
DESTROYED JAPANESE
LIGHTHOUSE

Kadaay
O'Keefe's Island
Maa

COAST GUARD
LIGHTHOUSE
HOSPITAL
Tamil
Harbor

Madrich
Colonia
Balabat
MEN'S HOUSE

YAP
AIRPORT
HIGH
SCHOOL
FORMER GERMAN
CABLE STATION

SWIMMING HOLE

BOMBER WRECK
WEATHER STATION
OLD
AIRSTRIP

OCEAN

MEN'S HOUSE
Dulkaan
Ngariy

MEETINGHOUSE

PACIFIC

0   2 mi

0   2 km

© MOON PUBLICATIONS, INC.

In 1869 the Germans set up a trading post. Their claims to the island prompted Spanish from the Philippines to occupy Colonia in 1885, which they ended up selling back to the Germans 14 years later.

One of the most unusual characters of the European period was Capt. David O'Keefe, an Irish-American who was shipwrecked on Yap in 1871. Nursed back to health by a Yapese medicine man, he caught a steamer to Hong Kong when he was able. He returned a year later with a Chinese junk, which he used to launch a successful 30-year trading career.

The highly developed Yapese culture of the time had an elaborate scale of values based on stone money. The type of stone used for this money didn't exist on Yap. Traditionally, the stones were brought hundreds of miles from Palau by raft, a perilous undertaking which, of course, gave the stone money its value. O'Keefe used his ship to bring the stone from Palau and traded it for copra and sea slugs, becoming very influential in the process. "His Majesty" built a residence from bricks imported from Hong Kong on Taraang, the little island you see in the middle of Tamil Harbor. Many years later, Burt Lancaster played O'Keefe in a movie about this adventurer.

The Japanese occupied Yap in 1914. As on other islands of Micronesia, the Japanese soon outnumbered the local population. World War II was a difficult time for the Yapese as the Japanese forced them to work on defense installations, breaking their stone money unless they cooperated. The United States bombed Yap, but bypassed it without an invasion. The remaining Japanese, now cut off from receiving supplies from Japan, expropriated Yapese food, making life even more difficult for the local population.

Government

By agreement, if the elected governor of Yap State is from Yap Proper, then the elected lieutenant governor will be from an outer island, and vice versa. The Office of Outer Islands Affairs assists the governor in coordinating outer island development.

There are two councils of chiefs: the Council of Pilung from Yap Proper and the Council of Tamol from the outer islands. The chiefs carry considerable influence in state and national

elections. The councils have veto power over legislation affecting traditional customs.

There are 10 municipalities on Yap Proper: two are separate islands (Rumung and Maap), Tomil and Gagil share an island, and Yap Island has six municipalities.

Economy

Yap continues more traditional economic activities, such as fishing and taro production, than any other major island in Micronesia. As in much of Micronesia, the government is the largest industry and bloated. It survives at this size only because of Compact payments from the United States. (See discussion in the "Introduction" to this chapter). When these cease, or even decrease, there undoubtedly will be layoffs, which could have dire effects on the whole cash economy of Yap. There is very little industry on the island, and even that tends to be foreign-owned enterprises using foreign labor, such as the textile plant not far from the airport. Goods thus

DAVID STANLEY

Stone money and betel palms flank the traditional meetinghouse at Okaaw on the path across Yap.

Yap Supreme Court Judge Constantine Yinuz in his home village of Kadaay

produced may be exported to the U.S. under a quota-free, tax-free status granted by the Compact. Several hundred foreign workers live in dormitories. The Yap government gets little more than tax revenue, while absorbing extra strain on the local infrastructure.

The People
Of the residents of the state, more than a quarter live on the outer islands, the rest on Yap. The population is 95% Catholic. At the peak of its empire, Yap may have had as many as 45,000 people. European- and Japanese- imported diseases probably reduced the population to about 10,000 in 1869 and to less than half that in 1950. Since then the population has rebounded.

The number of jobs available to high school graduates is limited, particularly outside the government. The best students go abroad for schooling and often fail to return. For the outer islanders especially, finding a way forward without economic dependence or the need to emigrate is not easy.

A rigid caste system governed Yap in the old days. The village accounted for the Yapese caste; those living in strong, powerful villages were of the highest caste. The people take their surnames from their land parcels rather than their parents, an example of how sacred land is to them. Each village has a chief, the highest chiefs coming from the highest caste villages.

The overlapping concepts of caste, village of origin, and property rights continue to exert an in-

fluence, sometimes pernicious, today. A child born on Yap to outer-island parents remains an outer islander. (Almost 600 outer islanders now live on Yap). Until the mid-1980's outer islanders, considered of lower caste than those from Yap itself, who moved to Yap were restricted to living in the crowded town of Madrich. Although things have loosened up somewhat today, no outer islander can obtain secure land rights on Yap. It is difficult for "lower" caste islanders, particularly women, to be considered for higher paying, higher prestige jobs.

Traditional society drew sharp distinctions between the roles of men and women. Women farmed, men fished. Even today, in some traditional families, a girl, or a mature woman, cannot begin to eat dinner until her brothers are finished. She also may not contradict statements made by brothers.

Traditionally, a village would have a *pebai* (meetinghouse) and a *faluw*. The *faluw* would be built beside the seashore on a large stone platform with a high thatched roof. It would serve as a school, meeting place, dormitory for young men, and a storage area for fishing gear. Many *pebai* and *faluw* were destroyed during World War II, and others were allowed to deteriorate since. But there still are large numbers of *pebai* and a smaller number of *faluw* that can be visited today. Women's houses *(dapal)* are found only on the outer islands. Always ask permission before approaching a *faluw*.

Note too the *wunbey* (stone platforms) and

malal (dancing grounds). Yapese dances include the bamboo, marching, sitting, and standing dances. The dancing could mark the inauguration of a new building, a high school graduation, or the commemoration of the death of an important person.

Today, only a small minority of women on Yap, mainly outer islanders, still walk in town bare-breasted, wearing *lava lava* made of hibiscus and banana fiber, or cotton cloth. You'll see these women shopping or chatting with friends. Why is it so surprising to see a bare-breasted woman hop into her Nissan Bluebird and drive off? *Lava lava* often have designs woven in which will tell a woman's history, such as her island of origin. Yapese culture is sufficiently flexible that appealing patterns from North American Indians recently have been incorporated into the design repertoire.

More men and many young boys and teenagers wear the *thu* (loincloth). The color of the *thu* tells of the origins, and thus the caste, of the wearer. A pure outer islander's *thu* will be blue. If a man is from Yap, the *thu* will probably be multi-colored. If he is mixed, he will wear red.

Betel nut chewing is universal, even among children, and for many, continual. All men and most women carry pouches made of coconut leaves in which they keep the necessary nuts, lime, and leaves. A green nut is split open, sprinkled with dry lime made from coral, and wrapped in a piece of a pepper leaf. The bundle is inserted into the mouth and chewed whole for 20 minutes or so.

If you are interested in trying betel nut, almost anybody on the island will be happy to help you. First-time users should not do so on an empty stomach. One's first experience will produce a sense of well-being, accompanied by a light-headedness that lasts for about 15 minutes. As with tobacco, after habitual use, the pleasure is less, but the absence of the drug may lead to feelings of deprivation and in some cases, depression. Betel nut chewing turns saliva and teeth bright red. The casual, though not the habitual, user can brush the color away. The red saliva should be spit out, not swallowed. All pavements have red stains from the continual spitting this activity entails. The new YCA building, knowing the futility of No Spitting signs,

merely used betel nut red-colored pavement. Top quality betel nuts are grown on the island and are an export item. Possession of betel nut is illegal in most American states and in many other Western nations.

Three languages are spoken in Yap State: Yapese, Ulithian, and Woleaian. In Yapese *mogethin* means "hello," *kefel* "goodbye," *sirow* "excuse me," and *kammagar* is "thank you."

Stone Money

Stone money *(rai)* was as much a pillar of Yapese society as gold is of ours. Although cash is used today for most commercial transactions, the big circular stone "coins" (and smaller stone and shell money for certain specific purposes) are still of considerable value to the Yapese. A Japanese count in 1929 revealed 13,281 pieces of stone money. About half that number survive today, and the money may be seen in every village. The money resembles a flat gristmill with a hole in the middle, so two or more men could carry it on a pole.

stone money coin resting on a meetinghouse

Yap Day festival,
Gagil

PAUL BÖHLER

The largest piece (on Rumung) is 13 feet across and takes a dozen men to move. Although important, size is not the only factor in determining the value of a coin. A smaller piece may be worth more due to its age and history. Thus the exact value of a stone, like paper money in the United States during much of the nineteenth century, is open to negotiation.

Stones are seldom moved, since who owns what is common knowledge. A particular piece of money might be owned by someone in another village. None of this should sound very odd to any modern Westerner, since it is much the method used by governments today. If, for example, the U.S. must make a gold payment to France, the gold is not shipped from the New York Federal Reserve Bank across the Atlantic Ocean to France. The gold is not even moved within the Federal Reserve building. It is much easier merely to change the ownership sign on top of a stack of gold. Sitting or standing on stone money is forbidden. Stone money cannot be taken out of Yap without the permission of the paramount chief and the state governor.

Crafts

Yap is an excellent place to purchase quality handicrafts. *Lava lava* are woven from hibiscus and banana fibers or from cotton, and usually have interesting lined patterns. There is a variety of basketry woven from pandanus and coconut, including women's soft handbags. Woven baskets for betel nuts make good souvenirs, as do

the distinctive combs with long teeth made of bamboo. The *yar,* a traditional form of currency, is a large, polished mother-of-pearl shell tied with a handle woven of coconut fiber. Other craft items include hair ornaments, carved spoons, shell belts, colorful hibiscus fiber necklaces, fans, model canoes, and woodcarvings.

Three main gift shops are located within walking distance of each other in Colonia. The **Women's Cooperative** has very reasonable prices. The **I.L.P.** store, on the north side of Chamorro Bay, dedicates half its shop to handicrafts. The newest shop, the **Tropical Touch,** in the YCA, is run by Mary Figir. It is exclusively a handicraft gift shop and has a wide selection of quality items at reasonable prices. Particularly outstanding is the collection of *lava lava,* made from traditional hibiscus and banana fibers or modern cotton thread. This shop also carries scenes of Yap, both in watercolors and prints, by expat artist Ruth Glenn Little.

Many small stores carry selections as well. Both the Manta Ray Bay Hotel and the Pathways Hotel have gift shops.

The **Ethnic Art Institute of Micronesia,** located near the Aces Market, runs a program in which elders teach craft skills to younger artists. Visitors are welcome and tours may be arranged in advance. Call 350-2604, or fax 350-4279. Inquiries can also be made to the center's sponsor, the Robert Bumbiner Foundation for the Arts (5456 The Todeo, Long Beach, CA 90803, tel. 310-433-5459, fax 310-439-2473).

Events

A *mitmit* is a traditional festival where one village hosts another in an exchange of gifts and obligations. The completion of a major village project and high school graduations can also occasion traditional singing, dancing, and feasting. Yap Day (1 March) is a celebration with sporting events, traditional dancing, contests, and feasts.

Conduct

Roads and stone walkways (except short paths leading directly to someone's home) are publicly owned. But most all other land outside Colonia is privately owned. Since land along the pathways is private, do not pick flowers or fruit. You need permission to use a beach, approach a *faluw,* collect shells, camp, or walk around a village, but it may be difficult to determine who has authority to give it. Do the best you can. If no one is there, use your own judgment to decide what to do. Off the main roads, if you smile and greet everyone you meet, you'll rarely be refused permission to proceed. At times, however, people with or without authority to do so may ask for several dollars in exchange for permission.

Don't infringe on fishing grounds or disturb fish traps. Many people, particularly older people, object to having their pictures taken. Don't take pictures of anyone without permission. Don't point at people or pat children on the head. The local custom is that women do not expose their legs above the knees. It's considered ill-mannered to step over another person's outstretched leg or betel basket or to walk in front of someone who is speaking. A group should walk single file rather than abreast. Yapese walking through a strange village will tell people they meet the purpose of their visit. They sometimes carry a piece of green vegetation in one hand to show peaceful intentions as they pass through a village; carrying a small basket called a *way* (pronounced "Y") serves a similar purpose. Traditionally, a Yapese not carrying the basket would be considered rebellious.

SIGHTS

Colonia and Environs

The Yapese name for Colonia is Donguch, meaning "Small Islands." The point where the government offices and legislature sit, once a tiny island, is now connected to the rest of Colonia by fill. The offices were built on the foundations of a **Spanish fort.** The state legislature nearby occupies the site of what once was a **Japanese shrine.**

Urban life in Colonia revolves around the two-story, modern **YCA** (Yap Cooperative Association) building. It contains the island's largest grocery store, a video store, the Bank of Hawaii, the Bank of FSM, and the Continental Micronesia Airline office. It also seems to be the place for Yapese to hang out in town in the morning, meeting friends and neighbors.

The Waab Mak'uuf is a produce market on the water that primarily sells local produce. It has an inexpensive restaurant behind it.

For a superb view of Yap, follow the jeep track from the Catholic mission above Colonia up Medeqdeq Hill to the **Coast Guard Lighthouse.** Beyond the lighthouse this track dead-ends at a power line in the valley.

You can take a beautiful walk on a traditional stone path right in town. It begins in the narrow space between a church and the Ocean View Hotel. At first, the path is a gentle uphill climb till it levels off above the mangroves. There are some houses along the path, but it gives a wonderful jungle feeling, remarkable considering you are still in town. In about a half mile, you will come to a fork in the road. To the right, the stone path falls into disrepair in another several hundred feet. It is a lovely walk though I have no idea what, if anything, lies beyond it. The left fork leads to a paved road. Heading left on that road will take you downhill and back to town; toward the right, the road leads up to Medeqdeq summit.

Directly south of Colonia is the outer islanders' colony of **Madrich.** A Spanish trading post was once here and the place is named after Madrid. Until the 1980s it was the only place on the island where outer islanders were allowed to live. It is crowded, vibrant, and a bit squalid. Less than a mile farther along, **stone money** lines each side of the road in front of the Ruul Municipal Office at Balabat. The road dead ends into a dirt road. Make a right turn and a few hundred feet beyond, the second small road to the left leads to another **stone money bank** and a *faluw.*

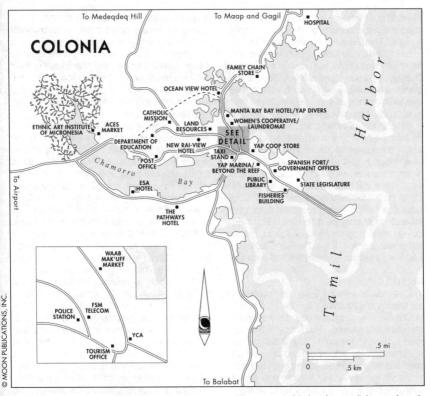

COLONIA

To Medeqdeq Hill
To Maap and Gagil
■ HOSPITAL

FAMILY CHAIN
STORE ■

OCEAN VIEW HOTEL ●

■ MANTA RAY BAY HOTEL/YAP DIVERS
● WOMEN'S COOPERATIVE/
LAUNDROMAT

CATHOLIC
MISSION ■
■ ETHNIC ART INSTITUTE
OF MICRONESIA
ACES ■
MARKET
LAND
RESOURCES ■

DEPARTMENT OF
EDUCATION ■
NEW RAI-VIEW
HOTEL ●
Chamorro
POST-●
OFFICE
TAXI
STAND
■
SEE
DETAIL
■ YAP COOP STORE

YAP MARINA/■
BEYOND THE REEF
SPANISH FORT/
■ GOVERNMENT OFFICES

ESA ■
HOTEL
Bay
PUBLIC ■
LIBRARY
■ STATE LEGISLATURE

FISHERIES
BUILDING

THE ●
PATHWAYS
HOTEL

Harbor

Tamil

WAAB
MAK'UFF
MARKET ■

FSM ■
TELECOM
POLICE ■
STATION
■ YCA
TOURISM ■
OFFICE

To Airport

© MOON PUBLICATIONS, INC.

To Balabat

0   .5 mi
0   .5 km

Continue to the south end of the road where a **dancing ground** rests between two stone platforms *(wunbey).* A stone path leads off to the right. All this can be seen on foot from Colonia in a couple of hours, or in less than an hour by car.

South of Colonia

The remains of an old **German cable station** still stand beyond the high school between Colonia and the airport. The Germans had an advanced undersea cable system linking Yap to Guam, Sulawesi, and Shanghai until World War I. The first message telegraphed around the world passed through this station. A British gunboat shot down the 200-foot-high steel radio mast in 1914, but you can still see the three huge concrete pylons that supported the tower.

The unused **old airstrip,** parallel to, and south of, the present strip, was built by the Japanese. Over a dozen Japanese planes are in fragments near it, most of them destroyed on the ground by Allied aircraft. Notice the gun half hidden in the vegetation between the weather station and the old airport terminal.

Beside the highway, just a few hundred feet south of the crossroads and to the west of the road, is a wrecked **Japanese bomber** with German engines. Notice the small insect-eating plants in this area. After exploring the old airport, cool off in the deep freshwater swimming hole at the rock quarry just southwest of the end of the new airstrip.

Driving farther south on the main road, a well-maintained dirt road, opposite St. Ignatius of Loyola Church is a dirt path to the left. This path hits a wider dirt road where, if you make a right, the road goes through mangroves to the ocean. It is not a place to swim, but a pleasant spot for a picnic. There is even a barbecue pit set up.

Less than a mile farther down the road is another left-hand turnoff that leads to the village of Dulkaan. The path down is lovely, lined with hibiscus. It is probably best to do this one-quarter-mile walk on foot, as the residents do not seem to appreciate tourists driving through town.

Better still is a visit to Ngariy, which one reaches by a path off to the left of the main road, about a mile farther south. The village has a new meeting hall and an old platform. The Ngariy road dead-ends into the unpaved coastal road. A few feet to the right lie the remains of a stone path lined with stone money. The path leads down to the water through the mangroves; the walk down from the main road is less than a quarter mile. Bug repellent is a must, but this trip is well worth it. It's extremely picturesque and gives a feel for how wealthy Yap once was.

North of Colonia

Two wonderful villages quite near each other are **Okaaw** and **Kadaay**. From the YCA building in Colonia, take the road toward the airport for approximately 1.4 miles. You will see a broad dirt road leading to the right. Take it and go right again at the next fork. About two miles farther, you'll see an unmarked road to the left that leads to the village of Kadaay. Unless you want to miss one of the most beautiful spots on the island, do *not* take the road. Instead park the car and get out. About 20 feet down the road to Kadaay, off to the left, lies a fantastic, restored stone walkway. It wanders through a vision of what tropical life was like when homes, jungle, and agriculture blended with each other and the earth.

The path is raised above fields of taro, banana plants, and betel nut trees. You pass magnificent banyan trees. There is one fork in the path; both branches lead to Kadaay, so whichever you take down, take the other back up.

Once in the village, check out the well-kept meetinghouse, set near a dancing area, and the stone money bank and sitting areas, complete with stone backrests. The village is one of the most peaceful spots I have ever seen.

In front of the meetinghouse, note the stone backrest with a carved lizard. To the people of

Yap, the lizard is the dumbest of animals because it climbs coconut trees for no apparent purpose. Therefore, to call someone a lizard is a supreme insult. Around the turn of the century, village morale was low, and the villagers ceased working together for the common good. One villager carved this lizard to show the rest the error of their ways and to encourage them toward better behavior.

The charge to walk through the village is $2, money that goes directly to the village. For prices ranging from $20 to $40, the village offers package tours. Such tours can include a dinner of local foods and traditional dancing by children. With advance notice, the village will arrange for a master to teach you the rudiments of local weaving. Either your hotel or the Tourism Office should be able to make arrangements for you.

If you return to the road and go another half mile, to the right you'll see an unmarked, broad stone path that begins near a house on the right, just before a small bridge. The beginning of the path measures a majestic 12 feet across. Most of the path is shaded by coconut palms. As is the custom in much of Yap, the sides of the path are lined with ornamental plants, such as hibiscus. On the trail, look for a piece of stone money serving as part of a bridge. This must have been a village of very high rollers.

It is a 10-minute walk to the village meetinghouse. It is quite large, but in a state of disrepair. The house is surrounded by stone money, one piece being at least eight feet in diameter. From here it's possible to continue on the stone footpath clear across the island. Follow the stream that winds through a bamboo forest punctuated with immense banyan trees and taro patches until you meet up with the road; take it down to Dugor on the east coast. This trip can be done in less than three hours on foot, if you don't get lost. But the trail is difficult to follow in spots and you may wish to hire one of the village children as a guide.

Gagil-Tomil

If you take the main road north from Colonia, in just over six miles there is a turnoff on the right marked Tamiling School that turns into a broad, good-quality dirt road. In about 1.5 miles, you reach the pretty hilltop village of Bogol. Make a right-hand turn in front of the bright blue church called St. Peter Chanel. About 50 feet farther, on your right, you will come to a beautiful meetinghouse. The meetinghouse is surrounded by a great deal of stone money.

If instead you take a left in Bogol, you will wind up in Maa, a village that organizes ceremonial dancing which hotels can arrange for their guests. The going price is $30 pp for the show.

The main road, if heading north, turns to dirt at the Maritime Academy, which is about a half mile past where a paved road comes in from the left. The United States Coast Guard once had a **LORAN station** here. In January 1990 the Micronesian Maritime and Fisheries Academy, operated by Pacific Missionary Aviation, opened.

Past the Maritime Academy, take the left fork and the road will end at the beach in the village of Wanyaan, one of the most charming spots in Yap. Past the modern concrete meetinghouse on the right are the remains of the old meetinghouse. Much stone money lies along the pathway. Many homes, even some modern ones, rest on high stacked-stone foundations. There are many thatched-roof homes.

The road then leads to a beach with four thatch-covered cabanas, voted by an international panel as the best spot to take a nap in the Northern Hemisphere. Behind the beach is an enclosed cabana for changing and a shower. The beach provides excellent snorkeling, though at high tide it is a *long* swim out to the deep waterholes.

As you arrive in Wanyaan, there is a small store to the right. Be sure to stop there on the way in or out to pay the $1 pp fee that benefits the community.

Maap

At **Bechiyal** near the north tip of Maap are three large traditional buildings including a men's house, set on a good beach. The larger building is a reconstructed *pebai* (meetinghouse), and in front of it is a *tabinaw* or residence. The *pebai* and a handicraft shop contain exhibits from the defunct Yap Museum in Colonia, including various kinds of shell money. All construction work here was supervised by Chief John Tamag, a master builder. The Endowment for Historic Preservation of the Micronesia Institute in Washington, D.C., supported this project.

The white sandy beach at Bechiyal slopes far out into the lagoon, which makes it very safe for children, but snorkelers have to swim quite a distance to reach the reef. Collecting live seashells is not allowed. There are several good short hikes in the vicinity, including walks along the beach to fish traps or to the mangrove forest.

The Bechiyal complex is part of a low-impact tourism plan. A $2.50 pp sightseeing fee is charged. Those with video or movie cameras are charged $25 extra, plus $20 for each local person involved in the filming, a price we assume was set to be prohibitive to anyone other than a Hollywood producer.

DAVID STANLEY

The Bechiyal men's house overlooks a sandy beach.

To stay in the men's house (women may stay also) or the guest cottage at Bechiyal, talk to Marietta T. Fathal at the Tourism Office in Colonia, or write Bechiyal Cultural Center, P.O. Box 37, Colonia, Yap, FM 96943. The charge is $10 pp in the men's house, $15 pp in the guesthouse, or $3 pp to camp on the green grass amid the whispering palms. The men's house and the guesthouse are nicer than you might expect, but do bring bug repellent and use the provided mosquito netting. The guesthouse is an unfurnished thatched cottage able to accommodate up to 10 persons on floor mats. Groups of three persons or more get a reduced rate of $10 pp in the guesthouse; in the men's house groups of six or more pay only $5 pp. Children are half price. Washing is done in a clean, enclosed bathhouse. Chief Tamag's kind family serves local meals of fried breadfruit chips, bananas, taro, and fish for $3-4; coconuts are 25 cents.

A bus runs into town early on weekday mornings and returns in the afternoon. A taxi from Colonia will be about $10 for the car (not pp). It's a 30-minute walk from the end of the road to Bechiyal. If you are driving, go straight when you come to a fork in the paved road—do not take the road to the left. The road you will then be on becomes a dirt road that ends at a wooden footbridge. To get to the Cultural Center, you walk through two of the most traditional villages on the island, Wanead and Tooruw. On the walk stay on the main track until it hits a T and only a small path lies ahead of you. Take that small path, which gets muddy when wet and leads to the center. Wear good walking shoes.

Bechiyal faces the forbidden island of **Rumung,** whose people have decided they're not ready for tourism yet.

ACCOMMODATIONS

Colonia is home to virtually all the state's hotels and restaurants. The tap water is not suitable for drinking, and during the dry season many hotels have water for showers only during certain hours a day. Add 10% room tax to the hotel rates. With two exceptions, **The Pathways** and the **Manta Ray Bay Hotel,** they are all budget hotels that require you to rough it a bit. *Be advised that many places on Yap do not take cred-*

FSM Country Code 691

it cards. Be certain to have sufficient United States dollars or traveler's checks with you.

Budget
The **New Rai-View Hotel** (Rose and Lonnie Fread, P.O. Box 488, Colonia, Yap, FM 96943, tel./fax 350-3527) is in an older two-story wooden building on a hill just above town, near government buildings. All basic but clean rooms now have private baths and are a good value at $40. The owner may negotiate a lower price for longer stays or for commercial travelers. In August 1995, the 10 rooms were being equipped with air conditioning.

The **Ocean View Hotel** (P.O. Box 130 Colonia, Yap, FM 96943., tel. 350-2279, fax 350-2339) is near the ocean, but few rooms have interesting ocean views. Run by Joe Tamag, the hotel has a familial feel, but the architecture also gives a crowded, close feeling. Rooms are $40 s, $50 d. Like the ESA Hotel and the New Rai-View Hotel, it has water problems.

The **ESA Hotel** (Elena and Silbester Alfonso, P.O. Box 141, Colonia, Yap, FM 96943, tel. 350-2139, fax 350-2310) is in a two-story, dreary concrete building on the south side of Chamorro Bay. It has 16 small rooms at $45. Water is only provided 6-10 a.m. and 4:30-8:30 p.m., even during the wet season. The common areas are not well kept.

More Expensive
The most charming stay in Colonia is at **The Pathways** (P.O. Box 718, Colonia, Yap, FM 96943, tel. 350-3310, fax 350-2066). Overlooking Chamorro Bay, its eight attractive thatched cottages are set on a hillside. The cottages rent for $85; a/c is an extra $10. Each rustic, individually screened unit has a private balcony overlooking the bay, a private bath, ceiling fans, and a king-size bed. The cottages are separated by lush vegetation, including such exotica as torch ginger and betel nut trees, and are connected by picturesque wooden walkways, all set into the hillside. There is a bar and a breakfast restaurant attached. The Pathways is owned by an American expat doctor, Don Evans, and

his Yapese partners, Stan and Flora Fillmed. Son John Fillmed is increasingly taking over day-to-day operations.

Beside the harbor in the center of town is the **Manta Ray Bay Hotel** (P.O. Box MR, Yap, FM 96943, tel. 350-2300, fax 350-4567), a modern three-story building opened in 1990. The 15 a/c rooms begin at $110 s, $130 d. The Manta Ray Bay serves the needs of divers admirably, as it also runs the leading dive shop on the island, Yap Divers next door, and boats leave from a dock behind the hotel reception area. If you plan to dive every day and can afford it, this is an excellent choice.

The Destiny (P.O. Box 428, Colonia, Yap, FM 96943, tel. 350-4188, fax 350-4187), formerly the Flying Fish Resort, is located in the village of Anooth, on the southern tip of Yap. There are plans for it to become a 24-unit resort with restaurant and bar. At present there are only two beautifully constructed cottages, each with a small kitchenette. They are isolated, with few surrounding services. Until (or unless) the resort's plans materialize, the cottages are extremely overpriced at $150 per night.

In addition to the places listed above, the **Tourism Office** (P.O. Box 36, Colonia, Yap, FM 96943, tel. 350-2298) can arrange stays in Yapese homes, costing about $25 pp a day including meals in villages near Colonia, or $15 pp in more remote villages. Among the local people receiving guests are Martin Datmagurun, Falownug Kenmed, Martin Dugchur (at Toruw village in Maap), and Robert A. Wuyoch (at Maa village in Tamil). This is a good way to meet the people provided you don't mind sacrificing privacy and roughing it.

In a pinch the best place near Colonia to look for a campsite would be up behind the water tank on the road to the Coast Guard lighthouse. **Campers** will do much better at the Bechiyal Cultural Center described above, the only place on Yap that caters to campers, including those in tents. ($3 pp).

FOOD

Until recently, there has not been a restaurant with truly good food on Yap. The new chef, Bill A.D. Munn, who joined the Manta Ray Bay Hotel

in December, 1995, is changing things, though. Some of the other restaurants have pleasant atmosphere and are good places to meet other travelers. Perhaps it is still best, however, to try to eat out no more than once a day. For locally grown vegetables and color check out the **Waab Mak'uuf Market.**

The pleasant restaurant-bar on the roof of the **Manta Ray Bay Hotel** overlooks the lagoon and usually has a delicious breeze. Now it may also have delicious food. Joining the hotel after leaving the Palau Pacific Resort, Jamaican-Canadian chef Munn is the new executive chef and brings with him promises of a much-improved dining experience.

The **Yap Marina** (tel. 350-2211), past the YCA, has a breezy terrace overlooking the bay where sandwiches, full meals, and cheap treats (cold coconuts for 75 cents, ice cream for $1.25) are served. Alcohol is also served after 1 p.m., and at happy hour the price of a Foster's drops to $1.50.

Kool Korner Restaurant (Vicky's), upstairs in the YCA complex, is a popular place for lunch. It's air conditioned, and the food, though not particularly good, is not particularly expensive.

The food at the **Queen B Restaurant** is pretty good, the service is lovely, and it's less expensive than most. From the YCA building in Colonia, take the road to the airport. In 1.4 miles you will see a broad dirt road leading to the right. Go about 300 feet past the dump and you will see a sign for a left turn onto a smaller dirt road that leads to the restaurant. It is located in a suburban tract-style home, in the middle of nowhere. The Filipina waitress thought she had signed on for a job in *the* States, not the Federated States. Two rooms lead off the dining room: one is a law office and the other an architect's. One-stop service at its best; I imagine ordering lumpia, a will, and a bathroom addition. Try the special—soup, salad, tuna sashimi, and fried tuna for $5.49.

The ESA Hotel Restaurant has air conditioning, no booze, and the most painful service on the island.

For your power breakfast on Yap, you can't beat **The Pathways.** For $5 you get unlimited coffee, a plate of hot muffins, and a huge assortment of local fruit served on a lovely outdoor patio. The only other food served at the Pathways is during Friday afternoon's happy hour (specials may include barbecued chicken for $4). Each week's food will be different. The other days of the week the bar is open 4:30-8:45 p.m., but for drinks only.

Drinkers staying on Yap for more than 30 days must obtain a drinking permit ($5) at the police.

OTHER PRACTICALITIES

Sports and Recreation

If you are going to dive in Palau, rightly famous for its diving, do yourself a favor and arrange a couple of days to also dive in Yap. Yap is one of Micronesia's most popular new scuba destinations and depending on the time of year, diving takes place at sites all around the island. One of the favorites is Gilman Wall off the southwest tip of the lagoon. From a depth of 35-40 feet a vertical wall plunges 650 feet. Large fish abound, including barracuda, tuna, and jacks, plus eagle rays, turtles, moray eels, and harmless sharks. The water is clear, prime diving spots are only a short boat ride away, and the hard corals are spectacular.

Yap is perhaps the best spot on earth to see manta rays. These beautiful and peaceful cousins to the shark return day after day to be cleaned of parasites by wrasses who make their living this way. By showing up at the cleaning stations, you can stay beneath them and see these graceful creatures, some with 12-foot wingspreads, swim by. Every manta has unique markings, and folks from the Yap Divers shop have identified and named 45 of them.

Yap Divers (Bill Acker, P.O. Box MR, Colonia, Yap, FM 96943, tel. 350-2300, fax 350-4567) is the oldest, largest, and most established dive shop on Yap. It's beside the Manta Ray Bay Hotel in Colonia and runs under joint management. The charge for a two-tank dive including a sandwich and beverages is $95 (minimum of two persons), night diving $45. Certification cards are carefully scrutinized. Snorkelers may go along with the divers for $45 pp.

A second choice, and a bit less expensive, is **Beyond the Reef,** managed by David Vecella. Located on the marina, advance arrangement can be made through P.O. Box 609, Yap, FM 96943, tel./fax 350-2537.

We cannot recommend the third dive shop, **Nature's Way.** We are troubled that it rents too much of its equipment from others to ensure proper maintenance.

Beyond the Reef and **Yap Angler,** another enterprise of Bill Acker's, also run fishing trips. Full-day charters are $130 pp and half day are $95. You can try trolling for tuna, wahoo, or mahi. Another experience is to go "whipping" for giant trevally. The boat will go out to the reef, where you will cast and pull the lure back very quickly. Hooking into a 20-50 pounder will be an experience you won't soon forget.

These Yap fishing companies encourage those fishing to "catch and release" unless the fish has been injured in the fight. They also do not use stainless steel hooks. That way, the hook will not permanently remain in a fish that gets away.

If you want to try surfing, the mouth of the harbor appears to be the best spot.

Shopping

The **YCA** (Yap Cooperative Association) store in the center of town sells Yap T-shirts. **Family Chain Store** offers a wide selection of goods and keeps the longest hours in Colonia (7:30 a.m.-8 p.m. daily). The hardware department sells masks and snorkels.

You can buy a Yap State "Island of Stone Money" license plate at the police station for $5. Stamps and first day covers are available at the post office.

Services

The Bank of Hawaii (tel. 350-2129) has a branch in Colonia and is open Mon.-Thurs. 9:30 a.m.-3 p.m., Friday 9 a.m.-5 p.m. The Bank of FSM (tel. 350-2329) is in the YCA Complex.

You can place long distance telephone calls at the Telecommunications Corporation (open 24 hours) up the road toward the New Rai-View Hotel. Rates are cheaper 6 p.m.-6 a.m. and on Sunday.

Address mail to Yap, FM 96943.

The FSM Immigration office (tel. 350-2126) is upstairs near Vicky's Kool Korner in the new YCA complex.

There are free public toilets in the Marina Center and the YCA building.

You'll find a laundromat (open weekdays 8

a.m.-4:30 p.m., Sunday from noon) in an unmarked building next to the Yap Divers office.

Information

Marietta T. Fathal in the Tourism Office, tel. 350-2298, has information leaflets on Yap, can answer questions, and will even arrange accommodations in local homes.

The Yap Public Library (P.O. Box 550, Colonia, Yap, FM 96943, tel. 350-2793) on the marina pier is open Mon.-Fri. 1:30-4:30 p.m. There is a covered basketball court behind it.

Radio station WSZA-AM broadcasts at 1490.

GETTING THERE

Yap Airport (YAP) is 3.5 miles southwest of town. All hotel keepers meet the flights at the airport and provide transfers at about $3 pp each way, or you can easily hitch a ride into town. There is a $10 departure tax.

Wednesday, Friday, and Sunday, Yap is a **Continental Air Micronesia** stopover between Guam and Palau, so the cheapest way to get there is to include Yap in a through ticket between Honolulu and Koror. From Southeast Asia, you can purchase a Continental ticket from Manila to Koror to Yap to Koror to Manila. Inquire whether there are any off-peak special fares.

Reconfirm your onward flight at the Continental Air Micronesia office (tel. 350-2127) at the YCA building.

GETTING AROUND

The terrain of Yap can be a bit confusing and roads are seldom marked. While driving or walking, you come upon many dirt lanes too small to place on most maps. The easiest way to reach your destination is by consulting the large *Topographic Map of Yap,* produced by the United States Geological Service in 1983. The Land Resources office near the New Rai-View Hotel sells it for $7.50. The map is extremely detailed and despite its age, it's still useful because most newer roads are merely upgrades of older roads or paths on the map. (Note: For some linguistic convention, the map frequently places the letter "Q" before or after "A" in place-names.)

local transport

Public buses connect the outlying villages to Colonia (50 cents) weekdays only, leaving the villages at the crack of dawn and departing the Waab Mak'uuf Market, Colonia, around 5 p.m. They are primarily for the use of students or people commuting to work.

Taxis are $1 anywhere in town. Price must be negotiated for longer trips. It is sometimes cheaper to hire a cab for an afternoon of sightseeing than to rent a car for the day. **Midland Taxi Service** can be reached at 350-2405.

The **ESA Hotel** (tel. 350-2138, fax 350-2310) and **New-Rai View** (tel. 350-2537, fax 350-2357) both rent a few cars each (automatics, with a/c and stereo). ESA is a little more expensive at $40 a day plus 10% tax compared to $30 a day plus tax at New Rai-View.

Pacific Bus Company (tel. 350-2266, fax 350-4116) in the hardware department behind Family Chain Store rents compacts at $40 a day plus 10% tax and sedans at $45 a day (all automatics, with a/c and stereo).

Target Store (tel. 350-3275) rents sedans

and pickups (standard with a/c and radio) for $37 a day plus 10% tax.

Island Rentals Company (tel. 350-2566, fax 350-2555) has sedans and pickups (all with a/c and radio, most standard transmission). Sedans rent for $38 a day plus 10% tax, and the pickups run $25-35 a day plus tax.

There is an excellent paved highway from the airport to Colonia, Tomil, Gagil, and Maap. When driving, observe the speed limit of 20 mph on roads, 15 mph in villages. Local chiefs often set "sand traps" (holes in the road filled with sand) in their villages to catch speeding cars.

To the Outer Islands by Air
Pacific Missionary Aviation (PMA; P.O. Box 460, Colonia, Yap, FM 96943, tel. 350-2360, fax 350-2539) flies Monday and Friday between Yap and Ulithi ($60 one-way); Friday between Yap and Fais ($75 one-way); every other Wednesday between Yap and Woleai ($150 one-way); and on Friday roundtrip between Ulithi and Fais ($25 one-way). Free baggage is limited to 30 pounds.

PMA was founded to support medical missionaries, but flights are available to visitors. This praiseworthy company carries out emergency medical evacuations and transports referral patients, bodies of deceased, and medical supplies at no charge.

Field Trips
The **Yap State Transportation Field Trip Service** (P.O. Box 576, Colonia, Yap, FM 96943, tel. 350-2240, fax 350-4113) in the radio room of the government offices in Colonia runs the fieldtrip ship MV *Micro Spirit* from Yap to Ulithi, Fais, Faraulep, Woleai, Ifalik, Eauripik, Sorol, and Ngulu about every five weeks. Actually there are two field trips: a short one from Yap to Ulithi and perhaps one other island, and a long one to the inhabited islands of eastern Yap.

Try to be there a week before departure to arrange required permits, extension of stay, and trip bookings. On an outer island the radio operator will know the estimated time of arrival of the ship.

Seven simple double cabins are available on the first deck, but 95% of the passengers travel deck. Fares are roughly five cents a mile on deck or 20 cents a mile cabin. Bookings have to

be made a few days in advance, otherwise an additional fee may be charged. Meals in the officers' mess are $3 for breakfast, $4 for lunch, and $4.50 for dinner.

Take plenty of food with you from Yap (soups, coffee, tea, canned food) and be self-sufficient. Locals always have rice, taro, breadfruit, dried or smoked fish, and bunches of fresh coconuts, and they're always inviting you to meals. In return offer them canned food or meat, which they can't get without spending their very limited money.

Take a few 10-quart plastic containers along to fill with fresh rainwater, or bring your own purification unit. The captain has a small shop to sell cigarettes, biscuits, and cold drinks, but these sometimes run out by the end of the trip.

On deck a straw mat and a thin sleeping bag will do for a bed and should be rolled out early upon boarding. The washing facilities are poor and only a half-hour of water daily is allowed for military-style showers. Be quick so you don't end up with a soapy body and no water.

The Field Trip Officer (FTO) is the one responsible for the itinerary, payments, and cargo. He also has a cupboard with medications. A doctor is often aboard to check the island people at short stops. A field trip can seem very long if you're not making friends on deck and taking the supply boat ashore at stops. Always make sure to get back to the ship on time, as they could easily leave without you. Keep in mind that the field trips are meant to serve the outer islanders, not tourists.

THE OUTER ISLANDS

The Outer Islanders
The Western Caroline Islands east of Yap are among the most traditional in the Pacific. The men still pierce their ears and noses and tattoo their bodies. They sing the chants of their forefathers and travel long distances by sailing canoe.

Women wear knee-length *lava lava* held in place by a string of shells or a girdle belt. Men wear a *thu* (loincloth) consisting of a long piece of cloth wrapped around the waist and between the legs. Neither men nor women wear any upper garment. Every outer island has a men's house or two. During menstruation women move to the *pal* (women's house).

Permissions

If you'd like to take the plane to Ulithi, Fais, or Woleai and stay a couple of days, you must first get clearance in Colonia. Apply at the Office of the Governor who may send you to meet with an outer island council in Madrich. The same procedure is required to spend time on an outer island between visits of the field-trip ship.

You're supposed to apply one month prior to your arrival at the outer island. If you're really serious about going, call ahead at 350-2108, or write two months in advance to the Office of the Governor, State of Yap, Colonia, Yap, FM 96943, stating precisely which atoll you'd like to visit, when, and why. Upon arrival in Yap check with the Outer Islands Affairs office at the governor's office. If you arrive in Yap not having applied for permission, with persistence, luck, and most of all a local contact, you may be able to obtain permission, sometimes with remarkable speed. You'll be expected to take enough food for the duration of your stay. Of course, take all medical supplies with you, and pay a courtesy call on the island chief upon arrival. An "entry fee" of $20 pp must be paid to the chief upon arrival at each island.

Advance permission is not required to visit the outer islands on a field-trip ship as a through passenger, provided you only get off for a couple of hours to look around while the ship's there. Tourists are not allowed to disembark for longer stays without consent.

People on the outer islands are not used to tourists. Arriving foreigners usually have been missionaries, Peace Corps volunteers, anthropologists, fisheries researchers, etc. Nobody is interested in tourism yet, so you'll be their guest. You will be offered food at many homes, and it is considered bad manners and suspicious behavior to decline. Don't eat too much at any one house as you may be called upon to eat at many. Coffee, tea, or betel nuts make welcome gifts to reciprocate the hospitality.

Ulithi

Ulithi (pop. 900), 106 miles northeast of Yap, has 49 small islets on its reef, which encloses a 183-square-mile lagoon. In 1731, a 13-member Jesuit missionary party under Father Juan Antonio Cantova landed on Ulithi. When the Spanish returned the next year, they found the islanders had wiped out the Jesuits.

The Japanese built an airstrip on Ulithi but evacuated to Yap when an American landing became imminent. On 20 September 1944, the United States Navy occupied Ulithi, unopposed. A thousand United States warships assembled in the Ulithi lagoon ("Flattop Row") prior to the landings on Iwo Jima and Okinawa in early 1945.

The presently inhabited islands of Ulithi are Asor, Falealop, Fatharai, and Mogmog. The airstrip, radio transmitter, administrative offices, post office, and Outer Islands High School are all on Falealop Island. The high school buildings were once part of a LORAN station, now closed. The school serves students from all the outer islands.

PMA (Pacific Missionary Aviation) flies in from Yap on Monday and Friday, and an outboard from Mogmog usually runs to Falealop to meet the plane ($60). PMA also flies in from Woleai on demand for $130. The field-trip ship calls at Ulithi on both the outward and inward journeys. It delivers supplies to all the villages on the way out, but may stop only at Falealop on the way back.

Mogmog is the chiefly island, where men once went to have their bodies covered in tattoos. The chief of Mogmog is the high chief of the atoll. There is rivalry between the government representative in Falealop and the chief.

Western clothing and alcohol are prohibited on Mogmog; on Falealop the women are covering up. As hurricanes destroy the old thatched

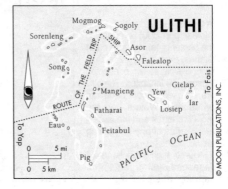

houses, dwellings of tin and concrete appear. Much work is still done communally. The men catch fish and the women cook vegetables from the gardens. If a fishing boat hasn't returned by dusk, the village launches a rescue mission.

If you are male, ask permission of the chief to stay in one of the two *fal* (men's houses). The stock in the couple of small stores often runs out, so bring food.

Fais

Fais (pop. 250) was once mined by the Japanese for its phosphate: the ruins of machinery and railroad can still be seen. Today the inhabitants live from fishing, vegetable gardening, and copra production, subsidized by assistance programs. This raised atoll has no lagoon. Access is fairly easy with weekly PMA flights from Yap ($75) and Ulithi ($35) on Friday, and from Woleai on demand for $110.

Eauripik

Large ships cannot enter Eauripik's long, fish-filled lagoon. The 100 inhabitants crowded onto the tiny islet at the east end of the atoll don't make copra because they need the coconuts to eat. Instead they smoke fish to exchange at Woleai, which they visit by sailing canoe. A passing freighter that lost a few big tropical logs recently was much appreciated by the skilled Eauripik canoe builders. They also make beautiful woodcarvings and other handicrafts of seashells. They build their houses on massive stone platforms to resist hurricanes, which flush waves over the islands.

Woleai

Woleai (pop. 800) is roughly in the center of the eastern outer islands. Five of the 22 islands around Woleai's two connected lagoons are inhabited. The others are used for copra and taro production. Woleai has the most breadfruit and the largest reef islands of any of the Yap atolls.

A junior high school and old Japanese airstrip remain on Falealop, where the high chief

resides. Thousands of bypassed Japanese soldiers starved on Woleai in 1945. Wrecked planes, cannons, bunkers, and dumped heavy equipment still rot in the bush. Former railway tracks are used as curbs along the roads or as supports for cooking pots.

Pacific Missionary Aviation flies into Woleai's wartime airstrip from Yap every other Wednesday ($150). The FSM government hopes eventually to have internal flights from Chuuk to Yap that needn't pass through Guam. Woleai would make an ideal stop. Many islanders fear the changes this would bring.

The Japanese government donated a modern ice plant to Woleai, but it's seldom in use due to maintenance problems and enormous fuel consumption. Aside from American education, the school on Woleai teaches youngsters skills such as weaving, rope and canoe making, fish trap manufacturing, and traditional dancing. The graduation ceremony is the biggest event on Woleai, with dance practice beginning weeks before.

Satawal

Many Satawal islanders, from the easternmost inhabited atoll of Yap, have emigrated to work on Yap, leaving Satawal with a population of about 500. Some of the best old Pacific navigators live on Satawal, setting their course by the ocean swells and relative positions of the stars. In 1988 Lino Olopai of Satawal sailed his outrigger canoe to Saipan in this way. A new

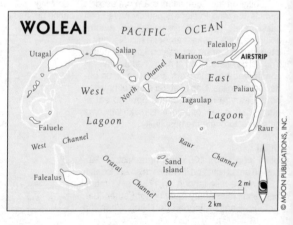

consulting industry has developed that supports inquisitive museums, writers, and filmmakers eager to learn the ways of Satawal. Mau Piailug, navigator of the famous Polynesian sailing canoe *Hokule'a,* is from Satawal. The *Hokule'a* sailed with a native Hawaiian crew and no modern navigational devices from Hawaii to Tahiti.

Other Islands

Sorol atoll has only two or three resident families, among the most isolated families on earth. Outboard motors are banned on highly traditional **Ifalik** atoll (pop. 475). Fish are mostly caught on an outer reef about 9.4 miles north of Ifalik, always by outrigger canoes. The Phallus of Maur stood in the meetinghouse (Tan Nap) on Ifalik until Catholic missionaries managed to engineer its removal.

Elato (pop. 70) and **Lamotrek** (pop. 300) are two of the most beautiful atolls of Yap, with an unspoiled traditional way of life and sailing canoes. Lamotrek is well known for the traditional magic still practiced there. Together with Satawal these islands have been hard hit by typhoons in recent years, and there still could be a serious shortage of food and water, so check before heading that way.

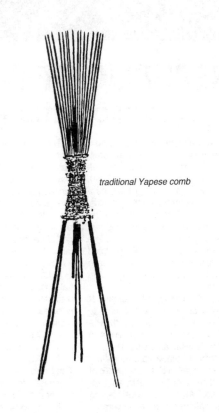

traditional Yapese comb

GORDY OHLIGER

REPUBLIC OF PALAU
INTRODUCTION

Quite simply, above water, below water, Palau is pure beauty. The great cities of the world present visitors with surprises at every corner or hillcrest. Koror, capital of the Republic of Palau, does the same in a town of only 10,000 people. It's not the buildings or the neighborhoods, of course, but the breathtaking setting of the town, a fantastic crazy quilt of islands, bridges, and water that is like nothing else on earth. The otherworldly Rock Islands, looming like sculpted green mushrooms, dot the horizons. If you have one day to spend in Micronesia, spend it in Palau's Rock Islands.

With about 15,000 citizens, the Republic of Palau is the smallest of the four political units to emerge from the former Trust Territory of the Pacific Islands. Much to their credit, this small nation was the world's first to issue an Elvis stamp.

Although the correct Palauan pronunciation of the country is as if spelled Belau, Republic of *Palau* is the official name of the country and, according to the Visitors Authority, it is the spelling most likely to get mail from abroad delivered.

The Palau cluster consists of 343 islands strewn along a line that begins with Kayangel in the northeast and ends with Angaur, 125 miles southwest, most within one encircling barrier reef. This spectacular group, at the southwest corner of the Western Caroline Islands, offers great diversity, from tiny dots to 153-square-mile Babeldaob, the second-largest island in Micronesia (Guam is bigger). In addition are the far-flung Southwest Islands, home to fewer than 100 people.

Only nine islands are inhabited. Two-thirds of Palau's population resides in Koror, the capital. Since this small island republic is equally distant from Guam and Indonesia, and only 550 miles east of the Philippines, its strategic position explains the bitter battles fought over it during World War II and the subsequent United States military interest.

The Land
The east side of the giant lagoon created by the barrier reef is riddled with hundreds of tiny umbrella-shaped islands, called the **Rock Islands**

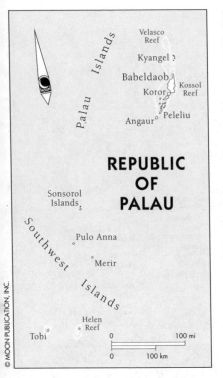

REPUBLIC OF PALAU

temperatures here tend to be slightly higher than elsewhere in Micronesia. Daily and seasonal variations in temperature are small. The heaviest rains occur early in the morning, with a second peak just after sunset.

Flora and Fauna

Palau's flora and fauna are the richest in Micronesia. The variety of habitats and proximity to the Indo-Malay faunal region explain the tremendous diversity of life in the lagoon. Scientists have found that as the distance from Southeast Asia increases, the number of species both above and below water decreases. Hawaii, for example, has only one-half to one-third as many varieties of fish and coral as Palau. Three nutrient-carrying ocean currents merge here. In all, some 1,500 species of tropical fish and 700 different types of coral and anemones may be seen at Palau. Collecting coral and seashells is prohibited.

Palau's seagoing crocodiles, which inhabit the rivers and mangroves of Babeldaob, as well as other locations, probably arrived from New Guinea. They grow up to 16 feet long. Like all wild animals, they're shy and will flee from people if they can. Not a single crocodile incident has been reported since 1965. But if you are

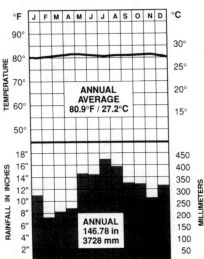

KOROR'S CLIMATE

(Chalbacheb is the Palauan name). These rounded, undercut mounds of limestone float like emerald mushrooms on a turquoise-fringed sapphire lagoon. Formed from the weathering of ancient uplifted reefs, the islands have secluded beaches, tranquil channels, clear water, and unbelievably rich coral formations and marinelife.

Babeldaob has a 700-foot-high volcanic center, fringed by mangrove forests. Add Babeldaob's freshwater Ngardok Lake (2,961 feet long) to Palau's perfect coral atoll (Kayangel) and two elevated limestone islands (Angaur and Peleliu), and you have one of the most compact and varied physical environments to be found in any ocean. Further, the Palau Visitors Authority promises, "At night the bright Southern Cross in clear sky will not fail to bring you a romantic mood."

Climate

Palau is alternately sunny and rainy, but always hot and humid. Due to its southerly location,

THE PALAU ISLANDS

Northwest Reef

West Entrance

North Entrance

Kossol Reef

East Entrance

Philippine

Sea

NGARDMAU STATE

Ollei

MTEULEOL DOCK

Mengellang

OKETOL DOCK

Ngardmau Bay

URRUNG DOCK

UCHERAEL DOCK

Ngaregur

Ngerbau

NGARCHELONG STATE

Chol

Chelab

NGARAARD STATE

NGEREMLENGUI STATE

Ngetbong

Ulimang

Kgkeklau

Babeldaob

Island

Ngermechau

NGIWAL STATE

West Passage

NGATPANG STATE

Ngermetengel

Imeong

Ngardok Lake

Melekeok

Ngeruikl

Ngerubesang

MELEKEOK STATE

Ibobang

Chimizu

Oisca

Ngchesar

NGCHESAR STATE

AIMELIIK STATE

Medorm

Ngchemiangel

Elechui

Imul

Rrai

Ngerngesang

Ngerkeai

Falls

Channel

Ngetkip

Arakabesan

Koror

Airai

Oikuul

Malakal Harbor

Arangel

AIRPORT

Aranget

Rock Islands

Malakal Pass

AIRAI STATE

Shark City

Augulpelu Reef

KOROR STATE

Orukuizu

PACIFIC

OCEAN

Ngemelis Islands

Eil Malk

Dengess Passage

Ngercheu

Barnum Bay

Ngerugelbtang

AIRFIELD

Peleliu

PELELIU STATE

0   10 mi

0   10 km

© MOON PUBLICATIONS, INC.

*an early
19th-century
view of Palau*

lucky enough to see one, a rare event, don't push your luck.

Palau, particularly Peleliu, is excellent for observing birds. Birdwatchers should purchase a copy of *Field Guide to the Birds of Palau* by John Engbring.

HISTORY

Creation

On the isle of Angaur lived a child named Uab, who had a voracious appetite. An average meal consisted of 50 large baskets of food, plus dozens of basins of spring water and coconut juice. Reaching manhood, Uab grew so fat he could no longer feed himself, and men had to climb ladders to force food into his mouth. His size increased to the point where only his head would fit into the large house built just for him. His body stretched out along the beach.

The people of Angaur became frightened and decided to kill him. One night while he slept, they tied him up and set fire to his house. Uab roared and kicked, and Angaur shook. The struggle was so fierce that his body broke into many pieces, which were scattered to the north, forming the islands of Palau.

One leg became Peleliu, another formed Aimeliik. Babeldaob was his body. Today's Ngiwal State is attributed to Uab's stomach, which explains why the inhabitants there eat seven times a day. Ngarchelong was his head, so its residents are the smartest and most talkative

in the republic. The location of Uab's pubic area explains why Aimeliik gets more rain than any other part of Palau.

Prehistory

People may have arrived from Indonesia as long as 4,500 years ago. Carbon dating of abandoned village sites on the Rock Islands proves human habitation for at least 3,500 years. Terrace culture on Babeldaob was at its height in about 1000 C.E. The terraces were abandoned by 1600 C.E. The function of these great earthworks and the reason for their abandonment is not known.

At the time of European contact, Palauans resided in inland villages, associated in regional alliances. The social system was complex and highly organized. A council of chiefs from the 10 clans was headed by two chiefs: High Chief Reklai of Babeldaob (Upper Ocean) and High Chief Ibedul of Youldaop (Lower Ocean), seated at Melekeok and Koror respectively. Traditionally the elder women chose the chief.

Palau was abundantly self-sufficient. Women tended taro pits while men hunted, fished, and harvested breadfruit and betel nuts. Foreign trade centered around exporting stone money to Yap. Bead money *(udoud)* was a symbol of wealth. Legends, which explained the universe to the people, appeared on men's meetinghouses *(bai)* and were painted in limestone caves.

European Impact

Although Spanish and Portuguese navigators visited as early as 1543, it was Capt. Henry Wilson of the East India Company's ship *Antelope*, wrecked in the Rock Islands in 1783, who first publicized Palau in Europe. A chief befriended Wilson and helped him build a schooner to return to Macau. This chief is known in the West as Abba Thulle, though it is probably not merely coincidence that the title for chief in Palauan is "Ibedul." His son, Prince Lebu (also Lee Boo), sailed to London with Wilson, and the published account of the events made Palau briefly as famous in contemporary Europe as Captain Cook's Tahiti. Sadly, Lebu died of smallpox after five months in England.

British traders introduced guns to the islands. During the century from 1783 to 1882, the population declined from upwards of 40,000 to only 4,000, primarily due to influenza and dysentery epidemics brought by Europeans. Early Spanish colonialists were mostly concerned with spreading Catholicism, while Germans, who succeeded them in 1899, concentrated on taking phosphates from Angaur and producing copra.

The Japanese Period

The Japanese, who seized Micronesia from the Germans in 1914, pursued economic development, largely for the benefit of the homeland, and sent over large numbers of immigrants. They paid Palauan laborers seven yen a month. Phosphate and bauxite mines, rice paddies, and pineapple plantations flourished. Palauans were taught to speak Japanese, their lands alienated and the traditional chiefs replaced by Japanese bureaucrats.

Koror became the capital of Micronesia. Its population, four times as large as at present, was overwhelmingly Japanese. Before the war, a streetcar line ran through the city. In the late 1930s the Japanese built military bases, and after 1938 the area was closed to outsiders, a status that continued under the Americans until 1962.

In September 1944, a brutal battle exploded over Peleliu, as Americans sought a base from which to launch their at-

tack on the Philippines. Rather than meet the landings on the beaches, as was the usual Japanese strategy earlier in the war, the Japanese entrenched themselves in caves on a tangled limestone ridge. In two and a half brutal months, some 11,000 Japanese and nearly 2,000 Americans died. These deaths were particularly tragic since most military historians believe today that Peleliu could have been bypassed.

The United States bombed and neutralized Koror and Babeldaob, but never invaded. The 25,000 Japanese troops were left there to sit it out. Prior to the Peleliu landings the Japanese concentrated the Palauan population in central Babeldaob, where 526 (almost 10% of the indigenous population of the time) perished.

Recent History

In 1993, Palau voted to accept a Compact of Free Association with the United States. In October 1994 the Republic of Palau became fully independent, after almost 50 years of trusteeship, and in December became the 185th member of the United Nations. Under the terms of the Compact, Palau will receive about $472 million over the next 15 years. But Palau's journey from trusteeship to independence was a rocky one.

In 1978 Palau voted to separate from the rest of Micronesia, and in 1979 the first Palau Constitutional Convention convened to write a constitution for a self-governing republic. The delegates incorporated provisions banning nuclear materials from Palau and preventing the government from using eminent domain powers for the benefit of any foreign entity. The United States, in its cold war mentality, would not agree to these provisions.

Over the next 15 years Palau was deeply divided on whether to accept a Compact of Free Association with the United States, which would have negated these provisions. There were continual referenda over the issue. There was political violence, including the assassination of President Remeliik. There were charges of governmental corruption. No one could build a consensus on terms on which to end the trusteeship.

Since Palau finally adopted a Compact that allows nuclear weapons to be stored on the islands as well as allowing access to the islands by the United States military, it can be said the antinuclear forces, consistently a quarter to a third of the population, lost their fight. But with the cold war over, unless the world paradigm dramatically shifts once again, it's unlikely the United States military would now want to store nuclear weapons or build a military base in Palau. Thus, the antinuclear forces may have lost the battle but won the war.

During the 1970s, it was not only the United States that had designs for Palau's future. Nissho-Iwai and the Industrial Bank of Japan, backed by United States and Iranian interests, sought to create a $325 million central terminal station for oil storage on Palau's Kossol Reef. "Superport" was to have been used to transfer and store oil from jumbo tankers between the Middle East and Japan. Eventually the U.S. Environmental Protection Act managed to halt the project because of the havoc Superport would wreak on the wondrous seas around Palau.

As reported in *Pacific Below,* Noah Idechong, cofounder and director of the Palau Conservation Society, recently won the internationally respected Goldman Environmental Prize, which awards $75,000 to "grassroots environmental heroes." Idechong's successful work to limit fishing and protect village reefs has reinstated conservationist values in the villages and in government policy.

GOVERNMENT

The three branches of government are executive, legislative, and judicial. The president and vice president are elected by the people for four years; the president chooses his cabinet. The Olbiil Era Kelulau is a bicameral legislature consisting of an elected house of delegates (one delegate from each of the 16 states) and a senate (14 senators elected from districts based on population). A presidential veto can be overridden by a two-thirds majority in both houses. There are two political parties. The chief justice

of the Supreme Court is appointed by the president and confirmed by the senate.

For its population Palau is one of the most overgoverned places on earth. Aside from the national government and chiefs, each of the 16 states has a governor, chosen according to its state constitution, and a legislature. Some state governors are elected directly by the people, while others are the highest-ranking traditional leaders of the states. One governor is picked from among members of the state legislature. In addition there's a traditional Council of Chiefs, with one chief from each state. The authority of the chiefs increased under self-government.

ECONOMY

Under the terms of the Compact, the United States made immediate payment of $172 million, with approximately $300 million to be paid over the next 15 years, in declining installments. These payments will be the central feature of Palau's economy during this period and, if the history of the other Compact nations follows, it will be used to maintain a bloated bureaucracy.

There is little commercial agriculture in Palau, except for illegal marijuana farming on Peleliu and Angaur. There is relatively little subsistence farming. Consumer-oriented sales outlets are flourishing as much of the United States payments, directly and indirectly, goes into imported goods. Merchandising is dominated by the locally owned Western Caroline Trading Company (WCTC).

Tourism has tripled over the last decade to about 40,000 visitors per year, though it is not yet clear whether Palau will go the route of Guam and Saipan or will prevent such massive development. The majority of tourists are Japanese, but there is also a large presence of American tourists and business travelers.

PEOPLE

Palauans walk with a pride that is sometimes missing in other parts of Micronesia. They *appear* to be the most Americanized of Micronesians; don't expect to see native dress. Beneath the surface, though, they are extremely tradition oriented. They're friendly people but will often check you out by waiting for you to smile or say hello first.

In 1990 Palau had about 15,000 citizens. In addition, some 3,000 Filipino and 1,000 citizens of other Asian nations work in Palau, remitting much of their income back to their home countries. About 500 Americans also live on Palau. Foreigners may lease Palauan land but not purchase it; in a 1990 decision the Palau Supreme Court ruled that 99-year leases by foreigners were the equivalent of ownership and therefore illegal. A fifth of all Palauans live abroad, many on Guam. Two distinct languages are spoken, Palauan and Sonsorolese-Tobian. Both Palauan and English are official languages. The Palau Community College, founded in Koror in 1969, provides two years of training.

Palauan culture was traditionally matriarchal, with women choosing which males would be the clan chiefs. Women owned and divided land. Chiefly titles were, and still are, inherited through the mother.

Palau maintains one of the only indigenous religious movements remaining in Micronesia, the United Sect or Ngara Modekngei, founded by Temedad on Babeldaob in 1915. In this movement, traditional Palauan beliefs are mixed with ancestor worship and faith in protective spirits. Almost a third of the population adheres to the religion. The Modekngei High School at Ibobang village in Ngatpang State, Babeldaob, was founded in 1974 with funding from the School of the Pacific Islands, Thousand Oaks, California. The school's emphasis is teaching self-sufficiency and preserving Palauan culture, history, and language. For more information call Mr. Otoichi Besebes at 488-2741 on Palau.

ARTS AND CRAFTS

Palau's rich artistic tradition produces some of the most notable art work in Micronesia. Communal meeting centers, *bai,* were fashioned with excellent carpentry and powerful visual embellishment. Constructed under the direction of master craftsmen, the *bai* feature interlocking pieces held together by a complex joiner system utilizing removable pegs. The internal pillars and crossbeams of these buildings are carved and painted with Palauan stories, legends, and historical events fashioned by master carvers. In the 1930s the Japanese artist and folklorist Hisakatsu Hijikata worked with Palauan carvers to adapt traditional woodcarvings in a smaller format. The items, called story boards, were then exported to Japan. Story boards are not only from carved flat pieces of wood but can be formed to represent various shapes, such as fish and crocodiles.

Replicas of traditional Palauan money *(udoud)* are made from pink and black coral and used as necklaces. The real money, still used in customary exchanges, was made from bits of glass or ceramic of unknown origin. Today, some island women wear a string of *udoud* as a necklace.

Tobi Island statues are another unique traditional item available for sale. These small squatting figures represent guardian spirits and ancestral deities. They were once placed in canoes with the deceased and set adrift for burial at sea. Other important Palauan art forms include distinctive carved wood containers and other objects, inlaid with beautiful shell designs.

an inlaid ceremonial vessel

HOLIDAYS AND EVENTS

Public holidays include New Year's Day (1 January), Youth Day (15 March), Senior Citizens' Day (5 May), President's Day (1 June), Nuclear-free Constitution Day (9 July), Labor Day (first Monday or Tuesday in September), Independence Day (1 October), United Nations Day (24 October), Thanksgiving (fourth Thursday in November), and Christmas (25 December).

Youth Day features open-air concerts and sporting events, while on Senior Citizens' Day there are dancing contests, handicraft exhibitions, and a parade with floats. Senior citizens are remembered on the fifth day of the fifth month because in Palau one attains official senior citizenship at age 55. The Palau Arts Festival on Nuclear-free Constitution Day is also great for its traditional dancing, popular music performances, an arts and crafts show, and a culinary competition featuring local produce and cuisine.

During the *ngloik* dance, lines of Palauan women, their bodies glistening with coconut oil, chant legends to rhythmic movements. The Palauan men dance the *ruk* to celebrate a victory or inaugurate a new *bai*.

PRACTICALITIES

Accommodations

Most hotels are in or near Koror. No obvious campsites present themselves in central Koror, but you could try the village behind the Hotel Nikko Palau at Ngermid, down by the water. There's no problem camping on Peleliu, Angaur, or Kayangel, and the likelihood of being able to stay with a family is good. On Babeldaob get permission before pitching your tent. Many of the states have offices in Koror that may be able to advise on village accommodations in their areas.

Peleliu and Angaur have small guesthouses. Most guesthouses offer meals, but clarify

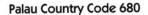

Palau Country Code 680

prices in advance. You may also be permitted to cook at a guesthouse. Bring along all supplies as the stores have little to offer. Buy ship biscuits for hiking or camping. Paradise Air (also known as Palau Paradise Air and Air Paradise) can be helpful in arranging a stay on either island.

All hotel accommodations are subject to a 10% room tax, which is added to the bill. Some hotels also add a five percent service charge.

Visas

All travelers are required to carry a passport, even U.S. citizens. No visa is required for a stay of 30 days or less, although you may be asked to show an onward ticket. Permission for stay extensions costs $50 each, so on arrival ask for all the time you expect to need. Extensions are not automatic and will only be done twice, so three months is the longest you'll likely be allowed to stay. A United States visa may be required if you'll be transiting Guam, but not if you're making a roundtrip from Manila.

Money and Measurements

United States currency is used. Restaurant tipping is usual. Credit cards are not universally accepted; many restaurants do not honor them.

Most government offices are closed 11:30 a.m.-12:30 p.m. When arriving in Palau from Guam or Yap remember that Palau is one hour earlier.

Although United States domestic postage rates apply, Palau issues its own colorful postage stamps bearing its name. Collectors can order sets from the Palau Philatelic Bureau, G.P.O. Box 7775, New York, NY 10116. They don't provide standing order accounts; issues must be ordered individually.

Services and Information

For a brochure and list of hotels write the Palau Visitors Authority (P.O. Box 256, Koror, PW 96940, tel. 488-2793, fax 488-1453). *Tia Belau* is published every other week and the *Pacific Daily News* is flown in from Guam. There's a government-run radio station, WSZB, at 1580 AM. CNN is now available, as well as pre-recorded San Francisco programming.

Visitors, particularly divers, will wish to check out Nancy Barbour's richly illustrated description of Palau's natural and cultural history, *Palau* (Full

Court Press, 511 Mississippi Street, San Francisco, CA 94107) and Tim Rock's *Diving and Snorkeling Guide to Palau* (Pisces Books, P.O. Box 2608, Houston, TX 77252). Also of interest is *A Guide to the Palau Islands* (available to U.S. addresses for $20 postpaid from NECO Tours, P.O. Box 129, Koror, PW 96940) by Mandy Thyssen, jammed full of color photos, line drawings, and useful information.

Getting There

Airai Airport (ROR) is on Babeldaob, 7.5 miles east of Koror by road. The taxi into town is around $15. Some hotels charge $10 for airport transfers; others are free. Car rental agencies are also located at the airport. The Visitors Authority operates a desk at the airport, which opens for arrivals. They'll give you a complete hotel list with current rates. A pay telephone (25 cents) stands against the wall beside the exit from the customs area. The departure tax is $10 on international flights.

Continental Air Micronesia has daily flights to Koror from Guam and flights from Manila on Tuesday, Thursday, and Saturday. Connections can be made easily from the major cities of Asia, Europe, and the United States by way of Guam or Manila. Yap is included as a stopover on the Guam to Koror flight Wednesday, Friday, and Sunday. Continental flies Koror to Saipan nonstop on Monday, but not Saipan to Koror.

Koror is the last stop on Continental Micronesia's Island Hopper. A through ticket from Honolulu to Majuro to Kosrae to Pohnpei to Chuuk to Guam to Yap to Koror costs about $1250 one-way; from California the same ticket is $1650. All passengers must change planes on Guam and often spend the night there at their own expense.

Off-peak hour Air Mike flights may be cheaper, so always check.

Getting Around

Palau Paradise Air (P.O. Box 488, Koror, Republic of Palau 96940, tel./fax 488-2348) manages to be both efficient and genial. It offers commuter service to Peleliu and Angaur on six-seater planes. The flight between Peleliu and Angaur allows you to combine both islands in a single visit. The Koror to Peleliu to Angaur service operates twice a day Monday, Tuesday, Thursday, Friday, and Sunday. On Saturday there is only a morning flight. Thus, even day trips from Koror are possible. On Wednesday, charters may be available.

Fares are $29 one-way Koror to Peleliu; $36 one-way Koror to Angaur; $18 one-way Peleliu to Angaur. The plane passes directly over the Rock Islands—in nice weather, the pilot often treats passengers to spectacular views from the air.

Paradise Air reservations must be reconfirmed. You're allowed 20 pounds of luggage free; $2 for each additional pound. Transfers between Airai Airport and Palau Paradise's Koror office are free.

LOUISE FOOTE

KOROR

Koror is the most scenic town in Micronesia. You get excellent views of the fabulous Rock Islands stretching out to the south. From Airai Airport on southern Babeldaob, a well-paved road leads to Koror, the political and economic center of the republic. About two-thirds of the country's population now lives in Koror. The bustling prewar Japanese city was leveled by American bombing, although isolated relics remain. Today Koror throbs again with a steady stream of traffic along the main road through town. There are even two traffic lights. Bridges and causeways linking Koror Island to Babeldaob, Arakabesan, Malakal, and other islands make it a perfect base and an interesting place to explore.

SIGHTS

The **Palau National Museum** (tel. 488-2265; open weekdays 8-11 a.m. and 1-4 p.m., Saturday 10 a.m.-2 p.m., admission $2), the oldest, most extensive and most interesting museum in Micronesia, is a short hike up a hill from downtown Koror. The displays, with their learned presentation, give a good look at Palau's rich artistic traditions.

In addition to paintings, exhibits include traditional shell-inlaid containers, native skirts, canoe models, traditional mourning money paid to relatives who come to mourn, cooking utensils, spears (used for both warfare and fishing), and traditional jewelry. The museum also has fragments and models of old *bai,* as well as photographs of old Palau and its people.

The spectacular wooden carvings, some three-dimensional, some flat story boards, some recent, some old, are the highlight of the collection. One three-dimensional carving, crafted several years ago by artist Petrus Sikyang, tells the story of the giant Uab who was burned and then fell down, forming the islands of Palau. Petrus sculpts without sketches: he sees the sculpture on the uncarved wood. Another three-dimensional story board, by Isaac Klewei, carved on a curving wooden crocodile, tells the story of

how taro growing came to Palau. Still another describes the division of work between men and women.

Upstairs is a room dedicated to the art of Hisakatsu Hijikata. Hijikata, a Japanese living on Palau in the 1930s, helped revitalize the Palauan story board tradition. This room shows how versatile the artist was with drawings, watercolors, and some carving.

A varied botanical collection and a statue of the late Pres. Haruo I. Remeliik (1933-85) spruce up the museum grounds. The traditional *bai* near the museum was erected in 1991 to replace an earlier one built in 1969 that burned down in 1979. A monument on the grounds states in English and Japanese:

> *May the souls of the people of Palau killed in the Pacific War rest in peace.*

Malakal

Malakal Island, Koror's industrial suburb and commercial port, has a cold storage plant for tuna exported to Japan. The nearby **Fisheries Co-op** sells fresh fish daily.

At the end of the road on Malakal is the **Micronesian Mariculture Demonstration Center** (MMDC), locally known as the "ice box" for a long-gone Japanese ice making plant. The MMDC, a major mariculture research center established in 1974, is the world's largest commercial giant clam farm. Through hatching and rearing, the MMDC hopes to save the giant clam (*Tridacna gigas*) from extinction. This species has been ravaged by Taiwanese poachers who take the clam's abductor muscle, supposedly an aphrodisiac. Millions of seed clams have been distributed throughout Palau as well as to foreign countries. In addition to four major clam species, hawksbill sea turtles are also reared in tanks here for release, and other marinelife such as commercial trochus and reef fish may be seen in outdoor tanks. Visitors are welcome weekdays 8-11 a.m. and 1-4 p.m., $2 admission.

Climb to the top of Malakal for a stunning view of the Rock Islands. Take the dirt road uphill from the sewage plant to the water tank,

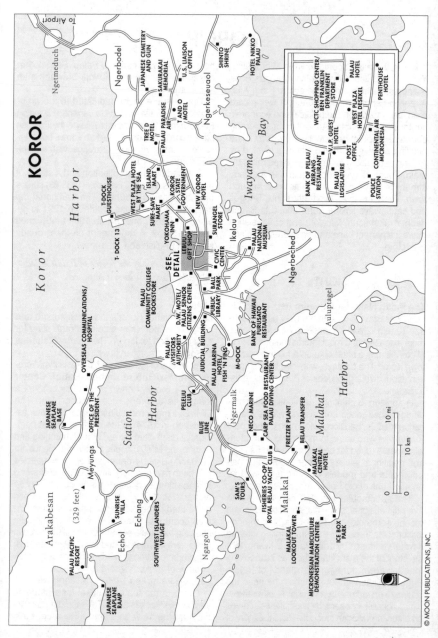

KOROR

then bushwhack through the forest to the high metal tower at the summit (408 feet), once used by the Japanese as a lighthouse. On one side you can see across Babeldaob; on the other you look down on the great green arms enfolding the harbor. Very few places in the Pacific give you as much of an eyeful as this tower.

Arakabesan

The Japanese evicted all Palauans from Arakabesan Island and turned it into a military base. Great concrete football fields sloping down into the water remain from the **seaplane bases,** one beyond a school at Meyungs village not far from the causeway from Koror, two more on the west side of the island by the Palau Pacific Resort. If you are not staying at the Palau Pacific, stop by to take a look and have a drink at their outdoor bar, set on a beautiful stretch of beach.

On the south side of Arakabesan is a Southwest Islanders village accessible via a dirt road. Notice the outrigger canoes.

East of Town

Going east along the highway from central Koror, in about a mile you reach the section known as **Top Side.** Opposite the Dragon Tei Restaurant is a paved road to the right that goes 1.5 miles down to the water. At the bottom is a basketball court and wonderful ruins of old Japanese brick buildings on a mangrove channel. The walk back up is a stiff uphill climb, through a lovely residential neighborhood.

Several hundred yards further, just beyond a couple of Japanese stone lanterns, go down a dirt track on the left beside the house marked QTR. NO. 03 to the evocative **Sakurakai Memorial.** The old Japanese cemetery and a cannon are just below.

Continuing east, past more stone lanterns, is a majestic stone stairway leading to a restored Japanese **Shinto shrine.** When opened in 1940 this was the largest of its kind outside Japan. Continuing along the road by the side of the shrine, you reach the Hotel Nikko Palau, which offers beautiful views of Iwayama Bay and the Rock Islands.

Ngermid village, beyond the turnoff to the Nikko Palau, is attractive and well worth strolling through. Halfway down to the dock at Ngermid

are some old stone platforms and pathways, and beyond the houses, in a field to the left, the stone figure of a woman and child frozen on this spot when caught snooping on a gathering of men in a *bai*. Visible on the hillside is a Japanese cave containing a double-barreled AA gun.

Rock Islands

The Rock Islands, south of Koror, are wonders of the world. These wonders are made of soft limestone; the action of the ocean undercuts their base, making them appear to be emerald mushrooms floating in the lagoon. Many have sandy beaches and virtually all are surrounded by astounding snorkeling and diving sites.

On some islands you'll find inland, brackish lakes. The best known is **Jellyfish Lake** on Eil Malk. Cut off from direct contact with the lagoon, two species of stingless jellyfish evolved here. Most jellyfish need stingers to kill their prey. But these two species became the ultimate vegetarians: they ingest algae, which remains alive in their translucent bodies. The jellies float to the surface during daylight hours, the algae photosynthesizes, and the jellyfish extract the energy produced. You can swim with and hold these otherworldly harmless creatures.

Many dive companies, fishing outfits, and tour companies arrange day trips to the islands. Do not come to Palau and miss such an excursion.

ACCOMMODATIONS

Koror has a wide choice of hotels from the luxurious Palau Pacific Resort to the best budget hotels in Micronesia.

Budget

The locally owned **D.W. Motel** (P.O. Box 738, Koror, PW 96940, tel. 488-2641, fax 488-1725), at $35 s, 45 d, is perhaps the best buy in Koror. It is in a clean three-story building nicely set back from the main street, next to the Senior Citizens Center, one of the cultural centers of the island. The 17 clean, a/c rooms have private baths and hot showers. Airport transfers are free.

The new **Tree D Motel and Apartments** (P.O. Box 1703, Koror, PW 96940, tel. 488-3856) is another excellent budget choice at $35 s, $45 d. Its 12 units are very clean with a pleasant atmosphere. There is a laundromat next door. Located in Top Side, location is its only drawback, unless you have a car.

You might also try the **T & O Motel** (P.O. Box 1383, Koror, PW 96940, tel. 488-2883, fax 488-1725), above T & O Enterprise, also in Top Side, near the place where Japanese stone lanterns are set on each side of the road. The five a/c rooms are $45 s or d, a bit more during peak seasons.

The **H.K. Motel,** formerly Ongdibel Bai (P.O. Box 61, Koror, PW 96940, tel. 488-2764, fax 488-1725), is located at a busy intersection opposite the Palau Visitors Authority. Rooms are plain and clean and rent for $40 s, $50 d. You can keep expenses down by using the on-premises kitchen.

The **Palau Hotel** (P.O. Box 64, Koror, PW 96940, tel. 488-1703, fax 488-1317) in central Koror is in a four-story building. The 38 rooms are air conditioned, but most do not have televisions or refrigerators. Rooms go for $35 s, $40 d and primarily cater to Asian business-people.

The bottom end **New Koror Hotel** (P.O. Box 339, Koror, PW 96940, tel. 488-1159, fax 488-1582) in the heart of Koror town has little to recommend it. The rooms are plain and the main lobby has a very unpleasant smell. Do not stay here if you, or anyone staying with you, is six or more feet tall; the retrofitted air conditioners extend over the walkway, as the six stitches in my scalp can attest. Rooms begin at $27 s, $33 d.

Moderate

The three-story **Palau Marina Hotel** (P.O. Box 142, Koror, PW 96940, tel. 488-1786, fax 488-1070) is located at M-Dock, next to the Fish 'n Fins scuba shop. The 28 a/c rooms begin at $65 s, $80 d; all overlook the water. The Southern Cross Restaurant at this hotel has a lovely bar with a great view across the water and a fairly lively dinner atmosphere. Most evenings there is live music.

The **V.I.P. Guest Hotel** (P.O. Box 18, Koror, PW 96940, tel. 488-1502) is located in the heart of central Koror, between the post office and the jail. The 10 a/c, balconied rooms in this pink three-story building are $65 s or d. It's a bit over-priced, but a good location for commercial travelers.

Slightly more expensive, but better value, is the modern **Penthouse Hotel** (P.O. Box 6013, Koror, PW 96940, tel. 488-1941, fax 488-1442), located in central Koror on a quiet back street. The rooms are small but clean and arranged well. The hotel has a nice warm feel to it. Rooms run $79 s, $89 d.

West Plaza Hotel, Inc. (a subsidiary of the Western Caroline Trading Company) operates three hotels in Koror. Each has a separate phone number, but reservations for all three can be made by faxing 488-2136 or writing to P.O. Box 280, Koror, PW 96940. All three hotels offer commercial discounts.

West Plaza Hotel by the Sea (tel. 488-2133) is located near T-Dock and is popular with divers. Rooms range $60-100. Many units have ocean views and kitchens. **West Plaza Hotel Desekel** (tel. 488-2521) is centrally located and a good choice if you need to be in town for business. Rooms are $50 and up. The third hotel, **West Plaza Hotel Downtown** (tel. 488-1671), is old and rather dreary. Some rooms have no outdoor window. Room rates begin at $55.

For a longer stay inquire at the mayor's office in the Koror State Government building (P.O. Box 116, Koror, PW 96940, tel. 488-2853 or 488-2576; ask for Scott Yano) about apartments for rent by the month ($150-600 a month).

Luxury

The **Palau Pacific Resort** (P.O. Box 308, Koror, PW 96940, tel. 488-2600) on Arakabesan is the most luxurious hotel in Micronesia. Its 160 guest rooms are located on 64 landscaped, ocean-front acres. The property looks out across a wonderful snorkeling bay. Single rooms start at $190 and suites go up to $650. "Commercial rate" discounts may be available. If you can afford it, PPR is an incredible place to stay. The hotel has two restaurants, a beachfront bar, a swimming pool, tennis courts, and its own hiking trails. All scuba boats pick up divers off the hotel's long concrete pier. The **Splash** scuba program operates from the premises, as does an underwater photography center.

The **Sunrise Villa** (P.O. 6009, Koror, PW 96940, tel. 488-4590, fax 488-4593) is a wonderful new hotel on a hillside on Arakabesan island. As you enter the hotel's front door, you look out at a sparkling view of town and water, the same view seen from each room. Service is good and the hotel is a great value at $105 s, $115 d. Suites, which easily can sleep four, start at $150 and have kitchens. The hotel has a small swimming pool, and its restaurant, Larry's, is quite respectable. Other than the more expensive Palau Pacific Resort, this is probably the best hotel on the island.

Until the Palau Pacific Resort went up in 1984, Palau's top hotel was the **Hotel Nikko Palau** (P.O. Box 310, Koror, PW 96940, tel. 488-2486), the former TraveLodge built by Continental Airlines in 1971. Now owned by Japan Air Lines, the Nikko Palau is spectacularly set on a hillside just east of Koror, with a breathtaking view of the Rock Islands. The hotel swimming pool is small and there's no beach, but dive boats can pick up and drop off passengers just below the hotel. The rooms are small and some are musty; rates start at $130, unless you can qualify for the commercial rate. It is probably a better place to enjoy a drink than to stay. There is a buffet, 6-9 p.m.

The **Airai View Hotel** (P.O. Box 37, Koror, PW 96940, tel. 587-3485, fax 587-3533) is on southern Babeldaob, the closest hotel to the airport. Its rooms start at $105 s, $115 d, but the view rooms are considerably more. The hotel caters mainly to Taiwanese and Japanese tourists. The nicest feature is the fabulous large story board sculpture in the lobby, which is a nice spot for a drink.

The four-story **Malakal Central Hotel** (P.O. Box 6016, Koror, PW 96940, tel. 488-1117, fax 488-1075) adjoins the commercial port, and for $140 s or d you can do better than this.

Island Base Camps

To avoid the long commute by speedboat from Koror to dive sites, some divers choose the **Carp Island Resort** (P.O. Box 5, Koror, PW 96940, tel. 488-2978, fax 488-3155) on Ngercheu Island near the fabulous Ngemelis Dropoff. The resort offers cottages with private baths, $60 s, $70 d, $80 t (slightly higher in peak season). Bunk bed accommodations are available in a large "divehouse" of 10 four-bed dorms with shared bath ($30 pp). The island restaurant serves breakfast ($7.50), lunch ($7.50), and

dinner ($20), but seafood specials ($30 pp) must be requested the day before. If owner Johnny Kishigawa is there to do the cooking you're in for a real treat; bring food if you want to cook for yourself. **Palau Diving Center** handles the diving. Boat transfers from Koror are $30 pp but free for scuba divers. Day trips are also available. You can make arrangements at the Carp Restaurant on Malakal.

You can also camp free on one of the Rock Islands, where shelters have been erected by the Koror government. Fish 'n Fins will drop you off at the end of a snorkeling tour with a promise to take you back to Koror a day or two later at no additional charge. Be sure to take enough water and pack out your garbage.

FOOD

Koror boasts quite a few restaurants, with new ones appearing all the time. As in much of Micronesia, many of the best restaurants serve Japanese food. Many restaurants do not accept credit cards.

Locally caught fish, fresh produce, and inexpensive plate lunches are often available. Buy local foods such as cold coconuts, hot tapioca, fried fish, fresh fruit, and betel nut at **Yano's,** just north of WCTC Shopping Center. Fresh fish is sold daily at the fish market on the Fisheries Co-op dock at Malakal. Another spot for a cheap snack is the **Palau Community College** bookstore, where you can get coffee, banana fritters, pizza, sandwiches, and hot dogs to go. A can of juice and two banana fritters costs 85 cents. In the same building as the Rock Island Cafe (see below) is a deli selling cold cuts and other things good for taking on picnics.

The locally oriented **Yokohama Inn** on Lebuu Street serves inexpensive lunches, including fried fish and Japanese dishes from around $5. The **Arirang Restaurant** above the Bank of Palau serves excellent Japanese and Korean dishes. Lunches run about $8 and dinners about $15. A good mid-priced choice is the **Furusato Restaurant** (tel. 488-2689) beside the Bank of Hawaii, a Koror favorite with an extensive menu, including good Japanese food as well as Filipino and American dishes. It's a breakfast and lunch place for local politicos.

The **Carp Sea Food Restaurant** (tel. 488-2978), near the Fisheries Co-op on Malakal, serves authentic Japanese dishes such as tofu stew, sukiyaki, and tempura. Included was a plate of fruit for dessert. The portions are large and prices very reasonable, with most dishes around $6. This rustic island restaurant, full of colorful Gauguin-style art by chef Johnny Kishigawa, is a great little hideaway; in fact you'll never find it at night unless you know the way. The restaurant is only open for lunch (11 a.m.-2 p.m.) and dinner (6-9 p.m.).

Another Japanese restaurant, which is a local favorite, is the **Dragon Tei,** located in Top Side. Open every evening except Wednesday; dinner will cost about $15, more if you order crab or lobster. Call for reservations at 488-2271.

Possibly the best meal on the island is the banquet at the **Fuji Restaurant** in the building south of West Plaza Hotel Downtown. Come very hungry. The special dinner for $25 includes mangrove crab, lobster, sushimi, and steamed fish as well as a host of other dishes. Call ahead for reservations at 488-2774.

Conveniently located downtown is the **Rock Island Cafe,** owned by Yutaka M. Gibbons, Ibedul, paramount chief of Palau. Next door to the law library, the cafe's location explains why so many local lawyers and government types hang out here. The great looking bar is one where you'll feel comfortable ordering a coffee, if that is your drug of choice. Pizza, Mexican dishes, and fried chicken are all good choices and will cost you about $7 per person. Rock Island Cafe T-shirts at $10 make great souvenirs.

Larry's is the hotel restaurant of the Sunrise Villa, serving breakfast, lunch, and dinner. During the daytime, the restaurant has exquisite vistas over the city and water. The cuisine is varied, but primarily American in tone. Dinner without drinks will run you $12-15. A good choice.

The following two waterfront restaurants offer hearty, basic food with a good selection of seafood dishes. The **Pirate's Cove Bar and Restaurant** is located on Malakal Island, at the port. It features a barbecue on Friday night. The

Southern Cross in the Palau Marina Hotel at M-Dock offers similar food and has live music most evenings. To find out if someone is playing call 488-2349.

The Palau Pacific Resort has two restaurants: the elegant and excellent **Meduu Ribtal** and the open air **Coconut Terrace.** The Meduu Ribtal can be very expensive, but it has been trying to include some less expensive meals. Seafood lovers will want to try their Taiwanese Steamboat special at $24. The Coconut Terrace serves breakfast, lunch, and dinner. Many nights they feature an excellent dinner buffet for $24. It's best to call for reservations at either restaurant (tel. 488-2600).

OTHER PRACTICALITIES

Entertainment
Koror's nightlife kicks in after 9 p.m. by the Malakal causeway. The **Peleliu Club** and **Kosi-il Landing** nightclubs are adjacent on an island off the causeway, easily visible from the road. It's a local scene and can get rough. Expats hang out at the **Royal Belau Yacht Club** on Malakal.

Everything closes down when midnight curfew rolls around, but you're given another hour to get home.

Palau Pacific Resort features traditional dancing by local children several nights a week at its 6 p.m. buffet. Call 488-2600 for information and reservations. Both **Pirate's Cove** and **Southern Cross** mentioned above have live music many evenings.

If you go down the alley between WCTC and Yano, you hit Lebuu Street. Turning toward the right, you come to a three-story building on your right, the first floor of which is **Q Ball,** a pool hall.

Sports and Recreation
Palau is one of the most sought after diving locales in the world. The diving season is year-round with visibility often 200 feet. There are a dozen blue holes along the southwest barrier

reef, along with 60 identified dropoffs; Ngemelis Dropoff on Barnum Bay is considered the world's best. One minute you're in knee-deep water on the reef, the next you're plunging into 1,000-foot-deep warm tropical ocean! This nearly vertical wall is covered with crimson and yellow sea fans, sponges, and soft corals. At Denges Dropoff is a plateau with giant tabletop corals.

Want to see fan coral, giant clams, or sharks? Just ask—the local divemasters know over 50 good diving spots including blue holes and at least a dozen channel dives (drift dives). Special trips can be arranged to the underwater cave system off Koror. Also ask about submerged Japanese ships and aircraft, including the well-preserved Zero sitting on a reef at Koror Road. The hospital has a recompression chamber if you need it.

Divers, of course, should carry their certifications. However, you can also speak to any of the following about introductory dives as well as their scuba certification programs. Palau is a great place to learn to dive.

Sam's Tour Service (Sam Scott, P.O. Box 428, Koror, PW 96940, tel. 488-1062, fax 488-5003) isn't quite as big as some of the other scuba operators, so you'll receive personalized, professional service. One-tank dive costs $50; two tanks, full day including lunch $85; night dive $50; all day snorkeling $45. Trips to northern Babeldaob are a specialty, but Sam is noted for taking divers to a wide variety of locales. He'll pick you up at your hotel.

The **NECO Marine** (Shallum and Mandy Etpison, P.O. Box 129, Koror, PW 96940, tel. 488-1775, fax 488-3014) on Malakal Island is Koror's largest dive shop: one-tank dive $65; two-tank dive $98; night dive $65. Transfers from hotels are free. Full day boat rentals to the Rock Islands are $350.

Fish 'n Fins Ltd. (P.O. Box 142, Koror, PW 96940, tel. 488-2637) beside the Palau Marina Hotel at M-Dock is a very experienced scuba operator. One-tank dives are $65; two-tank dives $85.

Splash (P.O. Box 308, Koror, PW, tel. 488-2600, fax 488-1601) is located at the Palau Pacific Resort. It offers an excellent program and will take divers who are not staying at the hotel. Prices are generally 15% higher than the other shops.

Palau Diving Center (discussed under "Island Base Camps" under Accommodations," below, will also take divers from Koror at competitive prices.

Palau is a wonderful place to spend evenings on land. But for those who care about nothing except diving, there are two live-aboard dive boats. Their big advantage is that there is no long trip out to dive sites in the morning.

The eight-cabin *Palau Aggressor* has Sunday to Sunday trips for $2000, meals included based on double occupancy. For information and reservations write Aggressor Fleet Limited, P.O. Drawer K, Morgan City, LA 70381, tel. (800) 348-2628 in the U.S., or internationally (504) 385-2628, fax (504) 384-0817.

The *Sun Dancer* is a similar sized boat. It runs some seven-day, Sunday to Sunday trips, and other 10-day trips, running from Sunday to Wednesday and Wednesday to Saturday. Prices, including meals and based on double occupancy, are $2000 for the seven-day trip and $2900 for the 10-day. Information and reservations can be made through Peter Hughes Diving, 6851 Yumuri Street, Suite 10, Coral Gables, FL 33146, tel. (800) 932-6237, or internationally (305) 669-9391, fax (305) 669-9475.

Ecotourism has been slow to come to Micronesia; as yet only two companies offer ecotrips in Palau. One is **Oceanic Society Expeditions** (Fort Mason Center, Bldg. E, San Francisco, CA 94123, tel. 800-326-7491 or 415-441-1106, fax 415-474-3395), a nonprofit environmental travel organization. Their 10-day snorkeling and natural history tour to Palau is offered in February and June and is limited to 12 people. An expert naturalist leads the expedition, and the $2490 cost per person includes airfare from Honolulu, accommodations, transfers, private boat excursions, picnic lunches, and guide.

The other company, **Adventure Kayaking of Palau, Inc.** (P.O. Box 225, Koror, PW 96940, tel. 488-1694), combines snorkeling and diving with a relatively new sport on Micronesia, sea kayaking. They offer various day tours for beginners and veterans for $35-65 per person, as well as outfitted camping packages that last from two to 10 days. Prices range $120-1000. Custom packages and tours are available upon request. Daily kayak rentals are also available.

Shopping

With its rich artistic traditions, Palau is an excellent place to shop. Story boards are a unique Palauan art form. Other handicrafts are also available, as well as beautiful stamps and first day covers.

The **Palau National Museum** in Koror sells quality story boards, Tobi Island statues, other handicrafts, and books on Palau. First day covers, postcards, and prints designed by noted local artists Simeon and Samuel Adelbai are available. By making purchases here you help support this worthy institution.

The talented prisoners held in the **Correction and Rehabilitation Division Jail** (open 8 a.m.-4 p.m. daily) behind the downtown police station carve outstanding story boards. Purchases can be made on the spot or work can be done to order. Prisoners on lesser charges may keep pets and are allowed to go home on weekends or attend courses. Medium-sized story boards cost $100-225 and up.

Ormuul Gift Shop at the Senior Citizens Center has a nice assortment of story boards and other handicrafts. The center is another key institution for keeping traditional cultural skills intact and is certainly worth a visit. You may see older men building a canoe or women weaving. It's located beside D.W. Motel.

The **Shell Museum** near the Bank of Hawaii has story boards, Tobi statues, and other carvings. In back, for $1 admission, you can view cases crammed with beautiful shells, as well as see shell souvenirs for sale.

Souvenirs at the **Hotel Nikko Palau** gift shop are expensive. It's also disappointing that the hotel sells tortoiseshell items. They're illegal to import into the United States, Japan, and most European countries. **Duty Free Shoppers** at the Palau Pacific Resort sells story boards, first day covers, T-shirts, and Palau videos ($30). The prices are high, but quality is good.

The post office offers Palau postage stamps and first day covers. They're only allowed to sell items less than one year old, however. Most souvenir shops on Koror sell older stamps and covers.

The **Ben Franklin Department Store** upstairs in the WCTC Shopping Center has a wide assortment of clothes and consumer goods, as well as souvenirs. There's a large supermarket downstairs at WCTC. **Sure-Save Mart** and **Surangel** are the other major supermarkets.

Services

The Bank of Hawaii (tel. 488-2602), Bank of Palau (tel. 488-2638), and Bank of Guam (tel. 488-2697) have branches in Koror. All are open Mon.-Thurs. 9:30 a.m.-2:30 p.m. and Friday 9:30 a.m.-5 p.m. There's seldom a line at the Bank of Palau where US$ traveler's checks are cashed, but there's no foreign exchange. To cash traveler's checks expressed in currencies other than US$ costs a hefty commission.

The post office in central Koror is open weekdays 8 a.m.-4 p.m. If you're considering mailing a story board, be aware it can't be over 108 inches total length and breadth. To the U.S. the maximum weight is 70 pounds ($75.35 by airmail), to Great Britain the maximum is 66 pounds ($97.25 for the first 22 pounds, then $3 for each additional pound, by air). Address mail to Koror, PW 96940.

Most hotels allow long distance calls. They also can be made from the PNCC Overseas Communications office just above the new hospital on Arakabesan. Charges are $9 for three minutes to Micronesia, $12 for three minutes to the Philippines and the United Sates, more to Europe.

The Immigration office (tel. 488-2498) is upstairs in the Judicial Building. Enter from the back side.

The Palau Hospital is in a clean, modern building on Arakabesan, just across the causeway from Koror. The hospital has well-trained doctors. At the emergency room, I had six stitches placed in my scalp and was gone 20 minutes after I arrived—total price, $13. Nobody even asked to see my credit card.

Tngeronger Laundromat is beside the National Development Bank of Palau on Lebuu Street below WCTC Shopping Center. There's also a small laundromat behind the reception area at D.W. Motel and another just past the hospital, on the opposite side of street.

Information

The **Palau Visitors Authority** (P.O. Box 256, Koror, PW 96940, tel. 488-2793) is at the junction of the Malakal and Arakabesan roads. Watch for William H. Stewart's *Tourist Map of Palau* and *Battlefield Map of Peleliu* at souvenir outlets.

There's an air conditioned public library (P.O. Box 189, Koror, PW 96940; open Mon.-Fri. 7:30-11:30 a.m. and 12:30-4:30 p.m.) opposite the old high school. Before the war, the Japanese administration building stood on the site of the present library.

Blue Line (tel. 488-2679) opposite the Mobil station on Malakal has topographical maps of Babeldaob and Koror for $10 a sheet, also a few nautical charts.

Radio station WSZB broadcasts at 1580AM.

GETTING THERE

Daily flights to Koror from Guam and flights from Manila on Tuesday, Thursday, and Satruday are offered by **Continental Air Micronesia.** You can make connections easily from the major cities of Asia, Europe, and the United States by way of Guam or Manila. Yap is a stopover on the Guam to Koror flight Wednesday, Friday, and Sunday. Continental flies Koror to Saipan nonstop on Monday, but not Saipan to Koror. For more information see the "Getting There" section in the Palau "Introduction."

GETTING AROUND

Field Trips
Belau Transfer (P.O. Box 318, Koror, PW 96940, tel. 488-2432) at the commercial port may have information on the quarterly field trip to the Southwest Islands (Sonsorol, Pulo Anna, Merir, Helen Reef, and Tobi). A Palauan fishing patrol boat also travels there occasionally.

Local Boats
Boats to Peleliu and Angaur leave from the dock by the **Fisheries Co-op** on Malakal. The state boat to Peleliu leaves Tuesday and Friday ($3, two hours); it also sometimes makes special trips. Due to varying tide conditions, it's best to check the precise departure times with the boat captain, either the night before or early on the morning of the day you wish to leave. Occasional fishing boats also head out from here to Ollei and Melekeok on Babeldaob.

Boats between Peleliu and Angaur are rare, although you might arrange for an Angaur boat to drop you off on Peleliu on its way back to Koror. Private boats to Peleliu leave from the anchorage beside the Peleliu Club.

Boats for Babeldaob and Kayangel leave from **T-Dock.** Although a few of the state boats to the north have regular schedules, the only sure way to get on is just to be there, ready to leave when they do. Friday afternoon and early Saturday morning are good times to look for speedboats to northern Babeldaob (up to $5 one-way).

Surprisingly, Monday is a good day to head north, as the crowds are smaller and some boats that brought commuters may be returning empty. There's a concrete waiting pavilion by the dock. Quickly accept a ride to any place in Ngaraard or Ngarchelong States, or to Kayangel if you're lucky.

Every other week a boat makes the four-hour trip to Kayangel ($6 pp). It usually leaves Koror on Saturday morning, returning Thursday after-

M.G.L. DOMENY DE RIENZI

an early 19th-century view of Peleliu

noon a week and a half later. On its way back, the boat calls at Ollei, the northernmost village on Babeldaob, and sometimes another village halfway down—a good connection for those wanting to get off. Rides are scarce on the off weeks but are sometimes available from speedboats and fishing boats.

By Road

There's no bus service, but since nearly everyone travels by car, hitching is possible. Taxis are not unreasonable. Standard fares from the center of Koror are $2 to Ice Box Park, $3 to the Hotel Nikko Palau, $4 to the Palau Pacific Resort, and $15 to the airport. Check the fare in advance. Taxis are individual, not shared, and the price is for the whole car, not per person. To call a radio-dispatched taxi, dial 488-1519, 488-2510, or 488-2691.

Car rentals are $35-40 a day with unlimited mileage. At the airport you can find: **1A Rent a Car** (P.O. Box 694, Koror, PW 96940, tel. 488-1113, fax 488-1115) and **Kings Car Rental** (P.O. Box 424, Koror, PW 96940, tel. 488-2964, fax 488-3273). **Toyota Rent-a-car** (P.O. Box 280, Koror, PW 96940, tel. 488-2133) and **Neco Rent a Car** (P.O. Box 129, Koror, PW 96940, tel. 488-1451, fax 488-2743) are two of the larger rental agencies located in town. Often car rental agencies will drop you off and pick you up at your hotel.

Most agencies want their sedans driven only along the paved roads on Koror and as far as the airport. If you want to explore Babeldaob by car, consider renting a pick-up or jeep. They run between $50 and $75 a day. Take care with uneven driveways, which can scrape car bottoms. The speed limit in Koror is 15 mph.

Sharp spines on its back make the butterflyfish hard to swallow.

OTHER ISLANDS

BABELDAOB

Southern Babeldaob

Since 1979 Koror has been connected to Babeldaob Island by the 775-foot-long cantilever **K-B Bridge,** one of the longest of its kind in the world. Ten states are on the coastal plains of Babeldaob. A network of roads covers the bottom half adjacent to Koror, as far as Ngatpang and Melekeok; beyond that, access is by boat only.

The **Palau Crocodile Farm** at the end of the causeway is open when it's open and closed when it's closed. At last count, it had 37 local crocs in captivity. Admission is $3 adults, $2 children. It additionally charges $5 to use a still camera and $10 to use a video, a bit excessive.

The paved highway passes the airport and extends almost as far as the concrete shell of the huge **Japanese Communications Center** at **Airai** (Irrai) village, split by American bombs in 1944. A Japanese tank and several AA guns lie dumped beside the structure. Half a mile beyond is an authentic old *bai,* built in 1890, with painted facades, thatched roof, and finely carved beams. One is sometimes, though not always, asked to pay $5 to walk around it, $10 to take photos inside. This is the only original building of its kind left in Palau.

Near the *bai,* at the junction of four stone pathways leading in from the cardinal points, is the compass platform. The south path leads to the modern concrete **Bai ra Mlengl** (1983), painted with traditional scenes (notice the quarrying of Yapese stone money). Below this new *bai* is a dock from which you'll get a good view.

Middle Babeldaob

A dirt road leads north from near the K-B Bridge to Aimeliik, Ngatpang, and Ngchesar States. You will see a sign pointing to the left. It is an unpaved road through beautiful green taro patches and hilly countryside. Don't drive too far on this road in anything less than a pickup. Traffic is light so this is a great road to hike, with just enough traffic that you stand a good chance of being able to hitch back.

Six miles north of the bridge the road divides, with Aimeliik to the left and Ngchesar to the right. If you keep left toward Aimeliik, after a half mile you'll reach a turnoff to the left to Ngerkeai village. One and a half miles beyond this turnoff is the Chinese Agricultural Mission at **Nekkeng,** with the Oisca agricultural training school one half mile to the right.

North from Nekkeng another road climbs to a lookout above central Babeldaob with a view of a large bay which at first appears to be a lake. Visible on the east side of the bay is the Belau Modekngei High School at Ibobang and south of it the solitary white triangle of a large Japanese war memorial. Four miles north of Nekkeng on this road is the **Ngatpang** State Office and a half mile beyond it, over a hill to the right, a fisheries dock constructed with Japanese aid money in 1990.

The road to the left from Nekkeng runs three miles to **Ngchemiangel** village and terminates at the **IPSECO power plant** on the coast, about 16 miles from Koror by road. You get a good view of the ancient Aimeliik terraces from here. A short feeder road to the north runs to **Medorm** village, where old *bai* platforms may be seen: one on the ridge just before the village, another accessible from the dock. There's a store at Ngchemiangel where you can buy cold drinks and food.

If back at the turnoff to Ngchesar you had turned right, after two and a half miles you would have reached a group of collapsed metal towers dating from Japanese times. Here the road divides again with **Ibobang** and the **Japanese war memorial** to the left and Ngchesar to the right.

At last report the roads beyond the collapsed towers were in bad shape and four wheel drive essential. Be aware that all the dirt roads on volcanic Babeldaob can get very muddy and even become impassable after heavy rains.

Northern Babeldaob

During the Japanese period, northern Babeldaob was connected to Koror by roads, but these have long been overgrown and the locals now commute by speedboat. You can sometimes walk along jungle trails from one coastal enclave to the next, but it's not easy and you'll probably need a guide. The east coast offers the most possibilities for hikers, but there too you will need a guide since there are rivers and mangrove forests with which to contend. A project is now underway to rebuild these old roads and causeways, so get recent information upon arrival. From Melekeok one can rent a boat to Ngiwal State for around $20.

Melekeok was once the seat of the high chief of Babeldaob; an old village and stone *bai* remain. You can also see a circle of huge stones in the vicinity, one carved into a great face.

South of Melekeok is **Ngchesar** village, which boasts a traditional war canoe and, inland, crocodile-inhabited **Ngardok Lake,** a two hour walk from Ngchesar. A trail once ran from the lake to Ngardmau State, on the northwest side of the island.

Ngardmau is noted for having the highest point in Palau (700 feet) and the tallest waterfalls. Also remarkable are the remains from the prewar Japanese bauxite mine. At Taki Falls the Ngardmau River tumbles 80 feet into a lush jungle pool. The trail to the falls follows the one and a half mile route of an old Japanese mining railway through the rainforest.

The highlight of Babeldaob is the northern tip; excellent **beaches** extend down the east coast from Ngaraard to Melekeok. A road crosses the narrow neck of Ngaraard State from Urrung dock to Chelab and Ulimang villages. Walking north from Ulimang to Ngarchelong State is easy and there are many stone paths to explore.

Visit the awesome five-ton Easter Island-like basalt **stones of Badrulchau,** on a hilltop between Mengellang and Ollei, the northernmost villages. The story goes that spirits were working in the night to build a great *bai* at this spot. Then the sun came up, roosters crowed, and the spirits scattered, so the building was never finished. Today all that remains are 37 monolithic blocks arranged in two rows, which may once have supported an immense *bai.* Carved faces are seen on six of the stones.

An old **Japanese lighthouse** stands on a hill at Ollei. Boats for Koror leave Ngarchelong and Ngaraard States fairly often.

Practicalities
The only official place to stay on Babeldaob is the **Ngaraard Traditional Resort** (P.O. Box 773, Koror, PW 96940, tel. 488-1788 evenings, fax 488-1725), run by Hanson Shiro on the beach at Ulimang village. They offer three thatched cottages, each with two bedrooms, sitting room, and kitchen (bring food). The toilets and washing facilities are outside and there's no electricity. The price is $25 s, $45 d. You can arrange for three meals a day at $19 pp extra. Getting there from Koror by boat costs $100 roundtrip per group. This locally owned resort has all the attributes of a genuine island hideaway, and it's reasonable if you can get a small group together. It can be difficult to reach the resort by phone so start making arrangements as early as possible.

KAYANGEL

The same geological movement that uplifted Angaur and Peleliu submerged Kayangel and the northern reefs. Kayangel, an idyllic atoll 16 miles north of Babeldaob, has only one village (137 people) and no electricity, plumbing, or cars—just peace and quiet, and beauty. Alas, motor scooters have appeared! Untouched beaches surround the four islands of the atoll

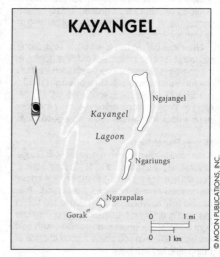

KAYANGEL

Ngajangel

Kayangel

Lagoon

Ngariungs

Ngarapalas

Gorak

0   1 mi

0   1 km

© MOON PUBLICATIONS, INC.

and you can walk from island to island on the reef at low tide. Snorkeling in the lagoon is exquisite. Unfortunately, in November 1990 Typhoon Mike destroyed the island's traditional *bai*, which was replaced by a concrete one.

Upon arrival, ask one of the two chiefs to help find a family willing to accommodate you; they would welcome the money. Although the island has two tiny stores, bring plenty of canned food, ramen, insect repellent, and your own water supply or purification device. Bread and coffee are appreciated but no beer is allowed. The islanders weave high quality pandanus handbags.

PELELIU

The little island of Peleliu, population 600, 31 miles southwest of Koror at the south end of the Palau lagoon, was a scene of intense combat from September through November 1944. Mercifully, the Japanese evacuated the Micronesian inhabitants to Babeldaob before the battle began. The defense of Peleliu marked a change in Japanese military tactics. Instead of defending the beaches, the 10,000 defenders holed up in entrenched positions in the island's

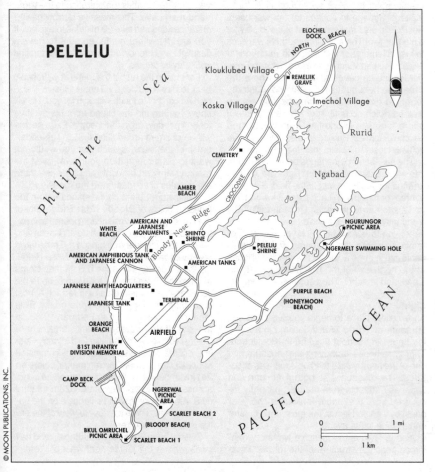

© MOON PUBLICATIONS, INC.

tangled rocky interior. This strategy led to a drawn out two-and-a-half-month struggle, with heavy U.S. casualties.

After the battle the United States made no attempt to capture Koror and Babeldaob, which remained in Japanese hands until peace came. Military historians now agree the whole campaign was ill-advised and the capture of Peleliu contributed nothing to the eventual defeat of Japan.

Today, Peleliu is a lovely, sleepy island once more. It is possible to visit Peleliu as a day trip, flying from Koror in the morning and returning in the afternoon. Many Japanese tourists do this to make pilgrimage to shrines for the war dead. But Peleliu also makes a great place to stay for a night or two. There are innumerable war sites to visit. Remember it is illegal to remove war relics. One can visit the invasion sites and interior limestone caves and tunnels where the Japanese held out till the fatal end. (One determined group of 34 Japanese soldiers remained holed up until April 21, 1947). Peleliu offers fantastic snorkeling from white-sand beaches. Some of Palau's greatest dive sites are actually closer to Peleliu than they are to Koror.

The six-seater plane lands on an airfield cut into surrounding vegetation. Paradise Air can arrange for you to be met at the field. Since it is a three- or four-mile hike to town, it's worth it to make such arrangements. Once in town, pay a courtesy visit to the island's governor. He can direct you to homes in which you can stay or to places where you can camp. Peleliu's residents live in three adjacent flower-filled villages at the north end of the island: Kosca, Klouklubed, and Imechol. The people are friendly.

Sights

An excellent place to begin your visit is at the **Museum of World War II**, located in a building below the school building in Klouklubed. There are hopes of moving the museum into one of the nearby still-standing Japanese structures. The museum has both American and Japanese artifacts from the war, patiently recovered from the jungle through a two-year quest by Tangie Hesus, the museum's curator and a guide to the island.

Also in town is the massive two-story reinforced concrete structure of the former **Japa-nese Communications Center** looming among the houses at Klouklubed village, just south of the school. Do not trespass to get to it. The large blue and white **grave** of Haruo I. Remeliik, president of Palau and a native of Peleliu, is on the corner opposite the baseball field in Klouklubed. Buried next to him is Mamoru Nakamura, Palau's first Supreme Court chief justice.

About a mile north of Klouklubed, a pleasant walk, is Elochel Dock. This is a nice spot to picnic. There is a **fisherman's cooperative** and public outhouses nearby. Several hundred yards south is a Japanese pillbox. Another hundred yards further south is the entrance to the **thousand man cave.** This massive burrow has 11 entrances and can take 20 minutes to explore. If you are not with a guide, be sure to have a flashlight and breadcrumbs so that you can find your way back out.

For touring the rest of the island, it is probably best to hire a guide: try Tangie Hesus. Paradise Air can get in touch with him for you. He will show you around the island from his minibus for $44 per day, up to four people. Extra people will be charged an additional $11. The underbrush of the island is such that you would not want to cut through it on your own. Even the road system can be confusing because there are remains of so many wartime roads.

A miniature Shinto shrine stands before the limestone cliffs of **Bloody Nose Ridge,** site of the fiercest fighting. Americans poured aviation fuel into caves sheltering diehard Japanese who refused to surrender and ignited it. Three large **war memorials** stand on Bloody Nose Ridge. On the lowest terrace is the U.S. Marine Corps monument. From there a road winds up to the Japanese monument on a high terrace almost surrounded by jagged limestone peaks. This monument was erected in February 1989 on the site of the Japanese last stand, where Colonel Nakagawa of the elite 2nd Infantry Regiment of the Imperial Japanese Army committed *seppuku* after burning the regimental colors on 24 November 1944. At the very top of the ridge, accessible by a stairway, is the 323rd Infantry (U.S. Army) memorial and a flagpole on the uppermost peak. There's a superb view of the entire island from up there.

Several huge **Japanese buildings** stand half swallowed in the jungle northwest of the airfield. **Orange Beach** is where the American landings took place on 15 September 1944. At **Camp Beck Dock** is an assortment of abandoned U.S. ships and vehicles, plus wrecked planes bulldozed into mangled heaps of bent aluminum sculpture.

Most beaches on Peleliu have color names, though some also have other names. Heading counterclockwise from Klouklubed are: Amber Beach, White Beach, Orange Beach, Scarlet Beach (Bloody Beach) and Purple Beach (Honeymoon Beach). The color names are the code names used during the American invasion.

The **Bkul Omruchel Picnic area** on the island's southwest corner is a Japanese pilgrimage site. At high tide you can often see blowholes on this stretch of coast. At the cove between Scarlet Beach I and Scarlet Beach II (Bloody Beach) there is good snorkeling.

There is spectacular snorkeling from shore at Purple Beach (Honeymoon Beach) at the spot where the two roads intersect. If the surf is small, walk through the breakers and you come to a steep drop-off with huge fish swimming amidst fantastic coral gardens. Watch the current. If it's running strong, it's best not to snorkel.

Continuing on the road heading north from Honeymoon Beach is the **Ngermelt Swimming Hole,** a natural limestone sinkhole full of water that rises and falls with the tides—dive into the clear salt water and enjoy a refreshing swim.

Practicalities

Peleliu has no restaurants, though most guesthouses will, for an additional fee, serve meals. There are a fair number of stores on the island, but they may be out of essentials. All things considered, if you are only spending a night on Peleliu, it may be best to bring in your own food and water. Beer and cold sodas are readily available.

Electricity is only on from 6 p.m. to 6 a.m. Each night at 9 p.m. a siren goes off to signal curfew for the kids. The island tends to be hot, sometimes extremely so in the afternoons.

Peleliu has no full-service hotel, but a number of guesthouses from which to choose. In most you rent a room with shared bath, often outhouses. A brief stay is an ideal way to observe contemporary outer island Micronesian life. There aren't any phones to Peleliu, which makes

it difficult to make arrangements. Paradise Air can help, and some establishments have Koror contact phone numbers. You can also just show up because the island's guesthouse rooms are seldom all filled. Camping is an option also. Ask the governor for permission. Orange, White, Amber, and Purple Beaches are all good places to camp.

Keibo's Place lies near the beach in Koska village. Mayumi and Keibo Rideb rent rooms beside their store for $15 pp. A new **annex** opened recently, the only place on the island to have both air conditioning and hot showers (at least from 6 p.m. to 6 a.m.). Rooms in the annex are $35 s, $50 d. Meals are available for $18 pp per day. Keibo offers minibus tours at $15 pp and sometimes has vehicles for hire.

On the beach in Koska is the **Story Board Beach Resort** (P.O. Box 1561, Koror, PW 96940, tel. 488-3280), with A-frame cottages. The rooms are clean and soft breezes come through the screened windows. The cottages have private indoor bathrooms. This is a very pleasant place to stay for $55 s or d.

In Klouklubed is **Reiko's Inn,** run by Tangie Hesus' family. Four rooms are in a building behind the family's home. The stay is $15 pp per night and meals are available for an additional $18 pp. You can try to contact Reiko's by calling 488-2348. Nearby, also in Klouklubed, is the five-room **Wenty Inn.**

Jackson's Inn rents several rooms in a modern house owned by Jackson Ngiraingas, the present governor of Peleliu. It is a bit out of town and you will probably want to arrange transportation if you stay here. The rooms are lovely however, and it overlooks the ocean. Rooms are $35 s or d.

ANGAUR

Angaur (pop. 206) is a quiet coral island, with few tourists and little traffic. This was also a major World War II battlefield, so you'll find the same sort of relics and caves as on the larger and more populated island of Peleliu, seven miles northeast. The 18 September 1944 American landings on Red Beach on the northeast side of Angaur were unopposed. The Japanese garrison had withdrawn to caves in the mined out area, which they held for over a month. The Americans built the huge airstrip, which runs right across Angaur, in just 30 days, and B-24 Liberators became the main occupants.

Today the island is noted for the casual life in the one village, the attractive coastal scenery and beaches, and Micronesia's only monkeys, macaques that bred from two escaped German pets. Large monitor lizards are also seen. Palauans consider the monkeys pests because they eat crabs, so it's illegal to take them to other islands. Like Peleliu, Angaur is a prime marijuana-growing area, and the producers tend to be rather suspicious of strangers.

Central Angaur

Several half-submerged **American tanks** reinforce the breakwater of Angaur's harbor. The Japanese government spent $2.2 million on the harbor's new pier, but this reduced the available space, making it difficult for large fishing boats to maneuver, and the entrance is still treacherous. **Phosphate mining,** begun by the Germans in 1909 and continued through the Japanese period, finally ended under the Americans in 1954. The ruins of the bulk loading pier are just north of the harbor. Follow the remains of the fallen conveyor belt back through the bush to the skeleton of the phosphate crushing plant.

A ruined **Japanese lighthouse** rises high above the harbor, but it's not visible from the road, so it can be hard to find. Get there by taking the coastal road north from the phosphate plant less than a half mile, to a point where the route cuts between cliffs and begins to drop. Retrace your steps a little till you find your way into a small coconut grove on the southwest

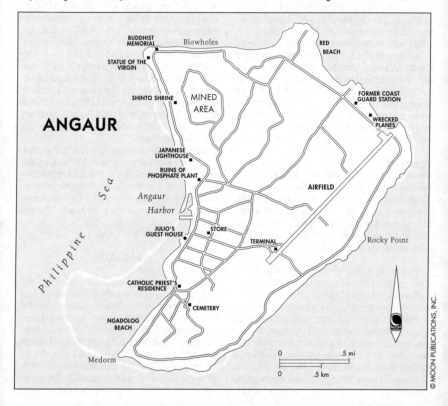

side of the road. Go in and look for a stone stairway leading past a square concrete water tank to the highest point. Your effort is rewarded with a good view of the island from the second-story roof. This place is perfect at sunset, and chances are you'll have a grandstand view of the antics of the local monkeys.

Northern Angaur

A pleasantly shaded coral road runs right around Angaur, which you can cover on foot in a day, but carry plenty of water. The most attractive stretch skirts the stark limestone cliffs at the northwest corner of the island. This is where the Japanese army made its last stand during the American invasion; Shinto and Buddhist memorials mark the event. The miniature **Shinto shrine** is especially striking, with a good beach opposite. The snorkeling is good here when the water's calm, but beware of surf and riptides when it's not. Today this area is inhabited by large bands of monkeys, which dwell in the many huge banyan trees.

The ocean crashes relentlessly into the northwest cape of Angaur. A statue of the **Virgin Mary** was erected at this point in 1954 to protect the islanders from rough seas. Several spectacular **blowholes** blow on the north coast, and the beat of the waves against the uplifted coral terraces can be hypnotic.

Between the abandoned buildings of the **former Coast Guard station** and the northeast end of the airstrip, a number of **broken aircraft** are found between the road and the coast. Included in this WW II aviation dump are fragments of a Corsair fighter and the wings of B-24 Liberators, half swallowed among the pandanus and ironwood trees.

Southern Angaur

Angaur is outside the protective Palau Reef. The impact of this can be appreciated at **Rocky Point** on the east side of the island: a blowhole and smashing surf. The far south end of the island is calmer with sandy beaches.

By the road at the north end of **Ngadolog Beach** is the former hospital, now the residence of a Catholic priest, just behind which are two large concrete platforms. Beyond the platforms look for a long depression in the ground near some large trees. The souls of all Palauans are

said to come to this pit after death to ascend to heaven up the trees or descend into hell through the ground. The place is thought to be haunted. Some hear screams in the night and see a ghost in the priest's residence.

Practicalities

The two guesthouses in the village are both within easy walking distance from the airstrip. **Julio's Guest House** (P.O. Box 261, Koror, PW 96940), the house beside the store closest to the airfield, has a few rooms at $15 pp. Meals are $5 (breakfast), $8 (lunch), and $12-15 (dinner). You can, of course, bring groceries. You share all facilities.

Masao's Guest House, a pleasant beach bungalow with a large veranda, has two rooms at $15 pp and floor space for groups. All meals are $18 per day extra or you can cook your own food. The water supply is variable. Here you're more or less on your own.

Camping is okay almost anywhere on the island. The pine covered southwest tip of Angaur beside Ngadolog Beach, the island's best, makes a perfect campsite. It's easy walking distance from town, yet far enough away from local houses. The beach is protected by a wide reef, so enjoy the swimming and snorkeling. Don't go off and leave valuables lying around, though.

Both camping and snorkeling depend on the direction of the wind: if it's out of the east Ngadolog Beach will be calmer, but when it's out of the west Rocky Point or the promontory between Red Beach and the former Coast Guard station will be preferable. Much of the year Ngadolog Beach will be best, except during the southwest monsoon season from July through October, when this side of the island gets the most rain and wind.

The two small stores on Angaur are not always well stocked and are closed on Sunday.

Transportation

The plane stops at the southwest end of Angaur's gigantic wartime airfield on the east side of town, a few minutes' walk from everything, or you can catch a ride with the Paradise Air agent for $2. **Paradise Air** offers convenient flights to Peleliu ($18) and Koror ($36).

The channel between Angaur and Peleliu can be rough. The *Yamato Maru,* a modern

Japanese-made motor vessel given to Angaur as war reparations, sails to Angaur from the Fisheries Dock, Koror, Monday and Friday afternoons, returning from Angaur to Koror on Thursday and Sunday, $5 one-way. It doesn't stop at Peleliu on the way.

THE SOUTHWEST ISLANDS

These five tiny islands between Koror and Indonesia are among the most remote in the Pacific. **Tobi Island** (Hatohobei), 372 miles southwest of Koror, is just 155 miles from the Indonesian island of Morotai. In 1990, Sonsorol State, which includes Tobi (148 acres) and Sonsorol (470 acres) Islands, had 61 inhabitants.

About a dozen people may be on **Pulo Anna** (198 acres) at any one time, while Merir (222 acres) and Helen (494 acres) are usually uninhabited. The main source of income is the sale of copra. **Sonsorol** consists of two islands, Fana and Sonsorol, about a half mile apart.

The people of the Southwest Islands speak the language of Woleai atoll, Yap State; Palauans cannot understand them. These islanders retain more of the traditional Pacific culture (leaf houses, canoe making, handicrafts, etc.) than any other group in Palau.

On remote **Helen Reef,** a sand spit east of Tobi, thousands of seabirds and turtles live in undisturbed bliss. Helen Reef has a 39-square-mile lagoon, but the other Southwest Islands are all low islands with only fringing reefs.

GORDY OHLIGER

TERRITORY OF GUAM
INTRODUCTION

As soon as you clear customs at Guam's International Airport, you see the symbol (dare I say it) of fin de siècle America, no longer a McDonald's, but an espresso bar, the Italian invention that Americans have made their own. Leaving the airport, you'll see a profusion of American junk food restaurants. But to come to Guam in the '90s and think of it as Waikiki West is like going to Hong Kong and thinking of it as London East—perhaps a kernel of truth in each thought, but they each miss the point.

Guam has wide streets and modern buildings. It does not have the exotic feel of the remote regions of Micronesia. But the sun is warm, the beaches beautiful; the streets are crowded, but clean; and the tap water is drinkable. United States military bases are physically and economically prominent. But increasingly, this is a land where brown-skinned islanders, Chamorros from Guam, Filipinos, and recent arrivals from the Federated States of Micronesia cater to Asian vacationers. People are busy spending or making money.

Guam is complex. It is a U.S. territory and military base. It is an Asian resort. But its southern half, still rugged from its volcanic origin, is a quiet place where modern Chamorro culture, a blend of indigenous Chamorro mixed with centuries of Spanish rule, thrives and rejuvenates itself today.

It's not easy to pinpoint who visits Guam today. Numerically far and away the most prominent are Japanese (and increasingly Korean and Taiwanese) vacationers seeking a fairly close, relaxing, short vacation. Some of these visitors are quite wealthy. Many others are young working people who, with the exchange rate of yen to dollars, can afford packaged tours. But Micronesians and expats living in Micronesia come here for urban errands and pleasures. Still other visitors are family and friends of Americans stationed or working here.

Finally, there are American and European travelers, usually in transit to or from more exotic destinations. Too often they are in a rush to leave. This is unfortunate. Guam is a great spot

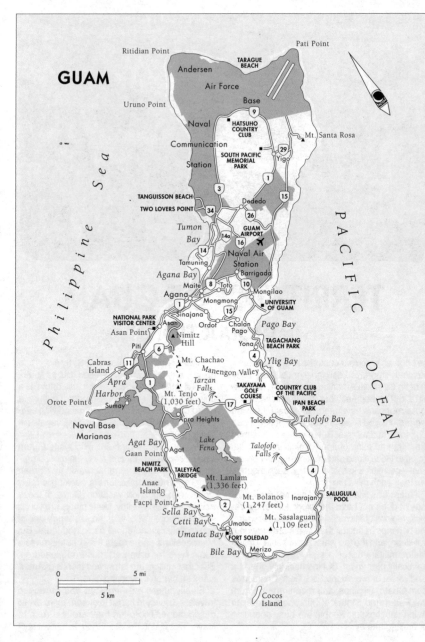

GUAM

Pati Point

Ritidian Point

TARAGUE BEACH

Andersen

Air Force

Uruno Point

Base

9

HATSUHO COUNTRY CLUB

Mt. Santa Rosa

Naval

Communication

29

Yigo

SOUTH PACIFIC MEMORIAL PARK

Station

3

1

15

TANGUISSON BEACH

Dededo

TWO LOVERS POINT

34

26

Tumon Bay

14a

16

GUAM AIRPORT

14

Naval Air Station

Tamuning

Barrigada

Agana Bay

Maite

8

Toto

10

Agana

Mongmong

Mongilao

1

UNIVERSITY OF GUAM

NATIONAL PARK VISITOR CENTER

Sinajana

15

Asan

Ordot

Chalan Pago

Pago Bay

Asan Point

Nimitz Hill

6

Yona

TAGACHANG BEACH PARK

Piti

Mt. Chachao

Cabras Island

Manengon Valley

Ylig Bay

4

11

Tarzan Falls

TAKAYAMA GOLF COURSE

COUNTRY CLUB OF THE PACIFIC

Apra Harbor

1

Mt. Tenjo (1,030 feet)

17

IPAN BEACH PARK

Orote Point

Sumay

Apra Heights

Talofofo

Talofofo Bay

Naval Base Marianas

Agat Bay

Lake Fena

Talofofo Falls

Gaan Point

Agat

NIMITZ BEACH PARK

TALEYFAC BRIDGE

Mt. Lamlam (1,336 feet)

4

Anae Island

Mt. Bolanos (1,247 feet)

Inarajan

SALUGLULA POOL

Facpi Point

2

Sella Bay

Mt. Sasalaguan (1,109 feet)

Cetti Bay

Umatac

Umatac Bay

FORT SOLEDAD

Merizo

Bile Bay

Philippine Sea

PACIFIC OCEAN

0   5 mi

0   5 km

Cocos Island

© MOON PUBLICATIONS, INC.

GUAM'S CLIMATE

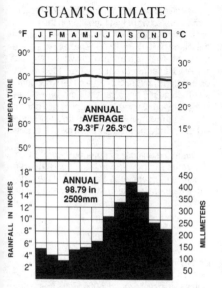

that rise hundreds of feet to a high limestone plateau with no permanent rivers or streams. Toward the center of this portion of the island, a second set of cliffs leads to a still higher plateau. The southern one-third consists of mountainous, volcanic terrain with a ridge of red clay hills.

In the south are crashing waterfalls, seldom-visited jungles, and easygoing villages along the coast (Umatac, Merizo, and Inarajan are the most picturesque). The best **surfing spots** on Guam are reputed to be Rick's Reef at Tamuning, the Agana Boat Basin, the entrance to Merizo harbor, and Talofofo Beach Park.

Climate

Guam is a land of endless summer, generally warm with little seasonal temperature variation. Like Hawaii, its air is liquid, though the humidity is not oppressive, as it can be in other parts of Micronesia. January through April is the dry season. Guam is located within the breeding grounds of western Pacific typhoons (June to November). Between 1948 and 1977 approximately 80 tropical storms and typhoons passed within 200 miles of Guam. Most rain falls during this southwest monsoon season.

to rest and relax after hard traveling in Micronesia or in Asia, or at the start of a vacation, to recover from jet lag.

THE LAND

The Pacific ends at Guam: on its western shores begins the Philippine Sea. This 209-square-mile island, the southernmost of the Marianas, is the largest in Micronesia. Guam's position on the Pacific Ring of Fire makes it prone to earthquakes.

Shaped like a footprint, Guam was formed by the union of two volcanoes: the older northern one was already capped with limestone when the southern volcano joined it. The island is less than five miles across its narrow instep, from the University of Guam to Agana, the commercial center. Legend holds that a great fish had been eating away at the middle of the island until the Virgin Mary restrained it with a hair from her head, saving Guam from destruction.

The northern two-thirds of Guam, where almost all development is, shows clearly its geologic history; it is a raised atoll. In most places, there is a narrow coastal plain, backed by cliffs

FLORA AND FAUNA

Salt-tolerant vegetation grows along the coastal strands, with swamps and marshes on some southern coasts and rivers. In the southern ravines are ferns and palms, then sword grass-sided valleys, which give way to high savanna. Dense forests once covered the northern limestone plateau, which today is mainly scrub brush.

The territorial tree is ironwood or *ifil,* a slow-growing evergreen. Its timber turns black with age. In 1947 *tangan tangan* brush *(Leucaena)* was seeded from aircraft to protect the defoliated island from erosion. *Tangan tangan* now grows in impenetrable thickets over much of the north end of the island, although it's seldom found on Guam's volcanic southern slopes.

The only indigenous mammals on Guam are bats. The fruit bat, locally known as the *fanihi,* has been having a rough go as it is considered a delicacy among Chamorros. (One local recipe for fruit bat soup specified that it could feed two

Chamorros or 25 *haoles,* foreigners). Other unique creatures are nonpoisonous centipedes and scorpions (though their bites are painful), stinging ants, large monitor lizards and a variety of crabs.

Guam has endangered species of sea turtles, including the green and the hawksbill. Guam's sharks rarely attack humans. Guam's reefs harbor one of the most diverse fish populations in the world, with 110 families and 800 species of inshore fish identified so far. Over 300 species of coral are present. The gathering of live coral is prohibited by law.

Guam may be one of the first places on earth to lose *all* its endemic birds, a disaster that could have serious ramifications on the pollination of native plants, dispersal of seeds, insect populations, and the whole ecological ladder. Introduced diseases, pesticides, hunting, and habitat loss have all been factors in the dramatic decline in birdlife over the past two decades. But in 1983 biologist Julie Savidge identified the main culprit as the brown tree-climbing snake *(Boiga irregularis),* introduced accidentally from the Solomon Islands from the hold of a navy ship or plane toward the end of World War II. The nocturnal snakes were first identified in the harbor area in the 1950s. Now some forested areas of the island have up to 12,000 snakes per square mile. The snakes can grow to over six feet but are of little danger to people. They feed mainly on eggs and chicks, but can also be a danger to small domestic animals. Until the brown tree snake arrived, Guam's only serpent had been a blind, earthworm-like snake. Guam's native forest birds were helpless in the face of this new predator.

Guam's electricity is notoriously unreliable. For years the power company used the tree snake as its scapegoat, claiming that the problem was those pesky creatures creating short circuits.

HISTORY

Early History

Guam's first people probably arrived from the Malay Peninsula around 5,000 years ago. They lived in small villages; the basic social unit was the extended, matrilineal family. After marriage the man moved to the woman's house; land was inherited from the mother's brother. There were three social classes: nobles, commoners, and outcasts. Spirits of the ancestors were venerated.

The most intriguing remains left by the *taotaomona* (spirits of the before-time people) are *latte* stones, megalithic monuments up to 20 feet high thought to have once supported residences of the *matua* (upper class). The *latte* were usually constructed in double rows of six to 14 stones, each composed of a *haligi* (pedestal) and a *tasa* (cap). The *tasa* are natural coral heads placed atop the *haligi* with the spherical side down, making them look like giant mushrooms with the tops inverted. Burial sites and artifacts are usually found in the vicinity of *latte*. *Latte* stones are found throughout the Marianas, the biggest on Tinian.

A Spanish Colony

Ferdinand Magellan, on the first known circumnavigation of the world, landed on Guam in 1521, his first stop after crossing the Pacific. Magellan landed three and a half months after rounding the tip of South America; his scurvy-ridden crew

M.G.L. DOMENY DE RIENZI

marines taking cover during the landings on Guam, 21 July 1944

had been reduced to a diet of rats and leather after crossing the Pacific without sighting land. He saw Guam as a source of badly needed supplies. Magellan named Guam the Isle of Thieves when his skiff was stolen. He recovered the boat after personally leading a raid ashore, during which seven or eight islanders were killed and their village burned. Two months later, Magellan was killed in a similar fracas in the Philippines.

Miguel Lopez de Legaspi, colonizer of the Philippines, claimed Guam for Spain in 1565, but it was not until 1668 that Jesuit missionaries arrived to implant their faith. When persuasion failed, the Spanish resorted to force. From 1680 to 1695, troops under Captain José de Quiroga waged a war against the native Chamorro people and, with the help of introduced diseases like smallpox and syphilis, reduced their numbers from 80,000 in 1668 to below 5,000 by 1741.

The survivors, mostly women and children, were relocated in controlled settlements where they intermarried with Spanish and Filipino troops and adopted much of those cultures, becoming the Chamorros of today. Clan-held lands were divided among individuals. In 1769 a power struggle between the king of Spain and the Jesuits led to the expulsion of the order from Guam (and all other Spanish colonies). The Chamorro population declined to 1,500 by 1783.

Today, a church-inspired monument to the pro-Spanish collaborator Quipuha graces Agana's Marine Drive, while resistance leader Chief Matapang is not commemorated. Father Diego Luis de San Vitores, who used Spanish soldiers to carry out forced baptisms of Chamorros until they killed him in 1672, is now in the process of canonization.

Changing Hands

For 200 years, Guam was a source of food and water for Manila galleons plying between Mexico and the Philippines. It took three months to sail from Acapulco to Manila and six months to return. The Spanish traded silver from Mexico for gems and spices from Asia. The annual journeys ended in 1815 when Mexico became independent from Spain. After 1822, Yankee whalers became regular visitors.

Guam, Puerto Rico, and the Philippines became American possessions as a result of the Spanish-American War. On 20 June 1898 the USS *Charleston* entered Apra Harbor, firing as she came. Informed that their country was at war, the Spaniards promptly surrendered.

Military Rule

From 1898 to 1941 Guam was run as a United States naval station; U.S. Marines were the constabulary. To avoid provoking Japan, already a rising power, no attempt was made to fortify the island. Just prior to World War II, Guam's defenses consisted of a few machine guns and several hundred rifles.

The Americans surrendered to a Japanese invasion force just two days after Pearl Harbor. The Japanese immediately forced the 2,000

Chamorro inhabitants of Sumay village on the Orote Peninsula to evacuate their homes. (They still live elsewhere on Guam; the area is a United States naval base today.) The Japanese renamed Guam Omiyajima, "Great Shrine Island."

In March 1944, the Japanese deployed 18,500 troops to Guam to meet an expected American invasion. Guamanians were conscripted to work alongside Korean labor battalions. On 12 July, the Japanese beheaded 30-year-old Father Jesus Baza Duenas and three others accused of aiding a fugitive United States Navy radioman. A few days later all 21,000 local residents were herded into concentration camps such as the one at Manengon near Yona, a move that separated the Chamorros from the crossfire of battle.

Some 55,000 Allied personnel landed at Agat and Asan on 21 July 1944. Organized resistance by the outnumbered and outgunned Japanese ended on 10 August, although some remained in the interior for years. The final cost to the United States came to 2,124 dead and 5,250 wounded, most of them marines. Only 1,250 Japanese were captured; the other 17,000 perished.

One diehard Japanese straggler, Sergeant Shoichi Yokoi, held out in the jungle near Talofofo until 24 January 1972, claiming he was unaware that the war had ended.

The United States turned Guam into a massive military base; by mid-1945 there were 200,000 servicemen on Guam. Large tracts of land appropriated at that time remain in the hands of the military today, and the private owners have not yet been fully compensated. In the late 1970s former landowners and their heirs launched a lawsuit against the United States demanding compensation. A $39.5-million out-of-court settlement was paid in 1986. But this settlement was not deemed fair by many landowners. Questions remain as to whether the landowners actually gave knowing consent to the settlement.

From 1945 to 1949, 144 Japanese defendants were tried by the United States in a Quonset hut on Nimitz Hill, Guam. Two Japanese lieutenant generals, two rear admirals, five vice admirals, and the commanding officers in the Marshalls, the Marianas, Tungaru, Bonin, Palau, and Wake were among the 136 convicted of war crimes. Fifteen of the 111 convicted of murder were executed. The rest served their sentences at Sugamo Prison, Tokyo.

In 1946 the United States granted independence to the Philippines but retained control of Guam. In 1950, the Department of the Interior took control of the island, at which time Guamanians became United States citizens. Until 1962, a military security clearance was required to visit Guam.

Military Use

During the cold war, Guam's strategic importance to the U.S. came from its proximity to Russia, Japan, and China. Guam became one of the most heavily fortified bases. Andersen Air Force Base, the main Strategic Air Command (SAC) base in the Pacific, had the only B-52s based outside the continental United States.

The navy still controls a 1.5-mile runway at the Agana Naval Air Station beside the international airport. Guam is the communications center for naval forces in the western Pacific. But with the collapse of the cold war, the closing of United States bases in the Philippines, and a reduced U.S. presence in South Korea, the military situation in the western Pacific is changing. The number of military personnel on Guam has been drastically reduced. Some military lands have been opened to public use, and there is enormous political pressure from the islanders to release more. Guam's future seems tied more to Asian business than to the American military.

GOVERNMENT

Guam is a permanent, unincorporated territory of the United States. In 1987 the Guam electorate approved a draft Guam Commonwealth Act, which was never approved by the United States Congress. The proposed Commonwealth Act would give Guam control over immigration, veto power over certain federal laws, and a say in defense policy relating to the island. In many ways, this proposal would give Guam more attributes of sovereignty than given in Commonwealth bills to the Northern Marianas or Puerto Rico. Negotiations on the future status of Guam have occurred sporadically over the past decade.

At present, Guam has only one level of government: a 21-senator unicameral legislature elected every two years. The people of Guam elected their own governor for the first time in 1970; both the governor and an elected lieutenant governor serve four-year terms. Since 1972 an elected, *nonvoting* member of Congress has represented Guam in Washington. Guamanians cannot vote in United States presidential elections, yet United States citizens living in Guam can vote in its elections. The government of Guam controls certain territorial departments and autonomous agencies such as the Commercial Port of Guam, Guam Airport Authority, Guam Power Authority, Guam Telephone Authority, and the University of Guam.

A "sovereignty" movement continues among Chamorros today. This concept has different meanings to different adherents, but for all, it means greater Chamorro autonomy. In the political realm, demands run the gamut from merely more local rule to complete independence. At least three members of Guam's legislature are dedicated to increased autonomy. In the cultural realm, the movement includes relearning and using the Chamorro language and employing art forms that reflect traditional Chamorro expression.

For more information on Guam's history, read Professor Robert Rogers's book, *Destiny's Landfall* (Honolulu: University of Hawaii Press, 1995)—an extraordinary discussion of the process of conquest and colonization, from the precontact era to the present day struggle for autonomy.

ECONOMY

Tourism is Guam's biggest business. Guam receives more tourists than any Pacific island destination except Hawaii. In 1995, Guam passed the million visitors a year mark for the first time. Over 80% of Guam's tourists are Japanese. Koreans are the second-largest group of visitors, and Americans are third. The Japanese tourists do not bring as much money to Guam's economy as might be hoped. Because so many come on three-day prepaid tours, much of the profit remains in Japan. Guam's high-impact tourism is similar to that of Saipan, yet Guam is much bigger than Saipan and not as overwhelmed by Japanese tourism.

Military spending has been greatly reduced since the end of the cold war. It remains significant, though segments of the economy that were heavily dependent on the military are still enduring hard times. As elsewhere, movement toward a peacetime economy causes economic dislocations. Large military reservations account for 30% of the surface area of the island; over half of this area is held for "contingency purposes" and is not currently being used. The Guam government holds another 25% of the land. There are increasing local demands for the return of unused military lands to domestic use.

Guam is a free port, not part of the United States customs area. Import duties are charged only on tobacco, liquor, and liquid fuel. Manufactured goods with at least 30% value added by assembling or processing on Guam can be exported duty free to the United States. This was intended to spur industries that would assemble component parts produced inexpensively in Asia, but such industry has not yet developed to a significant degree.

THE PEOPLE

The pre-European people of the Marianas were racially and culturally related to other Micronesians. The Chamorros of today are a mixed people with Micronesian, Filipino, and Spanish blood. Ninety-eight percent are Roman Catholic. Many continue to live in traditional flower-filled villages, but they commute to work by car or bus.

Under a succession of colonial rulers the focus of Chamorro life shifted from the traditional men's house to the village church, the school, and finally the shopping mall and office. The Chamorros underwent an assimilation crisis.

Today, Guam's total population is roughly 135,000, more than half of whom are not Chamorro. Guam is home to many ethnic Filipinos (about 25% of the population), Statesiders (about 15%), Chinese, Japanese, Koreans, and Micronesians from other islands. The number of immigrants from the Federated States of Micronesia is increasing. The Chamorros share a very real fear that the growing influx of immigrants from east and west will make them a small minority on their own island. In 1940 they comprised 90% of the total population; today they're less than 45%.

Language

Chamorro is a rhythmic, melodic language. A Spanish speaker has difficulty following a conversation, even though approximately 85% of the words in modern Chamorro derive from Spanish. Chamorros are always surprised and pleased by a visitor who attempts a few words of their language. Chamorro went out of general use a generation ago, but today there is a revival of its use and it is again being taught in the schools.

M.G.L. DOMENY DE RIENZI

Hafa adai sounds like "half a day" but means something like "hello, how are you?" If you'd like to ask how someone is, try *hafa* or *fa*. To ask the time, ask *Que hora?* Other easy phrases include *si yuus maasi* (thank you), *buenos dias* (good morning), and *adios* (goodbye). *Bai falak y...* (pronounced "bay-fa-LAK-ee") means "I'm going to...." Add the name of the place (*banko* is bank, *checho* is work, *tenda* is store) and you're speaking Chamorro! To stress something, simply repeat the last syllable or two. Hence *dikiki* is little, and *dikikikiki* is very little.

ARTS AND CRAFTS

Guam has a lively arts scene. Artists trained in Western art, often in the United States, are creating a new school of painting that combines Western techniques with traditional values and themes. The **Guam Gallery of Art** in Chamorro village shows local artists.

In addition, Guam has two art museums. The **Guam Museum** is located at the government complex in Adelup. At the University of Guam, 15 Dean's Circle, you'll find the **Isla Center for the Arts,** which contains a collection of Pacific and Pacific Rim art, both indigenous and modern. Though currently closed, the old Guam Museum, located in Plaza de Espana, did contain many artifacts relating to Shoichi Yokoi's 16 years of hiding on Guam. More

funding is needed to reopen the new Tumon location of this museum.

HOLIDAYS AND EVENTS

Banks and government agencies remain closed on the following public holidays: New Year's Day (1 January), Martin Luther King's Birthday (third Monday in January), President's Day (third Monday in February), Guam Discovery Day (first Monday in March), Good Friday, Memorial Day (last Monday in May), Independence Day (4 July), Guam Liberation Day (21 July), Labor Day (first Monday after the first Tuesday in September), Columbus Day (second Monday in October), Veteran's Day (11 November), Thanksgiving Day (fourth Thursday in November), Feast of the Immaculate Conception (8 December), and Christmas Day (25 December).

Around 6 March a fiesta at Umatac village commemorates Magellan's landing. Many events take place in July to celebrate Guam's liberation in 1944, culminating in a large parade and fireworks on 21 July. Merizo's Water Festival is held in August. Feasts are commonly held to celebrate anniversaries, marriages, and births. The biggest procession of the year occurs on 8 December in Agana, to honor Our Lady of the Immaculate Conception, patron of the island. Fireworks at the Hilton mark New Year's Eve.

All 19 Chamorro villages on Guam celebrate their patron saint's day; since some villages have more than one saint there are 32 recognized fiestas a year. The best known fiestas are those of the Santo Nino Perdido, Asan (January); Nuestra Senora de la Paz y Buen Viaje, Chalan Pago (January); Our Lady of Lourdes, Yigo (February); St. Joseph, Inarajan (May); Assumption of Our Lady, Piti (August); San Roque, Barrigada (August); Santa Rosa, Agat (August); Dulce Nombre de Maria, Agana (September); San Miguel, Talofofo (September); St. Teresita, Mangilao (October); St. Jude, Sinajana (October); Our Lady of the Blessed Sacrament, Agana Heights (November); and Santa Barbara, Dededo (December).

A complete three-month *Calendar of Events* is available from the Guam Visitors Bureau.

A complete list of village fiestas with exact dates is provided on the last page of the Guam telephone directory. Most of these feature a religious procession through the streets, followed by a feast. People are very hospitable on these occasions and you stand a good chance of being invited if you're in the right place at the right time. "Come and eat" is the usual greeting.

SIGHTS

AGANA

Looking at Agana from the sea, one realizes what a narrow band, above the ocean and below the cliffs, has been home to so much human drama. The town of Agana (pronounced "a-GA-nya") is primarily low rise, tucked in a small coastal strip below the cliffs to the central plateau. The town is pleasant looking and clean, though the buildings themselves are not picturesque. What is missing is anything old. The 1920s wooden structures one finds in the towns of much of the tropical Pacific are missing. They have been destroyed by earthquakes, typhoons, and the United States retaking the island in 1944. Old in Agana means before 1977, the date of a particularly severe typhoon.

Agana, particularly at night, is a sleepy town. Most of the action has moved up to Tumon Bay. However, some treats remain, tucked away. Nobody on Guam seems to know street names, even if they know every building on the island.

The Spanish founded a town at Agana in 1668. A few physical reminders of the Spanish era remain. The **Plaza de Espana** in the heart of downtown Agana was the center of spiritual and temporal power during Spanish colonial times. Of the Casa de Gobierno ("Governor's Palace"), built in 1736 and enlarged in 1885, little survived the war. However, one can still see the *azotea* (terrace), the arches of the arsenal (1736), and the "Chocolate House," a summerhouse where Spanish ladies once gathered for late afternoon *meriendas* (teas). The former Spanish garden house, also in the plaza, has served as the **Guam Museum.** It was closed in 1995 and it's not clear when it will reopen. It housed a collection relating to the amazing story of Japanese sergeant Shoichi Yokoi, who hid out from the end of World War II until 1972.

To one side of the plaza is the **Catholic Cathedral,** first erected here in 1669 and rebuilt in 1955. The image above the main altar is Santa Maria Camalin. Legend says that this statue miraculously floated ashore on the beach at Merizo over 200 years ago, guarded by two golden crabs bearing lighted candles in their claws. A revolving statue of Pope John Paul II (who said mass here in 1981) watches over Plaza de Espana.

Nearby, at the foot of Kasamata Hill, is **Latte Stone Park,** where eight ancient *latte* pillars, originally from the vicinity of Lake Fena in south central Guam, were re-erected in 1955. These timeworn monoliths could once have been the foundation stones of prehistoric buildings, though their precise history is obscure. The stones are impressive, but not their setting, which is next to a busy street. Along the cliffs behind the park are **caves** where the Japanese ensconced themselves during the 1944 invasion by American forces.

Above Latte Stone Park at Agana Heights is **Government House** (est. 1952), residence of the governor. Inside you may visit the Governor's Museum, with its interesting displays on Guamanian history, and enjoy the view from the terrace. Just beyond this is the site of **Fort Santa Agueda** (1800). Although very little is left of the

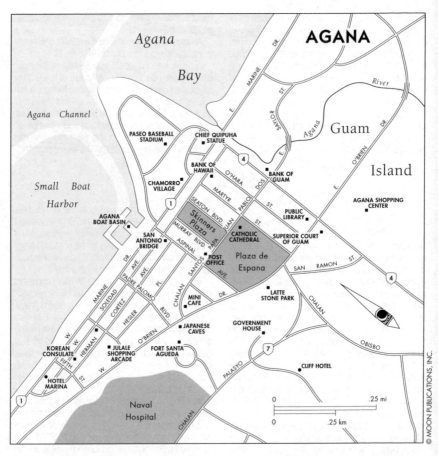

fort, you do get a splendid view of Agana from this hill. As with many attractions on Guam, you will enjoy the visit most if you can time it between tour bus arrivals.

Back near Marine Drive, northwest of the Plaza de Espana, is the **San Antonio Bridge** (1800). In 1676 the Presidio Agana, a small settlement surrounded by a stockade, was located between this bridge and the waterfront. The river itself was filled in after WW II.

The most interesting spot in town, particularly for the budget traveler, is **Chamorro Village.** It opened in 1994 and is located on fill from bulldozed World War II rubble, on a point opposite downtown, the former site of the public market. It is a great place to hang out, though unfortunately, not yet open at night. It contains a series of small kiosks, made to resemble traditional housing. Only local produce and products can be sold here. The fish store sells reasonably priced sashimi to go. There are all types of gift shops, selling goods made by local artisans, using local products to the degree feasible. There are many food shops featuring the different ethnic cuisines of the people of Guam.

My favorite shop here is Guam Chokolati, which sells fresh homemade chocolate. They do handicrafts in chocolate, such as chocolate baskets. A great, nonrenewable souvenir for $4.20 is a solid chocolate Great Seal of Guam. They will take phone orders at 472-9688.

Within the Chamorro Village, fronting Marine Drive is the Guam Gallery of Art, open during the day and in the evening by appointments (tel. 472-9659). Run by Fillamore Paloma, the gallery exhibits members of the Chamorro Artists Association. A recent exhibit featured works by well-known Anita D. Bento, a Guamanian of Filipino descent.

In the same room is a second gallery showing the work of the Castro family, perhaps Gaum's most renowned family of artists.

Right behind Chamorro Village is the **Paseo Baseball Stadium,** a charming, small stadium that makes you remember why people play baseball for less than $3 million a year. If you see the lights on in the evening, go take a look.

The **Paseo de Susana Park,** behind the stadium, is also worth a stroll. Some tourists have their pictures taken in front of the **miniature Statue of Liberty** in the park. The mouth of Agana Boat Basin is a prime surfing spot.

AROUND THE ISLAND

Guam, though a large island for Micronesia, is only 30 by nine miles. Agana is located at the narrow waist of the island. One can travel the northern portion of the island in two to three hours sightseeing included. A similar trip around the south takes four to five hours.

North of Agana
Above Tumon Bay, on Route 1 between 14A and 34 (pretty much opposite and above the Sotetsu Tropicana), is a small park dedicated to **Confucius.** There is a nice view of the bay, and it's about as restful as anything could be in this busy location.

Beyond the north end of Tumon Bay is **Two Lovers Point,** a 350-foot basalt cliff where two young Chamorro lovers are said to have tied their hair together and jumped to their deaths to avoid separation. A deep cave drops to the sea.

Gun Beach, beyond the Hotel Nikko on Tumon Bay, directly below the cliffs, is a favorite for swimming, snorkeling, scuba diving, and surfing. There is a parking structure just

past the Nikko. It is fairly easy to get past the reef here, but check for currents. Tumon Bay curves around between Two Lovers Point and the Hilton.

Heading north, Routes 3, 9, 1 and 15 create a loop around the island's northern plateau. The land here is flat, with dense scrub vegetation. The road is not near the ocean, because the coast is controlled by Andersen Air Force Base.

One of Guam's most beautiful beaches, **Tarague Beach,** is located on the base, east of Guam's northernmost spot, Ritidian Point. The road to the beach is not open to the public. However, if you make friends on the island who are in the military or even work for the federal government in another capacity, they can visit the beach and take you in as their guest. The beach is lovely and never crowded. Do not swim outside the reef here because of the powerful Rota channel. Military personnel and their guests can camp.

Northwest of and accessible from Tarague Beach is privately held land. With luck you will see some of the lovely fica butterflies that congregate here.

Another method of seeing this area is to go for the day to the **Star Sand Resort.** This private beach is mainly used by Japanese tourists. For $85 a person, you can relax on the beach and have a Chamorro barbecue buffet lunch. The excursions are 9:30 a.m.-2:30 p.m. or 11 a.m.-4 p.m. To make arrangements call 646-9230.

Toward the end of the battle for Guam in 1944, the Japanese withdrew northward. They made their last stand near Yigo; **South Pacific Memorial Park** marks the spot. Lieutenant General Hideyoshi Obata, commanding general of the Japanese 31st Army, had his headquarters in a network of tunnels below the park. On 11 August 1944 American soldiers tossed white phosphorous hand grenades into the tunnels and sealed the openings with blocks of explosives. When the tunnels were reopened four days later, 60 Japanese bodies were found inside, though Obata was never identified. Several of the tunnels can still be seen at the bottom of the hill behind the monument.

On Route 15, just past the junction with 29 (after the base) is the Mangilao Golf Club. From here you can see long stretches of the rocky coastline.

At Mangilao, north of Pago Bay and overlooking the ocean, is the **University of Guam,** founded in 1952 as a teacher's college. The university houses the Micronesian Area Research Center (MARC), the most important collection of material for serious Micronesian scholars. The university also has a big arena, called the Field House, that serves as a convention site for Guam. On the nearby new fine arts building is a large mural worth taking a look at.

If you follow Route 32 past campus to the end, you come to a parking lot in front of WERI, University of Guam Water and Energy Research Institute. Behind the building is a path to the ocean. There is often surf here good for boogie boarders; the waves look a little too tight for board surfers and the bottom too rocky for body surfers. Even boogie boarders should be careful and ask locals for advice on the rock situation. Alternatively, you can work your way around the shore to the right for some beautiful high tide snorkeling.

The South

You can cross to the east coast of Guam either on Route 4 out of Agana or Route 8 and then Route 10 from Tumon Bay. The following discussion traces a trip along Route 4, heading to the south of the island then back north on the west coast, where the road's name is changed to Route 2. The end of this section, particularly the **War in the Pacific National Historical Park**

Visitor Center, can be reached much more easily by heading west out of Agana.

Once you get away from the Tumon Bay/Agana area, the island is no longer overwhelmed by tourists. No simple primitive, unspoiled Guam exists. But down south, you see mostly Chamorro faces. In the countryside, houses are spread out and there is not the apparent, grinding poverty as on some other islands of Micronesia.

There are a good number of public beach parks, most with toilets and showers. Along the east coast there are also a fair number of beaches with family names on them. They are *private* and should not be used without permission. If you meet a family member, permission to use the beach will usually be given.

You can get a good view of the cliffs lining Guam's windy east coast from the road leading to **Tagachang Beach Park** just below Yona. The beach sign is behind some ironwood trees and is a bit difficult to see. There is a paved road heading down to it. The park has a pleasant covered picnic area. It is not a good place to swim. Waves break on a hard reef and there are frequently rips. **Ipan Beach Park,** about five miles farther south, is another family beach. The setting is not as pretty as Tagachang, but it is better for snorkeling.

Before reaching Ipan, however, Route 17 leads across to **Tarzan Falls,** near the center of the island. It takes 20 minutes to hike down a muddy track to the crest of the falls, and then

a view of Umatac in the early 19th century

M.G.L. DOMENY DE RIENZI

there's a slippery climb down the side through long, sharp sword grass to a pool. The bottom of Tarzan Falls is idyllic. Route 17 leads back to the west side of the island.

At the junction of Routes 4 and 4A, drive a bit up 4A, where you will be rewarded with one of the best views of the southern, volcanic portion of Guam. You will be looking down into Talofofo Bay and the river which flows into it.

Talofofo Bay Beach Park is at the mouth of the river. This makes the water a bit muddy for snorkelers or divers, but prevents coral growth creating a reliable shore break for surfing. On storm surge, a long right comes off the point and can get pretty hairy.

What is remarkable about this beach is that locals, military personnel, and tourists seem to coexist. The same can be said of body surfers, boogie boarders, and board surfers, all of whom use this wave. The shore break is soft mud, except for a couple of obvious rocks.

Saluglula Pool, a popular saltwater swimming hole, is right beside the road at **Inarajan**. Founded by Governor Quiroga in 1680, this is the best preserved village on Guam, so take time to stroll around. Father Jesus Baza Duenas, the Chamorro priest beheaded by the Japanese in 1944, is buried beneath the parish church.

The **Chamorro Cultural Village** is located here. This popular attraction has exhibits where elders explain and demonstrate traditional methods of living—such as using limestone ovens or fishing. This is an enjoyable spot where you can get snacks or purchase souvenirs.

Merizo is the halfway point around the island—about 22 miles either way from Agana. Busloads of Japanese tourists are sent over from Merizo to **Cocos Island** (P.O. Box 7174, Tamuning, GU 96911, tel. 828-8691) in a shuttle boat. There is good snorkeling off the island, but the trip is overpriced at $50, including lunch. It is difficult for any tourist to get the local rate of $10 without lunch.

The **rectory** (El Convento) in front of the Merizo village church was occupied by the parish priest beginning in 1856; across the road is a **bell tower** (Kampanayun Malessu) built in 1910. The **Massacre Monument** in front of the church memorializes 46 Chamorros murdered by Japanese troops near here as the American invasion became imminent.

Umatac village was the docking site used by the Manila galleons; several forts built here in the early 19th century protected the area from English pirates. **Fort San Jose** was on the north side of the bay, **Fort Soledad** on the south; not much is left of either, but the view from Fort Soledad is great. Magellan has been said to have landed at Umatac on 6 March 1521; there's a monument to record the event. However, more recent scholarship doubts that this was the actual landfall. (See *Destiny's Landfall* by Robert Rogers—Honolulu: University of Hawaii Press, 1995.)

The main road turns inland between Umatac and Nimitz. The road climbs through the rugged volcanic country of the slopes of **Mt.Lamlam** (1,336 feet), Guam's highest peak. A viewpoint above Sella Bay looks down on grassy red ridges trailing into the sea. A trail departing from the **Cetti Bay Overlook** leads up to the large cross atop Mount Lamlam (45 minutes one-way), with a sweeping view of the entire island. On Good Friday a religious procession parades to this cross. It's possible to hike south along the ridge back to Merizo or Inarajan.

A terrific but difficult hike is along the coast from Umatac to a point near **Nimitz Beach Park.** Although the coconut plantations at the heads of bays are private property, much of this area is within **Guam Territorial Seashore Park.** You'll have to wade on the reef around the points and ford knee-deep streams emptying into the bays, but you can make it through in a day. Wear shorts and old tennis shoes that you don't mind getting wet. It's also quite feasible to hike down to the coast from the **Sella Bay lookout**, which avoids a lot of houses but can be very slippery after rain.

The West

Apra Harbor, between Asan and Agat, is one of the largest protected harbors in the world. Guam's commercial port is here, though most of the south side of the harbor is taken up by a giant U.S. naval base. At **Gaan Point**, Agat, a couple of guns and tunnels recall the World War II fighting. Just south of Nimitz Beach Park is **Taleyfac Bridge** (1785), part of the old Spanish road from Agana to Umatac.

Three large 140mm **Japanese guns** are perched in a row up a concrete stairway and along a short trail behind the community hall on the north side of Piti Catholic Church. The mahogany trees near the guns were planted in the 1920s and 1930s.

From Nimitz Hill high above Piti, an excellent hike follows a jeep track south from Mount Chachao to the summit of **Mt. Tenjo** (1,030 feet) with panoramic views along the way. As you drive up to Nimitz Hill from Piti, turn right onto Larson Road, the next street after Trans World Radio, and right again on Turner Road. Keep straight as far as Mount Chachao where the road swings left to the relay station atop Mount Alulom. The rough jeep track to Mount Tenjo, impossible for a car, is straight ahead, a two hour hike roundtrip.

Heavy fighting took place near Agana in July 1944. The main landings were at Asan and Agat; the Japanese commander directed the defense from the Fonte Plateau above Asan. **War in the Pacific National Historical Park Visitor Center** at Asan, one and a half miles west of Agana, offers a photo display and a 15-minute slide show on the war (tel. 477-9362; open weekdays 7:30 a.m.-3:30 p.m., weekends 8:30 a.m.-2 p.m.). Even if you are coming from the south, rather than from Agana, go to this interesting center to get oriented, before you double back to the actual battlefields.

PRACTICALITIES

ACCOMMODATIONS

The geography of Guam controls its hotel scene. Most hotel rooms are along beautiful but developed Tumon Bay, or adjacent to it at the north end of Agana Bay. Hotels on the beach are luxury hotels at luxury prices. Many of the large, luxury hotels are Japanese-owned and quite expensive, yet do not have services for English-speaking guests. On the other hand, some luxury hotels, which also cater primarily to a Japanese clientele, work well for English speakers. It is not mere ownership, nor the language of the employees. Rather, at some "Japanese" hotels the staff's knowledge of dive shops, fishing boats, and other island activities may be limited to businesses where the proprietors speak only Japanese.

The hotels on the inland side of Pale San Vitores Road are lower priced, though they front a busy commercial street. Behind this beach area is a cliff, the remains of an ancient raised reef. Hotels on or above the cliff are close to the beach, though they may be several hundred feet above, a healthy climb in a wet bathing suit. Nonetheless, these are some of the best values on Guam and can provide an excellent choice for budget travelers. This area up the cliff is called Tamuning toward the south end of the bay and Upper Tumon toward the north.

Virtually all rooms in Guam have air conditioning, private bath, color TV, and in room phones. The most crowded months are February, March, August, and October to December.

Many of Guam's hotels, including luxury hotels, will offer substantial discounts. These discounts fall into four categories: corporate, local, military, and government. Nobody is clear about the exact requirements for each. For example, do you qualify if you are in Guam to visit someone in the military? Discount qualifications are determined, in part, by how many vacant rooms

the hotel has at the time. Be sure to inquire, particularly if you are calling from Micronesia to make the reservation.

For a long stay, check the yellow pages of the telephone directory under the heading "Apartments" and start calling. One agency with many such apartments is Six D Enterprises Inc. (tel. 646-5606, fax 646-5929).

Tumon Beach Enclave

Guam is a wonderful place to relax and enjoy yourself, in luxury if you wish. Tumon Bay is not a carbon copy of Waikiki. Yes, there are highrise eyesores. But the hotels do not crowd each other the way they do on Oahu. The beach itself is never crowded and appears to be cleaned every evening. Pale San Vitores Road, behind the beach hotels, has restaurants and both elegant and schlock shopping.

The bay itself, backed by green cliffs, is stunning. The water is quite shallow and most enjoyable for snorkeling at high tide. When the water is calm, and if you are ocean-wise, it is relatively easy to work your way outside the reef, where ocean life is more varied. As usual in shallow water, make sure your feet are covered to avoid injuries from the sharp coral. Also keep your feet up, to avoid injuring the coral.

The best luxury hotel for Westerners is the newly refurbished, 691-room **Guam Hilton** (P.O. Box 11199, Tamuning, GU 96931, tel. 646-1835, fax 646-6038). Rooms begin at $145 s, $175 d. The hotel is located on 32 acres along Ypao Beach on Tumon Bay. Its beachfront seems even longer because it sits next to a large beach park. Like all of Tumon Bay's hotels, the clientele is mainly Japanese. But there is a substantial number of other guests, and the Japanese guests are a bit younger and more likely to be independent travelers. It is fun to sit in the lobby with a drink or a coffee and watch the scene.

The Hilton's location and service make it an excellent place for a business stay as well as for a vacation. It has a health club and all necessary business equipment.

The **Pacific Star Hotel** (P.O. Box 6097,

Guam Country Code 671

Built in the late 1960s and recently refurbished, the Hilton International Guam is one of the largest hotels on the island.

ANTHONY CORN

Tamuning, GU 96931, tel. 649-7827, fax 646-9335) is an architecturally interesting 19-story pyramid. The hotel has a quiet atmosphere, less festive than most of the other hotels on this stretch. Rooms begin at $195 s, $205 d. Special features of the hotel are six restaurants and a 24 hour coffee shop, three bars, a computerized business center, and a complete health club on the premises.

The 448-room **Hyatt Regency Guam** (1155 Pale San Vitores Rd., Tamuning, GU 96911, tel. 647-1234, fax 647-1235) is a recently constructed luxury hotel. Despite the American name, this $150-million Hyatt belongs to EIE International of Japan. It appears able to provide good service to English speakers, however. Its grounds are lovely and worth a visit even if you are not staying there. The pricey rooms run $250 s, $270 d. Also fun to visit at the hotel is T.J.'s Mexican restaurant (open for dinner or drinks at 6 p.m., live music at 9:30 p.m.) or La Mirenda for buffet ($20-26, depending on the night).

The **Pacific Islands Club** (P.O. Box 9370, Tamuning, GU 96931, tel. 646-9171, fax 646-5762) is a 32-story eyesore on Tumon Bay. Not only is the hotel an eyesore, it is an ear sore, with messages continually blasted in English and Japanese with sufficient volume to disturb those relaxing on the beach. Forced "fun" runs rampant at this resort. Rooms, single or double without meals, are $246.

All hotels farther northeast on Tumon Bay are primarily for Japanese tourists.

On the beach is the **Fujita Guam Tumon Beach Hotel** (153 Fujita Rd., Tumon, GU 96911, tel. 646-1811, fax 646-1605), with its sprawling, low-rise 283 rooms at $140 s, $150 d. This was the first hotel along Tumon Bay. The outside of many of the buildings are decorated with fantastic tile mosaics, some 30 feet tall. The hotel has a 24-hour laundromat.

Tumon Holiday Plaza Hotel (P.O. Box 12639, Tamuning, GU 96932, tel. 649-8001, fax 646-3400) is across the street on the inland side from the Fujita Guam Tumon Beach Hotel. It is mainly set up for Japanese tour groups. Its regular rate is $150, but its "local rate" is $120 and its corporate rate is $85. Just down the road toward Tamuning lies **Dai-Ichi Hotel** (P.O. Box 3310, Agana, GU 96910, tel. 646-5881, fax 646-6729), with 333 rooms at $160 for ocean view, $140 hillside. Directly adjacent **Sotetsu Tropicana Hotel** (P.O. Box 8139, Tamuning, GU 96911, tel. 646-5851, fax 646-5583) has 198 rooms at $150.

Overlooking Tumon Bay is the 18-story **Guam Reef Hotel** (P.O. Box 8258, Tamuning, GU 96911, tel. 646-6881, fax 646-5200), owned by Japan Air Lines. You get excellent views from the balconies of the 458 rooms at the Reef. Rooms begin at $180.

The **Guam Hotel Okura** (185 Gun Beach Rd., Tumon, GU 96911, tel. 646-6811, fax 646-1403) is quite elegant with a large crystal chandelier hanging in the lobby and a convention/banquet facility seating 450 guests. The 366 rooms at the Okura begin at $140 s, $160 d in the South Wing and $240 in the Tower Wing.

Although the **Hotel Nikko Guam** (P.O. Box 12819, Tamuning, GU 96931, tel. 649-8815, fax 649-8817) is on a cliff, directly below it is the beach, at an excellent spot for low tide reef walking. It probably has the most luxurious grounds of any of Guam's hotels. The building is architecturally interesting with big open spaces. Not all staff speak English. The 500 rooms begin at $180 s, $190 d.

Palace Hotel Guam (P.O. Box 12879, Tamuning, GU 96931, tel. 646-2222, fax 649-5211), on Oka Point, offers some fabulous views, seen from within its vacuous architecture. It is overpriced at its regular rate of $210 s, $230 d, and its beach does not compare to those on Tumon Bay. However, see if you can qualify for the "corporate rates" of $130 per day with every fourth day thrown in free. At these rates, it is a reasonable choice if you are on business.

Closer to Agana and to be avoided is **Alupang Beach Tower.** This hotel is trapped behind a fortress-like parking lot. The hotel is set down on a narrow stretch of beach. It's a great place to go if your idea of fun is watching and listening to jet skis driven in incessant circles.

Near Tumon Bay

One of Guam's best bargains is the **Polynesian Hotel** (P.O. Box 9014, Tamuning, GU 96931, tel. 646-7104, fax 649-3230), with its 13 rooms above a convenience store, all units with kitchenettes. The hotel is not far from the airport. It is on Ypao Road, above the cliff, but only about one mile from the Hilton and the adjacent public beach park. Studios are $48, and bedroom units are $62. You will wish to rent a car if staying here.

Another choice for a less expensive hotel near the beach is the **Seoul Regency Hotel** (1475 Pale San Vitores Rd., Tumon Beach, Guam 96911, tel. 649-8000, fax 646-8738), on the road going up the cliff from the Reef Hotel. This Korean-run hotel is popular with expats traveling to Guam from other parts of Micronesia and strives to give personal service to all its guests. Most rooms have spectacular views of Tumon Bay and are quite reasonably priced, beginning at $85.

Behind the Seoul Regency is **Hotel Sunroute Oceanview** (1433 Pale San Vitores Rd., Tumon, GU 96911, tel. 649-9670, fax 649-0562). All units have kitchens. A one-bedroom unit is $128 and a two-bedroom $160. The hotel offers substantial discounts to corporate customers.

The 520 room **Guam Plaza Hotel** (P.O. Box 7755, Tamuning, GU 96911, tel. 646-7803, fax 646-7809) is up the hill from Pale San Vitores Road. It is relatively inexpensive for the Tumon Bay area at $76 s, $84 d.

Farther up the hill is **Tumon Bay Capital Hotel,** also primarily catering to a Korean crowd. This is a small hotel but a good buy at $90.

Inexpensive Hotels

Guam has a fair number of motels that Statesiders call "hot sheets motels," and the Japanese "love hotels." Rooms can be rented by the hour. The difference in Guam is that these hotels usually have a number of rooms, perhaps a whole floor, dedicated to legitimate use. Morality aside, most such hotels are not well kept, and the traffic is annoying. Hotels bearing a neon sign proclaiming "24 hours" fall into this category.

At any rate, there are a fair number of inexpensive hotels in and near Agana without the above drawbacks. However, check with your local contact to make sure the business will be in Agana. Much business is now in Tamuning—a better place to stay.

The three-story **Hotel Marina** (P.O. Box CK, Agana, GU 96910, tel. 477-8349, fax 477-2709) is located on the west edge of Agana, opposite the lagoon. The hotel had fallen on quite hard times but has been rehabilitated under new management. At $50 s, $55 d, the hotel is a good deal, particularly if you are able to get a lagoonfront room. Although this area is not usually thought of as the "beach," there is actually some good snorkeling in the lagoon, across the boulevard from the hotel.

On Route 8, about a quarter mile up from Marine Drive is the **Plumeria Garden Hotel** (P.O. Box 7220, Tamuning, GU 96911, tel. 472-8831, fax 477-4914), a pleasant, motel-style establishment with lots of parking. It has 78 rooms at $55 s, $60 d, and offers discounts for stays of a week and longer. A laundromat is on

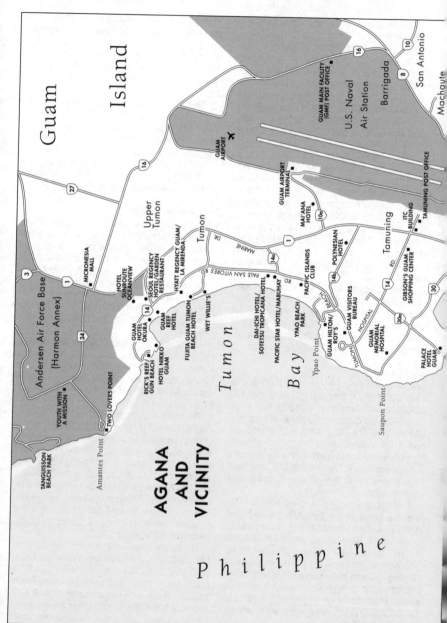

AGANA AND VICINITY

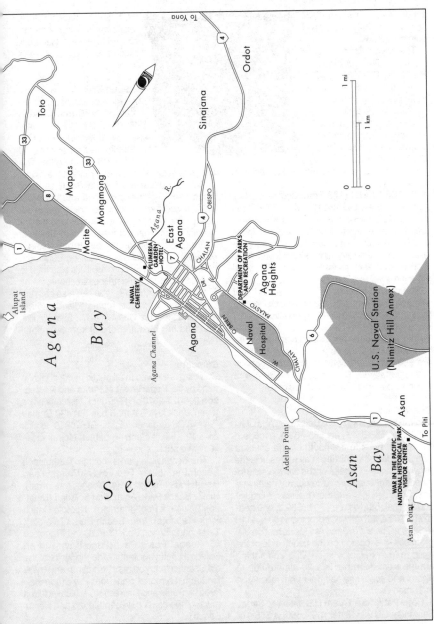

© MOON PUBLICATIONS, INC.

the premises. This is a decent place, built around a swimming pool.

The **Maite Garden Hotel** (P.O. Box 2925, Agana, GU 96910, tel. 477-0861, fax 477-0844) on Route 8, behind the Maite Shopping Town Plaza, has 47 units beginning at $55 s, $63 d. Suites begin at $75. Also sometimes available are units with kitchens for $650 per month. This is a good choice for a family visiting someone in the military.

The **Cliff Hotel** (178 Francisco Javier Dr., Agana Heights, GU 96910, tel. 477-767, fax 477-1044) is located near the old governor's mansion above central Agana. For $77 s, $93 d you'll get one of the 41 rooms, with cooking facilities, each complete with work desk and an individual balcony with a view of Agana. The office is frequently closed on the weekend.

The closest hotel to the airport is the **Hotel Mai'Ana** (P.O. Box 8957, Tamuning, GU 96931, tel. 646-6961, fax 649-3230), good if you need a place for one night. The U-shaped, three-story building (78 rooms) encloses a pleasant courtyard with pool. Studios with cooking facilities are $63, while spacious two-bedroom apartments go for $90. This hotel can be difficult to reach by phone. Fax ahead if you can.

Out of Town

The **Inn on the Bay** (P.O. Box 7387, Agat, GU 96928, tel. 565-8521, fax 565-8527), a modern beachfront hotel to the south on the coast at Agat, has kitchen facilities in all rooms. It is the only hotel south of Agana and is conveniently located for families visiting the nearby naval station. Considering the kitchen facilities, it is quite economical. Studios are $70 s, $80 d; one bedrooms $80 s, $90 d; two bedrooms $100 s, $110 d, $120 t. There's a Denny's Restaurant on the premises. It is located on the beach side of the main road. It has nice snorkeling and fishing out the front door, but is a 20-minute ride to Agana and about one half-hour from the airport or Tumon Bay.

Hotel Palmridge Guam (122 Hasalao Street, Barrigada, GU 96913, tel. 477-6666) is $65 s or d, but also offers a military discount. It is conveniently located for those visiting the University of Guam on the east shore.

Bed and Breakfasts

An excellent alternative to the hotels is the **Guam Garden Villa** (P.O. Box 10167, Sinajana, GU 96926, tel. 477-8166) at 193 Ramirez Dr., Ordot, off Route 4 southeast of Agana. This local homestay is run by Mrs. Herta K. Laguana, a German expat married to Romy, a local Chamorro. The charge for bed and breakfast is $40 s, $50 d with shared bath. Book well in advance—there are only three rooms and they're usually taken. Airport transfers are available at $10 each way, but you're better off renting a car upon arrival as the house, on spacious, flower-filled grounds, is isolated. It's also hard to find, so call Herta for detailed directions.

South of Agana in Piti, you can also call Ann Concepcion, who rents rooms adjacent to her shop, the Treasure Chest (tel. 472-8380) in Piti. Ann and her husband are extremely helpful hosts.

Camping

Camping is allowed in all public parks administered by the **Department of Parks and Recreation** (tel. 477-9620 or 477-7825). Visit their office (open weekdays 8 a.m.-5 p.m.) at 490 Chalan Payaso Rd., Agana Heights, GU 96919, to pick up a $2 a night camping permit. Not all facilities have public showers.

The accessible parks include Tanguisson Beach Park (near Two Lovers Point), Ypao Beach Park (Tumon Bay), Afflege Park (Agat), Nimitz Beach Park (Agat), Fort Soledad (Umatac), Saluglula Pool (Inarajan), Talofofo Beach Park (Talofofo), Ipan Beach Park (Talofofo), Tagachang Beach Park (Yona), and Francisco F. "Gonga" Perez Park (Pago Bay). At Fort Soledad pitch your tent inside the walls of the old Spanish fort. You may also camp anywhere in Guam Territorial Seashore Park (administered by Parks and Recreation), which includes much of the coast between Merizo and Nimitz Beach.

Remember that it's unwise to leave your tent unattended. Be prepared to be blasted by high volume music from cars parked nearby late at night.

FOOD AND ENTERTAINMENT

Guam has a large number of excellent restaurants. Since most food, other than fresh fish, is imported, restaurants in all price categories will be more expensive than comparable dining Stateside. Some rules to lessen the burden:

- Food is more expensive in luxury hotels than in freestanding restaurants.

- Japanese food, particularly in hotels, is very expensive. Don't expect to have dinner for less than $50. (In yen, these prices are cheap to tourists from Tokyo.)

- In hotels, a buffet is your best buy, particularly if it becomes your only serious meal of the day.

- Food is cheaper in town than by Tumon Bay.

- Beer is cheaper than wine.

- Stands are less expensive than sit-down restaurants.

Agana

In the **Chamorro Village,** by the Agana waterfront, are many food shops featuring the different ethnic cuisines of the people of Guam. They are located around a shaded center court with tables, a lovely spot to have an inexpensive lunch.

Shirley's Coffee Shop, located at the Hotel Marina on W. Marine Dr., is a local institution. Particularly at breakfast, it is a place that local businesspeople go to put together deals. Breakfasts are about $5. At lunch, sandwiches run $3-4. For lunch or dinner, Chinese dinners average about $7, a bit more for steak or salmon. Shirley's serves up good food at a reasonable price in a lively atmosphere.

For something different try the barbecue buffet at the **Mongolian Hut Restaurant** (tel. 472-8056; closed Sunday), also on Marine Drive. You pay according to the weight of food you select (about $10).

On Marine Drive, just east of the Chamorro Village, though on the inland side of the street, is the Sun Merry Restaurant, which serves an all-you-can-eat Chinese lunch buffet for $6.

Despite the unpretentious appearance, the **Mini Cafe** is very popular for its weekday Cantonese lunch combination specials.

Sizzler Steak House (tel. 477-7112) at the Agana Shopping Center has a good salad bar and fairly inexpensive steaks.

Opposite the main post office on the corner of Chalan Santos Papa and Aspinal is the recently opened **Olie's Restaurant.** It specializes in vegetarian dishes, though it also serves some meat dishes. Try their falafel, or lentil burger, each at $4.50, or the meatless lasagna dinner for $7.95.

*overlooking
Tumon Bay*

Downtown, on Herman Cortez Avenue, West of Aspinal is the **Mandarin Chinese Restaurant,** serving reasonably priced Chinese food.

In the Julale Shopping Arcade, the **Korea Palace** stylishly serves excellent Korean food. Its crowd is mainly local. Complete dinners will be $15-20. Lunches cost around $10. For budget eats in the same arcade, try the counter at the **Doughnut Tree,** where a two-choice lunch, including fried chicken, fried noodles, or fried rice will cost $5.

House of Chin Fee on the west edge of town serves Filipino dishes as well as Chinese. The best deal is the special for $16.95 that includes big portions of three dishes as well as two bowls of rice. It is surrounded by tacky nightclubs and massage parlors in an unsavory part of town. It does have a parking lot, however.

Perhaps the most innovative restaurant in Agana is moderately priced **Ivory's,** also located in the Hotel Marina. The food here is terrific, an eclectic mix of "New American" cuisine. Try the Jambalaya with fresh tuna and cumin, and for $2 the spicy onion rings. Leave room for the great desserts. The restaurant is always crowded with locals, so it is best to call for reservations (tel. 472-9590). Open for lunch and dinner.

Tamuning/Upper Tumon

Guam is loaded with American franchise eateries: **Taco Bell, Wendy's, Popeye's, Kentucky Fried Chicken, Shakey's, Pizza Hut.** They are inexpensive by Guam standards. Some upscale chains also have arrived—**Tony Roma's** and **Lone Star Restaurant.**

In **Gibson's Guam Shopping Center** are about a dozen shops around a central eating area. You can get Taco Bell there, but you can also get inexpensive Chamorro, Vietnamese, Korean, and Chinese dishes. **King's Restaurant** (open 24 hours) is also located at Gibson's. It offers weekday breakfast specials. The portions are huge and it's very popular with locals.

Food in the luxury restaurants can be excellent, but expensive. Perhaps the most inventive food is at elegant **Roy's** at the Hilton. As we discussed above, most of the luxury hotels offer scrumptious buffets at least some of the days of the week. The meals will not be inexpensive, but often offer very good value. **La Mirenda** at the

Hyatt has a buffet each night. Most nights the buffet is $20, but on Wednesday and Sunday when there is even more seafood than usual, the price is $26. The **Mabuhay,** located in the Pacific Star Hotel, has a Filipino buffet on Saturday night for $22.

Many hotels have dinner shows including Polynesian-style music and dancing. Staged primarily for Japanese tourists, these shows are usually quite expensive and have nothing to do with Chamorro culture.

Wet Willy's Beach Pub caters mainly to an American, military, and surfing crowd, and tries to cultivate a redneck flavor. It is on the beach with beautiful views.

Chuck's Steak House (tel. 646-1001) off Marine Dr. in Upper Tumon serves good, filling weekday lunches and thick, juicy steaks in the evening. Their bar is worth a visit anytime, but particularly at happy hours.

Ocean City Restaurant (370 South Marine Dr., tel. 649-2988) is an excellent (though not inexpensive) Hong Kong-style Chinese restaurant. At lunch it serves wonderful dim sum, and it's open till 2 a.m.

The rooftop **Garden Restaurant** at the Seoul Regency Hotel serves up great Korean food in an outdoor setting, overlooking Tumon Bay. The prices are moderate if you stay away from the pre-arranged dinners served to Korean tour groups.

Around Guam

The **USO,** in Piti near Cabras Island, has a cheap public snack bar. The **International United Seaman's Service Club** (tel. 472-4247), beyond the power plant on Cabras Island, has a good inexpensive dining room open till 9 p.m. daily and a bar open till 11. Turn off the main coastal highway at the USO.

One of the only places to get lunch (chicken and steaks) on the way around Guam is **Jeff's Pirates Cove** (tel. 789-1582; closed Monday), just north of Ipan Beach Park on the east coast. All the Japanese bus tours stop here, so it's not cheap, but the cold beer at the bar is fairly priced. Between tour buses, it is a pleasant a place to sit and watch the scenery. The bar is open air, and there is a volleyball court you are welcome to use.

Entertainment

Karaoke (video sing-along) is still the rage at many bars and restaurants on Guam and Saipan. Customers are offered a microphone and the chance to sing songs, following the text displayed on a video screen. It's great fun and hostesses are often available to do the singing for tips.

Tumon's most glitzy dinner theater and discotheque is the **Sand Castle** (tel. 649-7469), next to the Hyatt Regency Hotel in Tumon. This $30-million entertainment center features a Las Vegas-style musical revue dinner show at 7 p.m. nightly except Wednesday. It's $100 pp, $50 for the show alone. The Sand Castle also contains the 750-person capacity **Onyx Disco.**

A good local bar complete with shuffleboard and pool table is **Mom's Place** (tel. 477-7585) on Route 8, Maite. **Ninings Tavern** (no sign), on a side street down from Mom's, has lots of local atmosphere and very cheap beer.

The luxury hotels have bars and usually discos. In Tamuning is the **Haf Adai movie complex.**

SPORTS AND RECREATION

Guam is one of the best places for scuba diving in Micronesia. There is much to see in the waters around Guam. Moreover, it is a good place for a "shakedown" dive if you are just arriving in Micronesia. If you have any difficulty with your equipment, it can often be repaired in Guam, which is not the case on more remote dive sites. If you need to replace equipment, it can be purchased duty free. And for the more casual diver, without equipment, it's safe to rent from the established dive shops.

Prices are competitive among the major dive shops. A two-tank dive will cost around $90. Most shops will offer "locals" a cheaper price, especially if the diver is experienced and needs less supervision.

Guam Tropical Dive Station (P.O. Box 1649. Agana, GU 96910, tel. 477-2774, fax 477-2775) is run by the knowledgeable John Bent, whose dive shop is on Marine Drive opposite Ace Hardware at the south end of Agana. This excellent and very professional shop offers one-tank night dives, as well as the more usual two-tank day dives.

One of the biggest scuba operators on Guam is the **Micronesian Divers Association** (P.O. Box 24991, GMF, GU 96921), founded in 1975 by Pete Peterson. They frequent Blue Hole, Haps Reef, Crevice, and the twin shipwrecks in Apra Harbor. MDA has two locations: Pati, tel. 472-6321, and Andersen AFB, tel. 366-4220.

Scuba Locales

Guam's greatest attraction is its surrounding sea—a virtual paradise for snorkelers, scuba divers, surfers, or just plain swimmers and beach loafers. For accessibility, cost, and ease of diving, Guam is outstanding. Proximity to the Marianas Trench means the offshore waters are constantly flushed, resulting in 200-foot visibility in the dry season, 100-foot plus in the wet. There are also 15 to 20 good walk-in locations.

For beginners, **Bile Bay** on the southwest coast provides a gradual slope out, and some cave diving. Farther north a Japanese **Zero aircraft** rests in 60 feet of water off Umatac Point.

Blue Hole just off the south side of Orote Point, right under the cliffs, is also only 60 feet down. You pass through the 16-by-33-foot entrance and drop 130 feet, then make a 90-degree turn straight ahead out an immense opening onto a sheer drop-off. Near Blue Hole is the Crevice, also an exciting experience.

A navigational buoy in **Apra Harbor** marks two wrecks next to each other at about 100 feet: the WW I German auxiliary cruiser SMS *Cormoran* and the WW II Japanese freighter *Tokai Maru*. This is one of the few places in the world where vessels from two different wars can be seen on a single dive. Visibility, however, is usually better at the wreck of a sunken U.S. tanker one and a half miles farther out. Apra Harbor also has several nice reef dives.

Guam's most colorful scuba spot is **Double Reef** off Uruno Point near the northwest end of the island. Two parallel reefs about 1,000 feet apart have a channel 40 to 60 feet deep between them, with excellent visibility of the fine coral beneath.

Yachting

The **Marianas Yacht Club** (P.O. Box 2297, Agana, GU 96910, tel. 472-1739), behind Dry Dock Point at Apra Harbor, provides two-week guest privileges for visiting yachts and temporary membership at $100 a month. Facilities include washing machines and showers, and the Friday night barbecues here are fun and open to everyone. An annual race and regatta calendar is available from the club. The Continental Cup from Japan to Guam occurs around Christmas, with the Guam Japan Goodwill Regatta in February or early March.

Golf

Guam has many 18-hole public courses to accomodate golf enthusiasts. The most "local" and established of them is the **Country Club of the Pacific** (tel. 789-1362), which opened in 1971. It's in pleasant rolling countryside just north of Ipan Beach on Route 4 south of Yona. Greens fees are $85 weekdays, $110 weekends. If you want to do only nine holes it's cheaper. The clubhouse is impressive.

Similar, though slightly less impressive, is the **Takayama** or **Windward Hills Golf Club** (tel. 789-2474). It's located west of Talofofo in the center of the island, and primarily serves Japanese tourists. Greens fees are $75 weekdays, $85 weekends.

Another slick modern course popular with Japanese tourists is the **Hatsuho International Country Club** (tel. 632-0361) on Route 9 in northern Guam. A round of golf here will cost $110 weekdays and $150 weekends and holidays.

On Route 15, past the junction with 29, is the **Mangilao Golf Club** (tel. 734-1121) overlooking the ocean. With its rocky coastline and magnificent sights, it's not quite Pebble Beach, but close, which probably accounts for the high fees. Prices are $130 weekdays, $180 weekends. This is $10 a hole, or for most golfers, approximately $2 per shot. Off-island visitors must make reservations.

The **Leo Palace Resort** (tel. 888-0001) in Manengon Hills, Pulantat, Yona charges similar fees of $130 weekdays, $170 weekends.

You should call ahead to each course to check whether reservations are necessary. A dozen golf tournaments a year are held on Guam.

INFORMATION AND SERVICES

Shopping

Guam provides a good number of shopping malls and department stores if you need to restock and refit. Try **Gibson's Guam Shopping Center** in Tamuning, the **Agana Shopping Center,** the **Ben Franklin Department Store,** or the **Micronesia Mall** at the intersection of Routes 1 and 16 in Upper Tumon. This mall is Guam's biggest shopping center. A shuttle bus connects Tumon Bay tourist hotels to Micronesia Mall every 30 minutes—ask a hotel door attendant.

In Tumon Bay you can find goods by Chanel, Lorenz, Hermes, Cartier, Gucci, Ferragamo—all the usual suspects of world hot spots. **Duty Free Shoppers** has more than 10 stores on Guam. For most United States citizens, prices, even without sales tax and duty, are seldom cheaper than would be available Stateside, and are sometimes more expensive.

Visas

Entry requirements are similar to those of the rest of the United States: anyone not American requires a passport. People from most countries also need a visa. Visitors from certain countries now do not need a visa for stays of up to 15 days, and visitors from a few countries can stay without a visa for 90 days. Check with an American embassy or consulate in your home country.

American citizens need only show proper identification, such as a certified birth certificate or voter's registration card, if arriving directly from the States. Nonetheless, we urge any American traveling here to avoid possible confusion by carrying a passport. All passengers flying from Guam to Hawaii must pass U.S. Immigration controls at Honolulu.

Money, Measurements, and Services

Guam has many banks, the most ubiquitous one being the Bank of Guam. Banking hours are most usually Mon.-Thurs. 10 a.m.-3 p.m., Friday 10 a.m.-6 p.m., and Saturday 9 a.m.-1 p.m. Major credit cards are accepted at most business establishments. The American Express office is at 207 Martyr St., Agana, GU 96910, tel. 472-5777. You can receive mail at this office provided you have American Express traveler's checks or credit card; registered letters and parcels are not accepted.

United States domestic postal rates apply in Guam, making this a cheap, dependable place to mail things. General delivery mail is held at the inconveniently located Guam Main Facility

(GMF) post office on Route 16 in Barrigada. The Tamuning post office behind the ITC Building is open weekdays and Saturday morning. For postal information call 734-2921. For Guam postal codes see the appendix at the back of the book.

Long distance phone calls can be made at IT&E Overseas Inc., on Marine Drive between Agana and Tamuning. A direct dial call to Hawaii or the U.S. mainland from a booth at their office will cost only $1.75 for the first minute, plus about $1 per additional minute—cheap. Prices are a few cents lower evenings and weekends. To call direct from the United States to a telephone number on Guam, dial 011-671 and the regular seven digit number. Remember, Guam's a day ahead of the rest of the United States, so if it's noon Monday in Merizo it's 6 p.m. Sunday in Seattle.

The consulates general of Japan (tel. 646-1290) and the Philippines (tel. 646-4620) are in the ITC Building at Tamuning. If you have a personal problem and need help, call the Crisis Hot Line (tel. 477-8833), which is answered 24 hours. The electric current is 110-120 volts AC, 60 cycles.

Information

The **Guam Visitors Bureau** (401 Pale San Vitores Rd., Tumon, GU 96911, tel. 646-5278) can supply many tourist brochures. Their accommodations list only includes their members, however, not the cheapest places. Ask for their excellent *A Guide to the War in the Pacific Sites,* the *Island of Guam Highway Map,* and William H. Stewart's *Pacific Explorer's Map of Guam,* all available free of charge. You can obtain the same material through the mail by writing the Guam Visitors Bureau.

For an informative brochure on Guam's WW II history write: War in the Pacific National Historic Park, P.O. Box FA, Agana, GU 96910.

Weather information is available by dialing 117.

The **N.M. Flores Memorial Library** (254 Martyr St., Agana, GU 96910, tel. 472-6417) is open Monday, Wednesday, and Friday 9:30 a.m.-6 p.m.; Tuesday and Thursday 9:30 a.m.-8 p.m.; Saturday 10 a.m.-4 p.m.

Faith Book Store (tel. 472-1265) in the Agana Shopping Center specializes in books of Christian interest. It also has a first-rate section on Guam and Micronesia, including topographical maps. Located in the same center is the **I Love Books** store. In addition to its selection of books, the Sunday *New York Times* is available on the following Tuesday. For a list of academic publications write: Micronesian Area Research Center, University of Guam, UOG Station, Mangilao, GU 96923.

Guam has a good newspaper, the *Pacific Daily News* (P.O. Box DN, Agana, GU 96910), owned by the Gannett chain. It circulates throughout Micronesia. The monthly *Guam Now!* tourist magazine (free) includes extensive restaurant ads. *Guam Business News* can fill you in on the local business and economic scene. *Pacific Below* magazine will fill you in on interesting water-related activities in Guam, as well as in the rest of Micronesia.

If you need to see a doctor, you can try the new **Guam Memorial Hospital,** located on Oka Point, near the Palace Hotel at 850 Governor Carlos Rd., Oka, Tamuning, Guam 96911, tel. 646-2444.

There are seven radio stations on Guam: KGUM-AM (570), KUAM-AM (610), KTWG-AM (800), KUAM-FM (93.9), KSTO-FM (95.5) KZGZ-FM (97.5), and KOKU-FM (100.3). All but KTWG-AM broadcast 24 hours a day.

Volunteers

Youth With A Mission (YWAM) (P.O. Box 1245, Agana, GU 96910, tel. 646-7180), an international, interdenominational Christian missionary organization with close ties to United States fundamentalism, has been operating on Guam since 1977. YWAM welcomes young volunteers interested in performing a three-month summer of service as Christian missionaries. Their mobile teams travel constantly throughout Micronesia—an excellent way to see the area and meet the people, provided you're a sincere believer. Volunteers take the two week orientation course at Youth With A Mission's Guam headquarters, beside the Palauan meetinghouse and baseball field at Harmon, just beyond the Two Lovers Point turnoff. The cost is $5 a day for room and board. Accommodations are limited, so it's important to write in advance to let them know you'll be arriving.

GETTING THERE

Won Pat International Airport (GUM) at Tamuning is four miles northeast of downtown Agana. There's no bus service and taxis to most hotels are about $10-15.

Strangely, there's no tourist information at the airport, nor any foreign currency exchange office for arriving passengers. The airport "bank" is in the departure lounge on the second floor, past the security clearance, but its only purpose is to change excess U.S. dollars back into foreign currency for those departing ($1 minimum commission). They won't cash U.S. dollar traveler's checks. Have some quarters ready for the airport pay phones. No coin lockers are available at the airport.

Reconfirm or change your onward Continental Air Micronesia reservations at the helpful Service Center (tel. 646-9101) opposite the check-in counters.

All travelers transiting Guam between Hawaii or the FSM and Yap, Koror, or Saipan will have to change planes here, and this often requires an overnight stay. If you aren't interested in leaving the airport, check your luggage straight through to your final destination and spend the night in the transit lounge. In the case of westbound passengers from the FSM to Yap or Koror, this may entail a lengthy wait, so check the schedules carefully. The terminal is open 24 hours a day.

The transportation hub of the Central Pacific, Guam's airport receives most flights through Micronesia. Continental Air Micronesia (tel. 646-0220), Air Nauru (tel. 649-7107), All Nippon Airways (tel. 646-9069), Japan Air Lines (tel. 646-9195), Korean Airlines (fax 649-9683), Northwest Orient (tel. 649-8384), and Philippine Airlines all provide service.

All **Continental Air Micronesia** flights terminate on Guam. San Francisco and Los Angeles passengers must change planes in Honolulu. If an overnight stay at any of these points is required between connecting flights it will be at your own expense. Continental flights stop at Majuro, Kwajalein, Kosrae, Pohnpei, and Chuuk between Honolulu and Guam. Continental also serves Yap and Koror. Points in Asia served by

Continental directly from Guam include Denpasar (Bali), Hong Kong, Manila, Seoul, Taipei, and many Japanese cities.

Regular one-way Continental fares from Guam are $756 to Los Angeles or San Francisco, $342 to Koror, $342 to Japan. Certain off-peak flights from Guam offer reduced one-way fares.

Many airlines fly between Japan and Guam/Saipan (compare prices). All Nippon Airways, Continental, Japan Air Lines, and Northwest Airlines fly from Tokyo. Continental also serves Fukuoka, Nagoya, Okinawa, Osaka, Sapporo, and Sendai, and Japan Air Lines has nonstop flights from Nagoya and Osaka. Northwest arrives from Fukuoka and Nagoya. JAL and Northwest offer direct connections to Guam from many North American cities via Tokyo (Narita), instead of the usual Los Angeles to Honolulu routing.

Both Continental Air Micronesia and Freedom Air have regular service to Saipan.

You can charter a four seater Apache plane from Guam direct to Pagan in the Northern Marianas from **Freedom Air** (tel. 646-8009, fax 649-0729) for $1600 roundtrip plus $30 an hour waiting time on the island.

GETTING AROUND

Unless you are planning never to leave your hotel and its grounds, you should consider renting a car. Cabs are quite expensive, and even two short roundtrips a day will probably cost more than a car rental for the day.

Many car rental companies such as Avis (tel. 646-1801), Budget (tel. 646-5494), Dollar (tel. 646-7000), Gordon's (tel. 565-5827), Hertz (tel. 646-5875), Islander (tel. 646-8156), National (tel. 649-0110), Nippon (tel. 646-1243), and Toyota (tel. 646-1876) have offices on Guam. Their rates are fairly standard: about $40 a day with unlimited mileage, plus five percent tax. Always ask if they have any special discounted or business rates, or lower rates for older cars without air conditioning. Avoid any agency that tacks a mileage charge onto the daily rate. Avis, Hertz, Islander, and Toyota have locations at the airport. Tourist magazines like *Guam Now!* advertise special deals on car rentals.

Guam has an extensive **public bus system.** To use it, be prepared to spend a lot of time waiting. The system operates along nine routes, with important transfer stations at Micronesia Mall, Gibson's Guam Shopping Center, and the Agana Shopping Center. One of the most useful routes for visitors is the hourly Express Line from Micronesia Mall to the Tumon Bay tourist strip, then up to Gibson's, Tamuning, and down Marine Drive to the Agana Shopping Center. This service will stop anywhere along its route, so just flag down a bus.

Route PT-3 from Micronesia Mall to Gibson's

via Marine Drive runs only six times a day. Routes PT-4 and PT-5 from the Agana Shopping Center to the University of Guam run once an hour. Routes PT-6 and PT-7 from the Agana Shopping Center do a circular loop around southern Guam seven times a day in opposite directions. This two-hour ride is Guam's best bargain island tour and you can easily stop off at points along the way after confirming onward bus times with the driver.

Fares are $1 per ride or $3 for an all-day unlimited ride pass. Service ends around 7 p.m. and there are no buses on Sunday and holidays. For information call 475-7433.

GORDY OHLIGER

COMMONWEALTH OF THE NORTHERN MARIANAS

INTRODUCTION

The Commonwealth of the Northern Mariana Islands (CNMI) stretches north from Guam in a 426-mile-long chain. The 14 islands are weathered tips of a massive mountain range rising over six miles from the depths of the Marianas Trench.

Saipan is the business, government, and tourism center of the Northern Marianas, while Tinian and Rota are much less developed. These islands (along with northern Guam) are actually raised coral reefs, with level terraces and fringing coral reefs.

Saipan is also the largest and most populous island in the Commonwealth of the Northern Marianas. Because of the war, CNMI now has the same status and relationship with the United States as Puerto Rico. But over 85% of its tourists (tourism is the major industry) are Japanese, with less than five percent American. More store signs are in Japanese than English; fewer still are in Chamorro, the native language.

The Land

Saipan, the second largest of the Mariana Islands, is a 14- by five-mile block with towering cliffs on the north, east, and south, and gentle hills rolling toward white sandy beaches on the west. A barrier reef protects the wide western lagoon, making this side of the island the favorite of swimmers, snorkelers, and windsurfers. Sunsets seen from these beaches are spectacular.

Except for a short stretch at Laulau, no reefs are off the east coast. Huge waves fanned by the northeast trades often crash into this shoreline during Saipan's winter (November to April), cutting deep scars. Small bays, tidal pools, blowholes, and craters dot the rocky, broken east coast. The highest cliffs are in the Marpi area of northeast Saipan, entwined with the tragic events of war in 1944.

Rota and Tinian, the other big islands of the Marianas, are similar to Saipan, with Rota es-

THE MARIANAS AT A GLANCE

	LAND AREA (SQ. MI.)	HIGHEST POINT (FEET)
Northern Marianas	**184.51**	**3,175**
Agrihan	18.30	3,175
Aguijan	2.78	553
Alamagan	4.36	2,448
Anatahan	12.47	2,593
Asuncion	2.82	2,931
Farallon de Medinilla	0.35	266
Guguan	1.62	990
Maug Islands	0.81	750
Pagan	18.65	1,882
Rota	32.90	1,615
Saipan	47.45	1,550
Sarigan	1.93	1,806
Tinian	39.30	612
Uracas	0.77	1,050
Guam	**208.88**	**1,336**

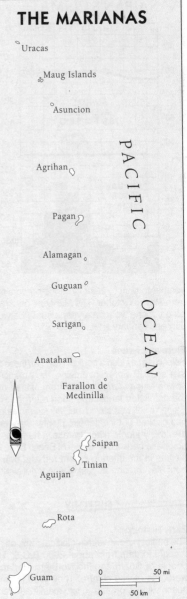

pecially noted for its beautiful, crashing coastline and upland plateaus. The towering northern islands, some still active volcanoes, are mostly uninhabited. There have been eruptions on Uracas, Asuncion, Pagan, and Guguan this century.

The Marianas Trench just east of the chain is the deepest of the world's trenches, a circular arc extending 1,865 miles from Japan to Ulithi atoll. The 47-mile-wide trench was discovered in 1899 when the Nero Deep was sounded at 31,702 feet. It's eight times longer, six times deeper, and two and a half times wider than the Grand Canyon, and as deep as Mount Everest is high. The islands of the Marianas are thus sitting on mountains taller than any on earth's surface.

Climate

The Marianas are the sunniest islands in Micronesia, though there is significant rain from July to September. From January to March conditions are best for swimmers and sailboarders. This is also the period when most tourists arrive to escape the Japanese winters. The northeast trades blow across the Marianas from No-

SAIPAN'S CLIMATE

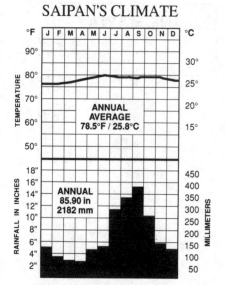

ANNUAL
AVERAGE
78.5°F / 25.8°C

ANNUAL
85.90 in
2182 mm

vember to March; easterly winds predominate from May to October. The Marianas get an average of one typhoon a year, usually between July and January.

Flora and Fauna

Saipan isn't as lush a tropical island as those farther south. To prevent erosion, the Americans sowed *tangan tangan* brush from aircraft over the defoliated landscape soon after the war. Saipan's soil was saved, but the *tangan tangan* has choked out indigenous plants. Still, there are lovely jungle hikes to take. The flame or poinciana trees along Saipan's Beach Drive, as well as in the interior, bloom red and orange from May through August, a wonderful sight.

HISTORY

Early History

The earliest known archaeological remains are thought to date from about 2000 B.C.E. The people of Guam and the Northern Marianas were one of one culture. They lived in small beach villages organized into matrilineal clans. Children belonged to the clan of the mother,

and inheritance was through the female line. Colonialism altered this organization, and the present Chamorros are primarily patrilineal.

In 1668 Charles II of Spain dispatched Jesuit missionaries to Guam and named the group for his mother, Queen Maria Ana of Austria. The Spanish defeated the Chamorros in 1689, after decades of heroic resistance, and relocated them to Guam where they could be more easily controlled. There they intermarried with the Spanish, adopting much Spanish culture.

In 1816, Chamorros began to return to the Northern Marianas, where they found communities of Carolinians from Lamotrek and Woleai had established themselves in their absence. The two cultures have lived peacefully through the generations, but to a considerable degree maintained separate identities to this day.

Germany purchased the Northern Marianas in 1899 from Spain, which was afraid of losing the islands to the Americans. Governor Fritz built roads and required every family to plant food crops.

Japan seized the islands from Germany in 1914. An influx of Japanese, Okinawans, and Koreans led to the development of sugarcane and pineapple cultivation. The Nanyo Kohatsu Kaisha (South Seas Development Co., Ltd.) built sugar mills fed by extensive rail networks on Saipan, Tinian, and Rota.

By 1935 as many Asians as Micronesians were present; by the outbreak of war Japanese nationals outnumbered Chamorros two to one. Garapan on Saipan was both the German and Japanese capital of the Marianas. Just before World War II the town had a Japanese population of 15,000.

The War

In 1941, the Japanese took a calculated gamble—they bet they could destroy the United States' ability to make war at sea in one decisive battle, allowing Japan to continue with her primary objective of domination of Indonesia and mainland Asia. The gamble failed. Over the next three years the United States simply out-produced Japan. By 1944 the outcome of the war was clear, as was the fact that the United States would accept nothing less than an unconditional Japanese surrender.

In June and July 1944 the United States took the Marianas from the Japanese. The landings

It is difficult to reconcile the beauty of Suicide Cliff with its deadly history.

at Chalan Kanoa on the southwest side of Saipan led to a brutal three-week struggle for the island. After securing the south, the GIs began fighting their way up both sides of the island, hoping to meet on the Marpi plain below what was to become known as Suicide Cliff.

On 19 June the Japanese Navy sent three Zero-laden aircraft carriers to rescue their forces. The United States had no less than 16 carriers waiting west of the Marianas. During the Battle of the Philippine Sea, 402 Japanese planes and all three carriers were destroyed in a single day, against a loss of only 17 U.S. aircraft.

On 6 July the remaining Japanese troops, with little firepower left, launched a fanatical charge across the Tanapag plains, which continued until all 5,000 Japanese attackers had been killed. Of the 30,000-man Japanese garrison on Saipan, only about 600 survived to be repatriated in 1945. Thousands of Japanese soldiers died making suicide attacks on the American forces. Hundreds of Japanese civilians tragically leapt to their death, jumping into the ocean from Banzai Cliff or onto land beneath Suicide Cliff, pushing their children ahead of them. Over 3,000 Americans were killed and another 11,000 wounded during the campaign. Some 419 Saipanese also died. Memorials now stand at the base of Suicide and Banzai Cliffs. They praise loyalty, sacrifice, and courage, but no memorial attests to the blatant stupidity of a world in which children are pushed off cliffs.

With Saipan in their hands, the United States landed on Guam on 21 July and Tinian on 24 July. Rota was bombed but not considered worth invading, so it remained in Japanese hands until the end of the war.

The islands became airbases from which American B-29s leveled the cities of Japan. At the height of the bombing campaign, North Field on Tinian was the busiest airfield in the world, with two B-29s taking off abreast every 45 seconds for the seven-hour ride to Japan. The nuclear age began here when the *Enola Gay* left Tinian for Hiroshima.

WASTE DUMPING

In 1979 the Japanese government announced plans to dump 10,000 cement solidified metal drums of dangerous nuclear wastes into the Marianas Trench halfway between Tokyo and the Northern Marianas. This was to be an "experimental" dump, followed by larger and continuous dumping in the future. After widespread opposition erupted throughout the Pacific, Japan dropped its plan. A 1983 law created a 200-nautical-mile no-dumping zone around the Northern Marianas, but the proposed Japanese dump site is outside this area. An open-ended moratorium on nuclear waste dumping at sea, adopted by the London Dumping Convention in 1983, hopefully put an end to this ill-conceived idea.

Americanization

With the rest of Japanese-held Micronesia, these islands became part of the Trust Territory of the Pacific Islands in 1947. Until 1962 the Northern Marianas were under U.S. naval administration and used as a training facility by the CIA.

Political-status negotiations began in 1969. In February 1975 the Marianas Covenant was signed, slicing the Northern Marianas from the Trust Territory to become a part of the United States Commonwealth, akin to Puerto Rico. Of the approximately 5,000 voters, 79% approved the Covenant. One factor in the favorable vote was a desire by the residents to remain eligible for federal entitlement programs. On 24 March 1976 President Ford signed the Covenant. The Commonwealth elected a governor and legislature in 1977, and on 9 January 1978 the Commonwealth constitution came into effect.

The Covenant creates a political union between the United States and the Northern Marianas. The U.S. controls defense and foreign affairs, while the Commonwealth is internally self-governing. The agreement can only be terminated by mutual consent. On 3 November 1986, the United States implemented the Covenant, and the inhabitants of the Northern Marianas were declared American citizens.

GOVERNMENT

The autonomous Commonwealth of the Northern Marianas has a governor and lieutenant governor elected every four years. The bicameral legislature is made up of nine senators, three elected at large from each of the main islands every four years, and 15 representatives elected every two years, two each from six districts on Saipan and one each from Rota, Tinian, and the northern islands. A two-thirds vote in both houses is required to impeach a governor. Each of the four municipal jurisdictions is headed by a mayor. Commonwealth residents aren't represented in the United States Congress and can't vote in presidential elections. Both the Democratic and Republican political parties are active.

ECONOMY

The Commonwealth of the Northern Marianas' greatest resource is its location, near Japan, Guam, and the Philippines. The beaches, relaxed entry requirements, and easy access bring more than a half million tourists a year, the greatest bulk from Japan. About 37% of the Commonwealth's income comes from tourism. Tourism income could be even greater, but Japanese tours are largely prepaid in Japan. Furthermore, most of the major hotels, tour companies, and restaurants on Saipan are owned by Japanese. Locals have been given few opportunities to assume managerial positions in these businesses. A recent federal district court decision interpreted a Japanese-American friendship treaty as allowing Japanese-owned companies to ignore most of CNMI's local hiring preference laws.

Built by the Republic of Nauru, the Nauru Building at Susupe is Saipan's largest office building.

DAVID STANLEY

TROPIC BIRDS

Although graceful in the air, the white-tailed tropic bird *(Phaethon lepturus)* must crawl on its belly to move about on land. During courtship male and female glide and circle one another high in the air, the upper bird sometimes touching the back of the lower with its two long, streaming tail feathers. Tropic birds often spend months at sea when not nesting, ranging hundreds of miles in search of food. Their bills have teethlike notches to help them hold their catch.

Covenant payments and United States aid have equalled almost $3000 per capita, much of it going to finance CNMI's government. The education system, however, is overwhelmed by the population explosion. Because of a lack of qualified local teachers, Statesiders and Filipinos make up a substantial percentage of the teachers. A Covenant provision prohibits the sale of land to persons of non-Marianas descent until 2011. However, a substantial amount of prime beachfront property is under long-term lease to Japanese interests.

While wages on Guam are close to those on the United States mainland, the minimum wage in CNMI is only about half the United States' minimum rate. Despite widespread local underemployment, foreigners (mostly Filipinos, but also Chinese and Koreans) compose 82% of the workforce in the private sector. Many of the jobs they hold are exempted from the minimum wage; maids, construction workers, fishermen, and farmers get under $200 a month. Filipinas are often brought in under false representations to work in Saipan's karaoke bars or to serve as housekeepers.

THE PEOPLE

Present-day Chamorros differ considerably from their ancestors, whose skeletal remains indicate a taller, larger-boned people. Modern Chamorros are clearly recognizable and do have a sense of ethnic identity. But they are descendants of not only the original Chamorros, but also of the Spanish, Filipino, Chinese, German, Japanese, and American citizens with whom they intermarried through three centuries. Culturally, Spanish influence is perhaps the strongest. Family names, social customs, and physical appearance reveal a deep Hispanic legacy. Estimates indicate over four-fifths of the words in the modern Chamorro language derive from Spanish roots.

One-fourth of the Micronesian population of the Northern Marianas is descended from Carolinians who arrived over a century ago by canoes. You can sometimes spot the Carolinians by the flower leis *(mwarmwars)* they wear in their hair. Since citizens of the FSM gained free entry to the United States and its Commonwealth in 1986, there has been a second wave of Carolinian immigration to Saipan.

About 50,000 people live in the Commonwealth, mostly on Saipan (45,000), Rota (2,500), and Tinian (2,500). Included in the total are almost 20,000 registered alien residents. During the 1970s the population of Saipan doubled, and it jumped 158% from 1980 to 1990. Nonresident alien workers are not allowed to stay in the Marianas for more than four years.

ARTS AND ENTERTAINMENT

The Commonwealth Council for the Arts sponsors exhibits throughout the year showcasing the arts, customs, and culture of all of Micronesia. Plans exist to open a CNMI Museum of Culture at the Japanese hospital, through the auspices of the Department of Historic Preservation. Until then you can view Chamorro and Caroline arts and crafts in display cases at the airport.

Crafts
Unfortunately you'll mainly find grotesque lacquered and mounted turtles and coconut crabs for sale, as well as jewelry, dolls, wall hangings, and carved coconut masks. Most of these souvenirs are imported from the Philippines.

Fiestas
As on Guam, village fiestas take place every month of the year, except during Lent. These offer an excellent opportunity to try typical

Chamorro food and to meet local people in an informal atmosphere. Since most of the population is Catholic, each fiesta begins with a procession and mass on the Saturday closest to the day of the village's patrón saint, followed by feasting into the night. Sunday is the village open house when people open their homes. You can find the precise dates of fiestas from the Marianas Visitors Bureau, or just watch for a large group of cars parked beside a rural road.

St. Joseph's Day (early May) is celebrated with great fervor at San Jose villages on both Saipan and Tinian. Other important fiestas include those dedicated to Our Lady of Lourdes (early February), San Vicente (early April), San Isidro (at Chalan Kanoa in mid-May), San Antonio (June), Our Lady of Mt. Carmel (at Chalan Kanoa in mid-July), San Roque (late August), San Francisco de Borja (on Rota in October), and Christ the King (at Garapan in mid-November). Other similar gatherings might commemorate a marriage, birth, or funeral. If you get invited to one, you'll long remember the hospitality of the local people.

Holidays

Public holidays include New Year's Day (1 January), Commonwealth Day (9 January), President's Day (third Monday in February), Covenant Day (24 March), Good Friday (March/April), Memorial Day (last Monday in May), Liberation Day (4 July), Labor Day (first Monday in September), Columbus Day (second Monday in October), Citizenship Day (4 November), Veteran's Day (11 November), Thanksgiving Day (fourth Thursday in November), Constitution Day (8 December), and Christmas Day (25 December).

Commonwealth Day (9 January) gives occasion to arts and crafts displays, entertainment, and feasts. Liberation Day (4 July) commemorates the day in 1946 when Chamorros were released from Camp Susupe, the U.S. internment camp at Chalan Kanoa, *not* the American Independence Day. The Flame Tree Festival occurs the week leading up to 4 July, with sporting events, handicraft shows, an agricultural exhibition, traditional food, and arts performances. On Liberation Day itself, expect a parade, firecrackers, carnival events, and feasting on Saipan. On All Souls' Day (1 Novem-

ber), cemeteries are visited and the graves are cleaned and adorned with candles and flowers.

Sporting Events

Hobie sailors and sailboarders should write the Northern Marianas Amateur Sports Association (Bill Sakovich, P.O. Box 2476, Saipan, MP 96950, tel. 234-1001, fax 234-1101) for information on sailboat and sailboarding races off Saipan. There are regular league games in basketball (Jan.-May), baseball (Feb.-June), soccer (April-May), volleyball (June-Nov.), and softball.

Annual events include the Saipan Sails Hobie Cat Regatta (January) and the Hobie Cat Laguna Regatta (February). The Tagaman Triathlon in May includes a one-mile swim, a 37-mile bicycle race, and a nine-mile footrace.

PRACTICALITIES

Food

A Chamorro feast might consist of roast suckling pig cooked on a spit, red rice (white rice colored with achote seeds), a selection of fish, taro, crabs, pastries, and *tuba*—a coconut wine fermented from sap drawn from a palm sprout. Another favorite is chicken *kelaguen* (minced and prepared with lemon, onions, shredded coconut meat, and a touch of that super-hot *finadene* sauce that goes well on everything).

Also try *cadon guihan* (fish cooked in coconut milk), *lumpia* (pork, shrimp, and vegetables in a pastry wrapping), *pancit* (fried noodles), *poto* (rice cake), *bonelos aga* (fried bananas), and *bonelos dago* (deep-fried grated yam served with syrup). For dessert it's *kalamai* (sweet coconut milk pudding) or *ahn* (grated coconut boiled in sugary water). Those familiar with Filipino cooking will recognize many similarities.

Visas

Since this is American territory, United States citizens are allowed to live and work in the Northern Marianas without restrictions. We do, however, advise Americans to come with a passport as this will speed entry.

Everyone but American citizens must have a passport to enter the Commonwealth. Passports must be valid 60 days beyond the date of entry. Visas are not required for tourist visits of

COCONUT CRABS

LOUISE FOOTE

The coconut crab (Birgus latro) is a nocturnal creature that lives under logs, in holes, or at the base of pandanus or coconut trees. The females lay their eggs in the sea and the tiny crabs float around a few months, then crawl into a seashell and climb up the beach. When a crab is big enough, it abandons the shell and relies on its own hard shell for protection. Its food is ripe pandanus or coconut. The crab will appear dark blue if it's a coconut eater, rich orange if it feeds on pandanus. First it will husk a coconut using its two front claws, then break the nut open on a rock. It might take a crab two nights to get at the meat. Coconut crabs can grow up to three feet across. Although tasty, they are endangered in much of Micronesia and should not be eaten.

up to 30 days, provided you hold onward or return tickets with any necessary visa and sufficient funds.

Money and Measurements
United States currency, credit cards, and postage stamps are used (there are no local stamps). The electricity is 110 volts, 60 cycles. There's no sales tax in the Northern Marianas.

Information
Before arrival you can obtain a packet of colorful brochures and a "Travel Information Sheet" listing hotel prices by writing the Marianas Visitors Bureau (P.O. Box 861, Saipan, MP 96950, tel. 234-8325, fax 234-3596). Ask for a copy of their *Historic and Geographic Map of Saipan,* by William H. Stewart, which contains a wealth of information on the island's war record. Mr. Stewart has also produced a *Geographic Atlas and Historical Calendar of the Northern Marianas,* which you can get from the Office of the Governor, Commonwealth of the Northern Marianas, Saipan, MP 96950.

Address mail to Saipan, MP 96950; Rota, MP 96951; Tinian, MP 96952.

CNMI Country Code 670

Getting There
Saipan International Airport (SPN) is eight miles south of Garapan. Some hotels offer free transfers, others charge up to $12 one-way, so ask. A taxi to Garapan would be about $15. Numerous car rental companies have offices in a kiosk in front of the airport terminal. Freedom Air flights leave from the commuter terminal next to the main terminal.

This is the former Aslito Airfield of World War II vintage, and over a dozen Japanese bunkers are scattered around the airport. One of them is now occupied by the Marianas Visitors Bureau, on the left side of the road leading from the airport. The money exchange counter is in the departure lounge and only intended for foreign tourists wishing to get rid of leftover dollars. There's no bank, nor are there coin lockers. There is one duty free shop in the departure lounge. The terminal building is open 24 hours a day. There's no departure tax.

Saipan is linked to Tokyo by **Continental Air Micronesia, Japan Air Lines,** and **Northwest Airlines.** Continental also arrives nonstop from Fukuoka, Guam, Koror, Manila, Nagoya, Osaka, Okinawa, Sapporo, and Sendai, and Japan Air Lines from Nagoya and Osaka. Both Japan Air Lines and Northwest Airlines have direct connections in Tokyo to and from Atlanta, Cincinnati, Los Angeles, New York, Seattle, and other North American cities.

Continental passengers can connect in Guam with flights to and from Honolulu. To fly Continental between Saipan and San Francisco or Los Angeles involves changing planes in both Honolulu and Guam. Those continuing on Continental to the Federated States of Micronesia or Palau may have to overnight on Guam.

Getting Around
Freedom Air (P.O. Box 239 CK, Saipan, MP 96950, tel. 234-8328, fax 649-0729) flies Saipan to Tinian, $25 one-way, several times a day. This commuter airline does not require reservations; just be at their office 45 minutes before flight time. Flights from Saipan to Rota on Freedom Air cost $50 one-way.

Dark with twisted paths,
canals of the mangrove swamp.
—An egret soaring.

SAIPAN

Saipan is a pleasant island where tourists go to relax in the sun and in warm ocean waters. As you look toward the lagoon from the beach between the old sugar dock and the Saipan Grand Hotel, you'll see a partially submerged tank several hundred feet from shore, its turret and gun out of the water even at high tide. I snorkeled to it, hoping the young Japanese tourists crisscrossing the lagoon on their jet skis would notice me in the water.

From looking at the tank I could not tell whether it was American or Japanese, but I knew it must be American because on 15 June 1944 it was the Americans who were attacking Saipan from the sea and the Japanese who were defending it from the land. The men in the tank most certainly died when their tank became stranded during the invasion.

Arriving at the tank, I rested, sitting on the main body, which was a foot or so beneath the water's surface. The tank was covered by algae and sea grass. Once rested, I snorkeled around the tank, which seemed larger in the sea than on land. Fish darted in and out through holes and ports.

Apparently other snorkelers had discovered this spot before me. The surrounding sand was covered with beer cans. Viscerally I hated this litter. But certainly it was more benign than the litter I had come to see: a weapon of war that had become a death trap.

Most of the island's tourist facilities run up the sunny west coast, from the commercial center of Chalan Kanoa to the entertainment district of Garapan. Some self-contained resorts are farther north. Near the north end of the island, in the rugged Marpi area, are Banzai and Suicide Cliffs, pilgrimage sites for many Japanese and a major attraction for all.

SIGHTS

Garapan

Little that is old remains in Garapan. This town, the Japanese capital of the Marianas, was destroyed during the war, but it has been rebuilt and is again the major town on the island. Gara-pan's commercial center has the heaviest concentration of restaurants, karaoke bars, and souvenir shops on Saipan. In the evening, the area is lively, with many tourists milling about. Bars have bar girls out in front, inviting customers to enter. Japanese tourists call this area Little Ginza.

Nearby **American Marianas Memorial Park** and adjacent **Micro Beach Park** with its gentle lagoon are great places to catch the sunset or have a swim. In the memorial park is a small **WW II Museum.** There are plans to open a larger museum in the remains of the old Japanese hospital.

Just south of the main tourist center you'll find **Sugar King Park,** complete with a 1934 statue of Haruji Matsue, head of the South Seas Development Company, which developed the sugar industry in the Marianas prior to the war. In

the cold, forbidding walls of the old Japanese prison at Garapan

DAVID STANLEY

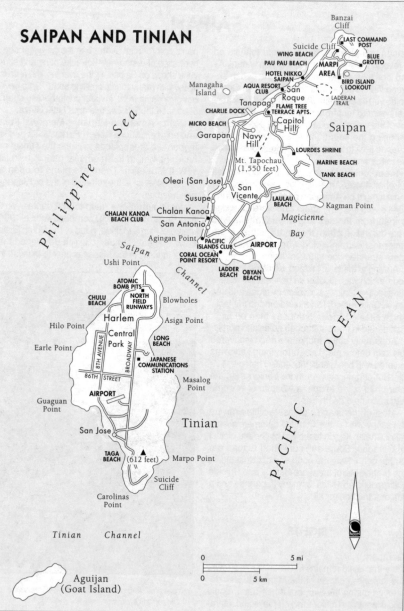

SAIPAN AND TINIAN

Banzai Cliff
LAST COMMAND POST
Suicide Cliff
WING BEACH
PAU PAU BEACH
BLUE GROTTO
HOTEL NIKKO SAIPAN
MARPI AREA
AQUA RESORT CLUB
BIRD ISLAND LOOKOUT
San Roque
Managaha Island
LADERAN TRAIL
Tanapag
CHARLIE DOCK
FLAME TREE TERRACE APTS.
Saipan
MICRO BEACH
Capitol Hill
Garapan
Navy Hill
LOURDES SHRINE
Mt. Tapochau (1,550 feet)
MARINE BEACH
TANK BEACH

Philippine Sea

Oleai (San Jose)
Susupe
San Vicente
LAULAU BEACH
Kagman Point
CHALAN KANOA BEACH CLUB
Chalan Kanoa
San Antonio
Magicienne Bay
Agingan Point
PACIFIC ISLANDS CLUB
AIRPORT
CORAL OCEAN POINT RESORT
Saipan Channel
LADDER BEACH
OBYAN BEACH
Ushi Point
ATOMIC BOMB PITS
CHULU BEACH
NORTH FIELD RUNWAYS
Blowholes
Harlem
Asiga Point
Hilo Point
Central Park
LONG BEACH
Earle Point
8TH AVENUE
BROADWAY
JAPANESE COMMUNICATIONS STATION
86TH STREET
Masalog Point
Guaguan Point
AIRPORT
Tinian
San Jose
TAGA BEACH
(612 feet)
Marpo Point
Suicide Cliff
Carolinas Point

PACIFIC OCEAN

Tinian Channel

0   5 mi
0   5 km

Aguijan (Goat Island)

© MOON PUBLICATIONS, INC.

the same park is a red **Japanese locomotive** used to haul cane to the old sugar mill at Chalan Kanoa. This park is now a botanical garden featuring a reconstructed Japanese shrine with examples of various tropical trees (open daily 8 a.m.-4 p.m., free).

Across the road are the imposing ruins of the **old Japanese hospital,** and nearby on a back street to the south, the **old Japanese jail.** In a 1966 book, author Fred Goerner claimed aviatrix Amelia Earhart was held here after being captured on a spy mission in the Marshall Islands in 1937. Several decades later Goerner has thrown out the spy theory, but he's still seeking evidence to place Earhart on Saipan.

On the street leading to the Sugar King Hotel is the **Saipan International House of Prayer** (not, to my knowledge, referred to as the IHOP). This hexagonal building, crafted in Japan, maintains a beautiful and peaceful elegance. In the center is a large bell, "the bell of peace, the bell of love." Coming here at sunset can make you believe striking the bell will bring peace to you and to the world at large. Do not miss this experience.

San Roque

La Fiesta San Roque, about five miles on the road north from Garapan, is a large tourist shopping center with many gift shops. The **Boga Micro Brewery and Restaurant** is a nice spot for a beer and lunch. Opposite the shopping center is **Pau** beach, a lovely safe beach to snorkel.

Nearby is the **Laderan Trail,** one of the nicest hikes on the island. It gives you a feel for the interior of this tropical island with its plant- and birdlife. As you head north from La Fiesta, the road to the trailhead is not marked, but it is the right turn immediately past the center. In a quarter mile, at a one-million-gallon water tank, make another right and proceed three-quarters of a mile to a turnoff to the trailhead. There are few parking spots at the trailhead itself, so it may be best to park the car before this last turn.

Despite several exceptions, the trail is well marked by blue and orange plastic ribbon, usually on your left, though sometimes on the right. If you are hiking with someone, as you should, and cannot see the next marker, send one of the group ahead to find it before leaving the last one. There is a heavy canopy, and once off the trail it is easy to become disoriented.

The trail is on ancient raised coral so the bottom is rough. Wear good walking shoes. Though the trail is not technically difficult, the second half can be tiring because the ground becomes rougher and there are several long uphill stretches. The entire trail is about three miles.

There are 14 numbered markers but no explanation of what they are marking. (Make up your own—it's called interactive hiking.) Past marker 13 is a fork; one trail leads down to the right, the other slightly uphill to the left. To get back to the trailhead take the path to the left. After ascending a hill, you come to a small grass meadow. Take the grassed-over dirt road to the right, which leads back to the trailhead.

An alternative is merely to hike to marker 6 and return. This is the easiest part of the hike, and probably the most interesting as you won't have to watch your footing as much.

Managaha Island

Off of the northwest coast lies Managaha Island, in the Tanapag lagoon—the most popular snorkeling site on Saipan. Captured from the Japanese only after the main island had fallen, a white sandy beach runs around Managaha. Three Japanese artillery pieces are still there, and an array of sunken barges, landing craft, ships, planes, and guns can be seen among the coral heads near the island, on a sandy bottom in only 20-40 feet of water. Look in particular for the Japanese Zero, the sub chaser, and the four-engine bomber.

Because of building and irrigation on this coast, and the runoff they create, the reef here is clearly distressed. It would be a tragic loss for Saipan if it does not take steps to reverse this process.

Numerous local tour operators run glass-bottomed boat trips over to Managaha Island, $43 pp with barbecue lunch. A good swimmer can make it out without too much difficulty. The greatest danger is from passing boats.

Northern Saipan

The north end of Saipan was the scene of the last desperate Japanese resistance in mid-1944 as well as mass suicides by Japanese soldiers and civilians to avoid capture. Later this area became an ammunition stockpile zone that was only cleared and reopened to the public in 1968.

To the Children
Who Died at Banzai Cliff

How stupid is war.
Children pushed to early death.
Fish can swim away.

DAVID STANLEY

No stores are in this area so come prepared with drinks and snacks.

The **Last Japanese Command Post** is in a cave just below high cliffs next to the **Okinawa Peace Memorial.** Here, General Yoshitsugo Saito ordered his men to take seven lives each for the emperor, then committed hara-kiri. From this post you can follow the Banadero Trail for an hour up to the top of **Suicide Cliff** where, high above the post, hundreds of Japanese soldiers jumped 820 feet to their deaths rather than surrender. You can also drive the three miles to the top of Suicide Cliff by another road.

At **Banzai Cliff,** near the north end of the island, entire families lined up and jumped off, elders pushing the young. The Saipanese claim the white terns that ride the winds over these cliffs didn't exist before the war, that they bear the souls of the dead.

At times during the morning and afternoon, a great number of tour buses disgorge large numbers of Japanese tourists. If possible visit the cliff early in the morning or late in the afternoon. You will be profoundly moved, and perhaps in the presence of Japanese mourning loved ones.

Continuing around the point and heading south it is a three-mile trip from here to the **Bird Island lookout** from which you get a good view of the small cliff-girdled island the Japanese more poetically called Moon Viewing Island. On the way to the lookout, the road passes the turnoff to the **Blue Grotto,** a sunken pool connected to the ocean by twin underground passages. Steep concrete stairs lead down to this cobalt blue pool where a variety of fish reside—a favorite spot for divers. Because of odd tidal effects occurring in the grotto, do not swim here until you discuss it with locals.

Central and Southern Saipan

From 1951 to 1962 the CIA had a $28-million base on **Capitol Hill,** where Nationalist Chinese guerrillas were trained. Later Capitol Hill became the headquarters of the High Commissioner of the U.N. Trust Territory, and a ghetto for American expatriates. Today this is the location for most Commonwealth government offices.

From behind the Civil Defense Energy/MPLC office (the former Congress of Micronesia building) at Capitol Hill, follow a rough road two miles up to the top of **Mount Tapochau** (1,550 feet) for a good 360-degree view. A small statue of Christ was erected on the summit in 1987, and the Saipanese carry wooden crosses up every Easter. A sturdy car could navigate the road, but you may have to park and walk when it gets too difficult.

Southeast of Capitol Hill is **Our Lady of Lourdes Shrine,** marking an area where the Saipanese took refuge during the American invasion. It's a half mile off the main highway. Remote beaches on the east coast are accessible from the Cross Island Road. **Laulau Beach** near San Vicente has good coral and tends to be calm.

Some of the best conditions for walk-in diving and snorkeling are at Ladder and Obyan beaches in southern Saipan. Don't leave valuables unattended on the beach. **Obyan Beach** features harmless garden eels. An ancient Micronesian settlement at Obyan has been carbon dated to 1500 B.C.E. The remnants of *latte* stones can still be seen.

ACCOMMODATIONS

Most of Saipan's hotels are along the west coast sunbelt. New hotels are popping up on Saipan all the time. Hotel rates in the Northern Marianas and on Guám are higher than elsewhere in Micronesia. As on Guam, at many Japanese hotels the staff's knowledge of dive shops, fishing boats, and other island activities may be limited to businesses where the proprietors speak only Japanese.

Separately listed with more details are the budget, midrange, and expensive hotels (some Japanese owned) that do better with English-speaking guests. Many of the least expensive are under Korean or Chinese management.

Many luxury hotels and car rental agencies on Saipan will have special "local" or "corporate rates." These mean different things at different hotels. Discount application often reflects the vacancy rate of the hotel rather than the status of the guest. However, these rates usually only are given to Americans and Micronesians—not Japanese. You stand a better chance of getting them by asking in person, rather than over the phone.

Saipan can fill up during the summer and during the Japanese winter vacation periods. It is advisable to have reservations during those times.

Budget

Contrary to popular belief, there are some nice budget hotels on Saipan. Perhaps the best, if you do not need to be by the beach, is the **Garden Motel** on Middle Rd. (Caller Box PPP 134, Saipan, MP 96950, tel. 234-0320), with 17 rooms at $44 s, $55 d. It has a warm, old-time feel, as if you were in someone's home. The rooms all open to a lovely enclosed patio. The front desk is in the same room as the restaurant and TV.

Another great buy is the **Micro Beach Hotel** (P.O. Box 1328, Saipan, MP 96950, tel. 233-1368, fax 233-0301) in the midst of Garapan. It is only one block from the beach, reached directly by walking down the alley north of the Hyatt. The rooms are small, but clean and cool for $50 d, including tax.

The **Remington Club** (P.O. Box 1719, Saipan, MP 96950, tel. 234-5449, fax 234-5619) is another good budget choice. The 14 regular rooms are on the second floor above their bar, and cost $49 s or 60 d; rooms with cooking facilities begin at $77. The hotel is near the beach and right in the heart of the action in the Garapan entertainment district.

The **Sun Inn Motel** (P.O. Box 920, Saipan, MP 96950, tel. 234-6639, fax 234-6062) is one of the least expensive places to stay on Saipan, located behind the ballpark beside Susupe's Marianas High School. The 18 a/c rooms here are $40 s, $50 d.

The **Sugar King Apartment Hotel** (P.O. Box 1939, Saipan, MP 96950, tel. 234-6164, fax 234-6154) near Garapan is set back a few blocks behind Sugar King Park. The 27 cottage-style units, each with its own veranda, fridge, and double bed, are $48. The cottages are basic, rather than rustic, but there is a swimming pool. Long-term rates of $288 weekly and $450 monthly are sometimes available.

The **Islander Hotel** (P.O. Box 1249, Saipan, MP 96950, tel. 234-6071, fax 234-6619) is right on a busy stretch of Beach Road in Garapan. It has 32 rooms on the second floor of a commercial building. A single room with fridge but no cooking facilities costs $53 d. A double with kitchen facilities and living and dining areas is $72 d. This is not a pleasant spot for vacationers, but might serve if you need to do business in Garapan.

Moderate

The **Pacific Gardenia Hotel** (P.O. Box 144, Saipan, MP 96950, tel. 234-3455, fax 234-3411) at Chalan Kanoa calls itself "Saipan's Biggest Little Hotel." The 14 spacious rooms with cooking facilities and TV are $77 s or d. There's a coin laundry. Usually on Friday evening, a local band plays on the sandy beach behind the hotel as guests wine, dine, and dance. Happy hour at the beach bar is Mon.-Sat. 4:30-6:30 p.m.

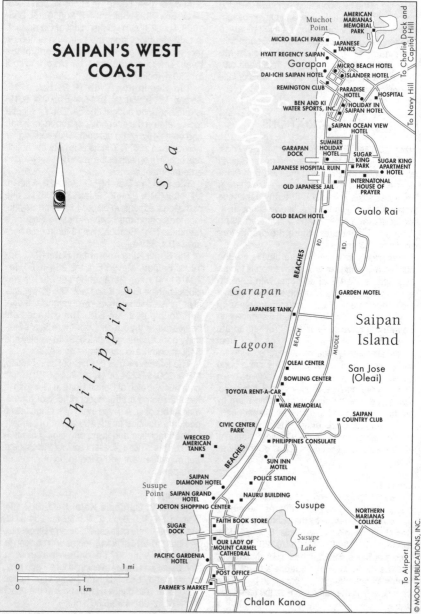

SAIPAN'S WEST COAST

Philippine Sea

Philippine Sea

Muchot Point

MICRO BEACH PARK

AMERICAN MARIANAS MEMORIAL PARK

JAPANESE TANKS

HYATT REGENCY SAIPAN

Garapan

MICRO BEACH HOTEL

DAI-ICHI SAIPAN HOTEL

ISLANDER HOTEL

REMINGTON CLUB

PARADISE HOTEL

HOSPITAL

BEN AND KI WATER SPORTS, INC.

HOLIDAY IN SAIPAN HOTEL

SAIPAN OCEAN VIEW HOTEL

GARAPAN DOCK

SUMMER HOLIDAY HOTEL

SUGAR KING PARK

SUGAR KING APARTMENT HOTEL

JAPANESE HOSPITAL RUIN

OLD JAPANESE JAIL

INTERNATONAL HOUSE OF PRAYER

GOLD BEACH HOTEL

Gualo Rai

Garapan Lagoon

BEACHES RD.

RD.

GARDEN MOTEL

JAPANESE TANK

BEACH

MIDDLE

Saipan Island

OLEAI CENTER

BOWLING CENTER

San Jose (Oleai)

TOYOTA RENT-A-CAR

WAR MEMORIAL

SAIPAN COUNTRY CLUB

CIVIC CENTER PARK

PHILIPPINES CONSULATE

WRECKED AMERICAN TANKS

BEACHES

SUN INN MOTEL

SAIPAN DIAMOND HOTEL

POLICE STATION

Susupe Point

SAIPAN GRAND HOTEL

NAURU BUILDING

Susupe

JOETON SHOPPING CENTER

NORTHERN MARIANAS COLLEGE

SUGAR DOCK

FAITH BOOK STORE

Susupe Lake

OUR LADY OF MOUNT CARMEL CATHEDRAL

PACIFIC GARDENIA HOTEL

POST OFFICE

FARMER'S MARKET

Chalan Kanoa

To Charlie Dock and Capitol Hill

To Navy Hill

To Airport

0   1 mi

0   1 km

© MOON PUBLICATIONS, INC.

The Korean-operated **Gold Beach Hotel** (P.O. Box 2232, Saipan, MP 96950, tel. 235-5501), south of Garapan, has 46 rooms at $88 and offers a 15% "local rate" discount. The rooms have cooking facilities, but you may have to supply your own pots and pans.

Locally owned **Summer Holiday Hotel** (P.O. Box 908, Saipan, MP 96950, tel. 234-3182, fax 234-3077) is behind Club Imperial on Beach Road, Garapan. The 26 rooms in the attractive three-story building are an economical $69, cooking facilities included. A nice beach park is a two-minute walk from the hotel. A coin-operated laundromat is on the premises, and Martha's Store next to the hotel is open 24 hours.

The **Saipan Ocean View Hotel** (P.O. Box 799, Saipan, MP 96950, tel. 234-8900, fax 234-9428) is a three-story hotel on Beach Road, Garapan. The 20 rooms with fridge are $72. The hotel stays on a busy stretch of road, but faces a park.

The **Holiday in Saipan Resort Hotel** (P.O. Box 5308, CHRB, Saipan, MP 96950, tel. 234-3554, fax 234-5023) is *not* a Holiday Inn. It has nice rooms with balconies, $65 s, $85 d, in the building that had been the Hotel Blueberry Saipan. It is about a 10-minute walk from the beach.

The **Paradise Hotel** is near the hospital and has rooms for $55 s, $71 d.

Luxury

The **Hyatt Regency Saipan** (P.O. Box 87 CHRB, Saipan, MP 96950, tel. 234-1234, fax 234-7745), formerly owned by Continental Airlines, serves an international clientele in its plush seven-story hotel. The 255 rooms with balcony and fridge begin at $200. It's nicely set on landscaped gardens facing Garapan's Micro Beach. Three wings of the hotel face a lush tropical garden with parrots in cages and colorful fish in the ponds. During happy hour 6-7 p.m. drinks in the lobby lounge are half price. Most nights there's a "Tahitian" show that includes dinner.

Pacific Islands Club Saipan (P.O. Box 2370, Saipan, MP 96950, tel. 234-7976, fax 234-6592) in San Antonio has 220 standard rooms at $370 d, including all meals, airport transfers, and a wide range of recreational activities. This hotel caters primarily to Japanese package tourists, but its staff is mainly American. Like its counterpart on Guam, its loudspeakers bark out "fun" activities, but at a much less frenetic pace. Many American expats working in the far east vacation here. There is a rate of $130 without meals and activities for "local" Americans.

Saipan's smallest luxury hotel is the **Chalan Kanoa Beach Club** (P.O. Box 356, Saipan, MP 96950, tel. 234-7829, fax 234-7005) at the south end of Chalan Kanoa. The 28 deluxe units arranged in two-story buildings around the swimming pool are $155. There's a cocktail lounge and restaurant on the premises.

The elegant **Aqua Resort Club** (P.O. Box 9, Achugao, Saipan, MP 96950, tel. 322-1234, fax 234-1220), a low-rise complex, stands on the beach between Tanapag and San Roque in northern Saipan. The 91 rooms begin at $175 and airport transfers are $12 roundtrip.

Additional luxury hotels, primarily for Japanese tour groups include:

Hotel Nikko Saipan (P.O. Box 5152 CHRB, Saipan, MP 96950, tel. 322-3311, fax 322-3144) near San Roque, $200.

Saipan Grand Hotel (P.O. Box 369, Saipan, MP 96950, tel. 234-6601, fax 234-8007), Susupe Beach, rooms from $130.

Saipan Diamond Hotel (P.O. Box 66, Saipan, MP 96950, tel. 234-5900, fax 234-5909), Susupe Beach, $175.

Hafadai Beach Hotel (P.O. Box 338, Saipan, MP 96950, tel. 234-6495, fax 234-8912), south of Garapan, $160-205.

Dai-ichi Saipan Beach Hotel (P.O. Box 1029, Saipan, MP 96950, tel. 234-6412, fax 234-7064), Garapan, $175.

Mariana Resort Hotel (P.O. Box 527, Saipan, MP 96950, tel. 322-0770, fax 322-0776), Marpi, near golf course, from $200.

Coral Ocean Point Resort Club (P.O. Box 1160, Saipan, MP 96950, tel. 234-7000, fax 234-7005), Marpi, near golf course, $160.

Plumeria Resort (P.O. Box 5228 CHRB, Saipan, MP 96950, tel. 322-6202, fax 322-6217), $180.

Apartments

Flame Tree Terrace Apartments (P.O. Box 86 CHRB, Saipan, MP 96950, tel. 322-3366;

fax 322-3886) in Lower Capitol Hill rents nicely furnished condominiums on a monthly basis only. There are 35 units available, as well as a swimming pool. The condos cost $700 for a one bedroom, $1050 for a two bedroom, and $2000 for a three bedroom. Everything tends to be fully booked, so write or call as far in advance as possible to get on the waiting list.

Camping

The parks along the west side of Saipan are for day use only, so if you want to pitch a tent consider the more remote east coast beaches, such as Laulau. On the south coast, Ladder Beach, less than two miles from the air terminal, has caves with picnic tables. Otherwise camp by the Bomb Wing Memorial nearby. Obyan Beach would be a better campsite, but it's two miles farther along.

No permit is required at these beaches and none of them have facilities. Try to keep out of sight of motorists and don't go off and leave your gear unattended.

OTHER PRACTICALITIES

Food

Food in Saipan can be very expensive. Prices are highest in the luxury hotels. But prices could also be high at a restaurant along Beach Road, even if its front makes it look like a dive. Check prices before sitting down. Often restaurants will post a menu, visible from the outside. If the menu is in Japanese, as is frequently the case, walk in and ask to see an English menu. Saipan is one of the few places on earth where a perfectly fine but modest Chinese meal can cost $30 pp, without drinks. Tips are expected on Saipan, but there is no sales tax on meals.

To beat the high price of restaurant food on Saipan, try the takeaway food at **Marge's Kitchen,** a specialty bakeshop. You can buy fresh bagels or excellent local bread. Bento box lunches start at $2.50. The bakery is also a great place to cure a sweet tooth. It is located on the side street immediately north of Our Lady of Mount Carmel Cathedral, north of Chalan Kanoa. It is open 6:30 a.m.-7 p.m.

Herman's Modern Bakery on the airport road serves breakfast and lunch specials (open 6 a.m.-3 p.m. Mon.-Sat.) and is popular among locals.

The large **supermarket** at Joeten Shopping Center is open until 7 p.m. on Sunday, 9 p.m. other days. **Aiko's Coffee Shop,** in the corner between this supermarket and Ace Hardware, serves a good breakfast, ramen soup ($2.45) and sandwiches anytime. Ask for the plate lunch (which may not be on menu), $4.25 for two scoops of rice, beef entree, and salad. It's open till 7:30 p.m. daily except Sunday, when it closes at 2 p.m.

J's Restaurant, at the Bowling Center in San Jose, is open 24 hours a day. It's good for breakfast and has cheap lunch specials.

The **Marianas Trench Restaurant** (P.O. Box 1074, Saipan, MP 96950, tel. 234-3146), above the *Marianas Review* office on Beach Road just south of Garapan, has a lunch special, weekdays 11 a.m.-1 p.m. The international special is $4.50 (lunch), and a local Chamorro plate is $3. A different plate is offered every day but there's no choice. The attractive dining room overlooks the lagoon.

Another choice is the **Canton Restaurant** (tel. 234-7236) opposite the Mobil station on Beach Road near central Garapan. The weekday lunch special includes a choice of six different dishes for about $5.

Poon's Restaurant, on Middle Road just north of Sugar King Park, serves Indonesian dishes.

And of course, there are **Winchell's Donuts, McDonald's, Kentucky Fried Chicken,** and **Pizza Hut.** Garapan has any number of inexpensive snack shops.

There is a large number of poker parlors on Saipan. As a come-on many of them serve quite inexpensive food. Such a meal will only be inexpensive if you can resist the urge to gamble.

Moving up in price, Saipan has several excellent Korean restaurants. The **Korean Restaurant** located in the Gold Beach Hotel serves full dinners, each with many side dishes for $15-18. **Korea House Restaurant** is also excellent and is similarly priced.

Brewhouse Pub and Restaurant (tel. 322-7662), connected to the Micronesian Brewers Corporation on the road to Capitol Hill, serves three fantastic beers brewed on the premises. The views out over the ocean are exceptional, particularly at sunset. Dinners go up to $20, but some good sausage plates are much less.

Rudolpho's (tel. 322-3017), located at the intersection of Capitol Hill Road and Middle Road, bills itself as a Mexican and pizza restaurant. Although the food is mediocre, it is not too expensive. It is *the* place to meet young local haoles on the weekend; it has a good bar and a lovely outside terrace. There is often live music on Saturday night.

For a delicious Sunday brunch, try the **Hyatt Regency Saipan.**

Entertainment

The Carolinian residents of Saipan transmit their oral traditions through dance songs; one group, the **Aghurubw Society Dancers,** performs stick war dances *(dokia)* and marching dances *(maas).* Try asking for venues and times at the Marianas Visitors Bureau, though your chances of seeing them are slim since the big hotels stage the "more dramatic" expensive Polynesian dance shows tourists expect.

Many of the large tourist hotels have happy hours at their bars with reduced drink prices, usually beginning around 5:30 p.m. Tourist discos have stiff admission charges. There are also plenty of karaoke clubs, most with Filipina hostesses.

JM Cinema (tel. 234-6950) beside the post office in Chalan Kanoa shows fairly current films. It opens at 7:30 p.m. daily ($6 pp).

Sports and Recreation

Saipan's oldest locally owned dive shop is **Ben and Ki Water Sports Inc.** (P.O. Box 31 CHRB, Saipan, MP 96950, tel. 235-5063, fax 235-5063). They charge $90 for beach diving (two tanks) or $100 for boat diving (two tanks). Snorkelers can join the divers for $25 pp, lunch and gear included. A seven-hour scuba expedition to Tinian and Goat islands is $120; a four-day scuba certification course runs $500. Waterskiing is $30 for 20 minutes, and trolling costs $350 for four hours (up to six persons). The manager, Ben Concepcion, his son Lawrence, and son-in-law Duanne Pangelinan are very helpful. Visit their shop in Garapan or their kiosk facing the beach just south of the Hyatt. They pick up at hotels anywhere on Saipan. Recommended.

Also well suited for English speakers is **All American Divers,** operating out of the Pacific Islands Club. Many of the 25 other scuba outfits on Saipan are geared mainly to Japanese tourists.

Because of environmental degradation the diving at Saipan is not as great as you might hope. On the other hand, Anatahan, Sarigan, and Pagan are wonderful and untouched.

The **surfing** is poor on Saipan, but the **windsurfing's** good in the wide western lagoon. Lessons and equipment are available from **Marianas Aqua Sports** (Bill Sakovich, P.O. Box 100 CHRB, Saipan, MP 96950, tel. 322-0670, fax 322-0672). Boogie boarders can try Obyan Point or Coral Ocean Point.

Of Saipan's four public golf courses, the nine-hole **Saipan Country Club** (Caller Box PPP 130, Saipan, MP 96950, tel. 234-7300) is the most "local." They have varying greens fees for varying clients: $20 for locals, $40 for Japanese tourists, $30 for other tourists. You can rent a full set of clubs for $15 and a pull cart for $7. On fairway four a ball passing to the left of a coconut tree is considered out of bounds, irrespective of where it comes to rest!

Saipan's top-end golf course is the **Coral Ocean Point Resort Club** (P.O. Box 1160, Saipan, MP 96950, tel. 234-7000, fax 234-7005) on the south coast at Koblerville. This golfers' paradise has 72 rooms at $165 d. The resort's fantastic 18-hole golf course right on the coast is $70 a round if you're staying at the hotel, $120 otherwise.

To the north **Mariana Country Club and Resort Hotel** (tel. 322-0770) at Marpi has another 18-hole golf course overlooking the sea. It's $100 a round for those not staying at the resort.

Midway between these two the Laolao Bay Gulf Resort offers the newest golf club (tel. 256-8888).

Services

The Bank of Hawaii (tel. 234-6102; open weekdays 10 a.m.-3 p.m., Friday 10 a.m.-6 p.m.) is in the Nauru Building in Chalan Kanoa. There are also branches of the Bank of Guam (tel. 234-6467), Bank of Saipan (tel. 234-6260), Marine Merchant Bank (tel. 234-7773), and the Union Bank (tel. 234-6559) on Saipan.

Many private companies on Saipan offer facilities for making overseas telephone calls. Always ask about lower direct dial rates. Rates may be lower Fri.-Sun. after 6 p.m. For example, try Key Communications just up Middle Road from the New Seoul Motel (open daily 8 a.m.-midnight), MTC Micronesian Tel behind Xerox just beyond Key Communications (only open during business hours), and Marianas Communication Services opposite the Garden Motel on Middle Rd. in San Jose.

The main post office is opposite the market in Chalan Kanoa and there's another, less crowded post office beside the CNMI Convention Center on Capitol Hill.

The Immigration and Naturalization Office (tel. 234-6178) is on the fourth floor at the Nauru Building in Chalan Kanoa.

The Japanese Consulate is on the fifth floor, Yarikuchi Building, opposite Garapan dock (open weekdays 9 a.m.-5 p.m.). The Philippines Consulate (tel. 234-1848) is in the CTC Building in Susupe (Mon.-Thurs. 8 a.m.-noon, 2-4:30 p.m.). You'll need a Philippines visa only if you want to stay longer than 21 days.

The main Continental Air Micronesia reservations office (tel. 234-6491) is in the back of the Oleai Center in San Jose. They also have an office at the airport.

Information

The helpful Marianas Visitors Bureau (P.O. Box 861, Saipan, MP 96950, tel. 234-8325; open 8 a.m.-5 p.m. Mon.-Sat.) is in a former Japanese communications bunker at the airport. Ask for a free copy of William H. Stewart's *Tourist Map of Saipan*. Their *Saipan Battlefield Map—1944* ($3.50) is also excellent. Unfortunately the Visitors Bureau's brochures only list their members (not the cheaper places), and the quoted room rates are not always current.

Faith Book Store opposite the Saipan Community Church on Beach Road has a large selection of books on Micronesia.

The *Marianas Variety* (P.O. Box 231, Saipan,

MP 96950) and the *Marianas Observer* are each published Mon.-Fri. and cost 50 cents. You can also get the *Saipan Tribune* (Caller Box AAA-34, Saipan, MP 96950), published every Wednesday and Friday, for free. The Guam-based *Pacific Daily News* is available daily.

The two Saipan AM radio stations are commercial KCNM-AM (1040) and nonprofit KSAI-AM (940); commercial KZMI-FM (93.9) dominates the FM bands.

GETTING THERE

Continental Air Micronesia, Japan Air Lines, and **Northwest Airlines** all fly from Tokyo to Saipan. Continental also arrives nonstop from Fukuoka, Guam, Koror, Manila, Ngoya, Osaka, Okinawa, Sapporo, and Sendai. Japan Air flies from Nagoya and Osaka. Direct connections in Tokyo to and from Atlanta, Cincinnati, Los Angeles, New York, Seattle, and other North American cities are provided by both Japan Air Lines and Northwest. To fly Continental between Saipan and San Francisco or Los Angeles involves changing planes in both Honolulu and Guam.

GETTING AROUND

By Boat

The **Commonwealth Marine Leisure Corporation** (CMLC, P.O. Box 369, Saipan, MP 96950, tel. 234-9157) at the Saipan Grand Hotel runs the ferry *Emerald* from Sugar Dock in Chalan Kanoa to San Jose village on Tinian daily at 8:15 a.m. It's $14 one-way for locals, $65 roundtrip for tourists. The tourist price includes a pickup at any Saipan hotel and free drinks on the boat. This red-and-white-striped motor cruiser caters mostly to Japanese tourists on day trips to Tinian.

Saipan·Rota·Tinian

MARIANAS

By Road
Taxi fares begin at $3 and go up to $42, depending on distance. Ask to see the official rate chart every taxi must carry. From the airport it's $11 to Joeten Shopping Center, $13 to Garapan. Hitching is much easier on Saipan than on Guam.

Unless you're really ready to rough it, rent a car upon arrival at Saipan. The main sights of the island can be seen in a day by rental car, and the car rental companies at the airport are competitive. The speed limit on Saipan is 35 mph unless otherwise posted. Your home driver's license is valid for 30 days after arrival.

There are several car rental companies with very nearly the same prices, usually $45-65 for most cars, about $80 for jeeps, vans, and station wagons. Most require advance reservations and renters must be 21 years old. Hertz, Islander, and Thrifty staff offices at the airport.

Companies include: **Automotion Inc.** (P.O. Box 569, Saipan, MP 96950, tel. 322-7467, fax 322-5852), **Dollar Rent-A-Car** (P.O. Box 1292, Saipan, MP 96950, tel. 234-8251, fax 234-2138), **Hertz** (P.O. Box 1989, Saipan, MP 96950, tel. 234-8336, fax 234-7930), **National Car Rental** (P.O. Box 562, Saipan, MP 96950, tel. 234-7259, fax 234-7948), **Pacific Island Motors** (P.O. Box 1551, Saipan, MP 96950, tel. 235-1979, fax 235-1982), **Islander Rent A Car** (tel. 234-8233), **Thrifty Car Rental** (P.O. Box 487, Saipan, MP 96950, tel. 234-8356, fax 288-0298), **Toyota Rent-A-Car** (P.O. Box 267, Saipan, MP 96950, tel. 234-5911 fax 288-6514).

Forget renting mopeds, which cost more than cars and are unreliable. At $15 per day, bicycles are also expensive.

OTHER ISLANDS

TINIAN

Only three miles south of Saipan, Tinian consists of a series of layered limestone plateaus covered by *tangan tangan*. Tinian was once a great sugarcane producer, but only scattered clumps of it grow wild today. The Bar K Ranch, built by Ken Jones on leased land, runs 4,500 beef cattle across a third of the island. Butterflies and dragonflies abound on Tinian.

United States and Asian fishing boats use Tinian's spacious harbor to transfer tuna caught in FSM and Papua New Guinea waters to refrigerated freighters bound for canneries. This presence, together with explosive-laden vessels of the U.S. Military Sealift Command, which often visit, helps explain the number of bars with Filipina hostesses in San Jose. Many Filipino laborers are employed in construction on Tinian.

Before World War II Tinian had a population of 15,000 Japanese and Korean civilians. Today it is a quiet backwater of several thousand, an island for a peaceful vacation. Tinian has had an on-again, off-again plan to develop gambling casinos. If the plans go forward, the pace of the island will undoubtedly change.

Sights
San Jose village has the air of a sleepy Spanish-American town complete with Mexican-looking church, flower gardens around the homes, and Spanish arcades on the larger buildings. The town's main sight is the **Taga House,** in a *latte* stone park not far from the harbor. These stones are much larger than the *latte* stones of Guam. Who carved the 12 mammoth *latte* stones then managed to erect them is a mystery of the Pacific. Next to the Taga House is a small Japanese war memorial.

Nearby lies the wreck of the freighter *Marianas,* thrown onto the beach by a typhoon in the late 1960s. From here you can look across to uninhabited Aguijan (Goat Island), five miles southwest. Another much larger shipwreck marks the entrance to Tinian harbor.

The **Korean Monument** off 8th Avenue just outside San Jose bears an evocative inscription on the back dedicated to the 5,000 Koreans who "suffered by chains of reckless imperial Japanese army, by whom they were deprived of their rights, and were taken to the islands here and there like innocent sheep, and then were fallen to this ground leaving behind them an eternal grudge."

Taga Beach at the foot of Broadway offers good views from the limestone bluff and is a good place to sit and watch the sunset. You can swim at **Tachonga Beach** about one-half mile south of Taga Beach. At **Suicide Cliff** on the southeast side of the island, Japanese troops held out in caves for three months after the rest of Tinian fell. There are Japanese and Okinawan peace memorials here.

On the east side of Broadway, halfway between San Jose and North Field, is the massive concrete structure of the former **Japanese Communications Station,** now the slaughterhouse of Bar K Ranch.

In 1944, even before the entire island had been secured, American Seabees began rebuilding a captured Japanese airstrip at the north end of the island in one of the largest engineering projects of World War II. Less than one year later **North Field** was the largest airfield in the world, with four vast 1.6-mile runways from which a total of 19,000 combat missions were against Japan. To carry the huge quantities of bombs up from the port at San Jose, American soldiers built two divided highways across Tinian. As the island is shaped something like Manhattan, the GIs gave the roads names like Broadway, 8th Avenue, and 86th Street.

On the north side of the runways a large concrete platform is flanked by two Japanese air raid shelters on the west side, another concrete Japanese building on the east side, and three American war memorials. In the bush behind the middle memorial is the Japanese **air opera-**

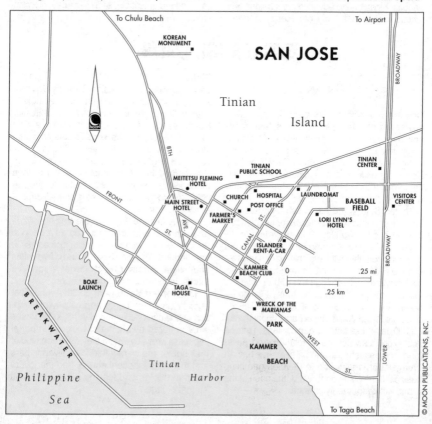

an old engraving of the latte stones of Tinian

M.G.L. DOMENY DE RIENZI

tions command post, a massive, two-story re-inforced concrete building complete with a Japanese bathtub. Beyond it a road to the right (east) leads to the poorly marked **atomic bomb loading pits.** At No. 1 Bomb Loading Pit an atomic bomb was loaded aboard an American B-29 dubbed *Enola Gay* on the afternoon of 5 August 1945, to be dropped on Hiroshima the next day. At nearby No. 2 Bomb Loading Pit a second atomic bomb was loaded on 9 August 1945 and dropped on Nagasaki. On 10 August 1945 Emperor Hirohito ended the Pacific war without his cabinet's consent.

West again is Chulu or **Invasion Beach,** where 15,000 U.S. soldiers landed on 24 July 1944. A concrete Japanese bunker stands watch.

Accommodations and Food

The best deal for accommodations is probably **Lori Lynn's Hotel** (P.O. Box 478, Tinian, MP 96952, tel. 433-3256), a little east of San Jose city center, where a comfortable, large a/c room with TV and fridge will be $40 s, $55 d. Reduced weekly and monthly rates are available. Lori Lynn's has more local atmosphere than the other hotels and a coffee shop with reasonably good Japanese food.

The five-room **Main Street Hotel** (P.O. Box 92, Tinian, MP 96952, tel. 433-9212) near the Fleming Hotel charges $46. The Japanese-oriented **Meitetsu Fleming Hotel** (P.O. Box 68, Tinian, MP 96952, tel. 433-3232, fax 433-3022) in central San Jose has 13 rooms at $60 s, $83 d. The Fleming complex also sports a restaurant, grocery store, laundromat, and bank.

No permit is required to **camp** on Kammer Beach near the Taga House in San Jose, which has a shower, toilet, and running water. The beach is good, and a few picnic tables down by the wrecked ship even have electric lighting. Many locals hang out here until late at night.

Camping is also possible at Taga and Tachungnya beaches. For something more secluded try Chulu Beach at the north end of 8th Avenue or Long Beach halfway up the east coast. Bring water to these.

The various restaurants and snack bars of Tinian are expensive. The best buy is probably **Mary's Bakery.** Also, **Kammer Beach Club** (tel. 433-0475) in San Jose has happy hour 4-6 p.m. daily except Sunday. The terrace is just the place to sit and watch the sun go down. Upstairs is an expensive restaurant.

Sports and Recreation

Suzuki Diving (P.O. Box 100, Tinian, MP 96952, tel. 433-3274), across the street from the Fleming Hotel, takes divers out. They know over 18 superb dive sites off the west coast of Tinian, including war relics, coral grottoes, and drop-offs. It's $80 for a one-tank dive, $100 for a two-tank dive. The price for snorkelers is less, but it will depend on how many are going out.

At high tide Long Beach is probably the best place for freelance snorkeling. You can also snorkel from shore at Tachonga Beach.

Services

The Bank of Guam (tel. 433-3258) is beside the Meitetsu Fleming Hotel. Overseas telephone calls can be made at the Tinian Center on Lower Broadway.

Transportation

West Field Airport (TIQ) is 2.5 miles north of San Jose village, but it's not hard to hitch into town. There's a pay phone in the terminal you can use to call your hotel to ask about airport pickups. The toilets at the airport are free and they're unlocked early. A couple of old Japanese guns stand outside the terminal.

Freedom Air's (tel. 433-3288) five-passenger Cessnas fly from Saipan to Tinian seven times a day. This commuter carrier runs extra flights when the traffic demands.

The CMLC cruiser *Emerald* departs San Jose for Sugar Dock, Saipan, at 2:45 p.m. daily, $14 one-way for locals. Due to the action of the northeast tradewinds the channel between the islands can get rough.

Car rental prices are in the range of $40-50 a day. Try **Tinian Rental Service** (tel. 433-3390), **Jim & Cris Co. Ltd.** (tel. 433-3207), **Islander Rent a Car** (tel. 433-3025) in San Jose, or **Hans Rent a Car** (tel. 433-9412) across the street from the Main Street Hotel.

Hitching to locales north of the airport or south of San Jose is dicey.

ROTA

Halfway between Tinian and Guam, Rota is an attractive, friendly island. Shaped like a hand with a finger pointing at Guam, the flat mountain atop the finger is known as Wedding Cake because that's what it looks like. The United States felt no need to recapture Rota during World War II, so the Japanese garrison was bombed and

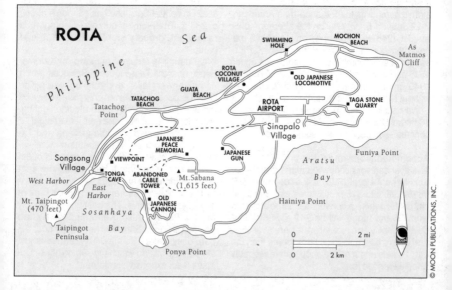

left to sit it out. Today Japanese tour groups hit the island on short excursions from Saipan and Guam.

The locals call their island Luta, and its flower-filled main Chamorro village, Songsong, offers a better glimpse of Chamorro life than the villages on Saipan. A second village is being constructed at Sinapalo near the airport by homesteaders. The best time for a visit is the Sunday before Columbus Day (in October), Rota's fiesta in honor of patron saint San Francisco de Borja. The sea around Rota is very clear and the sunsets superb.

Rota doesn't have a good harbor, which limits its development, though mass tourism is now threatening to flood the island. Golf courses and even gambling casinos are on the drawing boards.

Sights

Songsong is spread along a narrow neck of land between two harbors. The brick shell of an **old Japanese sugar mill** still stands beside Songsong's West Harbor, an old steam locomotive from the operation parked alongside. Local weightlifters use train wheels as barbells.

At the end of the road west of Songsong is **Tweksberry Beach Park** below Mount Taipingot ("Wedding Cake"). Tweksberry is very attractive and a good place to snorkel at high tide.

Just above Songsong is **Tonga Cave,** with stalactites and stalagmites. The Japanese used it as a hospital during the war. Locals still take shelter here during typhoons. There's a perfect short hike up the jeep track to the white cross directly above Tonga Cave. You'll get a great view of Songsong and Wedding Cake Mountain from this viewpoint, but it's too steep to drive a car up there.

The most complete collection of relics from Rota's history is at the **Rota Cave Museum,** a new museum privately owned by Mattias Taisican, and located in Antigo Cave on his property about one mile from Songsong village on the road to the airport. Admission is $5 for adults, $3 for children. The museum is located about a mile from Songsong Village along the main road from the airport.

A huge **Japanese cannon** in a bunker beside the road three miles east of Songsong overlooks Sosanhaya Bay. The abandoned **cable car towers** nearby once brought ore down from the phosphate mines in the interior.

The road along the south coast from Ponya Point to Hainiya Point is very rough but can be negotiated if you go slow. It's also a panoramic half day hike; you'll easily be able to hitch a ride back to Songsong from Sinapalo.

From Sinapalo a good dirt road climbs to the **Japanese Peace Memorial** on the Sabana Plateau near the highest point on Rota (1,615 feet), passing a Japanese cannon on the way. From the memorial the same deteriorating track continues northwest and eventually comes out on the coastal highway near Tatachog Beach. Rugged hikers could walk all the way from Sinapalo to Tatachog in about five hours and see a good cross section of Rota's vegetation, though scenic views from the plateau are few. Now a proposed golf course threatens the wild beauty of the Sabana.

At the **Taga Stone Quarry** east of the airport are the massive shapes of nine megalithic *latte* stone pillars, and seven capstones still lie unfinished in their trenches.

If you have a car, the stalactite-covered cliffs and blowholes (best at low tide) of **As Matmos Cliff** at Rota's northeast point are worth the drive. The **swimming hole** west of here and two miles off the main airport highway is a large, natural swimming hole in the reef and a perfect campsite.

Accommodations

Rota is a small island with relatively few hotel rooms. **Penny's Meitetsu Hotel** (P.O. Box 539, Rota, MP 96951, tel. 532-0468), also known as the Blue Peninsula Inn or "B.P. Hotel," in the middle of Songsong village, charges $28 s, $32 d for one of the 21 rooms with a/c and private bath. Penny's is still pretty basic. Below the hotel is a bank and a supermarket.

The two-story **Rota Pau-Pau Hotel** (P.O. Box 503, Rota, MP 96951, tel. 532-3561, fax 532-3562) stands on a terrace below Mount Taipingot at the south end of town looking like a rundown TraveLodge. All 50 rooms have a fridge and bathtub. It is primarily a Japanese resort, which explains the prices: $160 s, $180 d. Its poolside bar is reasonable, and the setting below the cliffs of Taipingot is evocative.

Perhaps the best value on Rota is the well-managed **Rota Coconut Village** (P.O. Box 855,

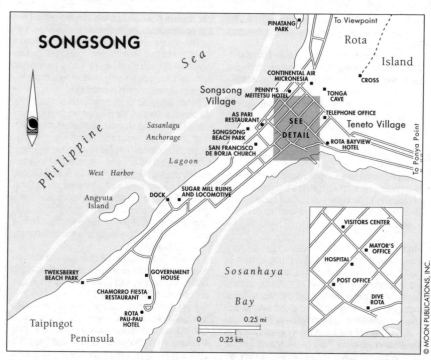

SONGSONG

Philippine Sea

PINATANG PARK

To Viewpoint

Rota Island

CONTINENTAL AIR MICRONESIA

CROSS

Songsong Village

PENNY'S MEITETSU HOTEL

TONGA CAVE

Sasanlagu Anchorage

AS PARI RESTAURANT

TELEPHONE OFFICE

SEE DETAIL

Teneto Village

SONGSONG BEACH PARK

SAN FRANCISCO DE BORJA CHURCH

ROTA BAYVIEW HOTEL

To Ponya Point

Lagoon

West Harbor

Angyuta Island

DOCK

SUGAR MILL RUINS AND LOCOMOTIVE

Sosanhaya

GOVERNMENT HOUSE

Bay

TWEKSBERRY BEACH PARK

CHAMORRO FIESTA RESTAURANT

ROTA PAU-PAU HOTEL

Taipingot Peninsula

0   0.25 mi

0   0.25 km

VISITORS CENTER

MAYOR'S OFFICE

HOSPITAL

POST OFFICE

DIVE ROTA

© MOON PUBLICATIONS, INC.

Rota, MP 96951, tel. 532-3448, fax 532-3449) on the coast west of the airport. An individual Japanese hot tub *(ofuro)* comes with each of the 18 bungalow-style rooms, $94 s, $105 d. There's a pleasant swimming pool on a terrace overlooking the sea, but no beach below, just a rocky shore graced by a shipwreck. Dive Rota bases its dive packages at the village, so divers will be well attended here. It is a little out of the way, so rent a car at the airport upon arrival. Airport transfers are $5 one-way.

The **Rota Bayview Hotel** (P.O. Box 875, Rota, MP 96951, tel. 532-3414, fax 532-0393) in Songsong village has nine rooms, $45 s, $60 d, and is just a walk to the beach.

Also in Songsong village and on the ocean is the **Coral Garden Hotel** (P.O. Box 597, Rota, MP 96951, tel. 532-3201, fax 532-3204). Its 22 rooms are $44 s $49 d.

Camping possibilities include the park in front of Tonga Cave, Tweksberry Beach Park, Guata Beach Park, Tatachog Beach, and the swim-

ming hole. A lot of traffic passes Guata and Tatachog, and Tonga Cave is probably better than Tweksberry as there are no picnic tables to attract late night visitors with loud radios. No permit is required to camp on Rota, though you could check in at the Parks and Recreation Division (tel. 532-4001), behind the police station on the hill in Songsong.

Food and Entertainment

There are several good restaurants in Songsong. The **Chamorro Fiesta Restaurant** beside the Pau-Pau Hotel serves breakfast, a good bowl of ramen for lunch, and reasonably priced steaks for dinner.

Leng's Restaurant (tel. 532-0717) near Penny's Meitetsu Hotel is a lot nicer inside than the exterior implies. It's a little expensive but they serve a very good breakfast.

Just a few yards away is the **As Pari Restaurant** (tel. 532-3356), with Rota's most extensive menu including everything from pizza to

Mexican food, though their specialties are steaks, lobster, seafood, and Filipino dishes. They close afternoons 1-6 p.m.

Also in Songsong, the **South China Restaurant** prepares tasty meals but the portions are small. The Pau-Pau Hotel and Coconut Village have restaurants, but they are expensive.

The Mobil station at the entrance to Songsong from the airport sells groceries and is open till 10 p.m. There are several grocery stores and even a coin laundry in Sinapalo village near the airport. The water on Rota is drinkable.

The **North Wind Restaurant and Bar** (tel. 532-0402) in Sinapalo isn't cheap but it's a good place to stop for drinks and *karaoke.*

Sports and Recreation

Dive Rota (P.O. Box 941, Rota, MP 96951, tel. 532-3377) at East Harbor, Songsong, charges $50 for a one-tank morning or afternoon dive ($75 for two dives the same day). Americans Mark and Lynne Michael also offer night dives, waterskiing, and trolling. They'll happily take snorkelers out in their boat for $20 pp. Dive Rota has a dive package including roundtrip airfare from Guam, two nights' accommodations at the Rota Coconut Village, three boat dives, and two picnic lunches. Even if you aren't a diver, visit their dive shop in Songsong for the wide selection of island T-shirts.

Most of the dive sites are near Songsong. The wreck of the WW II Japanese freighter *Shoun Maru* stands upright in about 100 feet of crystal-clear water in East Harbor. The wreck has been blown open to reveal trucks, bicycles, a deck crane, a bathtub, and two steam engines. Divers also can inspect the underwater debris near the phosphate loading cableway on the same bay and, of course, the usual marinelife on the reefs. It's possible to surface inside Senhanom Cave, among the moray eels, squirrel fish, and bronze sweepers.

Services

The Bank of Guam (tel. 532-0340) is below Penny's Meitetsu Hotel. International phone calls are more cheaply and easily placed on Saipan than on Rota and Tinian. There are several coin-operated laundromats in Songsong.

Information

The Rota office of the **Marianas Visitors Bureau** (tel. 532-0327) is up on the hill across the street from the police station in Songsong. The *Luta Pa'go* (P.O. Box 555, Rota, MP 96951) is published weekly on Rota.

Transportation

Rota International Airport (ROP) is eight miles northeast of Songsong. The excellent highway along the north coast from the airport to Songsong was built with United States dollars. Hitching to the airport is easy, but little traffic runs along the other roads. Car campers should note that the toilets at the airport are open long hours. The Mayflower Restaurant upstairs in the terminal is nice for a cup of coffee.

Rota's hotels offer guided island tours by minibus. It is also an easy island to rent a car and explore on your own. Most of the car rental companies have counters at the airport, including **Budget** (tel. 532-3535), **Islander** (tel. 532-0901), **ESPN** (tel. 532-0343), and **Paseo Drive Car Rental** (tel. 532-0406). Expect to pay around $40 with unlimited mileage.

NORTHERN ISLANDS

Pagan, 201 miles north of Saipan, has a formidable volcano, hot springs, and winding beaches of glistening black sand. Bandeera village is on Apaan Bay, backed by the narrow isthmus that separates explosive Mount Pagan (1,875 feet) in the north from the two dormant volcanoes in the south. When the mountain exploded in May 1981, blowing a section off the summit, the 54 Chamorro inhabitants of Pagan escaped the flow of molten lava by huddling together in bat-infested caves until they were rescued by a Japanese freighter. A wrecked Japanese bomber and AA gun remain beside Pagan's airstrip.

Only a handful of people live on **Agrihan** and **Alamagan.** The group on Agrihan are Carolinians, while Chamorros reside on Alamagan. The Chamorros made a last stand against the Spanish conquistadors on Agrihan in the 17th century. A hot spring is at the north end of Alamagan's west coast.

A wide caldera was created at the center of **Anatahan** when its volcano blew up. On the crater wall are two peaks, 2,349 and 2,593 feet high, on its northeast and west sides, respectively. In 1990 all 22 inhabitants evacuated the island due to continuing volcanic activity.

Asuncion's active volcanic cone rises to 2,931 feet. **Maug** comprises three steep islands, which remained when its volcano exploded and the sea flooded the caldera. The Japanese once used the submerged caldera as an anchorage and had a weather station here, but Maug is now abandoned. The Tropic of Cancer slices through Maug. **Uracas** (Farallon de Pajaros), northernmost of the Marianas, is a cinder-covered active volcano.

GORDY OHLIGER

REPUBLIC OF NAURU
INTRODUCTION

Tiny, 21-square-km (eight-square-mile) Nauru is the richest island in the Pacific; its A$20,000 per capita annual income is among the highest in the world. This wealth came mainly from large deposits of easily accessible, high-grade phosphates. For millions of years billions of birds nested on Nauru, and the excrement or guano (phosphoric acid and nitrogen) they left behind reacted through leaching with the coral (lime) of the upraised atoll to form a hard, odorless, colorless rock, averaging 85-88% pure phosphate of lime. This outstanding fertilizer has kept the fields of New Zealand green and the farms of Australia productive. Ironically, the phosphate has no impact on the fertility of Nauru itself, as it must be treated with sulfuric acid before it's used as fertilizer.

The Land
Oyster shaped Nauru is one of the three great phosphate rock islands of the Pacific (the others are Banaba in Kiribati and Makatea in the Tuamotus). A fringing reef, bare at low tide, encloses glistening white-sand beaches. A 100- to 300-meter-wide (330- to 1,085-foot-wide) coastal belt and a small area around the Buada lagoon contain the island's only cultivable soil. Coral cliffs encircle an elevated interior plateau that reaches 65 meters (214 feet) in altitude. Punctuated by white coral pinnacles of worked-out phosphate fields, the barren, moonscape interior is a scene of utter desolation, in striking contrast to the lush, tropical coastline.

Climate
Only 53 km (33 miles) south of the equator, there's no seasonal variation in Nauru's temperature. November through February (the westerly monsoon) are the wettest months; drier northeasterly tradewinds blow the rest of the year. Rainfall varies greatly from year to year with periods of prolonged droughts. Decades of phosphate mining has decreased rainfall by stripping the interior of its natural cover, thus making cloud formation less frequent.

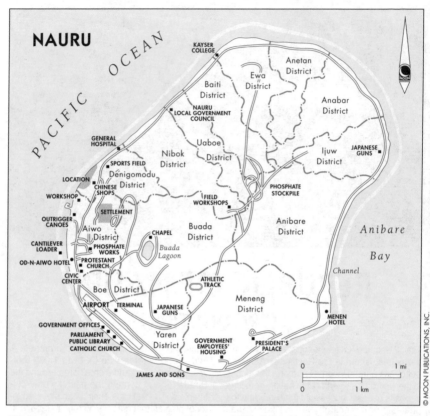

History

The first known European ship to arrive at Nauru was the British whaler *Hunter,* which arrived in 1798. Captain John Fearn named it Pleasant Island for the welcome he received. During the 1830s whalers began calling more often, a number of crew members deserting to remain on land. These men allied themselves with rival chiefs, and after 1878 there was continual fighting among Nauru's 12 tribes.

Germans from New Guinea landed in 1888 and suppressed the tribal warfare. Arms and ammunition were confiscated; liquor was banned. The Germans set about running their new colony as part of the Marshall Islands Protectorate, unaware of the wealth beneath their feet. The first missionaries showed up around 1899.

While visiting Nauru in 1896, trader Henry E. Denson picked up a stratified rock, assuming it was from a petrified tree. He took the rock back to Australia thinking perhaps it could be made into children's marbles. It kicked around the office of Denson's Pacific Islands Company for a couple of years and was being used as a doorstop when Albert Ellis, a young company employee in Sydney, noticed it. He had it analyzed and discovered that it contained 80% pure phosphate of lime. Today the original rock is in Auckland Museum.

The Germans had already claimed the island and set up a trading post and coconut plantation. As mineral rights negotiations proceeded on Nauru, an employee of the Sydney company found vast additional quantities of the same material on Banaba. Britain annexed Banaba on 28 September 1901. (The subsequent history of Banaba is given in the Kiribati chapter.)

It was finally agreed that the phosphates of Nauru would be exploited under joint British-German auspices, by the Pacific Phosphate Company. Profits were to be shared with the German firm on the Marshalls, Jaluit Gesellshaft. The agreement made no provision for direct compensation to the Nauruans. Mining began in 1907. The Germans lost their share when Australia took Nauru without a fight on 9 September 1914, at the beginning of World War I. A Japanese warship arrived soon after with the same intent, but turned back when it found the Australians already in control.

After the war, the League of Nations granted Australia the right to administer Nauru, on behalf of itself, New Zealand, and Britain. In 1920 the British Phosphate Commissioners (BPC), controlled by these three governments, bought out all rights to the deposits. Far from benefitting the Nauruans, the early days of phosphate mining witnessed a series of epidemics introduced by the foreign labor force: dysentery (1907), polio (1910), influenza (1919), and pneumonia (1920). Some 400 Nauruans died from these

NAURU'S CLIMATE

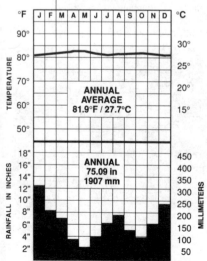

| °F | J | F | M | A | M | J | J | A | S | O | N | D | °C |

90° — 30°
80° — 25°
70° — 20°
60° — 15°
50°

ANNUAL AVERAGE 81.9°F / 27.7°C

ANNUAL 75.09 in 1907 mm

18" — 450
16" — 400
14" — 350
12" — 300
10" — 250
8" — 200
6" — 150
4" — 100
2" — 50

TEMPERATURE

RAINFALL IN INCHES

MILLIMETERS

diseases, lowering the population to only 1,200 in 1920. In 1927, agreement was reached between the company and the island chiefs that a royalty of seven and a half pence per ton of phosphate would be paid. Mining land was to be leased at £40 an acre and 25 shillings paid for any food-producing tree cut down.

World War II came to the island on 6 December 1940, when the German raider *Orion* captured and sank the BPC vessel *Triona* bound for Nauru. The next day the *Orion* and its companion, the *Komet,* arrived at Nauru and sank four more phosphate freighters drifting offshore. On 27 December 1940 the *Komet* returned to Nauru and shelled the cantilever loader, putting it out of commission until 1948. On 9 December 1941 a Japanese plane bombed the radio station on Nauru, and with the war situation deteriorating the British Phosphate Commissioners evacuated personnel and their families. The ship also took many Chinese laborers, but some 200 Chinese and 150 I-Kiribati were left behind.

On 26 August 1942 a Japanese invasion force landed on Nauru and began to build the present airport. Of the 1,850 Nauruans present when the Japanese arrived some 1,200 were eventually deported to Chuuk to serve as forced labor. It was not until 31 January 1946 that 737 survivors returned. The Japanese solved Nauru's leprosy problem by loading 49 people with the disease into a boat and sinking it. The Allies bypassed Nauru; some 500 Japanese Marines held it until the end of the war.

In 1947, Nauru became a United Nations Trust Territory administered by Australia. Phosphate shipments recommenced in July 1947, and payments to the Nauruans were increased. Despite the devastating effect of the mining, until 1965 only a 2.5% royalty was paid to the Nauruans for mining the phosphate.

The first elected Local Government Council was formed in 1951, at which time Nauruans began to press Australia more strongly for a greater share of the profits from phosphate mining. Expenditures by the BPC administration for health, housing, and education increased nearly fivefold between 1951 and 1955. In 1953 public service employees launched a four-month strike led by Hammer DeRoburt, who was elected Head Chief in 1956.

In 1963 DeRoburt turned down an offer of Australian citizenship for his people and resettlement somewhere on Australian territory, such as Fraser or Curtis Islands off the coast of Queensland. In January 1966, with the establishment of legislative and executive councils, Nauruans became almost self-governing. The next year, it was agreed that Nauru could buy itself back from the British Phosphate Commissioners for A$21 million, payable over three years. On 31 January 1968, the 22nd anniversary of the return from Chuuk, Nauru became the world's smallest independent republic. DeRoburt was elected president in May 1968 and on 30 June 1970 the mines were formally transferred to the Nauru Phosphate Corporation.

Government

Two levels of government coexist. The Nauru Government, run by the elected president and his ministers, owns the Nauru Phosphate Corporation and Air Nauru, while the Nauru Local Government Council (NLGC), under an elected head chief and his councillors, controls trade, including the Nauru Insurance Corporation, the Civic Center complex, the Menen Hotel, and the Lands Committee. Nauru has an 18-member Parliament, which elects the president from its ranks. The five cabinet ministers are chosen by the president. Elections are held every three years. The Nauru Party, founded in 1975, was reformed as the Democratic Party in 1987. The Nauru Local Government Council consists of nine elected members under a head chief. There are 14 districts, each headed by a councillor (formerly the chief of the clan).

Economy

Until recently Nauru exported two million tons of phosphate a year to Australia, New Zealand, Korea, and the Philippines, bringing in A$100 million. In 1990 shipments declined sharply, partly due to economic recession and alternative agricultural techniques, but more fundamentally because the phosphate reserves are quickly being exhausted. With Nauru's highest grade phosphate all but played out, the island could become a deserted hulk; 80% of its area is currently devastated.

The Nauru Government takes half the revenue from phosphate sales; the rest is split between the Local Government Council, the Nauru Phosphate Royalties Trust, and landowners. The trust fund is now worth over A$2 billion, designed to provide the inhabitants with a future income. Investments include flashy office buildings in Melbourne ("Birdshit Tower"), Honolulu, Manila, and Saipan, two Sheraton hotels in New Zealand, Fiji's Grand Pacific Hotel, and the highly successful Pacific Star Hotel on Guam.

Though financial reports are not published, other investments have been disastrous, like the never completed Eastern Gateway Hotel on Majuro. Nauru is believed to have lost A$70

These New Guinea soldiers made up the German garrison on Nauru at the outbreak of WW I.

AUCKLAND INSTITUTE AND MUSEUM

million on a fertilizer plant in the Philippines and millions more on a similar plant in India. Much money was also spent on Air Nauru's fleet of Boeing 737s. In 1991 Nauru filed a formal complaint with the Japanese government when the Japanese stock market crashed and they lost 40% of their investment.

In 1989 Nauru filed suit before the International Court of Justice to get the governments of Australia, Britain, and New Zealand to pay for damage to the land. In 1994 the suit was settled for A$107 million to be used to rehabilitate the island's interior.

In September 1995 the Republic of Nauru, showing more courage than most countries of the world, broke diplomatic relations with France because of France's resumption of nuclear testing in the Pacific.

The People

Of the 10,000 people living on Nauru, about 70% are indigenous Nauruans. The rest are a mix of Australians, New Zealanders, Chinese, Filipinos, and other Pacific islanders. Contract laborers, who make up almost 40% of the workforce, are housed in long, squalid tenements at Location, just north of the company's noisy Bottom Side phosphate crushing plant.

Native Nauruans, like Tongans, are huge. Most are a mix of Polynesian, Melanesian, Micronesian, and some European ancestry. The affluence and accompanying waste is astounding. Four-wheel-drive Land Rovers and fancy Australian cars rule the roads; blaring stereo and video systems dominate the airwaves. Not all families are rich. Those who come from smaller, more heavily populated districts where the phosphate was mined first receive less in royalties than people who possess large tracts of land with phosphate reserves.

Nauruans have the world's highest incidence of diabetes—a shocking 30.3%. Medical journals cite Nauru's epidemic as a classic case of junk-food-induced diabetes. High blood pressure, heart disease, alcoholism, and obesity are rampant, making a fiftieth birthday a big event.

The Nauruans reside in single-story, tin-roofed family dwellings strung along the coastline and around the Buada lagoon. It's fairly easy to distinguish the heavyset Nauruans, with their flattop Land Rovers and overpowered speedboats, from the guest workers, who ride big articulated trailer buses and fish for tuna just offshore in dugout canoes. For now, the Nauruans' education, hospitalization, electricity, and housing are provided free by the government, and there's no income tax, sales tax, or customs duties. School truancy has become an issue in Nauru. Affluent Nauruans may even send their children to Australia or New Zealand in an attempt to obtain a better education than they perceive is available on Nauru.

I-Kiribati, Tuvaluans, Indians, and Chinese are permitted to keep their families with them on Nauru. Filipinos must stick it out alone. And it's mandatory that foreign workers must marry any live-in companion.

The Nauru Phosphate Corporation still runs with no unions. Employees' wages often correlate with ethnic origin. The Pacific island and Chinese laborers are at the bottom of the scale, the Filipino tradespeople next up, and the European management and technicians near the top. Indians willing to work for lower wages are quickly replacing expatriate Europeans at the management level.

Conduct

Be aware that Nauruans do not take kindly to argumentative foreigners. Nauruans are large, strong, and not adverse to being physical. A friendly, low-key approach is usually best. Topless sunbathing and skimpy dresses are frowned upon. As in Kiribati, don't openly admire a possession of a Nauruan; he or she may feel obligated to give it to you, an old custom known as *bubuti*. Western males seen driving around late at night with Nauruan women receive special attention from the police. Be careful walking down the street after dark, as many Nauruans train their dogs to attack.

7c   REPUBLIC OF NAURU

Holidays and Events

Public holidays include New Year's (1 January), Independence Day (31 Jan.-2 Feb.), Easter, Constitution Day (17 May), Angam Day (26 October), and Christmas (25 December). The Independence Day celebration includes fishing competitions, sports events, a parade by students, and a speech from the president. Angam Day commemorates the times (in 1932 and 1949) when the local population regenerated to the 1,500 level, the minimum necessary for the maintenance of a collective identity, according to Nauruans.

Island activity virtually stops on the afternoon of the first Tuesday in November when the Melbourne Cup horse race is run and shown live on Nauru television.

SIGHTS

Bottom Side

The phosphate mined on the hot, dusty interior plateau (Top Side) is brought down by train to the works near the **cantilever loaders** (Bottom Side). Here the material is crushed, screened, roasted, and stored. A new **calcination plant** removes all carbon and most cadmium (a pollutant) from the phosphate.

The **buoys** off Aiwo are connected to the deepest water moorings in the world (518 meters, 1,704 feet). Two ships can be loaded from the cantilevers at a time. The **small boat harbor** nearby remains from the pre-1927 days when ships were loaded by lighter. **Location,** the workers' housing area, is just north of the boat harbor, while management housing sits on the hilltop above at Settlement.

Top Side

A look at the mined out **coral pinnacles** of the interior is an essential part of any tour of the island. You may also visit the **phosphate fields** on foot. There are no restrictions on entry. Head inland from the Od-N-Aiwo Hotel and turn right on the dirt road at the top of the hill. You may be lucky and get a lift for most of the way to the phosphate mining area, where great cranes load giant trucks at quite a slow pace due to the small size of the grab buckets on the crane. You'll often see lengths of steel cable protruding from the coral pinnacles with a grab bucket cut loose below. It's easier simply to abandon jammed buckets than to spend time trying to retrieve them. One of the few **railways** in the central Pacific operates here. The long phosphate trains traverse the narrow gauge tracks from the interior loader at Stockpile to Bottom Side below.

The interior of Nauru is in ecological chaos. Photographers will be especially intrigued. There's no water on Top Side, so take something to drink. Cross-country hiking off the road

through the pinnacles is challenging, but very dangerous. If you fall into a pit you might never be found, so don't go alone. Unaccompanied women should pay attention while wandering about the mining area, especially on weekends.

War Relics

To the northeast just beyond the garbage dump, about a kilometer along the dirt road to the phosphate fields, are a couple of big **Japanese AA guns** to the left of the main roadway, clearly visible at the top of a hill. There's also an excellent view from there, and a stone fort is hidden in the undergrowth just behind. Backtrack to the paved road and continue down to the **Buada lagoon,** where banana and coconut trees border the brackish water. Many Nauruans live in houses around the lagoon; fishing rights are divided according to family. There's a small store where you can buy a cold drink.

Between the lagoon and the west coast is **Command Ridge,** accessible via a dirt track to the right just before the road to the phosphate fields. If you miss it, follow the railway line that crosses the track about 20 minutes inland. A short distance inland to the left of the track is a huge **machinery dump** hidden in the undergrowth. Machinery is discarded here, cheaper to replace than to repair. Carry a stick, as wild dogs frequent this area.

The dirt track then takes you across the railway line, where you start to climb Command Ridge. The Japanese had their headquarters up here during the war, and the ridge is still riddled with trenches, bunkers, and intact naval guns, although much is hidden among the thick growth. The extremely deep **pits** between the adjacent coral pinnacles were dug out with pick and shovel by Chinese workers during the early days of phosphate mining. Take a shortcut down to **Settlement,** along the pipeline that feeds three large water tanks at the end of the access road. You can see some intact concrete pillboxes around these tanks. The management housing you'll pass contrasts strikingly with the crowded workers' lodgings on the coastal plain directly below. Carry a big stick for the dogs.

Many wartime **Japanese pillboxes** dot the coastal fringe and more are slightly inland. Just a little north of Anibare Bay, on the inland side of the road adjacent to houses on the crest of a hill, are two large coastal defense guns. One is hard to find as a large workshop has been erected right next to it, but the other is in the open.

Many Japanese bunkers are around the Menen Hotel, including a well-hidden pillbox just off the steps to the tennis courts and a larger two-story observation post directly below the courts. An underground bunker is behind the volleyball court near the hotel entrance. A number of camouflaged bunkers are on the interior side of the airport runway.

A machine gun from an American Flying Fortress, shot down over Nauru during World War II, is mounted in the front yard of a private residence in Yaren, along the road from the airport terminal near the junction to Meneng.

Around the Island

The better part of a day can be spent walking around the island (19 km, 12 miles). A cement sidewalk borders the road much of the way, and small stores and restaurants are well distributed so you're never too far from a cold drink or snack. Although reserved, the Nauruans are friendly and will return a smile, wave, and word of greeting when you catch their eyes.

Frigate birds (some tame enough to eat fish from your hand) are often seen soaring above the shoreline. Until recently each district had its own **frigate bird roost,** huge elevated platforms on wooden legs where the birds would perch. Some can still be seen, sadly falling apart. One fine example remains at Anabar, to the right of the road near the beach; you're welcome to feed or photograph the 100 birds—preferably in the early morning or an hour before sunset. The perch is privately owned so ask permission of anyone there. President Dowiyogo announced plans in 1994 to revitalize the old Nauru custom of keeping frigate birds.

The Bureaucracy

If you've got some extra time, visit the government offices opposite the airport terminal. If **par-**

Nauru phosphates are loaded onto ships for Australia and New Zealand from these giant cantilever loaders at Aiwo.

liament is in session you may observe from the large public gallery; the meetings in May and June on the budget are the liveliest as backbenchers heckle and mudslinging matches start. The debates are supposed to be in English but some strong Nauruan can be heard when things get hot. Nearby is the **courthouse,** where you're welcome to sit in on a trial. A very limited public library is also here.

Waterfront
The swimming is good in the boat harbor at Aiwo, especially at high tide. **Surfers** should check out Gabab Channel, at the end of the airport runway closest to the Civic Center, and Menen Point near the hotel at high tide. **Reef walking** at low tide along the coast near the Menen Hotel is fascinating. Corals, sea urchins, crabs, and small fish can be seen in abundance at the edge of the intertidal zone.

The best beach on Nauru borders **Anibare Bay,** but beware of dangerous currents. Be especially wary when swimming in the cut channel (boat ramp), about 500 meters (a third of a mile) north of the Menen Hotel, when the tide is going out. There's a strong flow of water. Saturday after 4 p.m. watch for drunks and don't leave personal effects unattended.

PRACTICALITIES

Accommodations

There are two hotels on the island.

The government-owned **Menen Hotel** (P.O. Box 298, Republic of Nauru, Central Pacific, tel. 444-3300, fax 444-3595) was expanded and upgraded in 1993 to accommodate a meeting of the South Pacific Forum. With its modern facilities, it is now the hotel of choice, particularly for business travelers. It has 119 rooms, all air conditioned. It is located on the water at the south end of Anibare Bay, four km (2.5 miles) east of the airport terminal. Prices for rooms vary between A$70-100 s and A$100-130 d, depending upon whether the room is standard or deluxe and whether or not it has an ocean view. The less expensive rooms usually go first, so reserve ahead if cost is an important consideration.

Service has picked up at the hotel. It now has bars, restaurants, a gaming room, gift shop, swimming pool, and all-weather tennis courts. Reliable safety deposit boxes are available and should be used for your valuables. The hotel offers Thai, Chinese, and Indian meals along with popular outdoor barbecues (A$10) Wednesday and Friday nights.

The island's other hotel, the family-operated **Od-N-Aiwo** (Tim/John Enterprises, P.O. Box 299, Nauru, tel. 444-3283, fax 444-3555), near the Civic Center and phosphate works downtown, is best if you're into sightseeing and observing local life. The 20 a/c rooms go for A$45 s, A$51 d, A$70 t. The meals served in the restaurant downstairs have improved to meet the competition of the refurbished Menen Hotel. A small, well-stocked supermarket is on the premises, but no alcoholic beverages are sold. The free Od-N-Aiwo airport bus meets all flights.

Food

Nearly all food is imported from Australia; even water is shipped in. Nauru has a fair number of restaurants in addition to those at the hotels.

Several inexpensive Chinese restaurants are at the Chinese shops near the workers' housing area at Location. A good lunch of beef and rice goes for around A$3. The **Triton Restaurant** near the Od-N-Aiwo is good, and if you wish to spend a little more, the **Star Twinkles Restaurant** at Nibok is worth a try. The **Frangipani Cafe** at Boe is very reasonable. Small Chinese cafes dot the island, but no Nauruan cafes. Hot meat pies and fries, barbecued chicken, and hot dogs are available at Capelle and Partners supermarket at Ewa, open late most evenings.

Entertainment

Nauru is not organized for tourists, so you'll have to entertain yourself. A little imagination reveals plenty to do. The best bar is at the recently refurbished **NPC Staff Club,** just beside the larger cantilever at Aiwo. One of the "tropo" Aussies will probably offer to sign you in (it's a private club) if you look respectable enough. The beer is cheap and there's an excellent snack bar here.

The wildest places on Nauru are the **Bula Bar** behind the Civic Center, the **Ace of Diamonds Club** near the Menen Hotel, and the **Sailing Club** at Anabar. Beware of aggressive drunks at all three. The friendly **East End Club** almost opposite Kayser Church at Baiti has two good snooker tables.

Nauru's national sport is Australian Rules football. Games at the sports field by the road just north of the Chinese shops are played all day Saturday and some evenings. Admission is free. If you enjoy tennis or volleyball, go to the courts at Location any evening and ask the locals if you may join in a game. A nine-hole golf course is set among the phosphate buildings at Aiwo. A reader, John Connell, writes: "Setting off at 6 one morning I ran around the island without too much interference from dogs. I now claim to be one of the few people to have run around a country (even a republic) before breakfast!"

Other activities in Nauru include betting on Australian horse races that are broadcast live

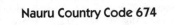

Nauru Country Code 674

over the radio. You can place bets at any one of the five or so technically illegal bookie joints. Many of the bookies provide patrons with a complimentary meal. Bingo games are ubiquitous on Friday and Saturday nights.

Sports and Recreation

Local expatriate Ian Chapman (tel. 555-4550, fax 444-3759 at Pacific Diving Company, Ewa), offers snorkeling and diving to certified divers only. Guided snorkeling is A$20 per person, with a two-person minimum, and diving is A$45. Ian will rent diving and snorkeling equipment. He also offers reef walks and guided tours of the island.

Shaun Oppenheimer, as well as Ian Chapman, can arrange fishing trips. Two modern vessels are available. The larger rents for A$75 per hour and can accommodate five, while the other is A$45 and can accommodate three.

Shopping

Nauru has a number of shops. Those operated by the Local Government Council, such as the ones in the Civic Center, have a poor selection of shoddy goods and keep irregular hours. The Chinese shops are better stocked. In recent years a few Nauruan general stores have been set up, one of the best of which is **Capelle and Partners** at Ewa with frozen foods, ice cream, liquor, fruit juices, film, and the like. A similar store is at the Menen end of the airport runway. Fresh fruit and vegetables can sometimes be found at **James and Sons** store between the airport and the Menen Hotel.

Most business needs can be tended to in the dilapidated **Civic Center** at Aiwo, which includes the Air Nauru office, the bank, the post office and Philatelic Bureau, and a barren but cheap supermarket, which features out-of-date canned goods and weevil-infested flour. The lack of local taxes means, among other things, cassettes (A$3-4), cigarettes (A$7-12 a carton), and alcohol are cheaper here than in their countries of origin.

The **Central Pacific Bookshop** near the Od-N-Aiwo sells magazines and some good postcards of Nauru. The post office may also have postcards. Color print film is available at a small store opposite the Civic Center with 24-hour processing available.

Visas

All visitors must have a passport. A visa is not required if you'll be continuing to a third country on the first connecting flight and hold a confirmed seat reservation. Since all flights begin or end in Nauru, a little planning will allow you a visa-free two- or three-day stopover. Even if your connection is immediate, Immigration might allow you to stay until the next flight a few days later, without a visa. Do not argue with the customs official if you are denied permission to do so. Mentioning the name of a Nauruan friend might work, however. If you know a Nauruan family willing to sponsor you, a one-month visa may be possible, but application must be made at a Nauruan diplomatic office before your planned arrival.

For longer visits, apply for a visa. If the stay is for business, the nature of the business and any Nauruan contacts must be detailed. Write to Principal Immigration Officer, Nauru. You can also apply for a visa in person or write: Consulate General of the Republic of Nauru, Level 50, 80 Collins Street, Melbourne, VIC 3000, Australia. Other consulate offices are:

Honorary Consul for Nauru, Level 5, 17 Castlereagh Street, Sydney, NSW 2000, Australia; Consulate General of Nauru, Sheraton Mall, 105 Symonds Street, Auckland, New Zealand; Embassy for Nauru, 7th Floor, Ratu Sukanu House, MacArthur Street, Suva, Fiji; Nauru Representative in London, Mairi Government Office, 3 Chelsham Street, London SW1-X8ND, U.K.; Consul General for Nauru, 7th Floor, Pacific Star Building, Makati Avenue, Makati Metro, Manila, Philippines.

Services

Nauru uses Australian currency. The hotels change traveler's checks at a worse rate than the Bank of Nauru. Credit cards are not generally accepted, though the Menen Hotel accepts American Express and Diners Club. Overseas telephone calls may be placed at the Telecom Nauru offices beside the satellite dish opposite the airport. Nauru uses the three-pin Australian plug and 240 volts, 50 cycles AC electricity.

Address mail to: Rep. of Nauru, Central Pacific.

Free consultations are available weekdays at the general hospital at Denigmodu just up the road from the NPC staff hospital. A haircut at Backside Barber No. 3 near the Chinese shops at Location is A$2. Nauru doesn't have a tourist information office. The Australian High Commission in the Civic Center has a decent library where you can relax in comfort and learn about the wonders of Oz.

Information
The government publishes the *Bulletin* once a week. There are no tourist brochures available in the country.

Radio station C2AM-AM broadcasts at 1320. Satellite TV with CNN is available for a rental fee from the telephone company.

Getting There
Nauru International Airport (INU), one km (two-thirds of a mile) southeast of the Civic Center at Aiwo, was extensively remodeled in 1993. Both hotels have courtesy buses meeting all incoming flights. The Menen Hotel operates a cafe at the airport that serves a continental breakfast for departing and arriving morning flights. Reynaldo's store next to the terminal building offers takeaway Chinese fare as well as cold drinks.

Air Nauru, the only airline to land on the island, has flights to Australia: Brisbane ($328), Melbourne ($369), Sidney ($369). It also flies to Guam ($257); Honiara, Solomon Islands ($138); Manila, Philippines ($414); Nadi and Suva, Fiji ($214); Pohnpei, FSM ($219); and Tarawa, Kiribati ($109). All prices are in U.S. dollars for a one-way, economy ticket.

Be sure to reconfirm your onward flight soon after you arrive. Get to the airport early, as the check-in counter often closes 30 minutes before departure time. If your Air Nauru flight is delayed or canceled, politely ask the employee at the airport to give you a voucher for a paid room with meals at the Menen Hotel.

Visiting yachts must tie up to a ship's buoy, and someone must stay on the boat at all times. It's much too deep to anchor. Spending the night moored here is not allowed, however, and yachts must stand offshore overnight if they wish to stay a second day. Dinghies can land in the shallow small-boat harbor, though it does experience quite a tidal surge. Diesel fuel is usually available, but little water.

Getting Around
Both the Menen Hotel and the Od-N-Aiwo offer guided tours, including trips to the phosphate diggings. Taxis on Nauru are not too expensive, once you've found them. The hotels serve as taxi stands. If plane connections allow only a couple of hours on Nauru, hire a taxi up into the interior.

Since the frigate bird doesn't have the oily waterproofing of other seabirds, it can't dive for its own food. Instead, it spooks other species into disgorging their catch in midair.

GORDY OHLIGER

REPUBLIC OF KIRIBATI
INTRODUCTION

Legend tells that the god Nareau picked flowers from the ancestral tree and threw them north of Samoa to create the islands of Tarawa, Beru, and Tabiteuea. These islands and 30 others now compose the independent Republic of Kiribati. The name, pronounced "KIR-i-bas" (also heard "kir-EE-bas"), is an indigenous corruption of the name "Gilberts." To further confuse you, the Kiribati name of the islands that form the Gilbert Islands group is Tungaru. The people of Kiribati, the Gilbertese, are known as I-Kiribati, and speak the language called Kiribati.

A visit to the republic is like stepping back to the Pacific of half a century ago. In this corner of Micronesia, outboards have not totally replaced sailing canoes and tourists still are extremely rare. The I-Kiribati are friendly, embarrassingly bold and inquisitive, and terribly hospitable. They are fun-loving, easygoing, and somewhat languorous. In Kiribati, visitors can participate in the daily activities of the village—mingling and observing customs, lifestyles, and behavior. But this is no place for the energetic, hyperactive traveler!

The Land
The 33 low-lying atolls and coral islands of Kiribati total only 810 square km (313 square miles) land area, but 3,550,000 square km (1,370,656 square miles) of sea are included within Kiribati's 200-nautical-mile Exclusive Economic Zone. No other political unit on earth is made up of such a large sea to land ratio. It is the largest atoll state in the world, straddling the equator for 3,235 km (2,010 miles) from Banaba to Christmas Island. Tarawa, the capital, is 2,815 km (1,750 miles) north of Fiji.

The islands are arrayed in three great groups: the 16 Gilbert Islands atolls (Tungaru), the eight Phoenix Islands, and the eight Line Islands, with little Banaba alone to the west between Tarawa and Nauru. Tungaru contains 280 square km (108 square miles) and most of the people of Kiribati. The flat, palm-studded Tungaru isles have a uniform environment of crushed coral surface, magnificent white beaches, lagoons, and reefs. Most of the atoll islands are no more than 200-300 meters (650-1000 feet) wide, but the atoll

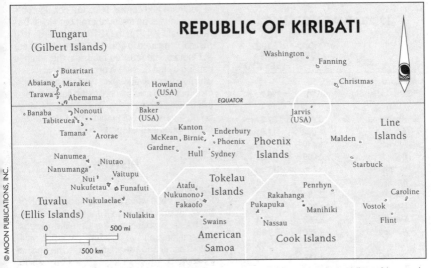

REPUBLIC OF KIRIBATI

Tungaru
(Gilbert Islands)

Washington Fanning

Butaritari
Abaiang Marakei Howland Christmas
Tarawa (USA)
Abemama EQUATOR

Banaba Nonouti Baker Jarvis Line
Tabiteuea (USA) (USA) Islands
Tamana Arorae Kanton
McKean Birnie Enderbury Malden
Gardner Phoenix
Nanumea Hull Sydney Islands
Nanumanga Niutao Starbuck
Nui Vaitupu Tokelau
Nukufetau Funafuti Atafu Islands Penrhyn
Nukunono Rakahanga Caroline
Tuvalu Nukulaelae Fakaofo Pukapuka Manihiki Vostok
(Ellis Islands) Niulakita Flint

0   500 mi
0   500 km

Swains Nassau
American Cook Islands
Samoa

© MOON PUBLICATIONS, INC.

lagoons are anywhere from 15 to 100 km (10 to 63 miles) long. Due to the action of the prevailing winds, the atolls' northeast coasts are generally higher than the west, but nowhere do they reach more than a few meters above sea level. The west sides are encumbered by shoals and reefs, making it safer for ships to navigate the east coasts. All except Makin, Kuria, Nikunau, Tamana, and Arorae have central lagoons.

Banaba, 443 km (275 miles) southwest of Tarawa, is a raised limestone island. To the southeast of Tarawa are the uninhabited Phoenix Islands, and farther east, the Line Islands stretch between Hawaii and Tahiti. Christmas Island, largest atoll in land area in the world, accounts for nearly half the republic's dry land.

A United Nations report on the greenhouse effect (the heating of earth's atmosphere and resultant rise in sea level due to industrial pollution) lists Kiribati as one of the countries that could disappear completely beneath the sea in the 21st century unless drastic action is taken. At the 1989 South Pacific Forum meeting on Tarawa, Australia agreed to fund monitoring stations to be established throughout the Pacific.

Climate

Robert Louis Stevenson wrote that the Gilberts enjoy "a superb ocean climate, days of blind-ing sun and bracing wind, nights of heavenly brightness." The best time to visit is March to November when the southeast trades blow; from November to March the westerlies bring more rainfall, in sharp irregular squalls. Droughts occur

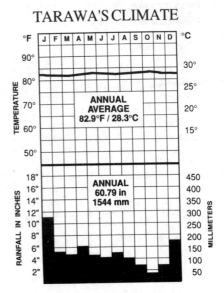

TARAWA'S CLIMATE

ANNUAL
AVERAGE
82.9°F / 28.3°C

ANNUAL
60.79 in
1544 mm

KIRIBATI AT A GLANCE

	POP. (1990)	LAND AREA (SQ. KM)
Tungaru		
(Gilbert Islands)	67,187	279.23
Abaiang	5,314	17.48
Abemama	3,218	27.37
Aranuka	1,002	11.61
Arorae	1,440	9.48
Beru	2,909	17.65
Butaritari	3,786	13.49
Kuria	985	15.48
Maiana	2,184	16.72
Makin	1,762	7.89
Marakei	2,863	14.13
Nonouti	2,766	19.85
Nikunau	2,048	19.08
Onotoa	2,112	15.62
Tabiteuea (North)	3,275	25.78
Tabiteuea (South)	1,325	11.85
Tamana	1,396	4.73
North Tarawa	3,648	15.26
South Tarawa	25,154	15.76
Banaba (Ocean Islands)	284	6.29
Phoenix Islands	45	28.64
Birnie	0	1.21
Kanton (Abariringa)	45	9.15
Enderbury	0	4.53
Gardner (Nikumaroro)	0	4.14
Hull (Orana)	0	3.91
McKean	0	1.21
Phoenix (Rawaki)	0	1.21
Sydney (Manra)	0	3.28
Line Islands	4,782	496.52
Caroline	0	2.27
Christmas (Kiritimati)	2,537	388.39
Fanning (Teraina)	1,309	33.73
Flint	0	2.43
Malden	0	43.30
Starbuck	0	16.19
Vostock	0	0.66
Washington (Tabuaeran)	936	9.55
TOTAL	72,298	810.68

in southern and central Tungaru; considerably more rain falls on the northernmost atolls: Butaritari gets 3,114 mm (121 inches) of annual rainfall, compared to only 1,177 mm (46 inches) at Onotoa. The reduced rainfall in the south is caused by the upwelling of cold oceanic water, which reduces evaporation from the ocean surface (nutrients also brought to the surface make this a prime fishing area). The climate of Kiribati is hot, but usually not humid; cool sea breezes often moderate the temperature.

HISTORY

Prehistory
Perhaps 3,000 years ago, the ancestors of the Micronesians arrived in Tungaru from Southeast Asia, probably via the Caroline Islands. Several thousand years later Polynesian navigators came and intermarried with the original inhabitants. I-Kiribati legends tell how spirits left Samoa and journeyed to Tungaru, where

Gilbertese warriors wielding shark-tooth swords once donned heavy armor made from coconut fibers and human hair.

INSTITUT ROYAL DU PATRIMOINE ARTISTIQUE, BRUSSELS

they remained a long time before changing into humans.

Continual contact among the atolls by canoe led to a homogenous culture. The inhabitants were fierce warriors, equipped with shark-tooth daggers and swords, body armor of thickly plaited coconut fiber, and porcupine-fish helmets. On the islands north of the equator district chiefs predominated; south of the equator, councils of old men *(unimane)* ruled.

European Contact

Some of the islands may have been sighted by Spanish explorers in the 16th century. In 1765, Commodore John Byron of the HMS *Dolphin* chanced upon Nikunau. Tungaru received its European name from Capt. Thomas Gilbert of the British ship *Charlotte,* who passed in 1788. The first detailed observations and charts were made by Capt. Charles Wilkes of the U.S. Exploring Expedition (1840).

By 1840, whalers were active in the area. Although they had many skirmishes with the islanders, they also traded with them, and some even deserted to become beachcombers. Resident Europeans maintained continual contact with the outside after 1850, trading bêche-de-mer (edible sea slugs), turtle shells, and coconut oil. Between 1850 and 1875, slave traders, known as blackbirders, captured I-Kiribati laborers to work European plantations in other parts of the Pacific.

American missionaries from Hawaii arrived in northern Tungaru in 1857; it was not until 1870 that the London Missionary Society sent representatives from Samoa to southern Tungaru. Catholic missionaries landed at Nonouti in 1888. When the Americans withdrew in 1917, the Catholics extended their influence in the north.

Colonialism

Britain established a protectorate over the Gilbert and Ellice Islands in 1892, to halt encroachment by American traders. When phosphate was discovered on Banaba (Ocean Island) in 1900, the British quickly annexed the island. From 1908 to 1941, the British governed the group from Banaba; the administration was not shifted back to Tarawa (where it had been before 1908) until after World War II. The protectorate became a colony in stages between 1915 and 1916. Britain annexed Christmas Island in 1919 and added the Phoenix Islands in 1937.

In the Guano Act of 1856, the United States claimed 14 islands in the Line and Phoenix groups, a subject of amicable dispute with the British until 1939, when they agreed to jointly control Kanton and Enderbury.

The British did end much factional and religious warfare. The people, who had always lived in scattered family *(kaainga)* settlements, were concentrated into compact, easy-to-rule villages, connected by roads. Land ownership was registered.

The War

Most Europeans and Chinese laborers were evacuated from the Gilberts after the outbreak of World War II. The Japanese occupied Tarawa, Butaritari, Abemama, and Banaba in late 1941 and 1942. They did not fortify the islands or establish large garrisons until after an American raid on Butaritari on 17 August 1942. That day, 221 marines under Colonel Carlson landed on the south side of the atoll from two submarines, in a move to divert Japanese attention from the concurrent invasion of Guadalcanal in the Solomons. The marines dug in and easily beat back an attack by the 150 Japanese on the island. The U.S. force then withdrew before the Japanese could retaliate from their strongholds in the Marshalls. Nine unfortunate marines left behind in a mix-up were captured and beheaded. Two days after the raid, Japanese planes bombed a Gilbertese village in which they thought some Americans were hiding, killing 41 islanders.

As a response to the Carlson raid, Tarawa's Betio islet was heavily fortified by the Japanese, who built an airstrip down its middle. On 20 November 1943 a strong force of U.S. Marines landed at Betio and cleared the island in a brutal three-day struggle. During the Battle of Tarawa 4,690 Japanese soldiers and Korean laborers were killed (only 17 Japanese and 129 Koreans were captured); the number of United States troops killed, wounded, or missing reached 3,314. This was the war's first great amphibious landing against fortified positions and, though costly, provided valuable lessons for later operations. The Americans retook Butaritari at a cost of several hundred lives; the 22 Japanese on Abemama

preserved British eight-inch naval gun at the eastern end of Betio

JACK D. HADEN

committed hari-kiri (ritual suicide) to avoid capture. The United States didn't consider it worthwhile to land on strongly defended Banaba and Nauru, which they bypassed but continued to bomb from the air.

Throughout the war Gilbertese civilians were used as forced labor by the Japanese. Later, the great quantities of supplies brought in by the Americans so impressed the Gilbertese that they developed a cargo cult and sent delegations to the military commanders requesting permanent American rule. This was denied, and several persistent petitioners were arrested. The British were not amused.

To Independence

The Gilbert and Ellice Islands Colony fell under the British colonial Western Pacific High Commission, headquartered in Fiji until 1953 and after in the Solomon Islands. In 1972 this administrative arrangement ended, and the British resident commissioner on Tarawa became a governor responsible directly to London.

The first formal steps toward self-government came in 1963 when the British appointed islanders to executive and advisory councils. In 1967 a House of Representatives with a majority of elected members replaced the Advisory Council. In 1971 the Legislative Council received greater powers. In 1974, the post of chief minister and a House of Assembly were created.

That same year the Polynesian Ellice Islanders voted in a plebiscite to be administered

separately from the Micronesian Gilbertese, and in 1975 independent Tuvalu was born. Banaba attempted, unsuccessfully, to secede from the colony about the same time. The British granted full internal self-government to the Gilbert Islands in 1977.

Official independence followed on 12 July 1979. The British timed this carefully to coincide with the playing out of the phosphate deposits on Banaba (the mine closed in 1980). With no other easy resources to exploit, and a growing, impoverished population, the British were more than happy to get out. Probably no other former British colony got a worse deal at independence; even Tuvalu had seceded from the Gilberts.

Also in 1979 the United States relinquished to the Republic of Kiribati all claim to the Phoenix and Line Islands in a Treaty of Friendship, which specified that none of the islands be used for military purposes by third parties without consultation. Kiribati didn't reach its present extent until 1982 when the country bought Fanning and Washington atolls back from transnational Burns Philp.

GOVERNMENT

The Republic of Kiribati has a 41-member Maneaba ni Maungatabu (House of Assembly), elected every four years. The speaker is not a member, but an outsider chosen by the Maneaba.

The Beretitenti (president) is elected by the people from among three or four candidates nominated by the Maneaba from its ranks. The Beretitenti chooses an eight-member cabinet from the Maneaba. Kiribati's first president, Ieremia Tabai, who served from independence in 1979 until his statutory retirement in 1991, worked toward the goal of national self-reliance.

The main political parties are partly divided along religious lines, with Protestants in the National Progressive Party and Catholics supporting the Christian Democratic Party. The Liberal Party and the New Movement Party complete the scene. Although government is centralized at Bairiki on Tarawa, small administrative subcenters are run by district officers on Abemama, Beru, Butaritari, Christmas, and Tabiteuea.

Kiribati was placed under a caretaker Commissioner in 1994 due to a vote of "no confidence" on the government of Pres. Teatao Teannaki. Opposition leader Teburoro Tito was elected president in the ensuing election, campaigning against corruption.

ECONOMY

Cash Economy

Kiribati has a simple agricultural economy based on copra production on the outer islands. Coconut Products Ltd. (P.O. Box 280, Tarawa, Republic of Kiribati) uses the copra to make coconut oil soap and cosmetics. In the Line Islands copra production is run by the government, while village cooperatives handle production in Tungaru. The large trading companies left the Gilberts during World War II and never returned.

Until 1980, phosphate from Banaba provided 80% of exports, over half the local tax revenue, and several hundred jobs. Since the loss of this income, Kiribati has faced financial hardship. A trust fund of phosphate revenues accumulated between 1956 and 1980 is presently worth more than A$200 million and brings in substantial income.

When Queen Elizabeth II visited Kiribati for 24 hours in 1982, the British government paid Kiribati a handsome sum to prepare for the visit by painting all houses along the road pink, among other absurdities, while cynically continuing to reduce aid grants. Aid from Britain has been replaced by development assistance from Australia (which also supplies most of Kiribati's imports), Japan, New Zealand, South Korea, and the European Community.

In 1989 a small garment factory opened on Betio (Tarawa) with South Korean aid, and a year later British aid was used to establish a small industrial center on Betio producing garments, footwear, and *kamaimai* (coconut molasses). Solar-evaporated salt is produced on Christmas Island. A seaweed farm on South Tarawa produces seaweed for use in food emulsifiers and pharmaceuticals.

Many I-Kiribati are still employed in the phosphate operation on Nauru, but those jobs will disappear when Nauru's mines are worked out in a short number of years. Remittances from I-Kiribati seamen serving on foreign ships are an important source of income for outer island families.

Kiribati's greatest resource is its EEZ, encompassing 3,555,000 square km (1,370,656 square miles) of the richest fishing grounds in the western Pacific. The royalties paid by foreign fishing vessels represent a significant portion of Kiribati's budget, though considerably less revenue than if Kiribati could exploit this resource itself.

Sales of stamps to collectors by the post office's philatelic bureau (P.O. Box 494, Betio, Tarawa) bring in a little revenue. Package tourism is insignificant and unlikely to develop due to competition from more accessible destinations and transportation difficulties within the republic.

Subsistence

Most I-Kiribati live from subsistence agriculture and by collecting seafood from lagoons and reefs. Small amounts of copra are made, and seaweed is farmed to earn extra cash for essentials such as sugar, flour and kerosene. Farmland is often divided into scattered miniholdings, and this, combined with the shortage of land, overpopulation, and a lack of services and opportunities, has led many to migrate to Tarawa where the best jobs are concentrated.

Away from the South Tarawa strip from Betio to Bikenibeu, however, life moves at a deliberately sedate pace. Activities are directed toward securing the few necessities of life, and most people seem not to exert themselves unnecessarily. Fishing, cooking, tending the *babai* (taro) pits, and socializing are the main preoccupations. The tranquility is disturbed only by the omnipresent motor scooters and infrequent Air Kiribati planes. Outside of South Tarawa, only the government compound at Beru and the main settlement on Christmas Island have electricity. Because of limited soil, the only vegetable grown is taro, and this must be cultivated in deep organic pits. Coconuts proliferate on all the islands (except some of the Phoenix group), and the pandanus palm, breadfruit tree, banana, and papaya trees all provide food. Pigs and fowl are common, and fish plentiful. It has been reported, however, that the use of drift nets by South Korean, Taiwanese, and Japanese trawlers has begun to deplete tuna stocks.

THE PEOPLE

About one-third of Kiribati's population lives in South Tarawa, primarily on Betio and the Bairiki-Bikenibeu strip. Most other Tungaru atolls have several thousand inhabitants each. The Phoenix and Line groups were never inhabited by Gilbertese; people have only inhabited them since the arrival of Europeans. To relieve the population pressure on South Tarawa, the Kiribati government announced in 1989 that nearly 5,000 people would be resettled on outlying atolls, mainly in the Line Islands.

Between 1985 and 1990 the population grew at an annual rate of 2.24%; 40% of the people are aged 14 or under. The northern atolls of Kiribati are predominantly Catholic, the southern mostly Protestant. The total population is 53% Catholic, 39% Protestant, two percent Seventh-Day Adventist, and 1.5% Mormon. Most of the 155 resident Westerners and 360 Tuvaluans live in South Tarawa.

The ribbonlike I-Kiribati villages stretch out along the lagoon side of the Tungaru atolls. Although thatched roofs still predominate, tin roofs are becoming popular because they require little maintenance and can be used as water catchments. The *maneaba*, a community meetinghouse, is the focal point of the village. Its huge lofty thatched roof rests on low coral pillars with open sides. Place mats *(boti)* line the earth-

an old photo of an I-Kiribati couple

en floor, each belonging to a specified member of a clan or extended family *(ka-ainga)*. Intermarriage within a *ka-ainga* is not allowed, so an individual always has another family to turn to in case of domestic strife.

The I-Kiribati are excellent seamen and build large, swift, seagoing outriggers with canvas sails. To reverse direction one must lift the mast and sail and swing them around to the other end of the canoe. Pointed windward, the canoes are manned by the lightest men, who constantly shift their bodies to keep the outrigger skimming just above the surface of the water. Racers can exceed 16 knots and are able to turn at great speeds. At night, fisherman on smaller canoes net flying fish by the light of dried coconut frond torches or kerosene lamps.

Language

English is understood by many on South Tarawa. It's also the official language, but once you leave Tarawa, only government officials and a few men are willing to speak English. Others are reticent, stemming perhaps from the

I-Kiribati custom of not being boastful or desirous of elevating oneself above others. Egalitarian society: If everyone present does not understand English, it's not used. This custom is pervasive, and it can occasionally be difficult to get I-Kiribati to speak English in group situations. An English speaker may become more communicative in one-to-one situations. English is generally used in government departments and business, but not at home.

Kiribati is in the Malayo-Polynesian group of the Austronesian family of languages. It bears resemblances to both Micronesian and Polynesian languages. Pronunciation of Kiribati is divided into northern and southern Tungaru dialects. The northern dialect is used on Abemama, Aranuka, Kuria, and all the islands northward, while the southern version applies on Nonouti, Beru, and the islands to the south. It's interesting to note that the northern dialect is also used on Mili atoll in the Marshalls and the southern dialect in the Line Islands and Nui in Tuvalu. On South Tarawa both dialects are used.

Both pronunciation and spelling are different. In the north the word for "one" is spelled *touana* while in the south it's *teuana*. "To sit" is *takataka* in the north and *tekateka* in the south. A few common words are entirely different: "satisfied" is *buu* in the north and *ngae* in the south. If you stay on an outer island long, you'll soon pick up a few words and there will always be someone willing to serve as your teacher. Kiribati has no letter "s" or "c" in their 13-letter alphabet, so "ti" is used for these and pronounced as an "s". This explains why someone who doesn't already know cannot guess how to pronounce Kiribati.

Conduct

When outside South Tarawa, always have a supply of small gifts to repay anyone who invites you in for a drink of toddy or a meal. Matches, a package of tea leaves, and a tin of condensed milk could be presented to any family with whom you stay. If you stay more than one night with the same family, check out the village trade store and purchase something more substantial to give them. Those staying over a week somewhere should contribute a large bag of rice. Spend at least what you figure your

meals were worth, then a little more. *Te ga'am* (chewing gum) is popular with children and young adults.

If you're invited to a meal at a *maneaba*, cash has replaced products as a gift. The going rate seems to be about A$10 pp. The money should be placed in an envelope and given to whoever appears to be in charge. If it is a wedding, the gift should be given to the bridegroom, at a wake to the head of the family.

Don't verbally admire an islander's possession or that person may feel obligated to give it to you, a custom known as *bubuti*. I-Kiribati are curious people who won't hesitate to ask your age, marital status, or occupation. Don't react as if they're invading your privacy. Take care, however, of your rubber thongs (zoris), even in a private home, as "borrowing" another person's pair is not considered a sin at all. Keep all your personal gear locked in your bag; sharing is customary among I-Kiribati families, and the children may go through your things while you're out. Be careful too with your Western time values, as the I-Kiribati are likely to be more relaxed and easygoing than you, something you'll no doubt experience on most Pacific islands.

In the *Maneaba*

When moving about in the *maneaba* it's proper to stoop. Never stand upright, especially in front of seated people. Maintaining a low profile is a sign of respect to the *unimane* (old men) and others present. It's also polite to back out of the *maneaba* when exiting; never turn your back on the occupants. It's considered disrespectful to place your hands on the beams and roof or to point with an outstretched finger or arm; the locals point with their head and a wrinkling of the nose.

While business is being discussed in a *maneaba* everyone sits cross-legged; do not sit with legs outstretched pointing toward someone. After the official "business" is over, everyone relaxes and stretches out their legs. It's rude to step over someone's legs.

If a celebration or special event is in progress at a *maneaba*, you may be placed up front with the guests and dignitaries, even though you have nothing to do with what is occurring. You'll be expected to make a short speech as a formality. Someone will translate. Tell them why you've come and how you're enjoying their island.

the largest maneaba *in the Gilberts, Nonouti atoll*

ROD BUCHKO

When driving past a *maneaba* in a car or motor scooter, it's polite to slow down if something is happening inside. This custom appears to be in total decline, however, in crowded South Tarawa.

HOLIDAYS AND EVENTS

The I-Kiribati are renowned dancers; the emphasis is on movement of the hands, head, and eyes, rather than the body or feet. A classical Kiribati dance is the *ruoia*, while the more vigorous *batere*, parts of which resemble a Samoan *siva*, was introduced from Tuvalu centuries ago. Children learn the technique early and practice all their lives. The *ruoia* was banned by the missionaries, but it has made a comeback in recent years. It's said that *ruoia* composers had special powers and could inflict curses and spells through their songs and chants.

Traditional dancing is performed during Easter, Christmas, Independence Days, or on special occasions such as opening a new building or greeting a special visitor. Talcum powder may be sprinkled on the backs of the necks of guests and performers at these gatherings, as a gesture of appreciation. To maintain the purity of Kiribati dancing, the Cultural Affairs Office has prohibited the performance of Polynesian dances such as the *tamure, hula,* and *siva* before tourists.

The young and middle-aged love to dance *"te tuitit"* (the twist). It's hard to believe that

these seemingly languid people could have such a passion for this energetic dance, yet they go absolutely nuts doing the twist. The four-stringed ukulele is still the most common musical instrument.

Independence Day (12 July) features a parade at the Bairiki National Stadium (Tarawa), traditional dancing, and canoe races. Interschool sports and dance contests are held on Youth Day (first Monday in August). Other public holidays include New Year's Days (1 and 3 January), Good Friday, Easter Monday, Independence Days (11 and 12 July), Youth Day (1 August), Human Rights Day (10 December), and Christmas Days (25, 26, and 27 December).

PRACTICALITIES

Accommodations

The only hotels are on Abemama, Abaiang, Christmas, and Tarawa. They are often booked around national holidays. A five percent hotel tax is added to the bill.

Many of the Tungaru atolls have basic Island Council rest houses constructed from local materials, most charging between A$15 and A$40 per person. A number have been upgraded for overseas visitors, but electricity and hot water

Kiribati Country Code 686

are still an exception rather than the rule. Cooking materials are usually provided. To be on the safe side, bring your own mosquito nets and insect repellent. To book a rest house send an urgent telegram to the council clerk of your chosen island stating your estimated arrival time. Also mention if you require transportation from the airstrip. The Ministry of Home Affairs (P.O. Box 75, Bairiki, Tarawa, Rep. of Kiribati, tel. 21-092) on Tarawa can be of assistance in making these arrangements. An alternative is just to hope the facility is available and make arrangements on arrival, but you could be out of luck. There are no rest houses on South Tarawa or Abemama.

Another possibility is to stay with locals. In recent years, there have been times when this has been discouraged, and even forbidden, by Immigration and Home Office. Further, even if you can arrange permission, keep in mind that this means adapting to their way of doing things, including squatting on the beach to do your "daily business." Toilet paper is unobtainable on the outer islands, and visitors should also bring their own mosquito net and repellent because these are often not found in local trade stores. Extra pillows and mattresses may also be lacking. Beware of unboiled water.

The first evening you spend in a private home, neighbors will come to visit. As a guest, you will eat first, having the choice of the best food. Once you have finished, the men will be served. The women and children will receive the leftovers. Expect to sacrifice much of your privacy. Custom dictates that members of your host family accompany you everywhere, and you will be deemed rude if you resist. On Sunday, you will be expected to accompany the family to church.

Food

Te babai (swamp taro) is cultivated in large pits below the water table; it's eaten either boiled or made into several different puddings. Breadfruit is a staple which is boiled or fried in butter; fried as chips it makes a terrific snack. Boiled pumpkin, papaya, and plantain supplement the diet. The harsh dry climate of most of the atolls limits the variety of produce. On the southern islands *te roro,* a wafer-like food made from the boiled fruit of the pandanus tree, tastes like dates. It's eaten with coconut cream spread on the surface. Formerly, *te roro* was eaten only in the *maneaba.* Ripe pandanus fruit is dark yellow or orange and sweet like pineapple.

CAPSULE KIRIBATI VOCABULARY

mauri — hello
tiabo — goodbye
ko uara? — how are you?
i marurung — I'm fine
kua — tired
taiaoka — please
ko raba — thank you
te raoi — you're welcome
antai aram? — what's your name?
ko nako mai ia? — where do you come from?
iraua am ririki? — how old are you?
katokia ikai — stop here
i kan amwarake — I'm hungry
e kangkang te amwarake — the meal is delicious

teutana — a little
teutana riki — a little more
e a tau — that's enough
akea riki — no more
akea — none, nothing
eng — yes
tiaki — no
te ika — fish
kikao — octopus
te iriko — meat
te ben — coconut
te moimotu — drinking coconut
te tongo — fermented coconut milk
kabubu — pandanus drink
te babai — swamp taro
katei ni Kiribati — the Kiribati way

maneaba — meeting place
boti — place in a *maneaba*
uea — chief
unamane — group of elders
ka-ainga — group of extended families
utu — extended family
batua — eldest male in a *ka-ainga*
unaine — old woman
karimoa — the eldest son
I-Matang — Europeans
riri — woman's coconut leaf skirt
tibuta — woman's shirt-sleeved blouse
baangota — spirit-worshipping place

A fantastic variety of fish can be caught in the lagoon or on the reef. You'll usually eat fish fresh since there's no refrigeration, but salted or dried fish is also delicious. Eels, crawfish, and various other shellfish are also eaten.

Rice is consumed in phenomenal quantities, and when possible, canned corned beef. The latter is substandard—too salty and fatty. The I-Kiribati go to great lengths to please foreigners (I-Matang); for example, the frequent serving of cold, uncooked corned beef from the can! Chickens, eggs, and pork are not often served. Remember that food and all the basics can be in short supply on the outer islands due to erratic shipping. Take with you as much as you can.

Toddy

The drink of the islands is *te karewe* (sweet toddy), extracted from the coconut palm early in the morning and evening. The spathe of the tree is bound and cut, then the sap is collected in a coconut shell or bottle. It can be drunk immediately—not sweet, but very refreshing—or used in cooking. It's usually taken after meals and is even used to wean babies.

Te kamaimai, molasses extracted from boiled *karewe,* is great in rice; diluted with water it makes a pleasing drink called *te katete. Te kamaimai* mixed with grated coconut and coconut

banana tree (Musa cavendishi)

cream makes a tasty sweet called *kati ni ben. Te karewe* fermented for three days becomes *te kaokioki* (sour toddy), a very smooth, potent drink. *Te kaokioki* can be readily obtained on most outer islands. The color varies from a milky white to light brown. A local sweetbread is made from *te kaokioki* yeast. *Kabubu* is a mixture of toddy, pandanus, and grated coconut, dried in the sun and pounded. It can be stored for long periods.

Toddy-cutting is a male profession passed from father to son, and the cutters are well respected in their village. In the 1990 census 1,638 I-Kiribati men listed their occupation as "tree workers," the highest number in any occupational category. As they work high up among the coconut palms they often sing Christian hymns or songs of praise for toddy, wives, girlfriends, lost loves, or even the adventures of the previous night. Said Robert Louis Stevenson, "They sing with a certain lustiness and Bacchic glee."

Visas

All visitors must have a passport and an onward ticket. Visa regulations are simple: nationals of countries that require a visa of I-Kiribati travelers must themselves possess a visa to visit Kiribati. Thus, Americans, Australians, Dutch, French, Germans, and Japanese must obtain a visa in advance at a British diplomatic mission. Most British subjects and nationals do not require visas. In 1994, airlines were instructed not to board passengers unless correctly documented.

The visa costs anywhere from A$20 to £60 sterling (two photos required) and may be used anytime within three months of the date of issue. In Australia contact Bill Franken, Consulate General of the Republic of Kiribati (35 Dover Rd., Rose Bay, Sydney, NSW 2029, tel. 02-9371-7808, fax 02-9371-0248). At this office a visa costs A$20 and one photo is required, issuing time two days to bona fide travelers. In New Zealand contact Mr. Raymond D. Mann (P.O. Box 40205, Glenfield, Auckland, tel. 09-419-0404, fax 419-1414). Hawaii: Mr. William E. Paupe (Suite 503, 850 Richards St., Honolulu, HI 96813, tel. 808-521-7703, fax 808-521-8304). Japan: Mr. Tokugoro Kuribayashi, Consular Office of the Republic of Kiribati (Room 684, Marunouchi Building, 2-41 Marunouchi,

DIANA LASICH HARPER

Chiyoda-kr, Tokyo, tel. 03-3201-3487, fax 03-3214-1884). Germany: Frank Leonhardt, Leonhardt & Blumberg (Rodingsmart 16, 200 Hamburg 11, tel. 040-36-146-0, fax 040-36-146-123). Great Britain: Maurice Chandler CBE, Consulate of Kiribati (Faith House, Westminster SW1P 3QN, tel. 071-222-6952, fax 071-976-7180). South Korea: Mr. In Yung Chung, Consulate of Kiribati (Halla Building, 891-44, Daechi-Dong, Kang Num-ku, Seoul, South Korea, tel. 02-5591-114/837, fax 02 5591-699).

Otherwise contact any British consulate or write: Principal Immigration Officer, P.O. Box 69, Bairiki, Tarawa, Rep. of Kiribati.

You run some risk of being immediately deported if you arrive without a visa. However, upon arrival you'll usually be granted a stay until the date of your onward flights. You may even be allowed a stay up to one month. Extensions can be obtained from the Office of Home Affairs, Bairiki, one month at a time for up to four months in any 12-month period. Bring along your onward ticket. If you are on an outer island, you must cable your request to this office in advance. Extensions are free. The officials may not be overly pleased with visitors living with locals and may seek verification that you're staying at a hotel or rest house.

Ports of entry for cruising yachts are Banaba, Tarawa (Betio), Fanning, and Christmas. At Tarawa yachts can obtain permission to cruise the outer islands of Tungaru but must return to Tarawa again to clear out of the country. Occasionally yachts en route to Majuro are allowed to stop at Butaritari without having to return to Tarawa.

Money and Measurements

Australian paper currency is used, although some Kiribati coins circulate. Beware of the Kiribati $1 coin—exactly the same size as the Australian 50-cent piece. Most prices in this chapter are in Australian dollars. It's usually impossible to change traveler's checks on the outer islands, so take enough cash in small-denomination banknotes. It's nearly impossible to change A$50 and A$100 bills on the outer islands. Don't expect to be able to use your credit cards in Kiribati, although the Bank of Kiribati accepts MasterCard for cash advances. Tipping is not practiced.

Take stamps to the outer islands if you want to post any mail from there; local post offices are often sold out of all values. Know how much to put on—many island postmasters are only familiar with local rates. Never mail anything from Kiribati by surface: it could be months until the next ship leaves! Airmail between Kiribati and Australia takes about one week, and about two weeks to Asia or America. Mail service has improved since Air Nauru and Air Marshall Islands began carrying the mail.

The electric voltage is 240 volts, 50 cycles, and the Australian three-pin plug is used. On Tarawa both the metric and imperial measurement systems are in use, although distances are usually measured in kilometers.

Health

When walking about, be careful of the sun—coconut palms provide little continuous shade, and the white sand on the lagoon side creates a tremendous glare. Wear a broad-brimmed hat and sunglasses. There's no malaria in Kiribati, but outbreaks of dengue fever sometimes occur. After prolonged dry spells there are outbreaks of pinkeye on South Tarawa. This highly contagious eye infection is easily contracted through using the pillow or towel of another person, and during epidemics all medication may become exhausted. Anyone contemplating staying with locals should have a mosquito net.

With very few toilets in Kiribati, unless you're staying at a hotel or can find a government building with a bathroom, chances are you'll have to squat on the beach with the locals. This makes lagoons near population centers unsanitary and potentially dangerous. The overcrowding on South Tarawa has led to appalling sanitary conditions. Diarrhea and hepatitis are common, so take care with the water. Carry an antidiarrheal and do not drink untreated water. Typhoid fever, tetanus, and immune globulin (for viral hepatitis A) inoculations are recommended (but not mandatory). There are chronic medicine shortages on Kiribati. Take all medicines you may need with you, including those as common as aspirin.

Fish poisoning is also common in Kiribati. Take care with the small red ants common on South Tarawa; they have a nasty sting. Centipedes should also be treated with respect.

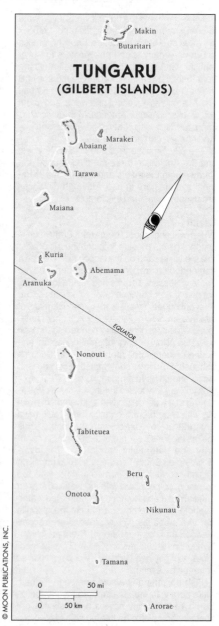

**TUNGARU
(GILBERT ISLANDS)**

Makin
Butaritari

Marakei
Abaiang

Tarawa

Maiana

Kuria

Aranuka

Abemama

EQUATOR

Nonouti

Tabiteuea

Beru

Onotoa

Nikunau

Tamana

0   50 mi

0   50 km

Arorae

© MOON PUBLICATIONS, INC.

Information

Tourist brochures on the country, with entire sections lifted from the 1985 edition of this book, are available from the **Kiribati Visitors Bureau,** Ministry of Natural Resource Development (P.O. Box 251, Bikenibeu, Tarawa, Rep. of Kiribati, tel. 28-287, fax 21-120). For information on Christmas Island, contact the Tourism Office (Ministry of Line and Phoenix Development, Christmas Island, Rep. of Kiribati).

Topographical maps of Kiribati can be ordered from the **Lands and Surveys Division** P.O. Box 7, Bairiki, Tarawa, Rep. of Kiribati). A good selection of books on the country is available from the National Library (P.O. Box 6, Bairiki, Tarawa, Rep. of Kiribati).

The bilingual newspaper *Te Uekera* (40 cents) is published twice a month by the Broadcasting and Publications Authority (P.O. Box 78, Bairiki, Tarawa, Rep. of Kiribati). The library in Bairiki sells books about Kiribati.

Getting There

Bonriki Airport (TRW) is five km (three miles) northeast of Bikenibeu on Tarawa. The airport bus to the Otintaai Hotel is free for guests with confirmed bookings, otherwise A$2 pp. Public buses only call on the terminal when Air Nauru or Air Marshall planes are arriving. If you arrive on an interisland flight, unless you have made prior arrangements to be picked up walk to the main road to catch a bus. A small, overpriced snack bar and a souvenir shop open for international flights. The airport tax is A$10 on international flights.

Air Nauru flies Nauru to Tarawa twice weekly. In peak traveling periods, they sometimes add an additional flight. At Nauru, one can fly on to Australia, Fiji, Guam, FSM (Pohnpei), and the Solomon Islands.

Air Marshall Islands has international flights that connect Tarawa to the Marshall Islands (Kwajalein and Majuro), Fiji (Suva and Nadi), and Tuvalu (Funafuti). Fares are much cheaper on roundtrip excursion fares, which require a seven-day advanced purchase. Be careful of the excursion ticket conditions, however, because of possible cancellation fees. A stopover at Tuvalu greatly increases the cost of a Fiji to Tarawa flight. AMI flights are often fully booked weeks ahead, so confirm your reservations. Baggage space is often limited.

Getting Around by Air

Air Tungaru operates a subsidized domestic air service to all the Tungaru atolls. Each island is allotted a portion of the seats along the route, and every atoll gets at least one flight a week, some several. It's best to book your flights before you leave Tarawa. The Air Tungaru "office" on the outer islands usually operates out of the agent's attaché case when a flight is due at the airstrip. Reconfirm your onward reservation with the local agent immediately upon arrival at an outer island. If you want to change your reservation, simply go to the airstrip when the next flight is due and ask the agent to radio in your request. At other times the radio shack will probably be closed. You could also try forwarding written requests to Tarawa with the pilot. Plan your itinerary carefully, as it will be hard to make changes. Fares from Tarawa vary between A$28 (Maiana) to A$153 (Arorae). Children ages two to 11 fly for half fare and infants fly for 10% of adult fare. The baggage allowance is 15 kilos (33 pounds).

Be prepared for schedule irregularities and canceled flights. Of more concern, there have been periodic charges, from members of the airlines' staffs, concerning safety issues.

Getting Around by Sea

The Shipping Corporation of Kiribati, now known as the **Kiribati Shipping Services Limited** (KSSL) (P.O. Box 495, Betio, Tarawa, Rep. of Kiribati, tel. 26-195), is located at Betio harbor and operates five cargo/passenger ships. Fares range from A$13 deck to Abaiang; A$49 to Banaba; up to A$148 to Christmas Island. Every four to six weeks voyages are made to Majuro (A$76 deck), Funafuti (A$94 deck), and Suva (A$175). Often a diversion is made to Nauru (A$76 deck). Children under 12 pay half fare

and cabin fares are usually double the quoted deck fare. Confirm all trips at the office. Don't trust local gossip!

MATS Shipping and Transport (P.O. Box 413, Betio, Tarawa, Rep. of Kiribati, tel. 26-355) in Betio runs its copra boat, the *MATS-1*, to the outer islands every couple of weeks with occasional voyages to Christmas Island, Fanning, Washington, Fiji, and Majuro. Fares are similar to those charged by KSSL. Another possibility is **Waysang Kum Kee** (tel. 21-036) above the Paradise Club on Betio.

Gilbertese *baurua* (large twin-sailed catamarans) travel between Tarawa and Abaiang (A$9 one-way) three or four times a week; visitors can arrange to go along by asking at the harbor at Betio. Also ask about a boat to Abaiang at Borata's Club in Bairiki.

A final possibility is to try traveling as unpaid crew on a cruising yacht. Most private yachts sail north from Fiji and Tuvalu to Tarawa, then continue on to Majuro. From Tarawa to Hawaii is a long haul. As yachts are required to clear customs at Betio on both the inward and outward journeys, you may be lucky enough to be accepted for a cruise around the Tungaru atolls. Be prepared to do your share of work and to contribute a per diem amount toward costs. Yachts anchor in the lagoon just off Betio, and the only way to get on is to convince a captain you're a hand worth having aboard.

Getting Around by Road

On the outer islands, ask the Island Council clerk if he knows of anyone who might be willing to rent you a motorbike *(te rebwerebwe)*. If you can borrow a bicycle *(te batika),* you've got great and leisurely local transportation, and a barrier-free way of meeting people.

TARAWA

Tarawa atoll, just 130 km (81 miles) north of the equator, is the main center of the Tungaru group and capital of Kiribati. Most people live along the bottom side of this huge open triangle of long, low islands facing a jade green lagoon. A single passage pierces the barrier reef along Tarawa's west flank, the route for contemporary shipping as it had been for the wartime American invasion force.

There is continuous ribbon development along the 24-km (15-mile) lagoonside road from Bonriki to Betio. Most of the structures are still traditional. The most important government offices are at Bairiki, though the health and education facilities are at Bikenibeu and communications at Betio. Densely populated Betio is the heart of Kiribati. It has stores, bars, war relics, and the port where the fishing and shipping industries are centered: commerce as well as squalor.

South Tarawa is overcrowded; the population has increased about 20-fold since the war. South Tarawa residents collect about three-quarters of the total cash income in the country, which explains the continuing influx of outer islanders toward its "bright lights." Along with the population explosion, South Tarawa is experiencing a religious explosion: a myriad of missions, churches, and theological colleges are

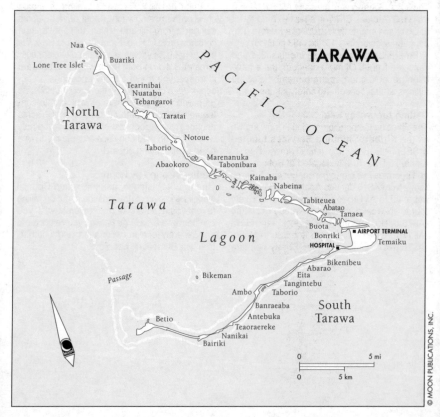

© MOON PUBLICATIONS, INC.

strung along the road from the airport to Betio.

The four-km (2.5-mile), A$10 million Nippon Causeway, built with Japanese aid, opened in 1987 connecting Betio to the rest of South Tarawa. The construction of causeways between the South Tarawa islands may be convenient for getting around, but a serious pollution problem has developed as wastes accumulate in the murky, trapped waters of the lagoon. Local fishermen complain that the causeways choke the lagoon and cause formerly clear passages to silt up. Large quantities of coral rock and sand are used to build the causeways, disrupting the ecology of reef and lagoon. Still, there's nice swimming under the Betio causeway bridge when the tide's coming in.

As of 1996, there were no causeways north of Buota. You can, however, wade to the north tip of Tarawa at low tide. To see more traditional Kiribati life, you must get out of South Tarawa.

Electricity currently (a not very bright pun) reaches only to Buota. There are plans to extend the grid to Buariki by 2000.

SIGHTS

Betio

In 1943, over 4,000 Japanese soldiers on Betio were sheltered underground in concrete blockhouses with walls 1.5 meters (five feet) thick, reinforced by palm trees and steel rails, roofed by a three-meter (10-foot) blanket of sand and coral. Facing the U.S. Marines, who landed on 20 November, was a solid wall of enemy gunfire coming from inside these pillboxes.

Today you can visit the four eight-inch **Japanese coastal defense guns** at the southeast and southwest ends of Betio. One of the guns has collapsed and is now half buried in the sand; another was restored in 1989. These guns bear British markings but were sold to Japan in 1904, *not* captured at Singapore as some assert.

You can find bunkers, dugouts, and trenches along the ocean side of the island, where the Japanese expected the landings, but the Americans came ashore on the northern and western beaches. About 20 rusting **landing vehicles** (LVT), visible at low tide, still lie stalled on the reef where they became stuck in 1943, due to a miscalculation of the tides. All that remains of them today is rusting engines and broken tracks. You can visit a fairly well-preserved Sherman tank at low tide on the beach just west of Betio hospital.

The two-story **concrete bunker** of Rear Adm. Keiji Shibasaki was captured only after a fierce struggle. Even a direct hit from an American warship just offshore failed to shatter the bullet-pocked walls. In 1989 it was announced that the bunker would be made into a war museum, but as yet nothing has been done. Even without any displays it would be a major point of interest if locals didn't use it as an outhouse—the stench is almost unbearable. Another large bunker containing the remains of an electric generator is behind the Betio police station between here and the port. Spent cartridges are scattered about.

On the south side of Betio, surrounded by smashed cement bunkers and fallen guns, is the local cemetery, with a simple **memorial** to the 22 British coast watchers beheaded here by the Japanese. Their epitaph reads, "Standing unarmed to their posts they matched brutality with gallantry, and met death with fortitude." Beware of drunks sleeping on the graves.

The **Marine Training Center** trains young islanders to work on vessels. This excellent program has given hundreds of I-Kiribati an opportunity to earn money, learn a trade, and see a bit of the world. Some of the buildings of the school are World War II vintage American. But also note the Japanese bunker converted into a squash court.

North Tarawa

The South Tarawa bus service extends from Betio to the end of Buota, just beyond Tanaea. A bridge links Tanaea to Buota Island (good swimming in the channel at slack tides). From the bus terminus at Buota, it's easy to wade northward at low tide through the knee-deep water, across passages separating the string of reef islands as far as Tabonibara. With luck, you may be able to hitch a ride with a local crossing the passage in a canoe. There, another continuous coral road begins, and you can walk right to Naa at the atoll's northern tip without getting your feet wet again. A few trucks ply irregularly between Abaokoro and Buariki. You can charter a minibus for about A$15.

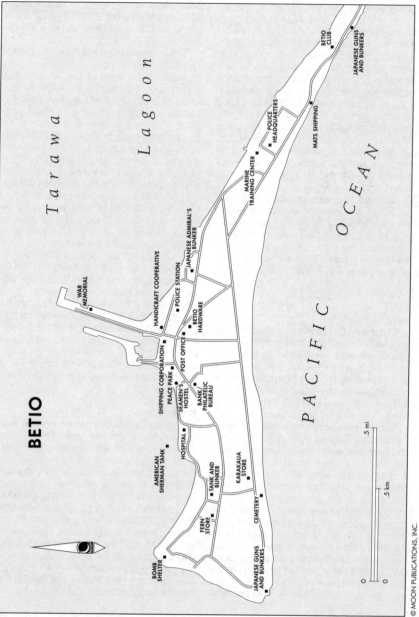

BETIO

Tarawa

Lagoon

PACIFIC OCEAN

WAR MEMORIAL
HANDICRAFT COOPERATIVE
POLICE STATION
JAPANESE ADMIRAL'S BUNKER
BETIO HARDWARE
SHIPPING CORPORATION
PEACE PARK
POST OFFICE
SEAMEN'S HOSTEL
BANK
PHILATELIC BUREAU
AMERICAN SHERMAN TANK
HOSPITAL
TANK AND BUNKER
KARAKAUA STORE
FERN STORE
CEMETERY
BOMB SHELTER
JAPANESE GUNS AND BUNKERS
MARINE TRAINING CENTER
POLICE HEADQUARTERS
MATS SHIPPING
BETIO CLUB
JAPANESE GUNS AND BUNKERS

.5 mi
.5 km
0
0

© MOON PUBLICATIONS, INC.

This excellent walk allows a glimpse of Kiribati village life, especially in Nabeina and Kainaba. There's a Catholic mission at Taborio. Set out from Buota three hours prior to low tide. You could camp on uninhabited islands, stop at the rest house in Abaokoro, or sleep in a village *maneaba*. Be prepared to sing or give a speech for your supper! An unreliable launch runs back to South Tarawa approximately twice a week from Buariki and Tearinibai (A$4 pp), or just walk back. This trip is the perfect way to spend a couple of extra days on Tarawa and meet some friendly people.

PRACTICALITIES

Accommodations

The **Otintaai Hotel** (Mrs. Aara Tekanana, P.O. Box 270, Bikenibeu, Tarawa, Rep. of Kiribati, tel. 28-084) has 40 air conditioned rooms with fridge and fan at A$77 s, A$88 d, A$103 t in the older eastern wing, A$88 s, A$99 d, and A$129 t in the newer western wing. There is a barbecue every Wednesday night from 7:30 to 9 that costs A$12 and often includes entertainment with Gilbertese dancing or singing by the local choir. On Friday night the hotel livens up with an all-night dance session starting at 10 p.m. and "officially" ending at 9 a.m. the next morning. It pays to have a room away from the conference center, if you are planning to sleep that night. Make sure your room door is locked.

The **Tarawa Motel** (Baakoa Ieremia, P.O. Box 59, Bairiki, Tarawa, Rep. of Kiribati, tel. 21-445) is near the Stewart Club by the ocean at Ambo. The four rooms with clean, shared bath and cooking facilities go for A$25 s or A$35 d. Long-term rates are negotiable. Baakoa runs a small store out front.

Mary's Hotel (Mary Teanako, P.O. Box 12, Bairiki, Tarawa, Rep. of Kiribati, tel. 21-164) is a neat, two-story, concrete-block building near the landing at Bairiki. All four rooms have a/c, private

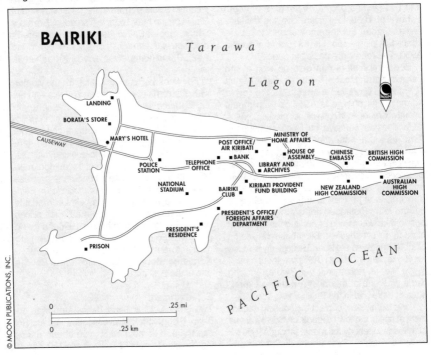

BAIRIKI

Tarawa Lagoon

LANDING
BORATA'S STORE
CAUSEWAY
MARY'S HOTEL
POLICE STATION
TELEPHONE OFFICE
MINISTRY OF HOME AFFAIRS
POST OFFICE/ AIR KIRIBATI
BANK
HOUSE OF ASSEMBLY
LIBRARY AND ARCHIVES
CHINESE EMBASSY
BRITISH HIGH COMMISSION
NATIONAL STADIUM
BAIRIKI CLUB
KIRIBATI PROVIDENT FUND BUILDING
NEW ZEALAND HIGH COMMISSION
AUSTRALIAN HIGH COMMISSION
PRESIDENT'S OFFICE/ FOREIGN AFFAIRS DEPARTMENT
PRESIDENT'S RESIDENCE
PRISON
PACIFIC OCEAN

© MOON PUBLICATIONS, INC.

0   .25 mi
0   .25 km

bath, and fridge. Rates are A$44 s, A$52 d. Meals in the restaurant downstairs are A$5 and up, and airport transfers in the hotel van cost A$7 per person. The walls are rather thin, so your comfort depends a lot on who your neighbors are.

Jong Kum Kee Brothers (Mr. Waysang Kum-kee, P.O. Box 463, Betio, Tarawa, Rep. of Kiribati, tel. 26-352) offers two air conditioned rooms with private bath adjacent to their restaurant for A$50. Unfortunately it's right next to the Club Paradise and on weekends the noise is deafening. Both rooms have two single beds as well as a small fridge inside and are well maintained. This place is handy if you have business in Betio town.

Seamen's Hostel (Mr. Teitia Binoka, P.O. Box 478, Betio, Tarawa, Rep. of Kiribati, tel. 26-133) has 10 rooms, A$20 pp, no double rooms available unless you sleep on the floor. The manager charges a A$5 key deposit.

Sweet Coconut Hotel (Mr. Nanimatang Karoua, tel. 21-487) has three double rooms and two singles on the ocean side of south Tarawa at Tebunia. Private cooking facilities are available, but the shower and toilet are shared. A single room is A$15 and a double A$30. The rooms are basic but peaceful.

Budget travelers can also do well at the **Tarawa Youth Hostel,** run by Mr. Biteti Tentoa at Antebuka opposite Tarawa Motors, the Toyota agency. The charge is A$15 pp with meals (mostly fish), or A$10 pp without meals. The toilet facilities are primitive, but Biteti (pronounced "BEE-tis") is a most attentive host who more than makes up for any material shortcomings. Once the leader of an I-Kiribati dance group, Biteti became a Seventh-Day Adventist in 1987 and gave up dancing, though. He'll still direct you to other dancers, though. He'll also teach you how to sail the *te wa* (outrigger) and arrange for someone to take you fishing or out into the lagoon at night to collect shellfish. Biteti has relatives on Nonouti and Kuria atolls, and he'll gladly arrange for you to stay with them (A$5 pp without meals) if you like. (A reader, Kik Velt, wrote, "Visiting Kuria was one of the most rewarding experiences I have had in the Pacific.")

For a longer stay, contact the housing department at one of the town councils on South Tarawa for houses to rent by the month (about A$500 for up to six people). Even if they don't have any available at the moment, someone working in the office may overhear your request and come forward offering private accommodations.

Food

At the **Fishermen's Restaurant** (tel. 26-314) close to the Betio fish market, prices are reasonable, service is good, and the place is clean. Just up the road, the restaurant atop the **Jong Kum Kee Brothers** store opposite the Co-op in Betio, is quite pleasant and relaxed although the service often leaves a lot to be desired. Takeaway is available. The Chinese restaurant very near Jong Kum Kee's store serves a mixed basic menu at fair prices. The place is dirty at times and draws local drunks who hang about the bar. It's open 24 hours a day.

Local expats dine on Chinese and European food at the **Tarawa Restaurant** (tel. 28-018), on the lagoon side at Bikenibeu. The food is good and takeaway is available. The Chinese food at **Susie's Restaurant** (tel. 21-280), adjacent to **Susie's Store** at the causeway end of Bairiki on the main road, is also good. **Borata's Store**, also at Bairiki, serves a limited fare of cold rice with either fish or chicken for around A$2.50, including sweetened I-Kiribati style tea.

For weekday lunches, watch for the women with pushcarts dispensing fish and rice with tea or *kamaimai* (A$2.50) opposite the library in Bairiki or around the high court offices in Betio. Throngs of hungry office workers congregate here, and beggar dogs take care of the leftovers. If you have access to cooking facilities, you can purchase fresh fish at the outdoor market in Betio or from vendors under the big trees near the Kiribati Provident Fund building in Bairiki. Downtown Bikenibeu has similar roadside vendors near the shopping area. Fish prices are set by the government. In 1996 the going price was 55 cents per pound. In the evening many stores sell fresh donuts for 30 cents— **Karakaua Store** near the cemetery at Betio is one of the best around.

Entertainment

Two groups of traditional dancers practice on Betio, though it takes investigation and luck to see them. If someone tells you about "dancing," be sure to clarify if it's traditional I-Kiribati or modern disco dancing—otherwise you could be in for a surprise!

The once-grand expat clubs at Betio, Bairiki, and Ambo usually have dances (cover charge) on Friday and Saturday nights that often go on till dawn. Temporary "guest" membership at a club will be A$5 to A$10 for the duration of your stay. The **Betio Club** is becoming run-down and the tennis courts are overgrown with vegetation, but it is still fine for a cold beer. The once-popular **Bairiki Club** has also fallen on hard times and is closed more than it's open. Still it is a good place to meet colorful expats and locals who drop in from the surrounding offices during their lunch break. Food is irregular and varies in quality when it is available. However, the beer is cold and you can play darts, snooker, and pool.

The **Ambo Lagoon Club** is the last bastion of the expat era, though it is changing as more jobs are localized. Come respectably dressed. Most activities around the club happen toward the weekend and on public holidays. Darts, snooker, table tennis, and pool competitions are often held on Friday nights along with an outdoor barbecue. Bring your meat and eating utensils. At high tide, the beach here is one of the best on South Tarawa for swimming. The **Stewart Club,** also at Ambo and only a short walk from the Ambo Lagoon Club along the main road toward the airport, is predominantly I-Kiribati.

There are a number of bars on Betio: **Paradise Club** next to the Bank of Kiribati, **Bonn Nikon Club** opposite the roundabout, and the **Seamens Club,** which has live music on Friday night. All three can get quite rough, particularly on Friday and Saturday nights, and tourists are best advised not to go without local escorts.

Most *maneaba* show kung fu or Rambo-style movies or videos in the evening (A$1.20). Bring your own mat and insect repellent. Each village has a large billboard hanging from a tree adjacent to the road, advertising forthcoming attractions.

Soccer matches take place most evenings at the Betio police headquarters sports field or the stadium at Bairiki. You'll be welcome to join in if you're able. In the villages, volleyball matches also occur most evenings, and if you hang around watching you're certain to be asked to play. They'll be thrilled to have you on the team.

On weekends you can watch model outrigger canoe races down the beaches at high tide. Look for these at Taborio, near the small causeway at Teaoraereke, or at Nanikai. You'll be amazed how fast they go when the breeze is right.

Scuba divers should bring all their own equipment as there's still no dive shop on Tarawa. Privately owned compressors do exist, and a good place to inquire about both diving and sportfishing is **Betio Hardware** (tel. 26-130) in Betio.

Shopping

Bikenibeu and Bairiki each have cooperative stores. Check out the small shopping plaza in the Kiribati Provident Fund Building next to the co-op in Bairiki for a variety of small shops. The best shopping is in Betio. Prices for the same items vary considerably. The **AMMS** stores at Antebuka, Bairiki, and Betio, and the **Fern Store** at Betio offer some of the best prices. When buying mosquito coils check to see that they aren't broken, and inspect the packaging of biscuits carefully for weevil infestation. Avoid plastic-wrapped cheese unless it's clearly dated. Every village and housing agglomeration has a small store selling tobacco, matches, kerosene, corned beef, rice, flour, beef drippings, tinned butter, sterile milk, and a small number of other items.

The **Territa Store** next to the Paradise Club has the best priced and freshest film on the island. But, it's still safer to bring all your own film as the supply here is variable.

The **Philatelic Bureau** (tel. 26-515) above the bank branch on Betio sells Kiribati postage stamps—excellent gifts or souvenirs.

Several places sell handicrafts at Bikenibeu, including the gift shop at the Otintaai Hotel (inflated prices), the **Cooperative Society** and **Girl Guide** shops across from the police station, and the **Women's Federation** shop, just a few hundred meters farther down the road. Hours are irregular, so just keep trying. Sleeping mats, sun hats, baskets, and fans are good buys. Check these shops regularly; new items are always coming in. Most Kiribati crafts are utilitarian, such as woven mats and thatch. There's no pottery or woodcarving, except for model canoes. On the outer islands, the co-op stores display items made by I-Kiribati families. Artifacts over 30 years old and traditional tools cannot be taken out of the country.

Services
The **Bank of Kiribati** branches at Bairiki and Betio open weekdays 9:30 a.m.-3 p.m., the Bikenibeu branch 9 a.m.-2 p.m. The Christmas Island branch closes for lunch from 12:30 to 1:30.

Bikenibeu, Bairiki, and Betio have post offices. When picking up general delivery mail, check under your first initial as well as your surname. Address mail to: Rep. of Kiribati, Central Pacific. Cables, telexes, and long distance calls can be placed at the Telecom Services Kiribati Limited office next to the medical clinic in Bairiki, at the Ministry of Communications next to Betio post office, or at Bikenibeu post office. Calls to Pacific countries are A$3/minute, to the rest of the world A$6. You can now direct dial from Tarawa to Christmas, Abaiang, Abaoko-

ro (North Tarawa), Marakei, Abemama, Kuria, and Aranuka.

The Immigration office is located at the Ministry of Home Affairs and Rural Development (tel. 21-092 or 21-087) in Bairiki. Australia, China, South Korea, New Zealand, and the United Kingdom maintain diplomatic missions on South Tarawa.

The recently established 120-bed **Tungaru Central Hospital** (tel. 28-081) is on the main road, between the airport and Bikenibeu. The branch hospital at Betio offers free medical service. Medical supplies are often limited. Due to chronic overcrowding patients may be transferred to the open-air *maneaba* next to the hospital, foreigners included.

Warning
The South Tarawa strip from Betio to Bikenibeu has crime. Drunks are becoming an increasing nuisance, and domestic violence and vandalism are growing. Clothes hung out to dry may be

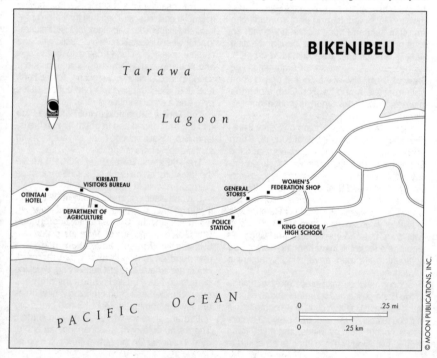

stolen from the line. Tarawa is still a safe place to visit; just keep an eye on your gear.

Information

The **Kiribati Visitors Bureau** office (P.O. Box 251, Bikinibeu, Tarawa, Rep. of Kiribati, tel. 28-287) is a five minute walk from the Otintaai Hotel, heading toward Bikenibeu. The receptionists at the Otintaai Hotel are also very helpful.

You also can pick up tourist information at the **Ministry of Natural Resources and Development** above the post office at Bairiki. The National Library and Archives at Bairiki stocks the latest magazines and newspapers. The library also sells some interesting books on Kiribati. The Lands and Surveys office above the archives has excellent colored maps of most of the islands.

The student bookshop in the forecourt area of the **Catholic Mission** at Teaoraereke has a comprehensive Kiribati dictionary (A$3.50). The University of the South Pacific Center is also at Teaoraereke. Visit the bookstore at King George V School, Bikenibeu, for books on the country and Kiribati grammar.

Radio Kiribati broadcasts from Tarawa seven hours a day over 846 AM and 98 FM.

GETTING THERE

Air Nauru flies to Tarawa twice a week from Nauru. An additional flight is sometimes added during peak travel times. **Air Marshall Islands** has flights that connect Tarawa to the Marshall Islands (Kwajalein and Majuro), Fiji (Suva and Nadi), and Tuvalu (Funafuti). **Bonriki Airport** (TRW) is five km (three miles) northeast of Bikenibeu on Tarawa. Public buses only serve the terminal when Air Nauru or AMI planes are arriving. The **Air Kiribati** office (tel. 28-088), formerly Air Tungaru, moved from Bikenibeu to the Bonriki Airport terminal in late 1995. The Bairiki and Bonriki branches handle international bookings; Betio handles only domestic flights.

GETTING AROUND

Tuesday and Saturday you can catch a launch to North Tarawa (A$4). You can also rent a small launch from people at the wharf in Betio for about A$5 an hour with driver. **Bikeman,** a small islet in the lagoon, is a nice destination for picnics.

By Road

Bus stops are indicated by black and white stripes painted on coconut trees. You can also flag them down anywhere along the road, provided they're not full. When you want out, just shout *kai.* Although buses are supposed to run between Bonriki and Betio every 15 minutes, you can wait five minutes or more than an hour. At rush hours, they're often overcrowded with workers and schoolchildren—it's not uncommon to see passengers spilling out of a jam-packed bus.

Buses run daily 5 a.m.-9 p.m., sometimes later on Friday and Saturday nights. The fare is about A$1.30 for the longest trip (Betio to Buota). On Betio there's a 40-cent flat fare. You pay the conductor, the person with the money box on his or her lap.

Unmetered taxis are also available, though more expensive than buses. If you hire a taxi for the day, agree on the price beforehand. Write it down. The biggest and most reliable taxi company is **T.J. Taxi** (tel. 21-350). It has small minibuses for group hire. You can also try **Coral Island Taxi** (tel. 21-391). Taxis are costly unless you get someone to share it with you. From Bonriki Airport to Bikenibeu is around A$7, to Betio A$15.

Avis (tel. 21-090, fax 21-451) rents modern Toyota cars. The **Otintaai Hotel** rents cars and motorbikes. The government **Plant and Vehicle Unit** (PVU) (tel. 21-174, fax 26-343) also rents vehicles to visitors from its compounds on Bairiki and Betio. The **Atoll Motor Marine Service** (AMMS) (tel. 21-113) and **Enna Taxi Service** at Mackenzie Point have vehicles for hire. Be prepared. What you see is what you get and make sure you settle on the price before driving off.

Some local I-Kiribati also rent cars to visitors. Ask around. The Visitors Bureau keeps a list of car rental companies and may offer to call around to help you find a car. A foreign driver's license is valid on Tarawa for two weeks, and driving is on the left. Beware of speed humps and police radar traps set to catch speeding motorists.

OTHER ISLANDS OF TUNGARU

Abaiang

Abaiang, 51 km (32 miles) north of South Tarawa, is the most easily accessible outer island, with Air Kiribati flights three times a week (A$29). The Island Council truck often meets the flights. More exciting is to journey over on the Island Council *baurua* (catamaran canoe), which departs Betio on Tarawa two or three times a week. It is a very pleasant three-hour journey in good weather. Fishing canoes also sometimes cross the narrow passage between Buariki on North Tarawa and Tabontebike on Abaiang.

In 1989 the Island Council built the **Nikuao Hotel** (Mr. Taata Tataua, tel. 27-102) on one of the best and cleanest beaches in Kiribati. It consists of four traditional thatched bungalows and is located at Tabontebike village near the southern tip of the atoll. The bungalows, which cost A$30-40 pp including one meal, are quite comfortable. Mosquito nets are provided; toilet and washing facilities are shared. The council can arrange fishing and snorkeling off an outrigger canoe and trips to uninhabited Teirio Is-

land. Traditional dancing is staged for groups and local meals are served. For reservations call the Abaiang Island Council clerk from South Tarawa.

There is an older rest house at Taburao, a few kilometers north of the airstrip. At Koinawa, further north, is an old Catholic church with a tower. Ask permission to climb up for the view. Heavily populated, villages are squashed together all the way up the thin strip of land along the lagoon's east side. Abaiang sour toddy has a distinct flavor. In 1991 Teatao Teannaki from Abaiang was elected president of Kiribati, but his government was suspended by a vote of "no confidence" in 1994.

Marakei

Marakei has an enclosed lagoon; two passages connect it to the sea at high tide, but at low tide it's entirely landlocked. It's customary for visitors to travel counterclockwise around Marakei (27 km, 17 miles). The airstrip is at the north end of the atoll, not far from Rawannawi village, which offers the rest house.

Butaritari

Due to regular rainfall, Butaritari is a very green island. The abundant vegetation and variety of food are in striking contrast with the dry, parched islands to the south. Butaritari is well known for its flavorful bananas, large quantities of which are shipped to South Tarawa. A causeway joins the two longest portions of the atoll, making it possible to walk the 30 km (19 miles) from Ukiangang to Kuma. At Kuma, near the east end of Butaritari, men call dolphins from the sea.

Butaritari has had long contact with Europeans; the first permanent European trading post in Tungaru was established here in 1846. At one time during the 19th century, 20 traders operated on the atoll. Many Western-style buildings remain today, intermingling with Chinese and local architectural styles. Americans and Japanese fought battles here during World War II, and rusted pillboxes still mar the island. The skeleton of a **Japanese seaplane** (minus wings

ABAIANG

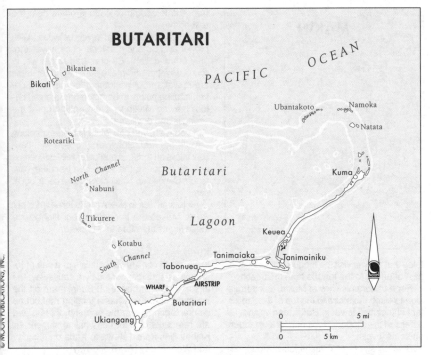

and tail) lies beside the lagoon, opposite the small hospital in Butaritari village.

There's good anchorage for ships in the lagoon. Father Gratien Bermond, the Catholic priest in Butaritari village, also runs a small two-room **guesthouse** (A$15 pp including all meals). There's a co-op and numerous privately owned shops on the island. Take care with the water, and always wear footwear, as the wetter climate encourages parasites such as hookworms. Air Kiribati flies to Butaritari three times a week (A$61).

Makin

Butaritari's near neighbor, Makin, is the northernmost Tungaru island, 191 km (119 miles) north of Tarawa. (Formerly, Butaritari was known as Makin and the present Makin was "Little Makin.") The rest house is at Makin village, south of the airstrip.

This small island is one of the least explored in the Gilbert group. Tourists are rare. Except for the island council and church trucks, the only other noise comes from an occasional motorcycle. You can walk around the island comfortably in a day. Start at the southern tip, opposite Aonbike, and walk north to Nakaa's gate. Tradition holds that the spirits of dead I-Kiribati pass this way on their journey to paradise or hell. Nakaa, the Watcher-at-the-Gate, waits at the northern end of Makin to catch the dead in his net. The adventurous, unafraid of ghosts, can stay the night in one of the two *maneabas* nearby. The one near Nakaa's gate is said to be haunted, and you may find it difficult to get local I-Kiribati people willing to stay the night with you; the caretaker's house, in between the two *maneabas,* remains abandoned.

By walking at extreme low tide a short distance to the beach due west of the haunted *maneaba,* you will be able to see **Nakaa's tongue,** a rocky outcropping. Should you see flies on the rocks it's a sign that a spirit is passing through the judgement net. Tradition dic-

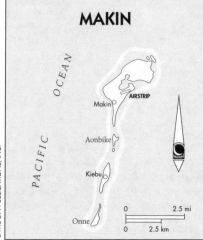

MAKIN

OCEAN

PACIFIC

Makin

AIRSTRIP

Aonbike

Kiebu

Onne

0   2.5 mi

0   2.5 km

© MOON PUBLICATIONS, INC.

tates that all who visit the tongue of Nakaa must cast offerings to the tongue from the beach.

For a panoramic view of Makin, ask permission to climb the stairs to the top of the Protestant church bell tower in **Bukintena** village. Be careful of the slippery steps and lack of ladders on some levels.

Small village stores can be found around the main center, although stocks are limited to basic I-Kiribati requirements: no cold Western drinks. Take a bicycle ride, or walk to the southern tip of Makin facing Aonbike island for a picnic and swim. Borrow a mat and sleep in the shade like the locals.

An ambitious undertaking is to walk from the tip of Makin through Aonbike to Kiebu at low tide, a two-hour walk. Both islands have small villages so if you get caught between tides there will be someone who can put you up for the night. The most southern island is uninhabited except for infrequent visit by local copra cutters. At low tide, you can walk there from Kiebu.

The Makin Island Council refurbished the local rest house in 1992. Five single rooms are available for around A$35 per night. There is no bar or restaurant, although a local woman will cook fish or chicken and rice meals for a little extra. Bring your own mosquito net; mosquitos swarm around Makin at sunset and sunrise. Telephone calls to Tarawa can be made

from the telecommunications office near the rest home.

A small motorized boat travels between Makin proper and Butaritari at least once a week for only a few dollars. Be prepared to get wet in rough weather and make sure important items are in waterproof packaging for the trip. Confirm landing points to be made on Butaritari before leaving Makin to avoid ending up at the wrong island or village.

If you wish, you can join a fishing expedition outside the reef. However, proceed with caution; this is an arduous and potentially dangerous activity because the seas can become very rough. Canoes and their crews have been lost at sea.

Air Kiribati flies to Makin two to three times per week. Make sure to confirm your flight since these flights are often fully booked.

Kuria

Kuria, north of Tarawa, consists of a pair of triangular islands connected by a causeway; the airstrip and rest house (at Buariki) are on the southern one. Kuria has a fringing reef but no central lagoon. Near the north tip of the island are remnants of a former whaling station. Air Kiribati flies from Tarawa to Kuria on Monday and Wednesday (A$48 one-way).

Banaba

Banaba (also known as Ocean Island) is a tiny, six-square-km (2.3-square-mile) raised atoll that claims the highest point in Kiribati—86 meters (283 feet). It lies 452 km (281 miles) southwest of Tarawa, closer to Nauru. Like the latter, it was once rich in phosphates, but from 1900-79 the deposits were exploited by British, Australian, and New Zealand interests in what is perhaps the best example of corporate, colonial exploitation of resources in the history of the Pacific islands.

After the Sydney-based Pacific Islands Company discovered phosphates on Nauru and Banaba in 1899, a company official, Albert Ellis, was sent to Banaba in May 1900 to obtain control of the resource. In due course "King" Temate and other chiefs signed an agreement granting Ellis's firm exclusive rights to exploit the phosphate deposits on Banaba for 999 years in exchange for £50 sterling a year. Of course,

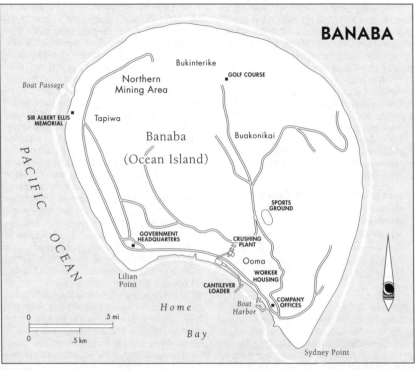

BANABA

Bukinterike

GOLF COURSE

Boat Passage

Northern
Mining Area

SIR ALBERT ELLIS
MEMORIAL

Tapiwa

Banaba
(Ocean Island)

Buakonikai

PACIFIC

OCEAN

SPORTS
GROUND

GOVERNMENT
HEADQUARTERS

CRUSHING
PLANT

Ooma

WORKER
HOUSING

Lilian
Point

CANTILEVER
LOADER

COMPANY
OFFICES

Boat
Harbor

Home

0   .5 mi

0   .5 km

Bay

Sydney Point

© MOON PUBLICATIONS, INC.

the guileless Micronesian islanders had no idea what it was all about.

As Ellis rushed to have mining equipment and moorings put in place, a British naval vessel arrived on 28 September 1901 to raise the British flag, joining Banaba to the Gilbert and Ellice Islands Protectorate. The British government reduced the term of the lease to 99 years, more than enough years for the Pacific Phosphate Company, formed in 1902, to strip out the resource.

Things ran smoothly for the British until 1909, when the islanders refused to lease the company any additional land after 15% of Banaba had been stripped of both phosphates and food trees. The British government arranged a somewhat better deal in 1913, but in 1916 changed the protectorate to a colony to prevent the Banabans from withholding their land again. After World War I the company was renamed the

British Phosphate Commission (BPC), and in 1928 the resident commissioner, Sir Arthur Grimble, signed an order expropriating the rest of the land, against the Banabans' wishes. The islanders continued to receive a tiny royalty until World War II.

On 10 December 1941, with a Japanese invasion deemed imminent, the order was given to blow up the mining infrastructure on Banaba, and on 28 February 1942 a French destroyer evacuated company employees from the island. In August some 500 Japanese troops and 50 laborers landed on Banaba and began erecting fortifications. The six Europeans they captured eventually perished as a result of mistreatment by the Japanese. All but 150 of the 2,413 local mine laborers and their families were deported to Tarawa, Nauru, and Kosrae. As a warning, the Japanese beheaded three of the locals and used another three to test an electrified anti-invasion fence.

Meanwhile the BPC decided to take advantage of this situation to rid itself of the island's original inhabitants to avoid any future hindrance to mining operations. In March 1942 the commission purchased Rambi Island off Vanua Levu in Fiji for £25,000 as an alternative homeland for the Banabans. In late September 1945 the British returned to Banaba with Albert Ellis the first to step ashore, to find only surrendering Japanese troops. The Japanese had destroyed all the local villages.

Two months later an emaciated and wild-eyed Gilbertese man named Kabunare emerged from three months in hiding and told his story to a military court:

We were assembled together and told that the war was over and the Japanese would soon be leaving. Our rifles were taken away. We were put in groups, our names taken, then marched to the edge of the cliffs where our hands were tied and we were blindfolded and told to squat. Then we were shot.

Kabunare had either lost his balance or fainted, and fell over the cliff before he was hit. In the sea he came to the surface and kicked his way to some rocks where he severed the string that tied his hands. He crawled into a cave and watched the Japanese pile up the bodies of his companions and toss them into the sea. He stayed in the cave two nights then made his way inland where he survived on coconuts until he was sure the Japanese had left. Kabunare said he thought the Japanese had executed the others to destroy evidence of their cruelties and atrocities on Banaba.

As peace returned the British implemented their plan to resettle all 2,000 surviving Banabans on Rambi. The first group arrived on Rambi on 14 December 1945 and in time adapted to their mountainous new home and traded much of their original Micronesian culture for that of the Fijians. They and their descendants live there today.

During the 1960s the Banabans saw the much better deal Nauru was getting from the BPC, mainly through the efforts of Hammer DeRoburt and the "Geelong Boys," who were trapped in Australia during the war and thus received an excellent education and understanding of colonialism.

In 1966 Mr. Tebuke Rotan, a Banaban Methodist minister, journeyed to London on behalf of his people to demand reparations from the British for laying waste to their island, a case that would drag on for nearly 20 bitter years. After some 50 visits to the Foreign and Commonwealth offices, he was offered (and rejected) £80,000 sterling compensation. In 1971 the Banabans sued for damages in the British High Court. After lengthy litigation, the British government in 1977 offered the Banabans a payment of A$10 million in exchange for a pledge that there would be no further legal action.

In 1975 the Banabans asked for their island to be separated from the rest of Kiribati and joined to Fiji, their present country of citizenship. Kiribati politicians, anxious to protect their fisheries zone and wary of the dismemberment of the country, lobbied against this, and the British rejected the proposal. The free entry of Banabans to Banaba was guaranteed in the Kiribati constitution, however. In 1979, Kiribati obtained independence from Britain, and mining on Banaba ended the same year. Finally, in 1981 the Banabans accepted the A$10 million compensation money, plus interest, from the British, though they refused to withdraw their claim to Banaba. The present Kiribati government rejects all further claims from the Banabans, asserting that it's something between them and the British. The British are trying to forget the whole thing.

Some 284 people now practice a subsistence life style on Banaba. There's no airstrip so the only way to get there is on the quarterly supply ship from Tarawa (A$25 deck one-way). Anyone wishing to spend three months on Banaba must obtain advance permission from the Home Affairs Office in Bairiki (Tarawa). No permit is required to visit the island for a few hours while the ship is in port.

Abemama

Abemama ("Island of Moonlight"), just north of the equator 153 km (95 miles) southeast of Tarawa, is a crescent-shaped atoll with a lagoon on its west side. No outlying shoals or reefs skirt the island, and two passages give access to an excellent anchorage. There's good snorkeling here, if you don't mind the company of a few black-tipped sharks.

ABEMAMA

AIRSTRIP

Tabiang

Tanimainiku

Tekatirirake

Kauma

Karekentekabaia

Baretoa

Tabontebike

Binoinano

Kariatebike

Western Passage

Abatiku

Lagoon

Southern Passage

Bike

Tebanga

Manoku

Kabangaki

Kenna

0   5 mi

0   5 km

© MOON PUBLICATIONS, INC.

Transportation on Abemama consists of two large church trucks and a few small private pickups belonging to the Island Council. One of them meets the plane, and you will have no trouble getting a lift. Kariatebike is the government center, with a small hospital, administrative building, police station, and co-op. Causeways have been built linking Kariatebike to the islets south, making it possible to drive all the way to Kabangaki.

Near Tabontebike, north of the Catholic *maneaba,* is the tomb of the tyrant chief Tem Binoka. Robert Louis Stevenson, who lived just north of

Kariatebike for several months in 1889, made Tem Binoka famous (read *In The South Seas*). War relics on Abemama include the airstrip at the north end of the atoll and a wrecked Corsair fighter aircraft set up in front of the hotel.

The **Captain Davis Hotel** (Henry Schutz, all correspondence via P.O. Box 415, Beito, Tarawa, tel. 26-279) offers six well-kept rooms and two family-sized bungalows on the lagoon side of Kariatebike. Facilities include a bar and dining room. Henry can arrange fishing or land tours on and around Abemama and offers airport transfers. Rooms are A\$30 s, A\$60 d with meals.

The Ruubao Lake Hotel on the lagoon side of Baretoa village is in a tranquil setting. A couple of rooms are available for A\$35 per person including three meals.

The Robert Louis Stevenson Hotel has closed.

Traditional dancing is popular and there are groups at most villages. A Chinese shopkeeper has a portable generator with which he runs a projector. He tours the villages, doing the circuit every two weeks or so: 20-50 cents for kung fu and Rambo-style movies.

Air Kiribati flies to Abemama three or four times a week (A\$45), but the flights are often full. After heavy rains the journey from Kariatebike to the airport can be very slow due to potholes and water on the road, so allow extra time when leaving.

Nonouti

The **government rest house** at Matang, four km (2.5 miles) south of the airstrip, faces the ocean and is cooled by the prevailing winds.

beach house on Abemama

JACK D. HADEN

The manager can provide food, if you need it. Nearby are a post office, a couple of small shops, and a local hospital with a nurse. The cooperative store is located at the government wharf at Aubeangai, just south of Matang. One bus, even if running, provides an erratic, unscheduled service the length of the road—two trips each way daily. Most people travel by motor scooter.

Visit Kiribati's largest *maneaba* at Umantewenei village. The Makauro *maneaba* is the oldest on Nonouti; visitors traditionally spent their first night on the island here, though this custom need not be followed today. A monument in the form of a ship at Taboiaki village recalls the arrival of the first Catholic missionaries to Tungaru in 1888. At the north end of the atoll are several small islets, accessible by boat, where large numbers of seabirds nest. Inquire at the council offices for a visit. Kiribati's first president, Ieremia Tabai, hails from Temotu village on Nonouti.

Tabiteuea

This 72-km-long (45-mile-long) island, 296 km (184 miles) southeast of Tarawa, is the longest in Tungaru. The name Tabiteuea ("Forbidden to Kings") was chosen for this island, since it traditionally had no kings. Fences erected around houses delineated private property. Anyone entering without first seeking the owner's permission could be attacked. You can still sees vestiges of this way of life in the well-maintained flower gardens surrounding houses, and in the more evident retention of fences.

In 1881 the population of Tabiteuea South was almost wiped out by an army from Tabiteuea North, organized by a pair of Protestant Hawaiian missionaries wishing to spread their faith by force. Most of the inhabitants of the atoll are now Catholic. Rest houses are at Utiroa, near the airstrip on Tabiteuea North, and at Buariki, near the airstrip on Tabiteuea South. Tabiteuea is known for its dancers.

Onotoa

Onotoa island is named for six giants who created it by throwing stones into the sea. Its houses and *maneaba* are still built on coral slabs. Much land has been reclaimed from the lagoon by building coral walls around an area, and then filling it in with broken shells and coconut husks. There's no causeway to the southernmost islands of the atoll, so you must wade at low tide or borrow a canoe. The postman delivers mail to the southern villages once a week and might give you a lift. The rest house is at Buraitan, seven km (4.5 miles) southeast of the airstrip. The mission truck charges 60 cents for the trip to or from the airstrip if it has already been hired, otherwise A$5 for locals and A$20 for tourists. The stores are poorly stocked. Ask about bingo games at the Catholic mission.

Beru

The bones of Kourabi, a famous 18th-century Beru warrior, hang in a basket in the Buota Maneaba Atianikarawa, with a huge turtle shell suspended above. Once every eight years they are washed in the ocean, and the villagers celebrate a great feast. The London Missionary Society ran its Tungaru mission from this island for many years.

Beru is the only place in Tungaru outside South Tarawa that has electricity. The well-furnished rest house is at Tabukiniberu, a few kilometers northwest of the airstrip. Ships cannot

TABITEUEA

Tabiteuea
North

PACIFIC

Tekabwibwi
Tekaman
Tanaeang
Buota   Terikiai
Eita
Utiroa   AIRSTRIP
Tauma
Kabuna

Tenatorua   Bangai

OCEAN

Aiwa

Tabiteuea
South

South
Tewai   Taungaeaka
Lagoon   AIRSTRIP
Buariki   Nikutoro
West Passage   Katabanga
Taku

0   10 mi
0   10 km

© MOON PUBLICATIONS, INC.

enter the lagoon. Every Tuesday evening an informal get-together at the *maneaba* in Tabukiniberu gives visitors and residents the chance to meet and perhaps learn something from one another. Ask the council clerk about this. It can be profoundly boring if you don't speak Kiribati, however.

Southern Tungaru

The three small islands at the southeast end of the Tungaru group, Nikunau, Tamana, and Arorae, are all without central lagoons. To stay at the rest house in Rungata village on **Nikunau,** see the manager of the co-op. The rest house on **Tamana,** smallest atoll of the Tungaru group, is cooled by sea breezes. The deep *babai* pits, about a 15-minute walk northeast of the government center, are impressive. **Arorae,** 624 km (388 miles) from Tarawa, has a basic rest house opposite the co-op at Taribo, three km (two miles) south of the airstrip. At the northwest tip of Arorae are the Atibu ni Borau, large coral "navigation stones." The ruins of an old village and a cemetery are nearby.

THE PHOENIX ISLANDS

Archaeological remains indicate that some of the Phoenix and Line Islands were once inhabited, probably by Polynesians. By the time the first Europeans arrived, however, these people had died or left. Guano was collected on these islands during the mid-19th century, but the deposits were soon exhausted. Britain annexed the group in 1889, although the United States had a vague claim dating from the guano-collecting era.

In 1937 Phoenix was joined to the Gilbert and Ellice Islands colony, and a year later, to reinforce their claim, the British resettled about a thousand people from overcrowded southern Tungaru on Gardner, Hull, and Sydney. Americans visited Kanton and Enderbury in 1938; in 1939, as their value as stopovers on the trans-Pacific aviation route between Fiji and Honolulu became apparent, the two islands were placed under joint British-American administration for 50 years.

By 1952 the strategic value of the islands had declined, and the colonists were undergoing serious difficulties due to saline well water and droughts. They also suffered from isolation and unrealistic expectations. Some returned to Tungaru, but most were taken to the British Solomon Islands Protectorate, where large numbers live today. By 1964 all the Phoenix islanders had left.

Kanton

Kanton (Canton) is the largest and most northerly of the Phoenix group. The 14-km-long (nine-mile-long) lagoon is surrounded by a narrow triangular strip of land, broken only on the west side. Despite strong currents, large ships can enter the lagoon. The island was named for the New Bedford whaling boat *Kanton,* wrecked here in 1854. The 32 survivors sailed from Kanton to Guam in an open boat, a distance of 2,900 nautical miles. (Captain Bligh's epic open-boat journey from Tonga to Timor totaled 3,618 nautical miles.)

Wildlife on Kanton consists mostly of birds, fish, and rats. Large colonies of white fairy terns and red-footed boobies nest on the atoll. Giant hermit crabs are plentiful all over Kanton and, together with the frigate birds, are useful scavengers. Tiny insect-eating lizards dart through the ruins of the base. A kaleidoscope of tropical

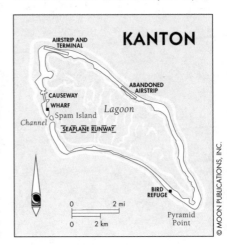

KANTON

AIRSTRIP AND TERMINAL

CAUSEWAY

WHARF

Channel

Spam Island

SEAPLANE RUNWAY

Lagoon

ABANDONED AIRSTRIP

BIRD REFUGE

Pyramid Point

0   2 mi

0   2 km

© MOON PUBLICATIONS, INC.

fish fills the lagoon: triggerfish, damselfish, puffer, parrot fish, sharks, and moray eels.

Pan American Airways used Kanton's lagoon as a stopover for its trans-Pacific seaplanes in the 1930s. In 1938 it built an airstrip on the atoll and cleared the coral heads from a seaplane runway in the lagoon. During World War II, the U.S. Air Force built a new airstrip at the island's northwest end. This was maintained as an emergency landing field until the 1960s when it was abandoned.

A NASA satellite tracking station established in 1965 closed in 1967, when the island passed to the U.S. Air Force. The unused facilities stand intact on Kanton, taken care of by an I-Kiribati family. An American-built wharf on Kanton is capable of handling large freighters. The United States has turned these abandoned facilities over to the Kiribati government.

In 1990 the government installed firefighting equipment and refueling capacity beside Kanton's airstrip to provide emergency landing facilities for flights between Tarawa and Christmas Island. There are no scheduled flights, but Shipping Corporation of Kiribati ships sometimes call on their way to Christmas Island every three months. On the return voyage the ship will bypass Kanton unless there's enough cargo or passengers to be picked up. Ask about this before disembarking or be prepared to pay a substantial "diversion fee" if the ship is forced to return only to evacuate you.

THE LINE ISLANDS

The five central and southern Line Islands, worked for guano over a century ago, are now uninhabited. None of the five (Malden, Starbuck, Caroline, Vostok, and Flint) has a safe anchorage, although landings have been blasted through the reefs at Starbuck and Flint, and an airstrip was built on Malden in 1958 as part of a nuclear testing program.

Plantation workers live on the three northern Line islands: Fanning, Washington, and Christmas. In 1983 the Kiribati government purchased the coconut plantations on Fanning and Washington from the Australian trading company Burns Philp, and leased them to the former employees, who produce copra for their cooperative on individual tracts.

The extremely isolated nature of these islands has created serious transportation and administrative problems for the government, yet a major resettlement program in the Line Islands to relieve the overcrowding on South Tarawa is underway. The deep seabed around the Line Islands contains some of the richest deposits of cobalt, nickel, platinum, and manganese in the world.

WASHINGTON

Washington is an oval-shaped island about seven km (four miles) long, with a large, Rep. of Kiribati freshwater lake surrounded by peat bogs on its eastern side. Washington is the wettest of the Kiribati Line Islands, and after heavy rains the lake drains into the sea through a sluice. Coconut palms cover the island, with pandanus in the damper areas. Taro and breadfruit do well on Washington, providing a steady food source. Tangkore and Nanounou villages are at Washington's west end. Landing can be difficult due to strong currents and heavy surf.

A 1,000-meter (3,281-foot) runway made from compressed coral reef mud was completed during 1994, and Air Kiribati has commenced commercial flights using a small propeller aircraft once a week from Christmas Island.

FANNING

Fanning is also known as Tabuaeran, a corruption of a Polynesian name meaning "sacred footprint." It is an 18- by 11-km (11- by seven-mile) atoll, 286 km (178 miles) northwest of Christmas Island and 141 km (88 miles) southeast of Washington. Three channels lead into the wide lagoon. In 1798 Capt. Edmund Fanning reached the island, 3,020 km (1,875 miles) east of Tarawa. It was once the mid-ocean station of the undersea cable running from Fiji to Vancouver, which is now closed. Most of the land area is planted with coconuts. The number of seabirds nesting here is limited due to the activities of feral cats. The main village, English Harbor, is on the southwest side of the island.

Since completion of the new runway in June 1994, Air Kiribati flights on propeller planes now link Fanning to Washington and Christmas once a week.

Visiting yachts are charged A$3 a day to anchor at English Harbor in the Fanning lagoon. The Shipping Corporation of Kiribati runs a supply boat to Fanning three times a year. One-way deck fares are A$17 from Christmas, A$116 from Tarawa, double fare for a B-class cabin, triple for A class.

FANNING

PACIFIC OCEAN

North Cape

Whaler Anchorage

English Harbor

Lagoon

AIRSTRIP   Grieg Point

0   5 mi
0   5 km

© MOON PUBLICATIONS, INC.

CHRISTMAS ISLAND

This large island, 2,110 km (1,310 miles) southeast of Honolulu, 2,715 km (1,690 miles) north of Tahiti, and 3,220 km (2,000 miles) east of Tarawa, accounts for nearly half the land area of Kiribati. Deserted beaches surround the 160-km (100-mile) perimeter, with many small lakes in the interior. The huge tidal lagoon on the island's west side covers 160 square km (62 square miles). Christmas's southeast "panhandle" has no palm trees, only bushes, and many seabirds.

Captain Cook reached the island on Christmas Day 1777; the British annexed it in 1888. (Another Christmas Island, a dependency of Australia, is in the Indian Ocean.) To the locals, it's known as **Kiritimati,** the Kiribati spelling of Christmas.

During World War II the United States built the airport on Christmas to refuel planes flying southwest toward Australia. From 1956 to 1962 the United States and Britain tested nuclear weapons in the atmosphere at Christmas and Malden Islands. The British tested their first hydrogen bomb at Malden on 15 May 1957; over the following 15 months they exploded six more, plus two atomic bombs. The British tests blinded millions of seabirds and exposed some 20,000 British servicemen to cancer and other radiation-related diseases.

The 1,265 present inhabitants are mostly indentured I-Kiribati laborers employed on the government copra plantation. They live in three villages: London, Banana, and Poland; Paris village has been abandoned. The roads on Christmas date from the testing period, while the airstrip was built during World War II. Ships must anchor off Cook Island; only small punts can enter the lagoon. There's a small wharf at London.

Sights
Large colonies of 18 species of rare migratory seabirds, all quite tame, nest on Cook Island and

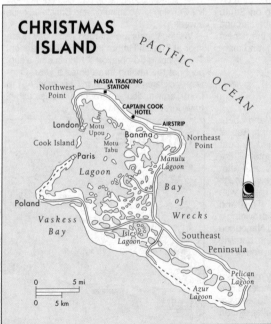

Motu Tabu. Christmas Island has the world's largest known colony of sooty terns; the eight million birds nest here in June and December. Other tame birds nesting on the ground at camera level include noddies, fairy terns, boobies, tropic birds, frigate birds, wedgetailed shearwaters, and petrels. The seabirds have breeding seasons spread throughout the year, though the best months to visit are March-July and October-December. It's illegal to hunt them, and possession of birds, nests, eggs, and even feathers is prohibited.

The island swarms with scavenging land crabs and the reefs teem with fish. Christmas Island is famous for sportfishing, particularly for the **Pacific bonefish** found on the coral flats of the shallow interior lagoon. Anglers wade out watching for a bonefish, then cast their fly toward it and experience the fight of their lives. Gray sharks are numerous along the drop-off. Beyond the reef papio, ulua, waho, marlin, stingrays, and lobster are abundant.

The lee shore between Northwest Point and London is the safest scuba diving or snorkeling area. It can be dangerous fighting your way through the pounding surf, but the coral "canyons" (surge channels through the reef) teem with fish. You can combine a little snorkeling with your visit to the bird sanctuary on Cook Island.

At the north end of the island, the National Space Development Agency of Japan (NASDA) has a downrange **satellite tracking station**, which controls satellites launched from Tanegashima, Japan, during the early stages of orbit.

Practicalities

Opened in 1994, the **Kirimati Hotel** (tel. 81-225, fax 31-316) offers a small number of rooms for A$40 to A$50, or A$65 to A$75 meals included (fixed menu European or Chinese cuisine). Motor vehicle hire can be arranged for around A$60 per day or a boat for A$50 per day.

The 36-room **Captain Cook Hotel** (Boitabu Smith, tel. 81-238, fax 81-230), four km (2.5 miles) northwest of the airstrip, has 12 air conditioned rooms. Formerly a Royal Air Force officers' quarters, its architecture and rates would not be out of place beside a motorway in Britain. All rooms have twin beds and private bath. Standard rooms are A$70 s or A$100 d. Air conditioned rooms are A$84 s, A$114 d. Fairly expensive American-style food and local fresh fish are served in the dining room. The bar is open every evening, and Monday is Island Night with typical food cooked in an *umu* (underground oven). Kiribati dance shows are arranged if a large enough group is present.

Camping on the island is prohibited.

There are plantation stores in all the villages, plus a hospital in London. A large map of the island is available from the Land Development Officer.

Getting There

Christmas Island is proof that there are still places for which it can be said, "You can't get there from here." As of early 1996, there was no regular airline service from Christmas to Tungaru, or for that matter, to any international destination. From time to time charter flights using Air Marshall Islands airplanes operate out of Honolulu with package tours. In the past, Air Marshall Islands provided regular service from Honolulu to Christmas. Current information should be available from the Consul of Kiribati in Honolulu. Contact Mr. William E. Paupe (tel. 808-521-7703, fax 808-521-8304), but be aware he can be difficult to reach.

Fishing tours to Christmas Island are offered by **Fish and Game Frontiers** (P.O. Box 959, Wexford, PA 15090, tel. 412-935-1577, fax 412-935-5388).

Kiribati's newest interisland container ship, the *Nei Matangare,* operated by Kiribati Shipping Services, serves Christmas from Tarawa at least once every two months to pick up copra. Cabins are often booked in advance.

Getting Around

To avoid disturbing breeding birds, access to some seabird areas is restricted. For example, Northwest Point, the area on the ocean side of the road between NASDA and London, is a bird sanctuary, and entry is prohibited unless accompanied by a wildlife warden. Escorted boat tours to the accessible reserves, including Cook Island and Motu Tabu, can be arranged through your hotel.

Other breeding areas can be reached in a rental Isuzu pickup truck (A$75 a day, A$450 a week, plus gas), available through the Captain Cook Hotel or from **J.M.B. Enterprises** nearby. Your overseas driver's license will be accepted. Motor scooters are sometimes available. Some of the vehicles are of dubious dependability, and traveling any distance with them is risky. However, J.M.B. also has some newer pickups for hire. Don't drive a vehicle onto the coral flats. It may sink in and damage the reef.

GORDY OHLIGER

AMERICAN POSSESSIONS

The United States government holds as possessions a number of scattered islands and atolls on Micronesia's northeast fringe. Although they cannot be visited by tourists, they are included here due to their historical and geographical links to the rest of the region. Midway atoll is geologically part of the Hawaiian chain, although it's not part of the State of Hawaii. Johnston and Wake atolls are stepping-stones to the Marshalls. Kingman Reef, Palmyra atoll, and Jarvis Island are part of the Line Islands (the rest of which are included in the Republic of Kiribati). Howland and Baker are just northwest of Kiribati's Phoenix Islands.

Originally uninhabited, many of these islands came under United States sovereignty about the same time as Hawaii and Guam (1898). They were not considered important until 1935, when they began to be used as aviation stopovers and military bases. Today they are administered by a number of different federal agencies. Howland, Baker, and Jarvis as well as Johnston form the **Pacific Islands National Wildlife Refuge** (P.O. Box 50167, Honolulu, HI 96850, tel. 808-541-1201). Entry to the refuge is restricted to scientists and educators, who must obtain a permit from the Refuge Manager prior to landing.

There have been periodic attempts to incorporate Baker, Howland, Jarvis, Kingman, Midway, and Palmyra into the State of Hawaii and annex Wake to Guam. To date, nothing has come of these proposals.

MIDWAY

Near the northwest end of the Hawaiian chain, 1,469 miles from Oahu, Midway measures two square miles. The 15-mile-long barrier reef around this circular atoll encloses two small islands, Sand and Eastern. The atoll is midway between California and Japan, hence the name. Captain N.C. Brooks of the Hawaiian ship *Gambia* arrived in 1859, and the United States annexed the atoll in 1867. In 1903 it became a station on a submarine cable that is no longer used. Since then it has been controlled by the U.S. Navy, under the command of Barbers Point Naval Air Station, Hawaii.

Pan Am China Clippers began refueling here in 1935. Soil was shipped in from Guam, and

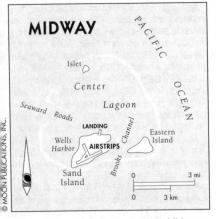

Norfolk pines were planted, giving Midway a manicured, military look. Pan Am's hotel is still standing, although dilapidated.

In 1941, the United States completed an important submarine base. The Battle of Midway took place early in June 1942, marking a turning point of World War II. In a massive sea battle, the United States halted Japan's eastward expansion. During the Vietnam War, Midway again became an important naval air station with several thousand residents. After 1978 the population fell sharply.

Hundreds of thousands of gooney birds (Laysan albatrosses) live on Sand, protected in a national wildlife refuge. As an experiment a few albatross were flown blindfolded to Alaska, San Francisco, Los Angeles, Australia, and other points. (There have been persistent reports that some of the birds may have peeked). Upon release, they flew back to Midway within 10 days.

Naturalists may visit Midway after obtaining naval security clearance; write: Officer in Charge, Naval Air Facility Midway Island, FPO San Francisco, CA 96516-1200, tel. (808) 421-6000.

Radio station KMTH 94 FM broadcasts 24 hours a day.

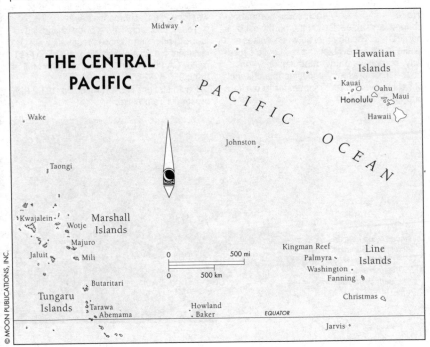

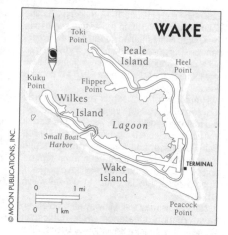

© MOON PUBLICATIONS, INC.

WAKE

Wake (Enenkio) is located between Guam and Midway, 750 miles north of Kwajalein. The three islands of this 2.5-square-mile atoll—Wilkes, Wake, and Peale—enclose a horseshoe-shaped lagoon, sealed on the northwest by a barrier reef. The channel between Wilkes and Wake islands, now blocked by a solid causeway, once gave entry to the lagoon. A small-boat harbor presently occupies this channel, but ships over 66 feet must moor to offshore buoys.

Although Enenkio traditionally probably had no permanent population, Marshallese navigators visited to hunt sea turtles and birds. Sighted by the Spaniard Mendana in 1568, Wake is nevertheless named for the British sea captain William Wake, who arrived in 1796. In 1840 the atoll was charted by Capt. Charles Wilkes of the United States Exploring Expedition; Peale Island was named for the expedition's naturalist. The Republic of the Marshall Islands claims the atoll, though the United States is unlikely to give it up.

The United States annexed Wake in 1898 for use as a cable station. A Pan American Airways refueling base and 48-room transit hotel opened on Peale in 1935.

At the outbreak of World War II, 1,200 civilian workers were on Wake, completing a major air and submarine base. On 11 December 1941 the construction workers and 523 marines repelled a Japanese invasion, but on 23 December, Japanese troops from Kwajalein landed in force. The Japanese forces took the surviving Americans to POW camps in China and Japan. The Japanese held Wake until the end of the war for use as a submarine base.

Today, civil aircraft are allowed to land and refuel, but prior permission is required; write Detachment 4, 15th Air Base Wing, APO San Francisco, CA 96501-5000, or call William Mull at (205) 955-5932.

Radio stations KEAD (1485 AM, 101.2 FM) broadcast from Wake.

smoke rising from an American installation on Midway, hit by Japanese aircraft in early June 1942

NATIONAL ARCHIVES, WASHINGTON, D.C.

A Pan American Airways Martin M-130 at Wake in 1936, the year Pan Am started trans-Pacific passenger service. The first airmail flight from San Francisco to Manila passed through a year earlier.

PAN AM

JOHNSTON

Johnston atoll, 828 miles southwest of Honolulu, is 12 miles around. Its four islets, Johnston, Sand, Akau (North), and Hikina (East), now total 1.1 square miles, increased from its natural state by dredging during the 1960s. Crew members of the brig *Sally* of Boston sighted this island in 1796. Charles James Johnston, captain of HMS *Cornwallis,* landed in 1807. In 1856 Johnston Island was claimed by both the United States and the Kingdom of Hawaii (which called it Kalama Island). That year, an American company began to extract guano. In 1934 the United States Navy as-

sumed jurisdiction of the atoll. Jurisdiction was transferred to the U.S. Air Force in 1948.

Since then, the United States military has converted this formerly idyllic atoll into one of the most toxic places on the planet, first by nuclear testing then by storing tons of mustard gas, nerve gas, and other chemical warfare weapons. The United States developed plans to use Johnston Island as a site to destroy obsolete chemical weapons. Pacific nations, fearing the potential for a mid-Pacific Ocean disaster, vigorously oppose this plan.

Since 1973, Johnston has been run for the Defense Nuclear Agency (DNA) by a U.S.A.F. lieutenant colonel, Commander, Johnston Island (address: Johnston Atoll, Field Command, APO San Francisco, CA 96305-5000). Overall command is exercised from Kirtland Air Force Base in New Mexico (NM 87115-5000, tel. 505-864-0011). The population consists of about 300 enlisted and 1,000 civilian employees. All personnel are required to have gas masks ready. All temporary guests are also issued masks and instructed in their use. Personnel on "J.I." have been known to go "island happy" and are often sent to Honolulu for "stress seminars."

Although some Continental Air Micronesia flights between Honolulu and Majuro touch down on Johnston, nonmilitary passengers are not permitted to disembark. It is virtually impossible for anyone without business to get permission to visit Johnston Island. This is not much of a problem because almost no one wants to.

JOHNSTON

Akau
Turning Basin · Hikina
Sand
AIRFIELD Johnston
Main Channel
West Channel

0   2.5 mi

0   2.5 km

© MOON PUBLICATIONS, INC.

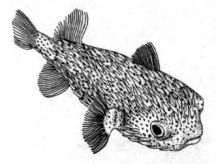

The dozens of sharp spines on the body of the porcupine fish (Diodon holacanthus) *make it almost inedible.*

KINGMAN

Kingman Reef, between Hawaii and Samoa, is a triangular-shaped atoll, the apex of which points northward. On the east side is a barren speck of sand about 130 feet long and only three feet above the high tide mark. This low profile makes the atoll a navigational hazard. An American, Captain Fanning, found Kingman Reef in 1798, but it is named for Captain Kingman, who visited in 1853. The United States annexed the reef in 1922, and in 1934 turned it over to the navy, which retains jurisdiction. Pan

Am China Clippers bound for New Zealand touched down in the lagoon from 1937 to 1938. Today the Kingman lagoon is abandoned.

Just 156 miles northwest of Kingman, within the United States Exclusive Economic Zone, is an extinct undersea volcano covered by a three-quarter-inch-thick manganese crust containing 2.5% cobalt, the richest deposit of its kind ever found. Other rich nickel and platinum deposits lie on the seabed near the Line Islands at depths up to 6,500 feet.

DIANA LASICH HARPER

PALMYRA

Palmyra atoll, 33 miles southeast of Kingman Reef, is at the north end of the Line Islands, 1,056 miles south of Honolulu. Dredging has been used to increase the acreage of the atoll's 50 tiny reef islets from 500 to 3,000 acres. The barrier reef encloses three distinct lagoons known as West, Center, and East. West Lagoon provides large anchorage areas and can be entered through a narrow dredged channel on the southwest side of the atoll, adjacent to Sand Island. A dredged seaplane landing area connects the West and Center lagoons.

Fish caught at Palmyra are often poisonous. Several years ago scientists in Tahiti determined that the cause of ciguatera (fish poisoning) is a microalgae called dinoflagellate. Nor-

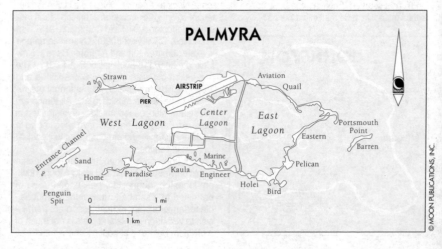

PALMYRA

© MOON PUBLICATIONS, INC.

mally this algae is found only in the ocean depths. When a reef is disturbed, as happened at Palmyra during World War II, the algae can multiply dramatically and enter the food chain.

Captain Sawle of the American ship *Palmyra* reached the atoll in 1802. It's rumored that Spanish pirates from Peru left buried treasure in 1816. Since the Kingdom of Hawaii claimed the atoll in 1862, the United States annexed it by annexing Hawaii. In 1911 Judge Cooper of Honolulu acquired title to Palmyra, which he used as a coconut plantation. Before his death in 1929 the judge sold all but Home Island to the Fullard-Leo family of Honolulu. During World War II Palmyra had a 6,000-man naval air station, becoming an important link in the aerial supply route to Kanton and Bora Bora in the South Pacific. The navy transformed the atoll, dredging the lagoon for a harbor and seaplane landing area while building an 6,000-foot coral airstrip on Cooper Island and connecting most of the islets by causeway. The sea has now severed the connecting causeways in several places.

In July 1990 Honolulu realtor Peter Savio (Suite 202, 931 University Ave., Honolulu, HI 96826, tel. 808-942-7701) leased Palmyra from the Fullard-Leo family. Plans to build "an away from it all resort" seem to have stalled. Cruising

yachts on their way from Hawaii to the South Pacific have long called here, though Mr. Savio now requires yachties to obtain advance permission. The island's huge wartime rainwater catch basin is usually full.

HOWLAND

Howland Island, 719 miles east of Tarawa, is only 385 acres in area. Pigweed and a few scrawny *kou* trees survive on this dry, flat island, 1.5 miles long, 2,928 feet wide, and nowhere over 15 feet high. There's no anchorage, but in emergencies small boats can land on the west side beach.

In 1937 three dirt airstrips were constructed so that Howland could be used as a refueling stop for Amelia Earhart and Fred Noonan on their around the world flight. They left Lae, New Guinea, on 2 July 1937, never to be seen again. A lighthouse (actually a day beacon painted with red and white stripes) called **Earhart Light** in memory of the aviator was constructed a year after the loss, some 500 feet inland on the western side of the island.

Just after Pearl Harbor, two colonists were killed during attacks on undefended Howland

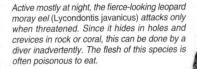

Active mostly at night, the fierce-looking leopard moray eel (Lycondontis javanicus) attacks only when threatened. Since it hides in holes and crevices in rock or coral, this can be done by a diver inadvertently. The flesh of this species is often poisonous to eat.

DIANA LASICH HARPER

by Japanese submarines and Kawanishi flying boats from the Marshalls. Although the Japanese didn't land, the remaining colonists were evacuated and the island abandoned for the duration of the war. In 1974 Howland, Baker, and Jarvis were placed under the supervision of U.S. Fish and Wildlife Service. The only inhabitants today are reptiles, crustaceans, green and hawksbill turtles, and millions of birds.

BAKER

Baker Island, just north of the equator, 36 miles southeast of Howland, is a flat, oval 320-acre island. Scattered herbs, grass, and low shrubs grace this hot, dry island. A 2,000-foot-long sandy beach runs along the southwest side, but Baker has no lagoon or anchorage. Feral cats were eradicated on Baker in 1964, and nesting brown noddies are now undisturbed.

In 1839 Capt. Michael Baker of the New Bedford whaler *Gideon Howland* discovered guano on the island while burying one of his crew and claimed the island for himself and the United States. The American Guano Company later

bought his rights and worked the deposits from 1859 to 1878; from 1886 to 1891 a British firm carried on the work. In 1935 American colonists landed and founded Meyerton to reassert the United States claim, but Japanese air raids following Pearl Harbor prompted their removal in early 1942.

JARVIS

Jarvis Island is located just below the equator, 250 miles southwest of Christmas Island. This saucer-shaped island of coral and sand is only 1.7 square miles in size and has no lagoon. The beaches slope steeply to a 20-foot-high ridge, which entirely surrounds the flat interior. Due to little rainfall, only sparse bunchgrass, prostrate vines, and low shrubs grow. Boat channels cut through the reef on the west and southwest sides of the island lead to landings, but there's no anchorage.

Captain Brown of the English ship *Eliza Francis* spotted Jarvis in 1821. The island has had many names: Brock, Brook, Bunker, Jarvis, and Volunteer. The American Guano Company dug guano from 1858 to 1879. Britain annexed Jarvis in 1889 and leased the island to a London and Melbourne guano company in 1906. Little was extracted and poor-grade deposits remain on the island today. In 1935 the United States landed colonists on Jarvis, who founded Millerville and erected a monument to make a point of the change in ownership. The British did not respond and the island remains in American hands today, uninhabited.

BOOKLIST

DESCRIPTION AND TRAVEL

Ashby, Gene. *Pohnpei: An Island Argosy*. Pohnpei: Rainy Day Press, 1993 (P.O. Box 574, Kolonia, Pohnpei, FM 96941 A comprehensive summary of the history, flora and fauna, culture, and attractions of Pohnpei. The numerous maps, illustrations, and complete subject index make this a very handy book.

Barbour, Nancy. *Palau*. San Francisco: Full Court Press, 1995. A wonderful, richly illustrated description of Palau's natural and cultural history.

Christian, F.W. *The Caroline Islands*. London: Frank Cass & Co., 1967. Christian's detailed account of his journey through Micronesia in 1896, when Spanish colonial rule was still in place.

Dawood, Richard. *Travellers' Health*. Oxford: Oxford University Press, 1989. Useful information on health risks for travelers abroad.

Evans, Julian. *Transit of Venus—Travels in the Pacific*. London: Secker and Warrburg, 1992. Colorful discussion of the underlying concerns of various islands.

Grimble, Sir Arthur. *A Pattern of Islands*. London: John Murray, 1952. Grimble served as British resident commissioner in the Gilberts 1926-32 and left behind this classic narrative of Kiribati life as he observed it during his first six years there (1914-20). In the U.S. the same book was published as *We Chose the Islands*. A sequel, *Return to the Islands,* dating from his second tour of duty, appeared in 1957.

Hinz, Earl R. *Landfalls of Paradise: The Guide to Pacific Islands*. Ventura, CA: Western Marine Enterprises, 1980. The only genuine cruising guide to all 32 island groups of Oceania.

Kahn, E.J., Jr. *A Reporter in Micronesia*. New York: Norton, 1966. An account of Kahn's travels through the region before the arrival of jet aircraft.

Kluge, P.F. *The Edge of Paradise: America in Micronesia*. New York: Random House, 1991. Kluge's long association with the region began with the Peace Corps and continued as speechwriter for Lazarus Salii, Palau's second president. This sweeping survey, bursting with vignettes of island players and politicians, is a full-length feature portrait of the place.

Lewis, David. *We, the Navigators*. Honolulu: University of Hawaii Press, 1972. A definitive work on the ancient art of landfinding as practiced by Micronesians.

Nakano, Ann. *Broken Canoe: Conversations & Observations in Micronesia*. St. Lucia, Queensland: Queensland University Press, 1984. A traveler's tale of Micronesia as it was a decade ago.

Price, Willard. *Pacific Adventure*. New York: John Day, 1936. A rare eyewitness account of Micronesia during the Japanese period. An updated abridgment of the same book appeared in 1944 under the title *Japan's Islands of Mystery,* then again in 1966 as *America's Paradise Lost: The Strange Story of the Secret Atolls.*

Rock, Tim. *Diving and Snorkeling Guide*. Houston: Pisces Books, 1994. Beautiful guides for Palau, Guam, and Yap, and Chuuk lagoon. Must-have book for divers.

Segal, Harvey Gordon. *Kosrae: The Sleeping Lady Awakens*. Kosrae: Kosrae Tourist Division, 1989. A 382-page compilation of all kinds of hard-to-obtain background information about the island.

Stanley, David. *South Pacific Handbook.* Chico, CA: Moon Publications, 1996. Covers the South Pacific in the same manner as the book you're reading. *Fiji Islands Handbook* and *Tahiti-Polynesia Handbook* are also by the same author.

Stewart, William H. *Business Reference Guide to the Commonwealth of the Northern Marianas Islands.* James H. Grizzard, P.O. Box 330 CHRB, Saipan, MP 96950. An economic atlas including 90 maps and 50 charts.

GEOGRAPHY

Coulter, John Wesley. *The Pacific Dependencies of the United States.* New York: MacMillan, 1957. A comprehensive, though dated, geography of Micronesia.

Couper, Alastair, ed. *The Times Atlas of the Oceans.* New York: Van Nostrand Reinhold, 1983. A superb study of the oceans of the world in their contemporary context.

Freeman, Otis W., ed. *Geography of the Pacific.* New York: John Wiley, 1951. Although somewhat dated, this book provides a wealth of background information on the islands.

Karolle, Bruce G. *Atlas of Micronesia, Second Edition.* Honolulu: Bess Press, 1993. A basic reference emphasizing the natural, manmade, and human resources of the Marianas, Carolines, and Marshall Islands.

Oliver, Douglas L. *The Pacific Islands.* Honolulu: University of Hawaii Press, 1989. Updated edition of the important 1951 study of the history and economies of the entire Pacific.

Ridgell, Reilly. *Pacific Nations and Territories.* Honolulu: Bess Press, 1988. One of the few high school geography texts to the region. Bess Press also publishes Bruce G. Karolle's *Atlas of Micronesia.*

NATURAL SCIENCES

Amesbury, Steven S., and Robert F. Myers. *Guide to the Coastal Resources of Guam: The Fishes.* Guam: University of Guam Press,

1982. A comprehensive, profusely illustrated handbook, useful to laypeople and specialists. Unfortunately, a matching volume, *The Corals,* is less comprehensible, as only scientific terminology is used.

Brower, Kenneth. *With Their Islands Around Them.* New York, Chicago, San Francisco: Holt, Rinehart & Winston, 1974. A 216-page discussion of efforts to protect Palau's fragile ecosystem.

DeLuca, Charles J., and Diana MacIntyre DeLuca. *Pacific Marine Life: A Survey of Pacific Ocean Invertebrates.* Rutland, VT: Charles E. Tuttle Co., 1976. An informative 82-page pamphlet.

Engbring, John. *Field Guide to the Birds of Palau.* Illustrated by Takesi Suzuki. Koror: Conservation Office, 1988.

Engbring, John, and Peter Pyle. *Checklist of the Birds of Micronesia.* Hawaii Audubon Society (1088 Bishop St., Suite 808, Honolulu, HI 96813, tel. 808-528-1432, fax 808-537-5294); $2. This excellent six-page publication lists both the scientific and common names of 244 species. A detailed bibliography and precise sighting information are provided. Hawaii Audubon also sells a *Checklist of the Birds of the Mariana Islands* (also $2).

Hargreaves, Bob, and Dorothy Hargreaves. *Tropical Blossoms of the Pacific.* Ross-Hargreaves (P.O. Box 11897, Lahaina, HI 96761). A handy 64-page booklet with color photos to assist in identification; a matching volume is titled *Tropical Trees of the Pacific.*

Hinton, A.G. *Shells of New Guinea and the Central Indo-Pacific.* Australia: Jacaranda Press, 1972. A photo guide to shell identification.

Lotz, Bev, and Dave Lotz. *Making Tracks in the Mariana Islands: A Guide to the Hiking Trails.* Guam: Marine Images, 1992. Useful guide for hikers in Saipan, Tinian, Rota, and Guam.

Martini, Frederic. *Exploring Tropical Isles and Seas.* Englewood Cliffs, NJ: Prentice-Hall, 1984. A fine introduction to the natural environment of the islands.

Mayr, Ernst. *Birds of the Southwest Pacific*. Rutland, VT: Charles E. Tuttle Co., 1978. A reprint of the 1945 edition.

Merrill, Elmer D. *Plant Life of the Pacific World*. Rutland, VT: Charles E. Tuttle Co., 1981. First published in 1945, this handy volume is a useful first reference in a field very poorly covered.

Mitchell, Andrew W. *A Fragile Paradise: Man and Nature in the Pacific*. London: Fontana, 1990. Published in the U.S. by the University of Texas Press under the title *The Fragile South Pacific: An Ecological Odyssey*. Andrew Mitchell, an Earthwatch Europe deputy director, utters a heartfelt plea on behalf of all endangered Pacific wildlife in this brilliant book. Micronesia is only briefly touched.

Myers, Robert F. *Micronesian Reef Fishes*. Coral Graphics, P.O. Box 21153, GMF, Guam 96921; $33 softcover. Three hundred pages of beautiful photos and thorough information on identification of coral reef fishes; new second edition. An absolute must for snorkelers and divers.

Nelson, Bryan. *Seabirds: Their Biology and Ecology*. New York: A & W Publishers, 1979. A fully illustrated manual.

Pratt, Douglas. *A Field Guide to the Birds of Hawaii and the Tropical Pacific*. Princeton, NJ: Princeton University Press, 1986. The best of its kind; essential reading for birders.

Tinker, Spencer Wilkie. *Fishes of Hawaii: A Handbook of the Marine Fishes of Hawaii and the Central Pacific Ocean*. Hawaiian Service, Inc. (P.O. Box 2835, Honolulu, HI 96803). A comprehensive, indexed reference work; $30.

HISTORY

Brower, Kenneth. *A Song for Satawal*. New York: Penguin Books, 1984. Discussion of three islanders, one each from Yap, Satawal, and Palau, and their efforts to preserve their cultures.

Burdick, Eugene. *The Blue of Capricorn*. Honolulu: Mutual Publishing, 1986. Chapter three, "The Puzzle of the Ninety-eight," describes the fate of 98 Americans imprisoned by the Japanese on Wake Island during WW II.

Carano, Paul, and Pedro C. Sanchez. *A Complete History of Guam*. Rutland, VT: Charles E. Tuttle, 1964. Comprehensive history, particularly important discussion of Spanish colonial rule in Guam.

Farrell, Don A. *The Pictoral History of Guam: 1898-1918*. Tamuning, Guam: Micronesian Productions, 1981. Discussion of the Americanization of Guam.

Gailey, Harry A. *Peleliu: 1944*. Annapolis, MA: Nautical & Aviation Publishing Company of America, 1983. This work discusses the bloody and costly U.S. invasion of the island of Peleliu in Palau.

Hezel, Rev. Francis X. *The First Taint of Civilization*. Honolulu: University of Hawaii Press, 1983. A History of the Caroline and Marshall Islands in precolonial days, 1521-1885.

Hezel, Rev. Francis X., and M.L. Berg, eds. *Micronesia: Winds of Change*. Saipan: Omnibus Social Studies Program of the Trust Territory, 1980. A huge book of readings on Micronesian history intended as a textbook for social studies and cultural heritage courses.

Grimble, Arthur. *Return to the Islands*. London: John Murray, 1970. Reprinted ed. A former British colonial officer discusses his deep affection for the Gilbert Islands and for colonial duty.

Kiribati: Aspects of History. Suva, Fiji: Institute of Pacific Studies, 1984. A collection of papers by 25 I-Kiribati writers.

Labby, David. *The Demystification of Yap: Dialects of Culture on a Micronesian Island*. Chicago: University of Chicago Press, 1976. Comprehensive work on the symbolic cultural significance of land.

Lavesque, Rodrigue. *History of Micronesia.* Honolulu: University of Hawaii Press, 1993. Two-volume historical resource book.

Lessa, William A. *Drake's Island of Thieves: Ethnological Sleuthing.* Honolulu: University of Hawaii Press, 1975. A fascinating examination of Drake's 1579 visit to Micronesia aboard the *Golden Hinde.*

Meller, Norman. *Constitutionalism in Micronesia.* Honolulu: University of Hawaii Press, 1986. An account of the factors that led to the fragmentation of the Trust Territory of the Pacific Islands.

Nevin, David. *The American Touch in Micronesia.* New York: W.W. Norton, 1977. A story of power, money, and the corruption of a Pacific paradise. Nevin provides good documentation on the U.S. educational system in Micronesia.

Nufer, Harold. *Micronesia Under American Rule: An Evaluation of the Strategic Trusteeship (1947-1977).* Hicksville, NY: Exposition Press, 1978. Includes interviews with Micronesians about WW II.

Oliver, Douglas L. *The Pacific Islands.* Honolulu: University of Hawaii Press, 1989. A new edition of the classic 1951 study of the history and economies of the entire Pacific area.

Oliver, Douglas L. *Native Cultures of the Pacific Islands.* Honolulu: University of Hawaii Press, 1988. A text for college level courses on the precontact societies of Oceania.

Parmentier, Richard J. *The Sacred Remains.* Chicago: University of Chicago Press, 1987. Myth, history, and society in Palau.

Peacock, Daniel J. *Lee Boo of Belau.* Honolulu: University of Hawaii Press, 1987. The story of a 20-year-old island prince taken to London by an English sea captain in 1784.

Peattie, Mark R. *Nan'yo.* Honolulu: University of Hawaii Press, 1988. The rise and fall of the Japanese in Micronesia, 1885-1945.

Prange, Gordon W. with Donald M. Goldstein, Katherine V. Dillon. *Miracle at Midway.* New York: McGraw-Hill, 1982. Account of the decisive battle of Midway during World War II.

Rogers, Robert F. *Destiny's Landfall.* Honolulu: University of Hawaii Press, 1995. Although dealing only with Guam, also an extraordinary discussion of the process of conquest and colonization.

Sanchez, Pedro C. *Guahan: The History of Our Island.* Guam: Sanchez Publishing, 1989. "Doc" Sanchez's *Complete History of Guam,* a primary source for over two decades, was updated in this well-illustrated new volume.

Sherry, Frank. *Pacific Passions: The European Struggle for Power in the Great Ocean in the Age of Exploration.* New York: William Morrow & Co, 1994. Thorough discussion of European explorers in the Pacific, although not very much on Micronesia in particular.

Stevensen, Robert Louis. *In the South Seas.* The writer's cultural observations during his travels through the Marquesas, Tuamotus, and Gilbert Islands between 1888-90.

Stewart, William H. *Ghost Fleet of the Truk Lagoon.* Contains 60 photos and maps of the February 1944 bombings, plus considerable general information on Chuuk. Other similarly well-illustrated books from Pictorial Histories Publishing Co. (713 South Third West, Missoula, MT 59801) include *A Glorious Page In Our History,* about the 1942 battle of Midway, and *Amelia Earhart: What Really Happened at Howland.*

Tetens, Capt. Alfred. *Among the Savages of the South Seas: Memoirs of Micronesia, 1862-1868.* Stanford: Stanford University Press, 1958. The account of a German sea captain in Palau and Yap.

White, Geoffry M., and Lamont Lindstrom, eds. *The Pacific Theater: Island Representations of World War II.* Pacific Islands Monograph Series, No. 8. Honolulu: University of Hawaii Press, 1989. An outstanding portrayal of what the war meant to the indigenous peoples of the Pacific.

PACIFIC ISSUES

Bradley, David, with a foreword by Jerome B. Wiesner. *No Place to Hide 1946/1984.* Hanover, NH: University Press of New England, 1983. A key book in the development of the antinuclear movement, written by a physician assigned to the Bikini atoll bomb tests.

Dibblin, Jane. *Day of Two Suns: U.S. Nuclear Testing and the Pacific Islanders.* New York: New Amsterdam Books, 1990. Dibblin links human rights and nuclear disarmament in this provocative review of American military activities past and present in the Marshall Islands.

Firth, Stewart. *Nuclear Playground.* Honolulu: University of Hawaii Press, 1987. The story of the nuclear age in the Pacific.

Johnson, Giff. *Collision Course at Kwajalein: Marshall Islanders in the Shadow of the Bomb.* Honolulu: Pacific Concerns Resource Center, 1984. Though dated, this referenced study continues to provide useful background information on the effects of U.S. nuclear and missile testing in the Marshall Islands.

Kiste, Robert C. *The Bikinians: A Study in Forced Migration.* Menlo Park, CA: Cummings, 1974. Anthropological discussion of Bikinians attempting to deal with their relocation.

Kluge, P.F. *The Edge of Paradise.* New York: Random House, 1991. Ex-Peace Corps volunteer writes about the impact and ironies of the American presence in Micronesia.

Marshall, Mac, and Leslie B. Marshall. *Silent Voices Speak: Women and Prohibition in Truk.* Belmont, CA: Wadsworth Publishing Company, 1990. Fascinating reading for anyone interested in the role of women in Micronesian society and the influence grassroots community groups can exert on the political process.

Report of the Global Conference on the Sustainable Development of Small Island Developing States, Bridgetown, Barbados, 26 April-6 May 1994. New York: United Nations Publications, 1994. A thorough discussion of ecological issues facing small island nations, such as those of Micronesia.

Robie, David. *Blood on their Banner.* London: Zed Books, 1989. Robie's incisive account of nationalist struggles in the South Pacific includes a chapter on Palau.

Robie, David. *Eyes of Fire: The Last Voyage of the Rainbow Warrior.* Philadelphia: New Society Publishers, 1985. Robie was aboard the Greenpeace protest vessel as the Rongelap islanders were evacuated to Kwajalein. His photos and firsthand account tell the inside story.

Walker, Ranginui, and William Sutherland, eds. *The Pacific: Peace, Security & the Nuclear Issue.* London and New Jersey: Zed Books Ltd., 1988. Published as part of the "Studies on Peace and Regional Security" program of the United Nations University, Tokyo. Among the 12 fully referenced papers is "Kiribati: Russophobia and Self Determination" by Uentabo Neemia.

SOCIAL SCIENCE

Alkire, William H. *An Introduction to the Peoples and Cultures of Micronesia.* Menlo Park, CA: Cummings Publishing Co., 1977. An anthropological survey.

Colletta, Nat J. *American Schools for the Natives of Ponape.* Honolulu: University of Hawaii Press, 1980. A study of education and culture change in Micronesia.

Cordy, Ross. *Archaeological Settlement Pattern Studies on Yap.* Saipan, CM: Micronesian Archaeology Report Series, 1982. Survey presenting pioneering work on islands of Yap.

Howell, William. *The Pacific Islanders.* New York: Scribner's, 1973. An anthropological study of the origins of Pacific peoples.

Kiribati: A Changing Atoll Culture. Fiji: Institute of Pacific Studies, 1984. A team of 14 I-Kiribati writers examines island life.

Kiste, Robert C. *The Bikinians: A Study in Forced Migration.* Menlo Park, CA: Cummings Publishing Co., 1974.

Koch, Gerd. *Material Culture of Kiribati.* Fiji: Institute of Pacific Studies, 1987. The English translation of a classic work; dozens of line drawings of everyday objects.

Oliver, Douglas L. *Oceania: The Native Cultures of Australia and the Pacific Islands.* Honolulu: University of Hawaii Press, 1989. A massive two-volume anthropological survey.

Ward, Martha C. *Nest in the Wind: Adventures in Anthropology on a Tropical Island.* Prospect Hills, IL: Waveland Press, 1989. Ward spent several years managing a scientific research project on Pohnpei in the early 1970s, and her very personal account of how she adapted to Pohnpeian ways will make fascinating reading for anyone thinking of "going native" in outback Micronesia.

ART

Browning, Mary S. *Micronesian Heritage.* Dance Perspectives, no. 43. New York: Dance Perspective Foundation, 1970. A historical overview of Micronesian dance.

Feldman, Jerome. *The Art of Micronesia.* Honolulu: University of Hawaii Art Gallery, 1986. This exhibition catalog, the definitive guide for art of Micronesia, includes three scholarly articles that discuss form, style, and ritual use in Micronesian art. The catalog also includes photographs and drawings of art objects.

Handicrafts of the Marshall Islands. Majuro: Republic of the Marshall Islands, 1993. This government brochure consists of color photographs of various handicrafts, but includes brief historical commentary as well.

Linton, Ralph, and Paul S. Wingert. *Arts of the South Seas.* New York: Arno Press, 1972. Brief overview of Micronesian art (pp. 67-74) with emphasis on the role of society and religion.

Mason, Leonard. "Micronesia and Micronesian Cultures." In Encyclopedia of World Art. New York: McGraw-Hill, 1987. An excellent survey (pp. 915-930, plates 543-548) of Micronesian material culture.

Montvel-Cohen, Marvin. "Craft and Context in Yap." Ph.D diss., Southern Illinois University, Carbona, 1982.

Mulford, Judy. *Decorative Marshallese Baskets.* Los Angeles, CA: Wonder Publications, 1991 (2098 Mandeville Cyn Rd., Los Angeles, CA 90049). A good book authored by a contemporary basketmaker on the process of Marshallese basket construction, including how to prepare plants and weaving techniques. Photos and drawings included.

Nason, James. "Tourism, Handicrafts and Ethnic Identity in Micronesia." *Annals of Tourism Research* 11 (1984): 421-449. Discusses traditional role of handicrafts in Micronesia and the changes that have occurred since European contact.

Owen, Hera Ware, ed. *Palau Museum Guide.* Koror, Palau: Palau Museum Publications, 1978. Reviews the art collection of the Palau Museum, which has perhaps the best art collection in Micronesia.

Wells, Marjorie D. *Micronesian Handicraft Book of the Trust Territory of the Pacific Islands.* New York: Carlton Press, Inc., 1982.

LITERATURE

Ashby, Gene, ed. *Micronesian Customs and Beliefs.* Pohnpei: Rainy Day Press, 1983 (P.O. Box 574, Kolonia, Pohnpei, FM 96941). A treasure trove of Micronesian legends and traditions, as related by the students of the Community College of Micronesia. This and the following entry are among the only cultural writings by Micronesians presently in print.

Ashby, Gene, ed. *Never and Always: Micronesian Legends, Fables and Folklore.* Pohnpei: Rainy Day Press, 1983 (P.O. Box 574, Kolonia, Pohnpei, FM 96941). Another 86 traditional stories by CCM students.

Knight, Gerald. *Man This Reef*. Majuro, Marshall Islands: Micronitor Press, 1982. This translated autobiography of a Marshallese storyteller takes more concentration to read than others of its kind because Knight went out of his way to retain the language patterns and structure of the original. This gives the book its depth and indirectly conveys the Marshallese concept of life.

Luelen, Bernart. *The Book of Luelen*. John L. Fischer, Saul H. Riesenberg, and Marjorie G. Whiting, eds. Honolulu: University of Hawaii Press, 1977. The old traditions of Pohnpei.

Nakano, Ann, photos by Tim Porter. *Broken Canoe*. St. Lucia, Queensland, Australia: University of Queensland Press, 1983. Narrative and photos describing the author and photographer's journey through Micronesia.

Tator, Elizabeth, ed. *Call of the Morning Bird*. Honolulu: Bishop Museum, 1985. This unique cassette bears the chants and songs of Palau, Yap, and Pohnpei collected by Iwakichi Muranushi in 1936. It's a basic document for the study of Micronesian music.

Te Katake. Fiji: Institute of Pacific Studies. Traditional Kiribati songs.

REFERENCE BOOKS

Pacific Islands Yearbook. Pymble, NSW, Australia: Angus & Robertson Publishers. A new edition of this bible of facts and figures for the Pacific has come out about every three years since 1932. Copies may be ordered through *Pacific Islands Monthly*, G.P.O. Box 1167, Suva, Fiji Islands.

Far East and Australasia. London: Europa Publications. An annual survey and directory of Asia and the Pacific. Provides abundant and factual political, social, and economic data; an excellent reference source.

Fenton, Thomas P., and Mary J. Heffron, ed. *Asia and Pacific: A Directory of Resources*. Maryknoll, NY: Orbis Books, 1986. Indispensable and complete survey of organizations, printed matter, and audiovisual resource material relating to Pacific issues.

Fry, Gerald W., and Rufino Mauricio. *Pacific Basin and Oceania*. Oxford: ABC-CLIO Press, 1987. A selective, indexed Pacific bibliography that describes the contents of the books, instead of merely listing them.

Goetzfridt, Nicholas J., and William L. Wuerch. *Micronesia 1975-1987: A Social Science Bibliography*. Westport, CT: Greenwood Press, 1989.

Haynes, Douglas, and William L. Wuerch. *Micronesian Religion and Lore: A guide to Sources, 1526-1990*. Westport, CT: Greenwood Press, 1995. Excellent comprehensive bibliography to all aspects of traditional Micronesian religion.

Jackson, Miles M., ed. *Pacific Island Studies: A Survey of the Literature*. Westport, CT: Greenwood Press, 1986. In addition to comprehensive listings there are extensive essays that put the most important works in perspective.

Layton, Suzanne. *The Contemporary Pacific Islands Press*. St. Lucia, Queensland, Australia: Department of Journalism, University of Queensland, 1992. Updated listing of print and broadcast media organizations, news services, and professional associations.

Marshall, Mac, and James D. Nason. *Micronesia 1944-1974: A Bibliography of Anthropological and Related Source Materials*. New Haven: Hraf Press, 1975.

Oceania: A Regional Study. Washington, D.C.: U.S. Government Printing Office, 1985. Extensive bibliography and index. This 572-page volume forms part of the area handbook series sponsored by the U.S. Army, intended to educate American officials. A comprehensive source of background information.

The Pacific Business Telephone Directory. Micronesian Publishing Co., P.O. Box 23097, Guam Main Facility, GU 96921 Includes businesses and government listings in the FSM, Palau, Guam, and the Northern Marianas in both alphabetical and classified sections. Revised annually.

Uludong, Francisco T. *American Pacific Business Directory.* Pacific Information Bank, P.O. Box 1310, Saipan, MP 96950 A telephone book directory, giving the addresses and phone numbers of businesses, government offices, and organizations throughout Micronesia and American Samoa.

Wuerch, William L., and Dirk Anthony Ballendorf. *Historical Dictionary of Guam and Micronesia.* Metuchen, NJ: The Scarecrow Press, 1994. An excellent compilation of historical terms and people of Micronesia.

BOOKSELLERS AND PUBLISHERS

Many of the titles listed above are out of print and not available in regular bookstores. Major research libraries should have a few; otherwise, write to the specialized antiquarian booksellers or regional publishers listed below for their printed lists of recycled or hard to find books on the Pacific. Sources of detailed topographical maps or navigational charts are provided in the following section.

Alele Museum Booklist. Alele Museum, P.O. Box 629, Majuro, MH 96960 A complete mail order list of books on the Marshall Islands.

Australia, the Pacific and South East Asia. Serendipity Books, P.O. Box 340, Nedlands, WA 6009, Australia. The largest stock of antiquarian, secondhand, and out of print books on the Pacific in Western Australia.

Books from the Pacific Islands. Institute of Pacific Studies, University of the South Pacific, P.O. Box 1168, Suva, Fiji Islands. A number of books on Kiribati are included in this 12-page catalog. Their specialty is books about the islands written by the Pacific islanders.

Books, Maps & Prints of Pacific Islands. Colin Hinchcliffe, 12 Queens Staith Mews, York, YO1 1HH, England. An excellent source of antiquarian books, maps, and engravings, mostly on the South Pacific.

Books & Series in Print. Bishop Museum Press, P.O. Box 19000-A, Honolulu, HI 96817-0916. An indexed list of publications on the Pacific available from the Bishop Museum.

Catalogue of Pacific Region Books. Pacific Book House, 17 Park Ave., Broadbeach Waters, Gold Coast, QLD 4218, Australia. A Queensland source of out of print books on the Pacific, including many on Micronesia.

Hawaii and Pacific Islands. The Book Bin, 2305 NW Monroe St., Corvallis, OR 97330, tel. (503) 752-0045. An indexed mail order catalog of hundreds of rare books on the Pacific. If there's a particular book about the Pacific you can't find anywhere, this is the place to try.

Hawaii and the Pacific. University of Hawaii Press, 2840 Kolowalu St., Honolulu, HI 96822. Lists many new and current titles on Micronesia.

Pacificana. Messrs Berkelouw, "Bendooley," Hume Highway, Berrima, NSW 2577, Australia (tel. 048-77-1370). A detailed listing of thousands of rare Pacific titles.

Pacificana. Books of Yesteryear, P.O. Box 19, Mosman, NSW 2088, Australia. Another good source of old, fine, and rare books on the Pacific.

Publications Price List. Micronesian Area Research Center, University of Guam, UOG Station, Mangilao, Guam 96923. Reprints or translations of old classics, bibliographical references, and specialized studies all figure in MARC's extensive mail order list.

Polynesian Bookshop Catalogues. P.O. Box 68-446, Newton, Auckland 1, New Zealand. Mostly new books on the South Pacific, but a good starting point for New Zealanders.

Map Publishers

American Pacific Islands Index. U.S. Geological Survey, NCIC, M/S 532, 345 Middlefield Rd., Menlo Park, CA 94025. A complete list of recent topographical maps of Micronesia.

Charts and Publications, United States Pacific Coast Including Hawaii, Guam and the Samoa Islands. National Ocean Service, Distribution Branch (N/CG33), Riverdale, MD 20737-1199. Nautical charts put out by the National Oceanic and Atmospheric Administration (NOAA).

Defense Mapping Agency Catalog of Maps, Charts, and Related Products: Part 2: Hydrographic Products, Volume VIII, Oceania. Defense Mapping Agency Combat Support Center, Attn: DDCP, Washington, D.C. 20315-0010.

Index to Topographic Maps of Hawaii, American Samoa, and Guam. Distribution Branch, U.S. Geological Survey, P.O. Box 25286, Denver Federal Center, Denver, CO 80225.

Pacific Historical Maps. Economic Service Counsel, Inc., P.O. Box 201 CHRB, Saipan, MP 96950. These fascinating tourist maps by William H. Stewart are packed with information. Copies often are available from local tourist offices.

PERIODICALS

Atoll Research Bulletin. Washington, D.C.: Smithsonian Institution. A specialized journal and inexhaustible source of fascinating information (and maps) on the most remote islands of the Pacific. Consult back issues at major libraries.

Bulletin of Concerned Asian Scholars. 3239 9th St., Boulder, CO 80302-2112. The volume 18, number two, 1986 issue is devoted entirely to the antinuclear movement in the Pacific.

Commodores' Bulletin. Seven Seas Cruising Assn., 521 South Andrews Ave., Suite 8, Fort Lauderdale, FL 33301. This monthly bulletin is loaded with useful information for anyone wishing to tour the Pacific by sailing boat.

The Contemporary Pacific. University of Hawaii Press, 2840 Kolowalu St., Honolulu, HI 96822 (twice a year, $25 a year). Publishes a good mix of articles of interest to both scholars and general readers; the country by country "Political Review" in each issue is a concise summary of events during the preceding year. Those interested in current topics in Pacific Island affairs should check recent volumes for background information.

Guam Business News. P.O. Box 3191, Agana, GU 96910. An informative newsmagazine published monthly on Guam ($36 a year).

Hafa, The Magazine of Guam. Local, Inc., Suite 211, Ada Commercial & Professional Center, 130 East Marine Dr., Agana, GU 96910 (monthly, $28 a year). Carries articles on island life.

Isla, A Journal of Micronesian Studies. Isla Editorial Office, Graduate School and Research, UOG Station, Mangilao, GU 96923 (twice a year, $15 a year).

Journal of Pacific History. Division of Pacific and Asian History, RSPacS, Australian National University, G.P.O. Box 4, Canberra, ACT 2601, Australia. Since 1966 this publication has provided reliable scholarly information on the Pacific. The volume XXI 3-4, 1986 issue includes several scholarly articles on recent events in Micronesia. Outstanding.

Micronesia. The Marine Laboratory, University of Guam, UOG Station, Mangilao, GU 96923 (twice a year, $15 a year). A journal devoted to the natural sciences in Micronesia.

Pacific Affairs. University of British Columbia, Vancouver, BC V6T 1W6, Canada (quarterly, C$25 a year).

Pacific Below. Sales office: P.O. Box 20088 GMF, Guam, GU 96921 (every other month, $15 a year in U.S. or Micronesia). Undersea magazine of the Pacific.

Pacific Arts Newsletter. Pacific Arts Foundation, P.O. Box 19000-A, Honolulu, HI 96817-0916.

Pacific Islands Monthly. G.P.O. Box 1167, Suva, Fiji Islands. Founded in Sydney by R.W. Robson in 1930, *PIM* is the granddaddy of regional magazines. In June 1989 the magazine's editorial office moved from Sydney to Suva.

Pacific Magazine. P.O. Box 25488, Honolulu, HI 96825 (every other month, $15 annual subscription). This business-oriented magazine, published in Hawaii since 1976, will keep you up-to-date on what's happening around the Pacific, and in Micronesia in particular. The January/February 1990 issue carried an excellent series of articles on Ebeye Island of Kwajalein atoll.

Pacific News Bulletin. Pacific Concerns Resource Center, P.O. Box 489, Petersham, NSW 2049, Australia. A 16 page monthly newsletter for use worldwide by members of the Nuclear Free and Independent Pacific Movement.

Skin Diver. Petersen Publishing Co., Circulation Division, 8490 Sunset Blvd., Los Angeles, CA 90069. This monthly magazine carries frequent articles on Micronesian dive sites and facilities.

Tok Blong Pacific. South Pacific Peoples Foundation of Canada, 415-620 View St., Victoria, BC V8W 1J6, Canada. Quarterly of news and views focuses on regional environmental, development, human rights, and disarmament issues.

The Washington Pacific Report. Pacific House, 1615 New Hampshire Ave. NW, Suite 400, Washington, D.C. 20009-2520 (twice a month, $150 a year, $175 outside the U.S.). An insider's newsletter highlighting the insular Pacific.

GLOSSARY

AIDS—Acquired Immune Deficiency Syndrome

archipelago—a group of islands

atoll—a low-lying, ring-shaped coral reef enclosing a lagoon

bai—a traditional Palauan men's meetinghouse

bareboat charter—the chartering of a yacht without crew or provisions

barrier reef—a coral reef separated from the adjacent shore by a lagoon

bêche-de-mer—sea cucumber; trepang; an edible sea slug

benjo—an overwater toilet

betel nut—the fruit of the areca palm, chewed together with pepper leaves and a little lime

blackbirders—European Pacific Ocean slave traders during the 19th century

breadfruit—a large, round fruit with starchy flesh, grown on a breadfruit tree *(Artocarpus altilis)*

cassava—manioc; a starchy edible root from which tapioca is made

Chamorro—the indigenous inhabitants of the Mariana Islands

ciguatera—a form of fish poisoning caused by microscopic algae

coast watchers—Australian intelligence agents who operated behind Japanese lines during WW II, spotting approaching planes and ships

coir—coconut husk sennit used to make rope, etc.

copra—dried coconut meat used in the manufacture of coconut oil, cosmetics, soap, and margarine

coral—a hard, calcareous substance of various shapes, comprising the skeletons of tiny marine animals called polyps

coral bank—a coral formation over 500 feet long

coral head—a coral formation a few feet across

coral patch—a coral formation up to 500 feet long

cyclone—also known as a hurricane (in the the U.S.) or typhoon (in the Pacific). A tropical storm rotates around a center of low atmospheric pressure; it becomes a cyclone when its winds reach 64 knots. In the Northern Hemisphere cyclones spin counterclockwise, while south of the equator they move clockwise. The winds of cyclonic storms are deflected toward a low-pressure area at the center, although the "eye" of the cyclone may be calm.

dapal—a Yapese women's meetinghouse

direct flight—a through flight with one or more stops but no change of aircraft, as opposed to a nonstop flight

ecotourism—a form of tourism that emphasizes limited impact participation in the natural environment

EEZ—Exclusive Economic Zone; a 200-nautical-mile offshore belt where a state controls mineral exploitation and fishing rights

endemic—something native to a particular area and existing there only

FAD—fish aggregation device

faluw—a Yapese young men's house

fringing reef—a reef along the shore of an island

guano—manure of seabirds or bats, used as a fertilizer

lagoon—an expanse of water bounded by a reef

latte **stones**—large limestone pillars left by pre-contact Chamorros

lava lava—a wraparound skirt

leeward—downwind; the shore (or side) sheltered from the wind; as opposed to windward

LORAN—Long-Range Aids to Navigation

maneaba—a Kiribati community meetinghouse

mangrove—a tropical shrub with branches that send down roots forming dense thickets along tidal shores

manioc—*see* cassava

matrilineal—a system of tracing descent through the mother's familial line

Melanesia—the high island groups of the western Pacific (Fiji, New Caledonia, Vanuatu, Solomon Islands, Papua New Guinea)

overbooking—the practice of confirming more seats, cabins, or rooms than are actually available to ensure against no-shows

Pacific Rim—the continental landmasses and large countries around the fringe of the Pacific

PADI—Professional Association of Dive Instructors

pandanus—screw pine with slender stem and prop roots. Fiber from the sword-shaped leaves is used for weaving.

parasailing—being carried aloft by a parachute pulled behind a speedboat

pass—a channel through a barrier reef

passage—an inside passage between an island and a barrier reef

patrilineal—a system of tracing descent through the father's familial line

pebai—a traditional Yapese community meetinghouse

pelagic—relating to the open sea, away from land

Polynesia—divided into Western Polynesia (Tonga and Samoa) and Eastern Polynesia (Tahiti-Polynesia, Cook Islands, Hawaii, Easter Island, and New Zealand)

purse seiner—a tuna fishing boat that encircles fish by using a net that is drawn up like a purse

Quonset hut—a prefabricated, semicircular, metal shelter popular during WW II

rai—Yapese stone money

reef—a coral ridge near the ocean surface

sakau—found on Pohnpei, this mildly narcotic drink is made from the root of the pepper plant; called *kava* in Polynesia

sashimi—edible raw fish

scuba—self-contained underwater breathing apparatus

shareboat charter—a yacht tour for individuals or couples who join a small group on a fixed itinerary

shoal—a shallow sandbar or mud bank

shoulder season—a travel period between high/peak and low/off-peak

SPARTECA—South Pacific Regional Trade and Economic Cooperation Agreement; an agreement which allows certain manufactured goods from Pacific countries duty free entry to Australia and New Zealand

subduction—the action of one tectonic plate wedging under another

subsidence—geological sinking or settling

tangan tangan—a thick brush found in the Mariana Islands

taro—a starchy, elephant-eared tuber *(Colocasia esculenta),* a staple food of the Pacific islanders

thu—a Yapese male loincloth

toddy—The spathe of a coconut tree is bent to a horizontal position and tightly bound before it begins to flower. The end of the spathe is then split and the sap drips down a twig or leaf into a bottle. Fresh or fermented, toddy *(tuba)* makes an excellent drink.

tradewind—a steady wind blowing toward the equator from either the northeast or southeast, depending on the season

trench—an ocean depth marking the point where one tectonic plate wedges under another

tridacna clam—eaten everywhere in the Pacific, its size varies between four and 40 inches

tropical storm—a cyclonic storm with winds of 35 to 64 knots

tsunami—a fast-moving wave caused by an undersea earthquake, sometimes called a tidal wave

TTPI—Trust Territory of the Pacific Islands

udoud—Palauan traditional money

windward—the point or side on which the wind blows, as opposed to leeward

wunbey—a Yapese stone platform

yam—the starchy, tuberous root of a climbing plant

zoris—a Japanese term still used in Micronesia for rubber shower sandals, thongs, flip-flops

APPENDIX

INFORMATION AND DIPLOMATIC OFFICES

REGIONAL

Pacific Asia Travel Association, Headquarters, One Montgomery St., Telesis Tower, Suite 1000, San Francisco, CA 94104-4539, tel. (415) 986-4646, fax (415) 986-3458

Pacific Asia Travel Association, Pacific Division, P.O. Box 645, Kings Cross, 80 William St., Level 2, Suite 203A, Woalloomooloo, NSW 2011, Australia, tel. 02-9332-3599, fax 02-9331-6592

Pacific Asia Travel Association, Asia Division, 138 Cecil St., #06-03, Secil Court, Singapore 0106, tel. 223-7854, fax 223-6842

Pacific Asia Travel Association, Europe Division, Les Eucalyptus (Block 1) 11 Avenues des Guelfes, Zone E Fontvieille, MC 98000, Monaco, tel. 392-056132, fax 92-056133

Northeast Asia Representative, The Contact, Inc., Shuwa Nishi-Golanda Building, 5-2-4 Nishi-Golanda, Shinagawa-ku, Tokyo 141, Japan, tel. 3-5487-0725, fax 3-5487-0726

Pacific Asia Travel Association, Micronesia Chapter, 970 South Marine Dr., Suite 10-PATA, Tamuning, GU 96911.

Office of Territorial and International Affairs, Room 4312, United States Dept. of the Interior, Washington, D.C. 20240

Office of Freely Associated States, Dept. of State EAP/FAS, Room 5317, Washington, D.C. 20520-6310

MARSHALL ISLANDS

Tourism Office, P.O. Box 1727, Majuro, MH 96960, tel. 625-3206

Embassy of the Marshall Islands, 2433 Massachusetts Ave. NW, Washington, D.C. 20008, tel. (202) 234-5414, fax (202) 232-3236

RMI Permanent Mission to the United Nations, 220 E. 42nd St., New York, NY, 10017, tel. (212) 293-3040, fax (212) 983-3202

Embassy of the Marshall Islands, 41 Borron Rd., Suva, Fiji Islands, tel. 387-899, fax 387-115

Embassy of the Marshall Islands, Moiji Park Heights, Room 101, 9-9, Minamimoto-Machi, Shinjuku, Tokyo, Japan, tel. (3) 5379-1701/1702, fax (3) 5379-1810

FEDERATED STATES OF MICRONESIA

Dept. of Resources and Development, National Government of the FSM, Capitol Postal Station, P.O. Box 12, Palikir, Pohnpei, FM 96941

Dept. of Conservation and Development, Division of Tourism, Kosrae State Government, P.O. Box R & D, Kosrae, FM 96944

Pohnpei Tourist Commission, P.O. Box 66, Kolonia, Pohnpei, FM 96941

Chuuk Visitors Bureau, P.O. Box FQ, Weno, Chuuk, FM 96942

Office of Tourism, Division of Commerce and Industries, Dept. of Resources and Development, Yap State Government, P.O. Box 36, Colonia, Yap, FM 96943

FSM Information Office, P.O. Box 490, Kolonia, Pohnpei, FM 96941

Embassy of the Federated States of Micronesia, 1725 N St. NW, Washington, D.C. 20036

Permanent Representative of the FSM to the United Nations, 820 Second Ave., Suite 800-A, New York, NY 10017

Federated States of Micronesia Consulate, 3049 Ualena St., Suite 408, Honolulu, HI 96819.

Federated States of Micronesia Consulate, P.O. Box 10630, Tamuning, GU 96911

Embassy of the Federated States of Micronesia, 2nd Floor, Reinanzaka Bldg., 14-2 Akasaka, 1-Chome, Minatu-Ku, Tokyo 107, Japan

Embassy of the Federated States of Micronesia, P.O. Box 15493, Suva, Fiji Islands

PALAU

Palau Visitors Authority, P.O. Box 256, Koror, PW 96940, tel. 488-2793, fax 488-1453

Palau/Washington Liaison Officer, 2000 L St., NW Washington, D.C. 20001, tel. (202) 452-6814

Palau/Guam Liaison Officer, P.O. Box 9457, Agana, GU 96911

GUAM

Guam Visitors Bureau, P.O. Box 3520, Agana, Guam 96910, tel. 646-5278

Guam Visitors Bureau, Kokusai Building, 3-1-1 Marunouchi, Chiyoda-ku, Tokyo 100, Japan

NORTHERN MARIANAS

Marianas Visitors Bureau, P.O. Box 861, Saipan, MP 96950, tel. 234-8325, fax 234-3596

Resident Representative, Commonwealth of the Northern Mariana Islands, 2121 R St. NW, Washington, D.C. 20008

CNMI Liaison Office, 1221 Kapiolani Blvd., Suite 348, Honolulu, HI 96814

CNMI Liaison Office, P.O. Box 8366, Tamuning, GU 96911

KIRIBATI

Kiribati Visitors Bureau, Ministry of Natural Resource Development, P.O. Box 251, Bikenibeu, Tarawa, Rep. of Kiribati, tel. 28-287

Tourism Office, Ministry of Line and Phoenix Development, Christmas Island, Republic of Kiribati

ALTERNATIVE PLACE-NAMES

Abariringa—Canton
Abariringa—Kanton
Babeldaob—Babelthuap
Babelthuap—Babeldaob
Banaba—Ocean Island
Belau—Palau
Bokaak—Taongi
Canton—Kanton
Canton—Abariringa
Christmas—Kiritimati
Chuuk—Truk
Dublon—Tonoas
Ellice Islands—Tuvalu
Emwar—Losap
Enenkio—Wake
Enewetak—Eniwetok
Eniwetok—Enewetak
Fanning—Teraina
Gardner—Nikumaroro
Gilbert Islands—Tungaru
Gilberts—Kiribati

Houk—Pulusuk
Hull—Orana
Jabat—Jabwot
Jabwot—Jabat
Kanton—Abariranga
Kanton—Canton
Kiribati—Gilberts
Kiritimati—Christmas
Kosrae—Kusaie
Kusaie—Kosrae
Losap—Emwar
Manra—Sydney
Moen—Weno
Mokil—Mwoakilloa
Mwoakilloa—Mokil
Ngatik—Sapwuahfik
Nikumaroro—Gardner
Ocean—Banaba
Onoun—Ulul
Orana—Hull
Palau—Belau

Phoenix—Rawaki
Pis—Pisemwar
Pisemwar—Pis
Pohnpei—Ponape
Ponape—Pohnpei
Pulusuk—Houk
Rawaki—Phoenix
Sapwuahfik—Ngatik
Tabuaeran—Washington
Taongi—Bokaak
Teraina—Fanning
Tonoas—Dublon
Truk—Chuuk
Tungaru—Gilbert Islands
Tuvalu—Ellice Islands
Ulul—Onoun
Wa'ab—Yap
Wake—Enenkio
Washington—Tabuaeran
Weno—Moen
Yap—Wa'ab

MICRONESIA COUNTRY CODES

To call Micronesia from the United States, dial the international access code 011, followed by the country code, then the phone number.

Country	Country Code
Republic of the Marshall Islands	692
Federated States of Micronesia (all)	691
Republic of Palau	680
Guam	671
Commonwealth of the Northern Marianas	670
Republic of Nauru	674
Republic of Kiribati	686

MICRONESIA POSTAL CODES

Note: When mailing a letter from outside the U.S. to the Marshall Islands, the Federated States of Micronesia, Palau, Guam, and the Marianas, include "via U.S.A." in the address.

Country		Postal Code
Republic of the Marshall Islands	Majuro	MH 96960
	Ebeye	MH 96970
Federated States of Micronesia	Kosrae	FM 96944
	Pohnpei	FM 96941
	Chuuk	FM 96942
	Yap	FM 96943
Republic of Palau	Koror	PW 96940
Guam	Agana	GU 96910
	Tamuning	GU 96911
	Dededo	GU 96912
	Barrigada	GU 96913
	Yona	GU 96914
	Santa Rita	GU 96915
	Merizo	GU 96916
	Inarajan	GU 96917
	Umatac	GU 96918
	Agana Heights	GU 96919
	Guam Main Facility (GMF)	GU 96921
	Asan	GU 96922
	Mangilao	GU 96923
	Chalan Pago	GU 96924
	Piti	GU 96925
	Sinajana	GU 96926
	Maite	GU 96927
	Agat	GU 96928
	Yigo	GU 96929
	Talofolo	GU 96930
	P.O. Boxes, Tamuning	GU 96931
Commonwealth of the Northern Marianas	Saipan	MP 96950
	Rota	MP 96951
	Tinian	MP 96952
Republic of Nauru		Rep. of Nauru, Central Pacific

INDEX

Italicized page numbers indicate information in captions, charts, illustrations, maps, or special topics. FSM is the abbreviation for Federated States of Micronesia

ABOUT THE AUTHOR

In the early '70s, Neil M. Levy and his bride Jane bought a Land Cruiser, drove from California to the Panama Canal, sold the car, and headed to South America.

They landed back in the San Francisco Bay Area several years later, Neil confident he had conquered his accursed wanderlust. For the next two decades he seemed to be right—he became a law professor, the father of three, and a homeowner.

Professor Levy is an expert on the legal rights of native people. He has spent summers in Hawaii, first researching then writing about the rights of Native Hawaiians. He later applied his knowledge by working for Native Hawaiian community groups. Some say, had there been better surf in South Dakota, he might have become an expert on the law of the Sioux tribes.

Neil fully intended to remain sedentary until all three children graduated from high school. He came close, but the islands of the Pacific broke his resolve. He has traveled extensively in the South Pacific and in Micronesia during the past three years. Jane accompanied him to Micronesia and contributed to the arts and crafts sections of this book. He and Jane still reside in the Bay Area. Neil likes to pretend his children understand his occasional need to disappear.

MOON TRAVEL HANDBOOKS
DISCOVER THE DIFFERENCE

Moon Travel Handbooks provide focused, comprehensive coverage of distinct destinations all over the world. Our goal is to give travelers all the background and practical information they'll need for an extraordinary travel experience.

Every Handbook begins with an in-depth essay about the land, the people, their history, art, politics, and social concerns—an entire bookcase of cultural insight and introductory information in one portable volume. We also provide accurate, up-to-date coverage of all the practicalities: language, currency, transportation, accommodations, food, and entertainment. And Moon's maps are legendary, covering not only cities and highways, but parks and trails that are often difficult to find in other sources.

Below are highlights of Moon's Asia and Pacific Travel Handbook series. Our complete list of Handbooks covering North America and Hawaii, Mexico, Central America and the Caribbean, and Asia and the Pacific, are listed on the order form on the accompanying pages. To purchase Moon Travel Handbooks, please check your local bookstore or order by phone: (800) 345-5473 Monday-Friday 8 a.m.-5 p.m. PST.

MOON OVER ASIA
THE ASIA AND THE PACIFIC TRAVEL HANDBOOK SERIES

"Moon guides are wittily written and warmly personal; what's more, they present a vivid, often raw vision of Asia without promotional overtones. They also touch on such topics as official corruption and racism, none of which rate a mention in the bone-dry, air-brushed, dry-cleaned version of Asia written up in the big U.S. guidebooks."
—*Far Eastern Economic Review*

AUSTRALIA HANDBOOK
by Marael Johnson, Andrew Hempstead, and Nadina Purdon,
913 pages, **$21.95**
Explore the "land down under" with Moon's *Australia Handbook*, providing comprehensive coverage of outdoor recreation, the hottest sights, and detailed travel practicalities.

BALI HANDBOOK
by Bill Dalton, 800 pages, **$19.95**
"This book is for the in-depth traveler, interested in history and art, willing to experiment with language and food and become immersed in the culture of Bali."

— *Great Expeditions*

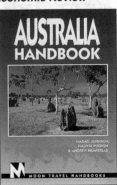

BANGKOK HANDBOOK
by Michael Buckley, 221 pages, **$13.95**
"Helps make sense of this beguiling paradox of a city . . .
very entertaining reading."

—*The Vancouver Sun*

FIJI ISLANDS HANDBOOK
by David Stanley, 275 pages, **$13.95**
"If you want to encounter Fiji and not just ride through it, this book
is for you."

—*Great Expeditions*

HONG KONG HANDBOOK
by Kerry Moran, 347 pages, **$15.95**
"One of the most honest glimpses into Hong Kong the Peoples
Republic of China would like never to have seen."

—*TravelNews Asia*

INDONESIA HANDBOOK
by Bill Dalton, 1,351 pages, **$25.00**
"Looking for a fax machine in Palembang, a steak dinner on
Ambon or the best place to photograph Bugis prahus in Sulawesi?
Then buy this brick of a book, which contains a full kilogram of
detailed directions and advice."

—*Asia, Inc. Magazine*

"The classic guidebook to the archipelago."

—*Condé Nast Traveler*

JAPAN HANDBOOK
by J.D. Bisignani, 952 pages, **$22.50**
Winner: Lowell Thomas Gold Award, Society of American Travel
Writers
"The scope of this guide book is staggering, ranging from an
introduction to Japanese history and culture through to the best
spots for shopping for pottery in Mashie or silk pongee in
Kagoshima."

—*Golden Wing*

"More travel information on Japan than any other guidebook."
—*The Japan Times*

MICRONESIA HANDBOOK
by Neil M. Levy, 330 pages, **$14.95**
"Remarkably informative, fair-minded, sensible, and readable . . ."
—*The Journal of the Polynesian Society*

NEPAL HANDBOOK
by Kerry Moran, 428 pages, **$18.95**
Winner: Lowell Thomas Gold Award, Society of American
Travel Writers
"This is an excellent guidebook, exploring every aspect of the
country the visitor is likely to want to know about with both wit
and authority."

—*South China Morning Post*

NEW ZEALAND HANDBOOK
by Jane King, 544 pages, **$19.95**
"Far and away the best guide to New Zealand."

—The Atlantic

OUTBACK AUSTRALIA HANDBOOK
by Marael Johnson, 432 pages, **$18.95**
Winner: Lowell Thomas Silver Award, Society of American
Travel Writers
"Well designed, easy to read, and funny"

—Buzzworm

PAKISTAN HANDBOOK
by Isobel Shaw, 660 pages, **$22.50**
Pakistan Handbook guides travelers from the heights of the
Karakorams to the bazaars of Karachi, from sacred mosques in
Sind to the ceasefire line of Azad Kashmir. Includes a detailed
trekking guide with several itineraries for long and short treks
across the Hindu Kush, Karakorams, and Himalayas.

PHILIPPINES HANDBOOK
by Peter Harper and Laurie Fullerton, 638 pages, **$17.95**
"The most comprehensive travel guide done on the Philippines.
Excellent work."

—Pacific Stars & Stripes

PRACTICAL NOMAD
by Edward Hasbrouck, 200 pages, **$13.95**
The Practical Nomad is a planning guide for travelers considering
extended, multi-stop international trips, including around-the-
world journeys. This how-to handbook features essential
information on understanding airfares and ticketing, working with
a travel agent, and handling required documentation such as
passports and visas.

ROAD TRIP USA
by Jamie Jensen, 800 pages, **$22.50**
Road Trip USA is a comprehensive travel guide to the "blue
highways" that crisscross America between and beyond the
interstates. This guide provides 11 cross-country, non-interstate
routes, many of which intersect, allowing travelers to create their
own driving adventure.

SOUTHEAST ASIA HANDBOOK
by Carl Parkes, 1,103 pages, **$21.95**
Winner: Lowell Thomas Bronze Award, Society of American
Travel Writers
"Plenty of information on sights and entertainment, also provides
a political, environmental and cultural context that will allow
visitors to begin to interpret what they see."

—London Sunday Times

SOUTH KOREA HANDBOOK
by Robert Nilsen, 725 pages, **$18.95**
"One of a small number of guidebooks that inform without being pedantic, and are enthusiastic yet maintain a critical edge . . . the maps are without parallel."

—*Far Eastern Economic Review*

SOUTH PACIFIC HANDBOOK
by David Stanley, 900 pages, **$22.95**
"Moon's tribute to the South Pacific, by David Stanley, is next to none. "

—*Ubique*

TAHITI-POLYNESIA HANDBOOK
by David Stanley, 243 pages, **$13.95**
"If you can't find it in this book, it is something you don't need to know. "

—*Rapa Nui Journal*

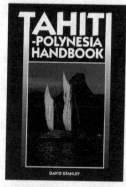

THAILAND HANDBOOK
by Carl Parkes, 800 pages, **$19.95**
"Carl Parkes is the savviest of all tourists to Southeast Asia."

—*Arthur Frommer*

TASMANIA HANDBOOK
by Jane King, 300 pages, **$16.95**
Tasmania Handbook is a comprehensive travel guide to Australia's island-state, covering sights and travel practicalities in a cultural context.

TIBET HANDBOOK
by Victor Chan, 1,103 pages, **$30.00**
"This is the most impressive travel handbook published in the 20th century."   —*Small Press Magazine*

"Shimmers with a fine madness."

—*Escape Magazine*

VIETNAM, CAMBODIA & LAOS HANDBOOK
by Michael Buckley, 650 pages, **$18.95**
The new definitive guide to Indochina from a travel writer who knows Asia like the back of his hand. Michael Buckley combines the most current practical travel information—much of it previously unavailable—with the perspective of a seasoned adventure traveler. Includes 75 maps.

STAYING HEALTHY IN ASIA, AFRICA, AND LATIN AMERICA
by Dirk G. Schroeder, ScD, MPH, 197 pages, **$11.95**
"Read this book if you want to stay healthy on any journeys or stays in Asia, Africa, and Latin America."

—*American Journal of Health Promotion*

PERIPLUS TRAVEL MAPS

Periplus Travel Maps are a necessity for traveling in Southeast Asia. Each map is designed for maximum clarity and utility, combining several views and insets of the area. Transportation information, street indexes, and descriptions of major sites are included in each map. The result is a single map with all the vital information needed to get where you're going. No other maps come close to providing the detail or comprehensive coverage of Asian travel destinations. All maps are updated yearly and produced with digital technology using the latest survey information. **$7.95**

Periplus Travel Maps are available to the following areas:

Bali	Kuala Lumpur
Bandung/W. Java	Ko Samui/S. Thailand
Bangkok/C. Thailand	Lombok
Batam/Bintan	N. Sumatra
Cambodia	Penang
Chiangmai/N. Thailand	Phuket/S. Thailand
Hong Kong	Sabah
Indonesia	Sarawak
Jakarta	Singapore
E. Java	Vietnam
Java	Yogyakarta/C. Java

MOONBELT

A new concept in moneybelts. Made of heavy-duty Cordura nylon, the Moonbelt offers maximum protection for your money and important papers. This pouch, designed for all-weather comfort, slips under your shirt or waistband, rendering it virtually undetectable and inaccessible to pickpockets. It features a one-inch high-test quick-release buckle so there's no more fumbling around for the strap or repeated adjustments. This handy plastic buckle opens and closes with a touch, but won't come undone until you want it to. Moonbelts accommodate traveler's checks, passports, cash, photos, etc. Size 5 x 9 inches. Available in black only. **$8.95**

ROAD TRIP USA
An Anti-Interstate of Mind

by Kevin Koe

ISSUE 17   FALL 1996   FREE

County road 640, state highway 45
life out off the interstate is way much alike.
There's magic in the mountains and music in
the valleys dear below.
And my song ain't through playing yet, so I believe
I'll hit the road andgo.

—JOHNNY CASH
"HIT THE ROAD ANDGO"

Travel Matters

Travel Matters is Moon Publications' free newsletter, loaded with specially commissioned travel articles and essays that get at the heart of the travel experience. Every issue includes:

Feature Stories covering a wide array of travel and cultural topics about destinations on and off the beaten path. Past feature stories in *Travel Matters* include Mexican professional wrestling, traveling to the Moon, and why Germans get six weeks vacation and Americans don't.

Transportation tips covering all forms of transportation by land, sea, and air. Transportation topics covered recently have included driving through Baja California, new Eurail passes, trekking in Tibet, and biking through Asia.

Health Matters, by Dirk Schroeder, author of *Staying Healthy in Asia, Africa, and Latin America,* focusing on the most recent medical findings that affect travelers. Learn about hepatitis A and B, critical travel supplies, and how to avoid common ailments.

Book and Multimedia Reviews providing informed assessments of the latest travel titles, series, and support materials. Recent reviews include The Rough Guide to *World Music, Passage to Vietnam* CD-ROM, and *I Should Have Stayed Home: The Worst Trips of Great Writers.*

The Internet page, which provides updates on Moon's WWW site, online discussions, and other travel resources available in cyberspace. A wide range of topics have been covered in this column including how to go online without going crazy, the Great Burma Debate, and details on Moon's *Road Trip USA* project.

Fellow Traveler, a reader question and answer column for travelers written by an international travel agent and world traveler.

To receive a free subscription to *Travel Matters,* call (800) 345-5473, e-mail us at travel@moon.com, or write to us at:

Moon Publications
P.O. Box 3040
Chico, CA 95927-3040

Please note: Subscribers who live outside of the United States will be charged $7 per year for shipping and handling.

MOON TRAVEL HANDBOOKS

NORTH AMERICA AND HAWAII

Alaska-Yukon Handbook (0161) $14.95
Alberta and the Northwest Territories Handbook (0676) $17.95
Arizona Traveler's Handbook (0714). $17.95
Atlantic Canada Handbook (0072) $17.95
Big Island of Hawaii Handbook (0064). $13.95
British Columbia Handbook (0145). $15.95
Colorado Handbook (0447) $18.95
Georgia Handbook (0390) $17.95
Hawaii Handbook (0005). $19.95
Honolulu-Waikiki Handbook (0587) $14.95
Idaho Handbook (0617). $14.95
Kauai Handbook (0013) $13.95
Maui Handbook (0579) $14.95
Montana Handbook (0498). $17.95
Nevada Handbook (0641) $16.95
New Mexico Handbook (0153). $14.95
Northern California Handbook (3840) $19.95
Oregon Handbook (0102) $16.95
Road Trip USA (0366). $22.50
Texas Handbook (0633) $17.95
Utah Handbook (0684) $16.95
Washington Handbook (0455). $18.95
Wyoming Handbook (3980) $14.95

ASIA AND THE PACIFIC

Australia Handbook (0722) $21.95
Bali Handbook (0730). $19.95
Bangkok Handbook (0595) $13.95
Fiji Islands Handbook (0382) $13.95
Hong Kong Handbook (0560) $15.95
Indonesia Handbook (0625) $25.00
Japan Handbook (3700) $22.50
Micronesia Handbook (0773) $14.95
Nepal Handbook (0412) $18.95
New Zealand Handbook (0331) $19.95
Outback Australia Handbook (0471). $18.95
Pakistan Handbook (0692). $22.50
Philippines Handbook (0048) $17.95

Southeast Asia Handbook (0021). $21.95
South Korea Handbook (3204) $14.95
South Pacific Handbook (0404). $22.95
Tahiti-Polynesia Handbook (0374) $13.95
Thailand Handbook (0420). $19.95
Tibet Handbook (3905) $30.00
Vietnam, Cambodia & Laos Handbook (0293) $18.95

MEXICO

Baja Handbook (0528) $15.95
Cabo Handbook (0285). $14.95
Cancún Handbook (0501) $13.95
Central Mexico Handbook (0234). $15.95
Mexico Handbook (0315). $21.95
Northern Mexico Handbook (0226). $16.95
Pacific Mexico Handbook (0323) $16.95
Puerto Vallarta Handbook (0250). $14.95
Yucatán Peninsula Handbook (0242) $15.95

CENTRAL AMERICA AND THE CARIBBEAN

Belize Handbook (0307) $15.95
Caribbean Handbook (0277). $16.95
Costa Rica Handbook (0358) $18.95
Jamaica Handbook (0706). $15.95

INTERNATIONAL

Egypt Handbook (3891) $18.95
Moon Handbook (0668). $10.00
Moscow-St. Petersburg Handbook (3913) $13.95
Staying Healthy in Asia, Africa, and Latin America (0269) $11.95
The Practical Nomad (0765). $13.95

PERIPLUS TRAVEL MAPS
All maps $7.95 each

Bali	Jakarta	Phuket/S. Thailand
Bandung/W. Java	E. Java	Sabah
Bangkok/C. Thailand	Java	Sarawak
Batam/Bintan	Kuala Lumpur	Singapore
Cambodia	Ko Samui/S. Thailand	Vietnam
Chiangmai/N. Thailand	Lombok	Yogyakarta/C. Java
Hong Kong	N. Sumatra	
Indonesia	Penang	

WHERE TO BUY MOON TRAVEL HANDBOOKS

BOOKSTORES AND LIBRARIES: Moon Travel Handbooks are sold worldwide. Please contact our sales manager for a list of wholesalers and distributors in your area.

TRAVELERS: We would like to have Moon Travel Handbooks available throughout the world. Please ask your bookstore to write or call us for ordering information. If your bookstore will not order our guides for you, please contact us for a free catalogue.

Moon Publications, Inc.
P.O. Box 3040
Chico, CA 95927-3040 U.S.A.
tel.: (800) 345-5473
fax: (916) 345-6751
e-mail: travel@moon.com

IMPORTANT ORDERING INFORMATION

PRICES: All prices are subject to change. We always ship the most current edition. We will let you know if there is a price increase on the book you order.

SHIPPING AND HANDLING OPTIONS: Domestic UPS or USPS first class (allow 10 working days for delivery): $3.50 for the first item, 50 cents for each additional item.

EXCEPTIONS: *Tibet Handbook, Mexico Handbook,* and *Indonesia Handbook* shipping $4.50; $1.00 for each additional *Tibet Handbook, Mexico Handbook,* or *Indonesia Handbook.*

Moonbelt shipping is $1.50 for one, 50 cents for each additional belt.

Add $2.00 for same-day handling.

UPS 2nd Day Air or Printed Airmail requires a special quote.

International Surface Bookrate 8-12 weeks delivery: $3.00 for the first item, $1.00 for each additional item. Note: Moon Publications cannot guarantee international surface bookrate shipping. Moon recommends sending international orders via air mail, which requires a special quote.

FOREIGN ORDERS: Orders that originate outside the U.S.A. must be paid for with an international money order, a check in U.S. currency drawn on a major U.S. bank based in the U.S.A., or Visa or MasterCard.

TELEPHONE ORDERS: We accept Visa or MasterCard payments. Minimum order is US$15. Call in your order: (800) 345-5473, 8 a.m.-5 p.m. Pacific standard time.

ORDER FORM

Prices are subject to change without notice. Be sure to call (800) 345-5473 for current prices and editions or for the name of the bookstore nearest you that carries Moon Travel Handbooks • 8 a.m.–5 p.m. PST. (See important ordering information on preceding page.)

Name: _____ Date: _____

Street: _____

City: _____ Daytime Phone: _____

State or Country: _____ Zip Code: _____

QUANTITY	TITLE	PRICE

Taxable Total_____

Sales Tax (7.25%) for California Residents_____

Shipping & Handling_____

TOTAL_____

Ship: ☐ UPS (no P.O. Boxes) ☐ 1st class ☐ International surface mail

Ship to: ☐ address above ☐ other _____

Make checks payable to: **MOON PUBLICATIONS, INC.**, P.O. Box 3040, Chico, CA 95927-3040 U.S.A. We accept Visa and MasterCard. **To Order**: Call in your Visa or MasterCard number, or send a written order with your Visa or MasterCard number and expiration date clearly written.

Card Number: ☐ **Visa** ☐ **MasterCard**

☐ ☐ ☐ ☐ ☐ ☐ ☐ ☐ ☐ ☐ ☐ ☐ ☐ ☐ ☐ ☐

Exact Name on Card: _____

Expiration date:_____

Signature: _____

THE METRIC SYSTEM

1 inch = 2.54 centimeters (cm)
1 foot = .304 meters (m)
1 mile = 1.6093 kilometers (km)
1 km = .6124 miles
1 fathom = 1.8288 m
1 chain = 20.1168 m
1 furlong = 201.168 m
1 acre = .4047 hectares
1 sq km = 100 hectares
1 sq mile = 2.59 square km
1 ounce = 28.35 grams
1 pound = .4536 kilograms
1 short ton = .90718 metric ton
1 short ton = 2000 pounds
1 long ton = 1.016 metric tons
1 long ton = 2240 pounds
1 metric ton = 1000 kilograms
1 quart = .94635 liters
1 US gallon = 3.7854 liters
1 Imperial gallon = 4.5459 liters
1 nautical mile = 1.852 km

To compute celsius temperatures, subtract 32 from Fahrenheit and divide by 1.8. To go the other way, multiply celsius by 1.8 and add 32.

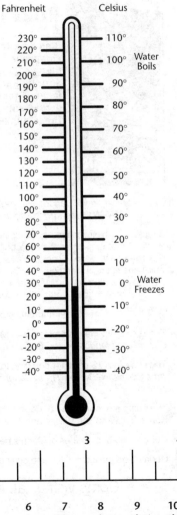

www.moon.com

MOON PUBLICATIONS

Welcome to <u>Moon Travel Handbooks</u>, publishers of comprehensive travel guides to <u>North America</u>, <u>Mexico</u>, <u>Central America and the Caribbean</u>, <u>Asia</u>, and the <u>Pacific Islands</u>, We're always on the lookout for new ideas, so please feel free to e-mail any comments and suggestions about these exhibits to <u>travel@moon.com</u>.

If you like Moon Travel Handbooks, you'll enjoy our travel information center on the World Wide Web (WWW), loaded with interactive exhibits designed especially for the Internet.

Our featured exhibit contains the complete text of *Road Trip USA,* a travel guide to the "blue highways" that crisscross America between the interstates, published in paperback in 1996. The WWW version contains a large, scrollable point-and-click imagemap with links to hundreds of original entries; a sophisticated network of links to other major U.S. Internet sites; and a running commentary from our online readers contributing their own travel tips on small towns, roadside attractions, regional foods, and interesting places to stay.

Other attractions on Moon's Web site include:

- Excerpted hypertext adaptations of Moon's bestselling *New Zealand Handbook, Costa Rica Handbook,* and *Big Island of Hawaii Handbook*

- The complete 75-page introduction to *Staying Healthy in Asia, Africa, and Latin America,* as well as the *Trans-Cultural Study Guide,* both coproduced with Volunteers in Asia

- The complete, annotated bibliographies from Moon's Handbooks to Japan, South Korea, Thailand, the Philippines, Indonesia, Australia, and New Zealand

- Current and back issues of Moon's free quarterly newsletter, *Travel Matters*

- Updates on the latest titles and editions to join the Moon Travel Handbook series

Come visit us at: http://www.moon.com

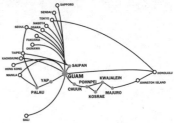

ISLANDS OF MICRONESIA

Postcard perfect island paradises. Unspoiled coral reefs and azure lagoons. Atolls teeming with vibrant life and color. Coral encusted shipwrecks and awesome drop-offs. A lively population of mixed cultures, tradition, legends and history.

The Islands of Micronesia. Experience them with Continental Micronesia. Call toll free for flight and tour information.

1-800-900-7657

Continental Micronesia
Fly with the warmth of Paradise